RAMPANT RAIDER

RAMPANT

An A-4 Skyhawk Pilot in Vietnam

RAIDER

STEPHEN R. GRAY

NAVAL INSTITUTE PRESS

Annapolis, Maryland

Naval Institute Press
291 Wood Road
Annapolis, MD 21402

First Naval Institute Press paperback edition published in 2017.
ISBN: 978-1-68247-198-2 (paperback)

The Library of Congress has cataloged the hardcover edition as follows:

Gray, Stephen (Stephen Roberts) 1942–
    Rampant Raider : an A-4 Skyhawk pilot in Vietnam / Stephen Gray.
        p. cm.
    Includes index.
    ISBN 978-1-59114-342-0 (alk. paper)
    1. Vietnam War, 1961-1975—Aerial operations, American. 2. Vietnam War,
1961-1975—Naval operations, American. 3. Vietnam War, 1961-1975—Personal
narratives, American. 4. Gray, Stephen (Stephen Roberts) 1942- 5. Skyhawk (Jet
attack plane) I. Title.
    DS558.8G734 2007
    959.704'348092—dc22
    [B]
                                        2007028624

Printed in the United States of America on acid-free paper ⊚

25 24 23 22 21 20 19 18 17   9 8 7 6 5 4 3 2 1

First printing

All maps are from the author's collection and were redrawn by Chris Robinson.

Contents

Preface

For a while, it seemed as if nothing much would ever be written about the Vietnam War. Most Americans did not want to be reminded about the first major military defeat in U.S. history. As far back as fall 1968 there were signs that public opinion had shifted against the war. The Tet Offensive launched at the end of January 1968 by North Vietnam and the Viet Cong stunned the American public. Even though the U.S. military had defeated the tremendous effort by the North Vietnamese to turn Tet into an American Dien Bien Phu, and despite the fact that Viet Cong losses during the offensive had eliminated them as an effective fighting force, Americans were left with the impression that we would never be able to thwart the North Vietnamese government's efforts to make all of Vietnam a communist state. Sickened by the unending parade of the horrors and images of American dead on the nightly news, and subjected to an intense antiwar barrage of news coverage that attempted to treat every action of the U.S. military in a negative light, most public opinion expressed disgust and disillusionment. Americans wanted an end to the war and withdrawal from Vietnam.

Early in 1968, while flying combat missions on my second combat cruise, the local Kiwanis Club in my small hometown in Oklahoma invited me to address its members upon my return to the States. Not many local boys were involved in Vietnam, and the local press had reported some of my actions, so the patriotic folks back home wanted to hear a firsthand account of my combat experiences. By the time I returned on leave in October 1968, the invitation had been forgotten. No one wanted to hear more about our ignoble debacle in Vietnam. They just wanted us out of there.

U.S. forces finally withdrew in 1973. Congress voted to cut off funds for the South Vietnamese, and in 1975 we were treated to the spectacle of the last retreat from Saigon, with Huey helicopters evacuating our embassy from the roof. The anti-U.S. and antiwar forces in the media and elsewhere in society had achieved complete victory. Although anticommunist voices in the United States had warned of the consequences of early withdrawal, few in this country were prepared for the extent of the revenge exacted on South Vietnam, Cambodia, and Laos after our capitulation. Images of fleeing "Boat People" and the squalor of overcrowded refugee camps began to fill our television screens.

The uneasy burden of responsibility for this debacle began to fall on the activist antiwar movement, and prominent voices in the movement began trying to deflect responsibility for the human tragedy befalling Southeast Asia. Wild fantasies such as the films *Apocalypse Now* and *The Killing Fields* attempted to focus the blame on the United States for its policies and on the U.S. military for teaching the peace-loving people of Southeast Asia to brutalize one another. It was not until the early 1980s, when President Ronald Reagan restored pride in our nation and in our military, that Vietnam veterans began to tell their stories to America. Books describing their experiences began to appear on bookstore shelves, and the history of U.S. involvement in Southeast Asia began to be reevaluated. The old anti-U.S. and antimilitary voices also began to stir. The film *Platoon*, directed by Oliver Stone, exemplifies their attempts once again to discredit U.S. involvement in Vietnam. This film, which received the Academy Award for Best Picture and was hailed as the definitive portrayal of the American military in Vietnam, highlights drug use by the soldiers, atrocities against civilians, maniac officers, and "fragging"—the practice of soldiers trying to murder their superior officers. These things did happen, but they were not the norm. To portray them as such does a terrible disservice to the thousands of American servicemen and servicewomen who performed their duties and fought for their country with honor.

New generations born after our involvement in Vietnam are reaching maturity and learning about that time in our history. Unfortunately, there has been very little reality and a lot of fantasy written for them to use to formulate their impressions of our nation's struggle against communism and of our military services during the sometimes not so Cold War. It is for this and other reasons that I wrote this book.

The experiences I describe here really happened, and what I say is as close to truth as my memory and memorabilia can make it. To fill gaps in my memory I have sometimes had to create details, but these are based on actual occurrences. For the most part, though, this account relates my experiences just as they happened. I use the actual names of real people, places, battles, and events, though the book is not intended to be a scholarly history. I was personally involved in most of what I describe here, although some events happened to others and were simply told to me.

However it is accepted, what I have written is the way it really was. Remember it, History, because in the course of human events things like these are bound to happen again.

———•———

To my huge embarrassment and everlasting gratitude, my wife, Alma, saved all the letters I wrote home, which amount to an almost daily diary of my time on cruise. The letters have been an invaluable source for dates and a great help in sharpening details blurred by time. Aviation writer and military historian Peter Mersky proved to be an amazing resource of photographs and valuable contacts whose assistance were vital in the production of this work. I am thankful to Alma and to my sons, Chad and Scott, for providing the encouragement to pursue publication in spite of obstacles, and to Chad's wife, Natalie, for proofreading the original manuscript. Many thanks go to my production editor and my copyeditor, Marla Traweek and Mindy Conner, for holding my hand during the process, and to Rick Russell for seeing value in my work.

RAMPANT RAIDER

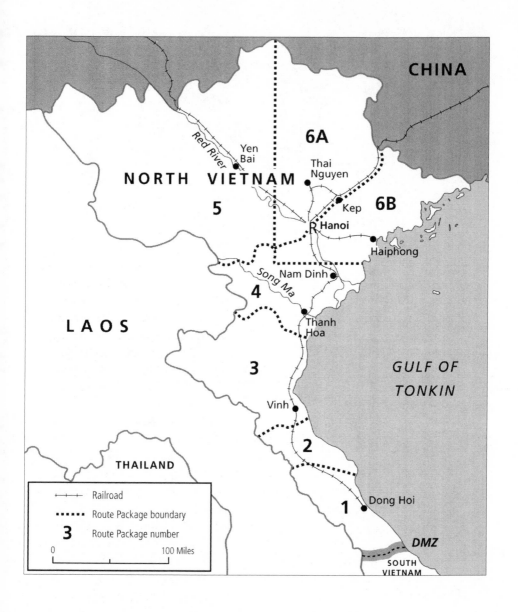

Overview map of North Vietnam showing the "route package areas" the Military Assistance Command (MACV) used to designate target areas in North Vietnam.

Prologue

The great gray side of the USS *Bon Homme Richard* (CVA-31) loomed above us like a prehistoric cliff dwelling as we stood in an unhappy little knot on the pier. It was late January 1967, and the weather in San Diego was living up to Southern California's reputation for having a near-perfect climate. The temperature was in the high sixties, under clear skies with gentle breezes. Red, white, and blue national bunting hung from the roofs of the dockside warehouses. The Naval Air Station North Island band played continuous marches and pop tunes in a futile attempt to lighten the mood of this singularly morose occasion. Departure day for the 1967 WESTPAC cruise for the *Bon Homme Richard*—nicknamed the "Bonnie Dick"—and Air Wing 21, which would be embarked in the Bonnie Dick for the duration of the cruise, had finally arrived. The colored clothing worn by the crowd of dependents, relatives, and well-wishers there to see us off swirled in marked contrast to the drab, haze-gray Navy paint on the ship and dockyard equipment. Dungaree-clad sailors of the line-handling parties stood by the thick, chest-high bollards that had the huge hawser ropes of the carrier's mooring lines draped around them. The sharp tang of fresh salt air mixed with whiffs of diesel oil, steam, and cooking smells—the body odor of any large ship. Across San Diego Bay I could see the light tan buildings of the Naval Training Center catching the first rays of the morning sun as it cleared the highlands east of San Diego. NTC, or "Boot Camp," was where I had started my life in the Navy four and a half years ago. It seemed as if all the hard things I had to do in my life occurred in San Diego.

1

Alma, my bride of six months, and my mother and father stood trying to make small talk to postpone the inevitable moment of my parting. The day after reporting to Attack Squadron 212 (or VA-212, the designation VA meaning "fixed-wing attack" in Navy parlance), I was assigned to fly an A-4 Skyhawk to San Diego to be loaded on board the ship. Mom and Dad had driven from Oklahoma to see their only son off to war, and Alma and my folks had driven from our apartment in Hanford to meet me. Perhaps only a handful of people in that crowd fully understood, as my father did, the significance of this day. My father had departed these same shores for battle in the Pacific at Iwo Jima and Okinawa twenty-three years before. Some of the people in that crowd were unknowingly bidding a final farewell to their loved ones. Some departing that day would not return, and some would return only after years in a POW camp. Alma was biting her lower lip to keep it from trembling and fighting back tears; Mother was already weepy; and Dad was trying to be Dad, ever-strong for me. I couldn't get a grip on my feelings. I felt the pain of imminent separation from my wife, the excitement of embarking on a great adventure, and apprehension about the unknown trials ahead. But I did not yet feel fear—I was still too ignorant of things to come.

After all, I had volunteered for this. My first choice for duty assignment on completing flight training had been A-4s, West Coast, a ticket to Vietnam. I had to "see the elephant," as they say. Compelled to continue the family tradition begun by my ancestral namesake who fought with Sam Houston at San Jacinto and continued by his son who fought the Comanche, I followed my father's footsteps into combat for my country. I was too young and idealistic to understand the price I would pay for this adventure.

The newness of the gold ensign's bar on my khaki cap, the single gold stripe on my shoulder boards, and the shiny gold naval aviator's wings pinned to my tunic made me self-consciously aware that I was the most junior pilot in my squadron. I had reported for duty to VA-212 only three days earlier and had barely met the other pilots. This was particularly upsetting to Alma because she had not met many of their wives. These "cruise widows," with the exception of a few who went to live with their parents for the duration, would be the support group for each other while their husbands were deployed. Alma had never been far from home before coming to the West Coast. Even though she had taught business at Sinton High School for two years before our wedding, Sinton was only a two-hour drive from her family farm in Weimar, Texas. Now she was twelve hundred miles away from her parents, in-laws, family, and friends, and her husband was leaving her alone for eight months. Alma and I believed that we should be independent from parental support after our marriage, so she had secured a teaching position at Tulare High School in California, and going home for the duration of the cruise wasn't an option. My new squadron had held a farewell dinner in San Diego the previous night, but it seemed that most of the wives Alma had a chance to meet were going home.

In an attempt to keep the small talk going, I let it slip that I didn't yet have a bunk to sleep in on board the ship. I had intended to make her laugh, but my mother was highly distressed by the prospect of my departure on a long cruise without a place to lay my head. As the junior ensign in VA-212, far too junior in the air wing to rate a stateroom, I was summarily assigned to the junior officers' bunkroom known as the "JO Jungle." This was a dormitory-like berthing space located just aft of the forecastle in the bow of the ship. All the bunks in the Jungle were taken when I reported for duty, however, so my gear lay in a forlorn little pile in a corner while the ship's First Lieutenant's Division decided how to rig me a bunk and find me a storage locker.

The shrill notes of the boatswain's pipe cut these musings short as the ship's PA system announced, "Now set the special sea and anchor detail. All departments make preparation for getting under way." The diesel engine of the dockside crane stuttered to life, and a sailor attached a shackle to a cable on the quarterdeck gangway. A stream of last-minute embarkers climbed the gangway. The moment had finally come. With a small sense of relief, I gave Alma a final short kiss, hugged Mom, shook Dad's hand, muttered a few appropriate things, and turned on my heel to join the last of the stragglers. The crowd had thinned considerably, the veterans of previous cruise departures having learned the painful folly of prolonging agony by watching the ship make its slow way out of sight down the bay. I stepped off the gangway onto the quarterdeck sponson, a weather deck extending beyond the bulkheads that formed the walls of the hangar deck. Self-consciously, I saluted the fantail colors and the quarterdeck watch and recited the traditional litany before boarding a U.S. naval vessel: "Request permission to come aboard, Sir." The officer of the deck watch was being transferred to the bridge, so my salute was returned by the quartermaster of the watch, a chief petty officer. "Permission granted, Sir." The chief smiled at me, no doubt noting the new gold bars of a "nugget" reporting for duty for the first time.

The quarterdeck gangway swung away and "Now single up all lines!" sounded over the PA. The line handlers slipped the big hawsers up and over the rounded tops of the bollards as tension was released, and now only a single line remained on each. Having not yet been assigned any collateral duties, I was free to watch the proceedings. I moved to a corner of the quarterdeck sponson to wave farewell to my family on the pier. A harbor tug nosed into the bow, which faced the Coronado Island ferry, and began to swing it out as the stern was nudged away from the pier. Suddenly, the ship became a live thing. She vibrated slightly as her own screws began to thrust her forward. The bow swung faster now, aided by the tugs, and the hills east of San Diego came into view. The side of the ship obscured the pier as the stern swung around, and I could no longer see my family. I walked into the hangar deck to cross to the opposite sponson. The bay was a cavernous open expanse at this time; most of the aircraft were still topside on the flight deck where they had been hoisted by crane from the dock. Working parties of air wing, flight deck, and hangar deck personnel would shortly begin the intricate task of "spotting" the decks, positioning aircraft and chaining them down for the four-day steam to Hawaii. The ship would undergo an operational readiness inspection (ORI) for four days, which would include two days in Pearl Harbor and liberty on the island of Oahu.

Feeling suddenly lonely, my spirits lifted when I spotted two other "nuggets" standing by the portside sponson. Ensigns Terry Rieder and Mike Wallace were watching as the ship completed her 180-degree turn, now placing the port side toward the NAS dock. We were too far out into the channel to distinguish faces, so I quit looking for Alma and my parents. Mike, Terry, and I had been naval aviation cadets (NAVCADs) in the same class. Terry and I had received our wings on the same day and were now squadron mates in VA-212. Terry had finished his initial carrier qualification landings ("car quals") three days before I had and was technically three days senior to me because a NAVCAD's date of rank was the date of his initial car quals. This made Terry the "bull ensign" in VA-212, but that didn't mean much because there were only two ensigns in the squadron. Still, Terry took great pains to remind me of this fact. Mike Wallace had been separated from us after preflight school and assigned to fly F-8 Crusader fighters. He was now attached to VF-24, or Fighter Squadron 24, which was also part of Air Wing 21, so our paths had converged again.

After a few words of greeting and expressing pleasure at being shipmates, we lapsed into silence. Each of us was still very affected by the beginning of our first combat cruise. Suddenly, Terry broke the silence, saying, "Now, you guys don't laugh at me," whereupon he threw a quarter into San Diego Bay and said, "For luck, so I'll come back." Nearly simultaneously, Mike and I said, "Damn, that's a good idea," and, reciting Terry's words, threw our own coins into the water. This was as close as we could come to admitting that underneath our swaggering bravado as carrier jet jocks we were really worried about our abilities and what lay ahead.

By now the *Bon Homme Richard* was well under way. The tugs had been dismissed and the bow began to swing around Point Loma and points west.

The ship's PA came to life with the boatswain's pipe whistling "Attention!" and the announcement of "Flight quarters, flight quarters, all hands man your flight quarter stations for re-spot." The three of us parted, Mike going to VF-24's ready room (a squadron's headquarters on board ship), and Terry and I to VA-212's. Terry said, "Well, at least you guys didn't laugh at me." "Laugh, hell," I answered. "I threw a silver dollar overboard. Now I have a four-times-better chance than you of coming back!" In fact, all three of us would come very close to dying, but we did indeed come home alive.

The bow completed the swing to west-northwest, the helmsman steadying up on a heading of 290 degrees magnetic. The Bonnie Dick's bow met the first of the long Pacific Ocean swells, and the 1967 WESTPAC cruise had begun.

1

Navy Beginnings

Many people can recall with great clarity moments when their lives took a dramatic turn that altered and shaped their future. I still remember the tang of the September air when, having just completed a long and frustrating day dealing with the bureaucracy of the University of Oklahoma, I made the first major decision of my life. It seemed that, after my rather poor academic performance the previous school year, the university—specifically, the College of Arts and Sciences—might not allow me to enroll for the fall term. Admittedly, my marks had fallen below minimum acceptable standards, but according to the university's own rules I should have been placed on academic probation for the fall semester, not forbidden to enroll. My poor performance was due in part to my extreme disappointment at not receiving an appointment to the U.S. Naval Academy. But during a summer of soul searching I had admitted that I was not academically qualified to attend the Academy and had determined to pursue a degree from OU with renewed vigor. Now, however, I had discovered that the university had placed a card in my enrollment packet preventing my enrollment for one calendar year. After spending the day bouncing from office to office attempting to appeal this action, I had finally been granted an audience with the dean of the college. He informed me that a panel would convene to consider cases such as mine. If I would appear before this panel and grovel appropriately, promising to do better, he said, they would probably allow me to enroll.

Later, standing on the steps leading away from the administration building and fuming at the way the university was treating me, I was still enough of a rebellious adolescent to decide, "The hell with this, I'll enlist in the Navy!" Though made in haste, it proved to be one of the best decisions I have ever made. In a few weeks, however, I came to regret that decision.

———•———

I had always wanted to go into the Navy. My father had been a "ninety-day wonder," as wartime officer candidate school graduates were known. He later became a gunnery officer in a destroyer, saw action at Iwo Jima, and was on radar picket duty off Okinawa during the height of the kamikaze attacks. Even though he did not remain on active duty after World War II, he always had a special love for the Navy. I was raised on sea stories and naval lore and history, and he would frequently break me out of bed in the morning calling, "Sweepers, sweepers, man your brooms." So when I left the university campus that September afternoon, there was no question; it would be the Navy. After being sworn in at the Navy recruiting office in Oklahoma City and my first jet airplane ride to California, I reported to the naval recruit depot in San Diego, California.

Boot camp was tough, but the sometimes brutal discipline was never sadistic; its purpose was always to turn raw recruits into military men. The Navy had but ten weeks to stamp us into the military mold, and it did so efficiently, albeit sometimes painfully. The first shock of boot camp came the second day when, after being stripped of all vestiges of civilian life, I stood naked in a barnlike building with a thousand other frightened young men as we were herded through the induction physical examination. After being poked, prodded, and pronounced physically fit for duty, we were issued every-thing we would need, from toothbrush to shoes. All our civilian things—the last remains of our civilian selves—were boxed up and sent home. On day three we were once again herded into a big room to take a battery of tests to determine our education levels and aptitudes. The tests lasted all day, and everything an enlisted man in the Navy could expect to do depended on the results of these examinations.

It took about a week to accomplish all the physicals, testing, and indoc-trination before we were able to begin training and the countdown to gradu-ation and boot leave. Time was measured in training days, with the one-one day being first week, first day. Graduation and departure day was the nine-five day, and it suddenly became the most important day of our lives. Time passed slowly for us even though frenetic activity filled our days and nights. But we were learning very valuable things—discipline, duty, honor, and pride. My graduation from boot camp was the proudest moment of my life up to then.

My first assignment after boot camp was six months' temporary duty at Naval Air Station Corpus Christi, Texas. As a high school graduate, I was guaranteed training at a technical school as part of my enlistment contract with the U.S. government. But my school start date was not until May 1963, and I spent the intervening six months doing menial tasks for the Navy. I really lucked out in the duty assignment at NAS Corpus Christi. Most of my contemporaries fresh out of boot camp were assigned to "mess cooking" duties or permanent KP (kitchen patrol) for their temporary duty—six months of plain hard labor, reporting for duty at 0400 and securing after 1900 most nights after being harangued by ill-tempered chief cooks in the interim. I had indicated typing abilities on my fact sheet on reporting, and this skill landed me a job as a clerk typist in the aircraft maintenance department. I was a find of pure gold to the harassed chief aviation boatswain's mate whose job it was to oversee the ground support equipment shop. The chief was responsible for compiling reports on the daily status of equipment, a task he found both arduous and time consuming. That I could type these reports at roughly three times his speed with dramatically improved grammar and accuracy clearly delighted him, and he treated me, an airman 2nd class, like a favored son and shielded me from some of the more odious working parties that occasionally befell junior enlisted men. He was clearly grieved when my orders for school finally came through.

When a U.S. Navy sailor decides to compete for a specialty, or "rating," as it is called in Navy parlance, he is said to have "struck" for that rating. I decided in boot camp to strike for the AX rating and train to be an air anti–submarine warfare technician. An AX was trained in the operation and maintenance of the high-tech electrical equipment used to detect and track submarines. The first step in training was aircraft fundamentals ("A") school, which taught us basic aircraft servicing, ground handling, security, and firefighting techniques. Then we began electronics fundamentals, where we learned how radio equipment worked, how signals were transmitted, and basic troubleshooting and repair of the equipment we would use in the fleet.

The school was highly technical and very compressed; the enforced discipline and study time built into the syllabus taught me how to manage my time and provided an atmosphere free from distractions. My grades were quite good and I was learning valuable skills. This training not only taught me how to use and maintain the equipment of my specialty, it also taught me how to learn and how to succeed in schools, among the most valuable lessons of my life.

During A school we were given the opportunity to fill out requests for the area and type of duty to which we would be assigned on completing our training. The Navy had three types of duty for AXs at the time: air crew on land-based P-3 Orion antisubmarine (ASW) patrol aircraft, air crew on carrier-based S2F Tracer ASW aircraft, and sonar operator on carrier-based ASW helicopters. One of the main bases for P-3 Orion aircraft was NAS Whidbey Island, Washington, just outside Seattle on Puget Sound. Whidbey was supposed to be a fabulous area surrounded by fine hunting and fishing, so naturally that was my first choice for duty. The Navy gave me helicopters at NAS Key West, Florida.

All of our training up to this point had involved theoretical classroom material. Now we would learn real-world operation of the gear. HS-1 (Helicopter Anti-submarine Warfare Squadron 1) was the East Coast Replacement Air Group (RAG) training squadron for new pilots and enlisted air crew, and it would be our introduction to the SH-3A Sea King, air crew duties, and sonar equipment. The SH-3A turbine-powered helicopter was new at the time, replacing the old HSS-1N reciprocating engine helicopter. The Sea King would become a familiar sight to most of the world as the primary recovery helicopter for the Gemini and Apollo Space Program missions.

After nearly three months of training I graduated from the RAG and reported in March to my operating squadron, Helo Antisubron 9 (HS-9), the "Sea Griffins." HS-9's homeport was at NAS Quonset Point, Rhode Island, and it was deployed on the USS *Essex* (CVS-9). While still in the RAG, I had taken and passed the exam for advancement in rank to air anti–submarine warfare technician, 3rd class, or AX3. My date of new rank would be effective on 1 June. Until then I was authorized to wear three green diagonal stripes with the AX rating badge over them on my left sleeve indicating that I was a designated striker for third class AX.

I had been in intensive training for nearly a full year now, but HS-9 had a policy that all new, nonrated enlisted men reporting on board would be assigned to the First Lieutenant's Division (or X Division), which was responsible for the housekeeping duties necessary to keep the squadron shipshape. Because my rating date was not official until June, I was considered nonrated and was assigned to compartment cleaning. Thus, after a year of highly technical and sometimes difficult education, my first assignment after training was to clean the enlisted men's restroom—or "head," in Navy parlance—in the squadron hangar.

The enlisted head was located on the ground level of the hangar next to the squadron leading chief's office, and it was a pit the day I reported to my new duty station armed with broom, swab, bucket, and various cleaning solutions. Dingy, grimy, and miasmic, it brought forth visions of the Black Hole of Calcutta. Obviously, the previously assigned custodian had not been diligent in performing his cleaning tasks, and the men using the facility were none too careful during their ablutions. Incensed by the lack of respect for my newly acquired technician status this assignment represented, I determined to make the head positively gleam.

Early on, I learned that the best way to cope with the vagaries of military service is to keep an active sense of humor. As I attacked the odious task of cleaning the urinals, a song from Gilbert and Sullivan's *HMS Pinafore* came to mind. I began to whistle the music that accompanied these words: "I polished up the handle so carefully that now I am the ruler of the Queen's Navy." This helped the work go faster and kept my mind off the drudgery. The leading chief of HS-9 was a master chief petty officer, the highest enlisted rank in the Navy. He couldn't help but hear my loud whistling emanating from the head and was intrigued by this most unusual cheer issuing from a person performing what was considered one of the worst tasks in the squadron. The chief was very familiar with the works of Gilbert and Sullivan and stepped into the head to see the source of this merriment. Unaware of his scrutiny, I continued whistling and polishing the brass drain pipes until they gleamed brightly. The deck was waxed, the porcelain toilet bowls and urinals sparkled, the sinks were clean, the mirrors spotless. The chief understood immediately the reason for my whistling, and when I finally turned from my task and noticed him, he pointed the stem of his pipe at me and said, "I see you know your *Pinafore*." I had just made a very favorable first impression on the leading chief.

I was stationed in the head for a week and did my best to keep it sparkling. I began to get genuine expressions of amazement and thanks from my squadron mates, who were delighted to have a clean head for a change. They entered now as if they were guests in someone's home and made every effort to try to keep it clean. Somewhere along the way, I had been taught that leadership begins by setting examples, and my example of doing my best to do a proper job of cleaning the head was having a positive effect on my squadron mates.

One day the division officer called me into his office and asked why I had not applied for a fleet candidate's appointment to the Naval Academy. He had my basic battery test scores in front of him, and I had scored very high in general comprehensive education and arithmetic. I had indicated a desire to try for any and all officer candidate positions when I filled out my boot camp questionnaire, but I had never been contacted and assumed that I hadn't scored well enough on the tests. The qualifying score for the Naval

Academy was 115 and I had scored 125. Now, however, at age twenty-one, I was too old to try for Annapolis. "How about NAVCAD?" he asked. "You can be twenty-five and try for NAVCAD, and it requires a score of 120." I didn't think for a moment that I had a chance for selection to the Naval Aviation Cadet program, but it didn't cost anything to apply so I decided to try.

The NAVCAD program, like the Naval Academy, was a source of naval aviators. Candidates who had successfully completed two years of college could apply for Navy flight training. Prospective Navy pilots and naval aviation officers who were college graduates could enlist in the Aviation Officer Candidate program and would be commissioned as officers after eleven weeks of training. They then would complete flight training as officers. The NAVCADs went through the same training as the AOCs, but they went through flight training as cadets—under cadet discipline and at cadet pay rates—until they graduated and received their wings. The NAVCADs were commissioned as ensigns, U.S. Navy Reserve, or if enrolled in the Marine Corps's twin program, MARCAD, second lieutenants, U.S. Marine Corps Reserve. The fleet candidate program under which I was applying allowed qualified enlisted men to enter flight training directly from active duty. Fleet candidates accepted into the NAVCAD or MARCAD program had the same status as the two-year college candidates. There was a caution, however: if the candidate washed out of the program, he served out the remainder of his enlistment at his old enlisted rank. In the case of the two-year college candidates, they would simply become enlisted sailors or Marines for the remainder of a four-year enlistment on active duty.

A few weeks after submitting my preliminary request for application to the NAVCAD program I was summoned to the NAS Quonset Point hospital to undergo the precandidate physical examination and the written aptitude test for flight training. The vision test was the most critical part of the process because while most young men who were accepted for military service were physically qualified, the flight-training program required perfect vision, and the eye exam was the Great Eliminator for many applicants. The Navy doctor snapped off the high-intensity, handheld examination light and flipped the room lights back on. "Well, son," he said, "you have the kind of eyes they are looking for. You have twenty-fifteen vision in both eyes with no astigmatism—in short, perfect vision."

The next step was the written aptitude test for aviation candidates. I don't remember much about the test except that the questions dealt primarily with cockpit presentations of various gauges for the candidate to interpret and contained a series of pictures showing houses, trees, and terrain features in various attitudes as they would be viewed from the cockpit of an airplane.

From the angles and tilt of the pictures I was to determine the attitude of the airplane. I wasn't sure of many of my answers, so I just answered according to what seemed correct to me. A few days later, I was recalled to the hospital. Four officers and a chief petty officer questioned me carefully. When had I taken this test previously? "Never before, Sir," I answered. Had I received any coaching from anyone before taking the test? "No, Sir," I answered. "What's this all about, Sir?" I asked.

"You're sure you haven't seen the test before or been in any way instructed about taking it?" he responded.

"No, Sir," I replied, again asking what was going on.

"Well, son," he said, "we had to check. It seems that you scored the highest score we have ever recorded on this test. Either you are a natural or you just guessed good. Anyway, if you make it to pilot training they will find out which it is soon enough."

There followed an exhaustive amount of forms and questions, character and credit references, and several appearances before a review board made up of the squadron officers. "Just relax, Gray, and tell us about yourself." They asked questions about me, my family, and my attitudes and thoughts on many subjects. The process took several months, and I became used to being called into the squadron personnel office to review some form or other for correctness, spelling, and grammar before signing it.

During this time I was assigned to the line crew and became a plane captain on a helicopter. The squadron deployed on board the *Essex* for a short six-week cruise to the Caribbean to practice for an upcoming operational readiness inspection. I flew a great deal and was very busy with my line duties, which were much more fulfilling than being a compartment cleaner, and I shoved the NAVCAD application to the back of my mind.

In late May the *Essex* was en route to Norfolk, Virginia, to pick up our operational readiness inspection team. One night our sister ship, the USS *Lake Champlain*, the last remaining straight-deck carrier in the Navy, was steaming up the Chesapeake Bay to pick up midshipmen from the Naval Academy to began their summer training cruise to Europe. The "Champ" was rammed by a freighter in dense fog and damaged too severely to make the European trip, so the ORI for the *Essex* was canceled and we were assigned to take the mids to Europe.

This was a fantastic deal, and most of the crew was ecstatic. Nearly all the enlisted men in the air wing were given the choice of remaining at Quonset Point for the summer or going on the cruise. The air wing had to cut strength by about 50 percent to make room for the midshipmen. Because I had never been to Europe, I enthusiastically volunteered for the cruise.

We visited Le Havre, France, for about a week; Copenhagen, Denmark, for nearly two weeks; and Portsmouth, England, for about a week. We conducted limited flight operations and even some anti–submarine warfare drills to provide summer training for the mids. En route to Copenhagen the Navy decided to give us the ORI anyway, and we had to pull double and sometimes triple duty to get all the flying done to qualify the air wing. So for four days we existed on minimal sleep and I literally lived in my helicopter. When I wasn't airborne in it I was responsible for it during flight quarters while it was on deck. But the extra duty seemed a small price to pay for all the fun I was having. My application to NAVCAD finally completed, the thick package containing the results of months of tests, interviews, and physical exams departed by Armed Forces Mail Service on 5 July 1964, from Copenhagen. It was under review in the Pentagon when the USS *Maddox* and the USS *Turner Joy* reported that they were under attack by high-speed surface torpedo boats out of North Vietnam.

The *Essex* returned to Quonset Point early in August after dropping the mids off at NAS Norfolk. I was due two weeks' leave by rotation, and I had to take it when my number came up or rotate back to the bottom of the list. The *Essex* and her air wing were on ASW alert status any time we were in port; sailors were restricted to a fifty-mile radius from the base while on liberty, and only 10 percent of the squadron was allowed to go on leave at any one time. These restrictions were necessary to allow the *Essex* to be "scrambled" in case our constantly patrolling ASW forces contacted a suspected Soviet submarine. This was not long after the Cuban missile crisis, and Cold War tensions were still high. It had been nearly a year since I had been home so I was glad for the leave.

My leave expired at midnight on Sunday, the week before Labor Day. HS-9 was due to load back on board the *Essex* on Friday, and she was due to depart for a thirty-day exercise with the Canadian navy off Halifax, Nova Scotia, the Tuesday after Labor Day. On Wednesday after morning muster, my division officer summoned me to his office. "Gray, your NAVCAD application came back and we need to go see the skipper to get his approval." About halfway across the hangar the lieutenant turned to me and said, "Well, Gray, I expected that you would be a little excited about getting accepted."

I had misunderstood the import of his remark about needing the skipper's approval and thought this was just another wrinkle in the application process—that we had neglected to get the commanding officer's signature on some of the paperwork. "Sir?" I stammered. "You mean I made it?"

"Yeah, you're going to Pensacola." He smiled as he said it.

"Hot damn!" I yelled, excitement overwhelming me.

"Relax, Gray. The skipper's real happy about it too—you know he's an ex-NAVCAD."

I didn't know that, but it was obvious that the skipper was very pleased and proud that one of his troops had been selected for the program. He was beaming when I was announced and ushered into his office. "Congratulations, Gray," he said, standing up and leaning across his desk to shake my hand. "A lot of people in this squadron really put a lot of effort into getting you selected."

"Thank you, Sir, I can't tell you how much I appreciate this."

"Well, son, just go down there and make it through the program and make us proud."

"I'll do my best, Sir," I answered.

"We know you will, Gray. We think you will make a fine naval officer."

"Thank you, Sir!" I replied.

So while the rest of HS-9 was bending to the arduous task of packing cruise boxes and moving out of the squadron spaces and back on board ship, I had my orders in my hand, my sea bag on my shoulder, and was heading out the front gate on thirty days' leave before reporting to NAS Pensacola to begin training as a naval aviator. I had reached the next turning point in my life, and no one on the planet was any happier than I was.

2

Naval School, Preflight

Naval Air Station Pensacola, Florida, is located on Pensacola Sound, with Santa Rosa Island forming a breakwater to the Gulf of Mexico. It is an area known for its sparkling clear Gulf water and dazzling white sand. I had never seen a more attractive military base. Huge oaks draped with Spanish moss lined wide streets. The red brick Naval Air Training Command buildings had an Old South charm with their large white columns and white gabled roofs. The air station was originally a seaplane base, and the old concrete seaplane ramps and hangars were still there, although no seaplanes were based at the naval station by 1964.

The orders transferring me to the cradle of naval aviation authorized me to delay in reporting by thirty days, and I was not to report to Preflight until 7 October 1964. Because my leave was up on 1 October, the base personnel office had to find something to do with me for a week, and because I was a petty officer 3rd class, I was assigned to the base's master at arms force, where I supervised working parties of sailors while they performed cleanup and maintenance duties. These were easy and short working days, so I had plenty of time to become familiar with the base and surrounding area. The administrative side of the base was the headquarters of the chief of naval air training (CNATRA). Vice Adm. A. S. Heyward Jr., USN, held the office of CNATRA, and he commanded both basic and advanced flight training. The school for the former was also located at main side Pensacola; the latter was at NAS Corpus Christi, Texas.

In 1964, the beginning of flight training for new cadets and officer candidates was a sixteen-week course known as U.S. Naval School Preflight. The first step into Preflight was the Indoctrination Battalion (Indoc), which lasted about three weeks.

The seventh of October was a beautiful fall day. At 1300, as my orders directed, I reported to Indoc, walking the short distance from the enlisted quarters in which I had been billeted while doing my temporary duty. Indoc occupied World War II–vintage wooden barracks, and the street leading up to the front of the barracks was quiet, residential, and tree lined. I walked into pandemonium. Frightened young men ran hither and thither, filling out forms, receiving issue gear, and being formed into ranks. Their faces expressed shocked disbelief at what was being said to and demanded of them. These men were raw recruits, panicked college boys getting their first taste of military life. In contrast, the fleet candidates wore expressions of bored resignation and performed their required tasks quietly and competently. We had completed enlisted boot camp and were old hands at this routine. I stood out because all the others in the squad bay had been issued the olive drab coveralls (called "poopie suits") that were the uniform of Indoc, and I was still in my enlisted dress blues. The men in charge of this organized chaos were sharply dressed in the working khaki uniforms of the Navy officer corps. These were cadet officers, men in their final week of Preflight who would be graduating next week. Part of the leadership training of Preflight was cadet officer week, during which the graduating cadets performed the duties of officers over the lower classes, conducting inspections and drills, and training the "poopies." I was faintly amused by the antics of the cadet officers because I, after all, was from the fleet and these people were mere schoolboys.

I donned my poopie suit and was swept into the swirl of registration with the rest of the class. We filled out forms and were issued "fore and aft" caps, or garrison hats; three pairs of shoes, one working pair called "boondockers" and two dress pairs called "low cuts"; two web belts and buckles; toilet articles and a canvas "ditty bag" in which to store them; shower shoes; undershorts; T-shirts; socks; and other items that would be necessary for life during the Indoc weeks. The rest of our uniform issue would come to us as the items were needed during the coming weeks of Preflight. We were then herded into a room to pack and mail home all our other worldly possessions, stripping us of the vestiges of our former lives. I was reminded of the feeling I had in boot camp after being stripped down to my skin and issued everything needed to sustain life, from shower shoes to hat; my former life seemed no more than a surrealistic dream.

All the arrivals were aboard by 1600 and we were herded out behind the barracks onto the "company street" and formed into ranks, a task accomplished after much shouting and invective by the cadet officers. I assumed the same air of bored indifference I had seen on the faces of the other "old salts" as the college kids struggled to comply with the confusing orders being shouted at them.We were called to attention, a position most of the men had first learned in the previous few hours. Standing in the second rank, I could see the approach of a perfect Marine between my classmates' heads in the front rank. From his drill instructor hat to his highly shined shoes, Gunnery Sergeant Minko was the absolute picture of military perfection. He delivered a short speech, but it was not so much what he said as the way he said it that got our attention. After the predictable observation that we were the most miserable collection of humanity he had ever seen, he informed us that the Marine Corps had given him the task of turning us into material from which officers and aviators could be formed, and he, by God, was going to accomplish his mission. We, by damn, had better pay close attention and shape up, or our lives would become unbelievably miserable. We would henceforth be known as class 39-64—the 39th class in the year 1964—and we had better start functioning as a team because, judging from the looks of us, it would take our collective efforts for each of us to survive. He then told us that at his command we were to fall out and assemble on the other side of the street, and it had better not be the clusterfuck he had seen when we first formed up. At the command "Dismissed!" there was a confused milling, and then the most incredible voice I had ever heard screamed: "You people are slow! Move, move, move! Fall in, fall in, fall in!" The voice carried the most urgent imperative and hinted at doom for all who failed at the task. Frightened poopies scrambled, collided, tripped, fell, got up, and somehow arrived across the street in a rough semblance of the original formation. After nearly thirty repetitions of this, with about ten seconds between each, we were beginning to get pretty adept at falling in. Sergeant Minko said then that if we ever again took more than twenty seconds to fall in, we would all rue the day of our birth. I glanced in the direction of some of the other "old salts" (out of the corner of my eye, of course—I was not about to move my head in ranks). Gone were the looks of bored compliance; now we all looked like scared college kids.

He then marched us to the barbershop for the traditional recruit haircut. While we marched, Minko called the most distinctive cadence of any of the drill instructors in Preflight. His count was clear, preparatory commands rolled off his tongue in parade-ground prose, and his commands of execution popped like rifle shots. It was inspiring to listen to such command, and since we had all just been highly motivated, everyone struggled to stay in step and march as best we could. By the time we had marched the mile or so to the barbershop, we were beginning to look like a military formation. Of course, in a very short time, we would look many times better.

Evening meal formation followed the haircut, and we learned how to line up for chow and when and where to fall back in after chow to be marched back to Indoc. We had thirty minutes from the time the first member of our class hit the door of the chow hall until our class had to be formed up again and ready to march. This left about ten minutes total in which to be served, find a table, stand at attention with tray in hand, take seats on command when the table was full, and finally eat. We learned early on that consuming a full meal required great economy of time, so we didn't talk. The upperclass cadets, those already "secured" to their battalions, were allowed to straggle back to barracks after chow, and took their meals in relaxed luxury compared with the Indoc poopies. We stole glances at them, in their highly starched khakis with gleaming brass belt buckles and collar device anchors, and wondered if we would ever look that sharp.

After marching back to Indoc and falling out and back in a few more times because we didn't do it fast enough the first time, we were secured to our rooms to unpack our issue gear and begin polishing new brass and spit-shining our new low-quarter shoes. Taps sounded at 2200 and reveille would sound at 0600. Thus ended our first day of Naval School Preflight. We fell into our bunks exhausted, amazed at how much we had accomplished in so short a time and filled with excitement, apprehension, challenge, and wonder at how we could possibly do it all. I doubt class 39-64 dreamed much that night.

"Reveille, reveille, reveille! Move, move, move!" The shouts amplified by the barracks PA system shattered sleep and jerked us to our feet. Stumbling to our lockers, we recalled what we had been told the night before: we had just five minutes to get dressed and form up out in the company street for morning physical training (PT). Actually, this was more than enough time; it was very easy to slip into our poopie suits and don boondockers. We remembered well the lessons of falling in formation from the previous day, and we formed up almost before the five-minute period expired. We were once again under the control of the cadet officers, and this morning they earned my respect.

After being right-faced and forward-marched, we were given double-time in ranks. Actually double-time is a misnomer: the cadet officers set the pace, and it was a swift jog-trot. At first it seemed kind of neat. With the cadet officer calling cadence, we ran in step, eighty of us in ranks with boon-dockers beating out a *clomp, clomp, clomp* tattoo that echoed off the darkened walls of the rows of barracks. The eastern sky was lightening rapidly as we ran a half-mile or so to an athletic field. Most of us were sadly out of shape. The majority of the college boys had never really been in shape, and the fleet candidates were amazed at how rapidly their boot camp physical training had evaporated. By the time we reached the field we were all breathing hard; after three circuits of the field we were hurting; after two more circuits we sprawled on the ground when given the command to halt and fall out for calisthen-ics. Push-ups, sit-ups, and jumping jacks followed; then we formed up again, ran around the athletic field a few more times, then back to the barracks to fall out and spend five minutes freshening up before the march to breakfast. Throughout the entire PT period, the cadet officers had been relaxed and obviously enjoying themselves. They weren't even breathing hard when they got us back to the barracks. We, on the other hand, were groaning, retch-ing, and wondering if we would be able to keep breakfast down. Our agony had been a pleasant early-morning stroll for the officers, and I wondered if I would ever be in that fantastic physical condition.

We spent that first week undergoing various tests, including the most thorough physical examination of my life. Some of the tests we were required to do seemed weird. For example, a number of white-smocked individuals would observe us while we stepped up and down on a stepstool, sometimes for a specified period of time, sometimes without a stated limit. This was quite strenuous because the step was about sixteen inches high and we were told to step up and down as rapidly as we could. No one told us who the white smocks were; we assumed they were doctors. We were all conditioned to obey by this time, and we were all somewhat afraid of flunking the physical, so we tried our hardest to achieve the stated goals and to keep up the pace until we almost dropped on the unstated goal tests. During it all the smocks sat mute, scribbling notes furiously, their contents never disclosed to us.

One test, though, the most memorable, was "the coriolis chair." The chair sat in a smallish room and resembled an old-fashioned barber's chair with head and foot rests. I was strapped into the chair and electrodes were attached to each finger on both hands. Another electrode was fastened to my forehead, held in place by a headband. As usual, the white smocks were present, sitting in a circle of chairs around the coriolis chair. I was told to close my eyes to avoid becoming dizzy when the chair began to spin and to keep my head absolutely still. I was very apprehensive about this. As a child I had always avoided merry-go-rounds because rapid spinning quickly gave me severe vertigo and caused me to throw up. But I did as I was instructed and wondered briefly if I would hit all the smocks in the room if I got sick while spinning. The flickering pattern of lights outside my eyelids blurred, and after only a brief moment of a turning sensation I had the feeling that I was motionless and the room was spinning rapidly around me. After a few moments of feeling stable, I was instructed to turn my head to the right and drop my chin toward my chest. The most amazing phenomenon occurred: I felt as if I had just done a complete forward somersault, chair and all! Next I was told to return my head to upright center; this time a complete back flip ensued. Various head position changes produced tumbling and twisting sensations, and far from feeling ill, I was delighted and intrigued by them. Finally, I was told to sit still with my head forward and reminded to keep my eyes closed until instructed to open them. The flickering lights slowed to a stop, and when I was told to open my eyes the chair was still and I had not the slightest feeling of dizziness. No one told me told the results of this test; I simply received curt instructions to rejoin my class. Later we learned that the sensations produced by the coriolis chair were caused by fluid displacement in the inner ear. The human body receives its balance information from a variety of sensors. The two most dominant are eyesight and fine hairs in the inner ear. Without eyesight, the body depends on the input from these hairs, called cilia. As the chair starts to spin, centrifugal force causes the fluid in the ear to rush to the outside of the spin. The cilia are bent outward with the current, but once the fluid stabilizes, the hairs return to an upright position and the body thinks it is upright and still. Each movement of the head causes the fluid to rush violently in a new direction, displacing the hairs and confusing the body's sense of balance. A thorough understanding of this phenomenon would save my life one dark night.

Looking back, I am convinced that many of these tests had nothing to do with the induction physical. The smocks were conducting some obscure medical studies and had us as a captive and compliant group of test subjects. It was with a sense of relief that we finished the physical exams, and those of us who remained realized that one hurdle had been cleared. After we had passed that physical, no one could ever question that we were fully medically qualified for flight training.

The three weeks of Indoc passed quickly. The days were full and there was never any real slack time. The regimen quickly became routine: PT after reveille, chow, morning inspection, drill, lectures, chow, more drill, gear issue, inspection, lectures, chow, evenings spent shining shoes and preparing gear for inspection, and finally taps. The final week of Indoc was spent preparing us to function in the normal routine of Preflight. We stood a final personnel inspection and now looked as sharp in our new khakis as the more advanced Preflight cadets. With the approaching end of Indoc, class 39-64 was split up among the three Preflight battalions. I was assigned to the third battalion, or Batt III.

The regular Preflight battalions were housed in large brick barracks much nicer than the "temporary" wooden buildings that housed Indoc. The barracks were two stories, with the bunkrooms on the second deck and the battalion offices on the first. Each battalion had a class sergeant and a class officer, usually a Navy lieutenant or Marine captain. The bunkrooms housed four men assigned alphabetically, so cadets Fisher, Fleming, Green, and Gray made up the complement of my room. The rooms were spacious, with two double bunks on each wall and a sturdy table in between. Four lockers stood along the third wall. The room was bright and airy, with one window looking out the back of the building and the other looking out onto a screened veranda.

The cadet officers of that week began squaring us away in the routine of Preflight. We learned that we should never walk into our rooms with shoes on. Black heel marks on the deck were devilishly hard to erase and would draw an "unsatisfactory" on a room inspection, so we lined our shoes up outside in the passageway, Japanese style, and padded around the room in stocking feet. Our lockers held all our gear and had shelves and drawers as well as hanging space behind the double doors. We were taught how each article was to be stowed and displayed for the daily, and sometimes surprise, room inspections.

Our bunks were made with two sheets, a bedspread, and a single blanket. The corners were tucked in hospital-style: where the sheet edge tucked in between the mattress and springs, no material could pooch out and the edge had to be straight. The bedspread had to be pulled tight enough to bounce a quarter. The blanket was folded in thirds the width of the bunk and placed at the foot of the bed. Because there was simply not enough time to remake a bed each morning, we slept in our PT gear on top of the bedspread with the blanket unfolded over us. On rising, we had only to fold the blanket twice on its creases and pull the bedspread tight. Thursdays were air bedding days: The bunk was stripped, the old sheets and bedspread were sent to the laundry, and the mattress was folded back on the springs to air. Because the bed wasn't made up again until Thursday night, Wednesday night was known as "hotel night," and we could enjoy the luxury of sliding down between the sheets to sleep.

The regular routine of Preflight soon became habit. Reveille sounded at 0600, and we had five minutes to dress and fall in for meal formation. The working uniform for a normal weekday was khakis with a black tie tucked in between the second and third buttons of the shirt. Each of us was issued three sets of uniforms, and the routine was for one to be worn, one to be hung in the locker, and the last to be at the laundry. We could get two days' wear out of each uniform, so the working uniform was called "highly starched" for the first wearing and "highly washed" for the second. The rigid time schedule was, as always, to train us in the proper management of time. We soon learned that we had to plan for the next morning before retiring for the night. The uniform for the next day was "set up": collar devices pinned on, belt threaded through the loops, shoes and socks underneath, hat clothes-pinned to the hanger, and tie pretied and ready to slip over one's head.

When reveille sounded, we leaped (literally) from the bunk, spun the combination lock the remaining two turns, and opened the locker. This took probably thirty seconds. The hat went on first, then the shirt, trousers, socks, and shoes. Straightening the gig line (a line formed by the fly edge of the trousers and the edge of the button seam on the shirt) and adjusting the belt buckle, squaring the hat away, and pulling the tie knot up snug completed the dressing process with an elapsed time of perhaps two minutes. Another two minutes were required to stumble down the stairs and pile into the group forming in the company street. The final minute was spent straightening the formation. Within a total of five minutes, we were formed and ready to march to breakfast. Laggards were conspicuous and were assigned demerits, which had to be marched off during one's precious liberty time and were therefore to be avoided.

After a few weeks of practice—with our bodies trained to react automatically—we were able to shave some time off our dressing routine and could almost saunter into the formation. At the click of the mike button, even before the cadet on watch had begun to announce reveille over the PA, we were on our feet and turning our combination locks. I was astounded once to wake up already in the process of dressing, with no recollection of having gotten out of bed. Two of the AOCs in our battalion were married and had installed their wives in town. They were totally isolated from their husbands, of course, until we were "secured" and got our first liberty. The men's only contact with their wives for the three weeks of Indoc was by telephone, and then for limited times. They wouldn't be allowed overnight liberty until they graduated from Preflight. Early one morning about 0200, one of the wives was confronting some domestic crisis and absolutely had to talk to her husband. She called the battalion watch office, and the cadet of the watch, in an act of incredible thoughtlessness, keyed the PA system and announced, "Cadet So-and-so, you have a telephone call in the battalion watch office." The entire battalion was dressed and people were halfway out to fall in when someone realized that it was only 0203 and that the PA had said nothing about reveille. There were a few comments directed toward the watch office as we straggled back to bed. I didn't know whether to be pissed off at being broken out early or relieved that we still had nearly four hours of precious sleep ahead.

After breakfast we straggled back to the room to prepare it for the daily room inspection and ourselves for the daily personnel inspection. Each of us in the room had assigned tasks on a rotating basis. If the room did poorly on inspection we would all suffer equally, so we were highly motivated to do our best. One roommate pulled the bunks tight and checked for loose bits of sheet protruding from beneath the bedsprings. Another dusted the walls, window-sills, tables, and so on. Two "Pledged the deck," which consisted of spraying wax onto an athletic sock pulled over one's hand and waxing the deck with it. The decks were highly polished concrete and glistened with a shine that appeared inches deep if done properly. We had to crawl under the bunks to be sure that no dust balls ("ghost farts" in the lexicon of Preflight) were hiding there. Formation for personnel inspection was at 0700, and academics began at 0730. Noon meal formation was at 1200, with classes resuming at 1300. We straggled back to the Batt to change into our PT gear after the 1300 class and fell in for PT at 1420. PT lasted until 1600, and after changing and showering we typically had free, personal time till 1800, which was evening meal formation. Mandatory study periods began at 1900, with a five-minute break every hour until taps sounded at 2200.

Academics at Preflight school were difficult but straightforward. The difficulty was due more to the pace of covering the material than the curriculum itself. The math required to perform navigation, plan problems, and study aerodynamics was no more advanced than trigonometry and basic algebra. We took classes in engineering, navigation, naval history and customs, meteorology, and aerodynamics. I managed to keep a respectable grade average but was nowhere near the top of the class. Cadets having difficulty—those who had failed one or more of the weekly tests given in each class—were assigned to extra study periods and tutoring. Dubbed "stupid study," these periods occurred while the rest of the battalion had liberty, but they saved several of our less academically inclined classmates from washing out.

Although academics caused problems for some of us, PT was tough for everyone. Even the fleet candidate Marines with their physical training background from boot camp struggled with the intensity of our training. We formed up outside the battalion and began marching toward the PT building, one of the old seaplane hangars located on the seawall about half a mile away. After a few feet to allow everyone to get into step, we began the double-time jog. After arriving at the hangar, we began the training session with calisthenics consisting of twenty-five push-ups, thirty sit-ups, and fifty jumping jacks. Then back into ranks for a one-and-a-half-mile jog in step up the seawall, and fall out to repeat the calisthenics—twenty-five, thirty, and fifty. This regimen was the warm-up for the day's main event, which was one of three courses: the "long distance run," a three-mile run up the seawall; the "cross country run," a one-mile course set up in sand and heavy woods with many sharp turns; and the "obstacle course," by far the most demanding of the three. The obstacle course wasn't very long, and it appeared deceptively easy. It began with a double row of old tires to jog through, then a short run of about thirty yards to a wall. The wall was about eight feet high and inclined down-course slightly beyond vertical. The trick was to time the run so that one could jump, plant one's right foot about four feet up the wall, and grab the top with one's hands to get over. After this there was another wall, somewhat higher, about fifty yards down the trail. This wall had knotted ropes hanging down to help in the climb. After dropping to the ground, one ran along a log lying over a shallow trench and then flopped down on one's belly to crawl through soft sand under a lattice of barbed wire. Next came a set of overhead "monkey bars," which brought one to a log trestle about twenty feet high. After scaling up and down the trestle, a short jog over a sand dune brought one to a pipe maze, which was the end of the course. Toward the end of Preflight the cross-country run became like a pleasant stroll in the woods, but the obstacle course was a trial for me until the end.

As one would expect for future naval aviators and naval flight officers, our training placed great emphasis on swimming and water survival skills. Fortunately, swimming was one of my strong points. My father had trained me to be an excellent swimmer when I was a youngster, and I excelled in swim sports in Boy Scouts. First we were given a swim test to separate the class into skill levels for future instruction; it was the most rigorous water test I had ever taken. It included jumping from a thirty-foot tower and treading water for fifteen minutes with one's hands clasped over one's head. We also had to demonstrate proficiency in the crawl, breast, side, and elementary backstrokes. The total distance swum during the test was close to a mile—fully clothed with tennis shoes on. We were also required to demonstrate making floats out of our trousers and shirts. I was able to pass the initial swim test, so I was exempt from taking further swimming classes.

Perhaps the most interesting, and for some the most terrifying, lesson in Preflight water survival was the device known as the "Dilbert dunker." ("Dilbert" was a pejorative term used by class sergeants and cadet officers to name the stupidest cadet in history.) The Dilbert dunker was a contraption of aluminum and steel mesh made up to resemble a cockpit mounted on rails and designed to slide down a forty-five-degree incline into a swimming pool. It had a standard cockpit seat, complete with lap belt and shoulder harness. Cadets strapped themselves into the dunker just as they would strap into an airplane seat. When they signaled readiness, the device was released and began a rapid descent toward the pool. Blocks at the end of the rails halted the device and flipped it forward into an inverted position.

The water impact was a solid jolt much greater than one might expect, and the inversion disoriented the dunker's occupant, who lost all sense of which way was up. We were instructed to just sit tight until the bubbles cleared, and then look at the lap belt to properly release the buckle. The buckle was designed so that all the straps released when the catch was thrown. Next, we were to look toward the top of the cockpit where the canopy rail met the windscreen, grab it, and pull ourselves out of the cockpit. We were to swim a few strokes toward the far end of the pool to clear the dunker, and then surface.

It sounded simple, and it was, as long as the cadet kept his head and didn't panic. It required holding one's breath for about thirty seconds and was performed while wearing a seat-cushion-style parachute pack. Scuba divers were standing by in the water to observe our actions and rescue anyone who couldn't make it out. A few cadets panicked and grabbed and fumbled frantically with the strap release, unable to unstrap. Some released the parachute harness as well as the seat belt and became hopelessly tangled in the straps. Another common mistake was to unstrap and then try to swim through the cockpit floor to reach the surface. There was a procedure to exit Preflight training called "DOR" (drop at own request). The first DORs from our class occurred after the Dilbert dunker training. It was tough and frightening for the poorer swimmers in our class, but this type of training could save your life someday if your airplane ever went over the side of your aircraft carrier.

───────

Once our class was "secured to the battalion" we were allowed liberty on weekends until 2400. The main attraction for cadets on liberty on the base was the ACRAC (Aviation Cadet Recreation Club) Club. Because we were not commissioned officers we weren't allowed the use of the officers' club, and because we weren't enlisted we couldn't patronize the enlisted men's club either—hence, the ACRAC club. The ACRAC offered beer and soft drinks only because some of our classmates were still shy of their twenty-first birthdays. One could buy hot dogs, hamburgers, and pizza there as well, so it had all the trappings of paradise for us. The club also provided a live band until it closed at 2345, allowing time for us to make it back to the Batt in time for mandatory taps and bed check at 2400. The base allowed young ladies from town free access to the ACRAC, and there was always a large supply of young females from the local area on hand to dance with the cadets. Preflight cadets had a slang name for these girls—"ACRAC Annies."

Saturday mornings in Preflight were occupied by mandatory intramural sports. If we had escaped incurring demerits during the week, we were allowed off-base liberty beginning at noon until bed check at 2400. Cadets got no overnight liberty until they passed instrument rating in advanced training.

Sunday morning church services were mandatory. The Protestant portion of our regiment formed up for a formal parade to the base chapel at 1030. Complete with field music from the Preflight band, the march to church service was an inspiring spectacle. The regiment trooped into the chapel and was seated by command after everyone had reached their places in the pews. The Preflight chapel was a beautiful place to worship, and the services were nondenominational and Navy oriented. The most moving portion was when the Preflight choir led us in singing the Navy Hymn: "Eternal Father, strong to save . . ." with its second stanza dedicated to aviation, "Lord, guard and guide the men who fly . . ." Memorials to departed comrades lined the walls and were a poignant reminder that Navy flying is sometimes dangerous and that some of our names might join those honored ranks.

Even with the regimentation and strict military discipline, the weeks flew by, and in the last week of January 1965 class 39-64 found itself in cadet officer week. We had enjoyed our Christmas leave, but now we were eager to finish Preflight. I was on the Indoc detail and was amused to remember my own Indoc experiences just fifteen weeks ago. All the physical training had me in superb condition and the early-morning Indoc PT was a lark. Our graduation parade was the next Friday, and the AOCs in our class would be receiving their commissions.

The graduation ceremony for class 39-64 was identical with all those in which we had marched over the previous four months. Preflight was over and class 39-64 was history, but nothing else changed for the cadets. The naval aviation officers (NAOs) would begin NAO school, and the pilot candidates would begin flight training. The newly commissioned officers would be leaving us to move to the bachelor officers' quarters (BOQ) or, if they were married, to off-base housing. The class would be fragmented, and we would never again see some of those whom we had come to know so well over the past sixteen weeks. Others would become wingmen for each other as we progressed through flight training, and we would be together for months to come.

The pilot candidates got an unpleasant surprise after graduation. Unusually poor flying weather had created a backlog of students waiting to finish primary flight training at Saufley Field, so the the NAVCADS and MARCADS of our class would receive temporary assignments to a flight pool and would remain in the wooden barracks we had inhabited during Indoc. In fact, we would be right next door to Indoc. It felt as if we were regressing.

There was one bright spot in this situation: we were now eligible for flight pay, and that was a huge increase in a cadet's salary. To actually receive flight pay, though, one had to accumulate at least four hours of flying time a month. We quickly discovered how to satisfy this obligation by cadging rides in the Navy transport aircraft that regularly flew dispatches, spare parts, internal paperwork, and the like to all the naval air stations in the southern United States. The round trip to NAS Jacksonville, Florida, was a particularly popular flight. The aircraft used for this support mission was a small, twin-engine, tail-wheel transport with the military designation C-45. In the civilian world it was known as a "twin Beech." Made by the Beechcraft Aircraft Company, this venerable light twin transport was the utility van of naval air. With seats for ten passengers and a crew of two pilots, the C-45 took a little more than four hours to make the roundtrip flight, thereby nicely filling our flight pay requirements in one shot.

With the increase in fortune that flight pay brought, I decided it was high time to purchase my first automobile. I calculated that it would be just possible to afford the payments and insurance on a very modest ride. Accordingly, I settled for the most inexpensive car I could find, a four-door Rambler American sedan. It was definitely not the image of a hot fighter pilot's car, but I could afford it, and it got me where I wanted to go. Spring was coming to north Florida, and with wheels and a lot of liberty time I was able to make the most of my sojourn in flight pool. Transfers finally came through, and in mid-March I packed my gear, loaded up the Rambler, and drove the ten miles north to NAAS Saufley Field to begin real flying.

3

Saufley Field

NAAS Saufley Field was a very small air base with barracks, mess hall, and administration buildings nestled in a wide V formed by the intersection of two of its eight runways. Everything there was designed to support flight training. I was assigned a room in the cadet barracks with two other cadets. One of my roommates was also just starting training, but the other, Mike Totten, was an advanced cadet in training for his first carrier landings. We viewed Mike with a mixture of awe and envy and constantly pestered him with questions about how to cope with the program. His advice was very helpful, and he patiently answered our questions. I hoped I would be in his place some day.

Saufley was home to two training squadrons: VT-1 and VT-5. The "V" in Navy squadron designations stands for fixed wing, versus "H" for helicopter. The second letter denotes the mission of that squadron: "T" for training, "A" for attack, "F" for fighter, and so on. VT-1 was a huge squadron with 123 T-34B Mentor primary trainer aircraft. Every naval aviation student began training in VT-1, so it had to be big. VT-5 was much smaller because its mission was to prepare students who had completed primary training for their first aircraft carrier landings before they began advanced training.

The remnant of class 39-64 was broken down into smaller groups for primary flight training. My group began training with ground school one day after reporting to Saufley. We would have three weeks of ground school before we began flying, then a half-day of ground school and half-day of flying for the next few weeks thereafter. We still studied aerodynamics and

28

engineering, but now what we learned was directly related to what we would be doing in the T-34B. For example, engineering dealt with the construction and function of the 220-horsepower Lycoming engine that powered the Mentor. Aerodynamics taught us about the airframe of the T-34B and the forces that would be acting on it while we performed the maneuvers prescribed for primary. Other ground school classes dealt with procedures and survival as related to the Mentor.

—————

In the event of airborne catastrophe, the final option for survival is the parachute. Standing up in the cockpit seat in a one-hundred-mile-per-hour (or more) windstream and vaulting over the canopy rail while wearing a heavy, bulky parachute is harder than it sounds, though. And if one bails out on the wrong side—the one toward which the airplane is spinning—one may end up going through the propeller, making egress both messy and unnecessary. To give us some idea of what it might be like to bail out, we spent several turns in the bailout trainer. The trainer was the nose and cockpit section of a T-34B, complete with engine and propeller, mounted on a pipe framework about six feet off the ground. The wings had been removed, and there was a heavy canvas net arrangement on the starboard side of the fuselage.

The first training session began when each of us climbed into the front cockpit, from which we would do all our training in the Mentor, and strapped in. We then went through the starting checklist and starting procedure under the watchful eyes of an instructor, giving us some training in starting and running the engine prior to our first flight. This was old hat for the few men in my group who were already private pilots, but for the rest of us it was the first time we had started an aircraft engine. When it was my turn, I carefully climbed into the cockpit, strapped in, and went through the checklist. I even remembered to call "Clear!" to warn the ground crew that I was about to crank the engine, avoiding the most common error of omission committed by neophyte students. I engaged the starter, counted the six propeller blades as the prop swung through its arc, brought the throttle out of "cutoff" to the "idle" position, and was rewarded with a throaty roar as the engine spun up to idle RPM. I accelerated the engine and set the prop pitch to "full increase RPM" to simulate the prop blast and wind I would encounter in flight. All that remained was to open the canopy, disconnect the radio plugs from my helmet cords, release the seat straps, stand up in the seat pan, place one hand on the top of the windshield and the otherhand on the canopy bow, and dive headfirst over the canopy rail into the net. As I was helped to my feet and down the ladder from the net to the ground, I realized I was shaking a bit from excitement and adrenalin. This was a blast!

The next survival exercise dealt with a parachute landing in the water. We assembled at the training swimming pool in flight suits and tennis shoes; our new steel-toed leather flight boots were too expensive to subject them to water practice. In turn, we each donned a parachute harness, which was then connected to a set of risers that were attached to bungee cords that had been pulled the length of the pool. The bungees were attached to a large, chain-driven take-up reel. Each cadet stood with his back to the pool. As soon as he indicated readiness the take-up reel was engaged. This yanked him rapidly backward into the pool and towed him across the water like a fishing lure to simulate being dragged by the parachute if the wind was high. The trick was to reach up to the riser attachment fittings on the parachute harness, located just below the shoulders, and squeeze the releases. This would allow one or both risers to fly free; the bungees were rigged so that if one side were released it would release tension on the other, just like air spilling out of the parachute canopy. We had to accomplish this before reaching the opposite end of the pool, or we did it again and again until we could. One can swallow a lot of water learning to do this.

Before our first flight we had to become intimately familiar with the location and function of all the controls and indicators in the cockpit of the T-34B. We accomplished this by spending several hours in cockpit mockups, touching each switch and gauge and repeating its name and function. Our final exam was a blindfolded cockpit check. We sat blindfolded in the mockup while an instructor called out the name of all the controls and indicators. We had to reach out and touch each item and describe its function as it was called. No mistakes were allowed.

———•—•———

Finally the day arrived—it was time for my first flight. All the training I had endured up to this point had been to prepare me for this event. I reported to the cavernous schedules hangar to meet my instructor, trying not to be nervous but still full of excitement and apprehension. It was 26 April 1965, and the weather was beautiful. Good weather was necessary for all primary training because it had to be conducted under VFR (visual flight rules) conditions. My instructor's name was listed alongside my own on the big schedules board: Lieutenant Lattimore. He was already waiting for me and began the brief for the hop right away. He explained that the first hop was intended to be more for orientation than instruction, and that I should relax and absorb all I could and not worry about how well I could fly. He said that he would be able to get a feel for my strengths and weaknesses and would know what to concentrate on teaching me after the hop. His remarks went a long way toward relaxing me, and I began to enjoy the experience.

We proceeded to the parachute room to check out our parachutes, then went to maintenance to check the airplane's logbook. Pilots perform this ritual of checking the aircraft's maintenance history—pilot write-ups and the mechanic's corrective action entries—before each flight, from primary trainers in Navy flight training all the way to jumbo jet transports in commercial aviation. We then walked out onto the flight line, where rows of white-and–day glow orange T-34Bs were parked. Mr. Lattimore indicated our airplane, number 0794, and walked me through this initial preflight inspection; I would be responsible for all succeeding preflight inspections at Saufley. We checked the oil; made sure the engine compartment was secure, with no loose wires or leaks; checked the condition of the tires and landing gear; drained the fuel sumps to check for the proper color avgas; made sure the control surfaces were free to move with no gust locks installed; and generally ensured that the airplane was ready to fly.

After strapping into the front cockpit and hooking up my radio cords, we went through the cockpit interphone check to see if we could communicate. I went through the prestart checklist and informed Mr. Lattimore that I was ready to start. The plane captain, standing by with a fire extinguisher in case of a carburetor fire on engine start, signaled clear and I started her up. After the engine settled down to a steady idle, I went through the poststart checklist down to the parking brake. Mr. Lattimore taxied us out of the chocks and away from the congested line area. The gentle vibration in the airframe from the spinning propeller made the airplane seem alive and eager to be away. Mr. Lattimore called Saufley Tower for a radio check. Saufley traffic was semicontrolled, in that the tower would transmit to aircraft only in the event of emergency. Normally a set of standard procedures regulated the traffic flow, and pilots visually cleared themselves in the traffic pattern. To ensure a good radio, though, we performed a mandatory radio check with the tower prior to every flight. As we taxied out we heard on the radio, "Saufley tower, Saufley 0808, soleo radio check," "soleo" indicating the pilot's nervousness. Mr. Lattimore chuckled over the intercom and said, "For some reason, when students key their mike, they frequently unkey their brains."

The first lesson was learning to taxi the airplane. Mr. Lattimore taxied us to a wide area of tarmac where the intersection of the runways formed a V. The main wheel brakes on most airplanes are actuated by pressing forward on the tops of the rudder pedals. The T-34B brakes were no exception, and because the nose wheel on the T-34B could freely rotate nearly 360 degrees, one could steer the airplane by alternately pressing on the toe brakes, and one could pivot the airplane about one wheel simply by locking that brake and applying a burst of power from the engine. My instructor told me to taxi straight for a few yards and then practice turning right and left, all the while maintaining adequate wing tip and tail clearance from several other first-flight airplanes practicing the same thing. Within a very short time I was turning smoothly and properly anticipating the extra power that was required to keep the airplane rolling while applying alternate brakes. Mr. Lattimore then took control and headed us for the duty runway.

The runways at Saufley were more than twice the length the T-34B needed for takeoff and landing; to expedite traffic, planes landed on the first half of the runway and took off on the last half. We held short of the runway while completing the taxi and pretakeoff checklists. Mr. Lattimore checked to be sure the T-34B that had just landed had slowed enough to turn off the runway short of our position, and then added full power and swung us smoothly onto the runway to begin our takeoff roll. He had me follow through gently on the controls with him as he used the rudder to correct the airplane's tendency to yaw into the torque created by the spinning propeller. As we rapidly gained speed, he kept up a running commentary on the interphone about what he was doing and checking. In what seemed like just a few seconds the airplane had reached rotate airspeed, and Mr. Lattimore eased back on the control stick. The airplane lifted smoothly off the runway and we climbed out west over Perdido Bay.

Mentally, I was still back on the runway. My instructor had said a great deal during the takeoff roll, and I didn't absorb half of it. Now we were "cleaning up" the airplane by retracting the landing gear and flaps, and he was describing how to set climb power and propeller RPM, and I had to concentrate on this and stop worrying about what I had missed earlier. Things were happening too fast, way too fast! I bleated this to my instructor: "Gee, Sir, I'm so far behind—I'm not getting all this!" Mr. Lattimore laughed and told me to relax. "Just let it wash over you," he said. "You're getting a lot more of this than you realize, and by your third or fourth hop this will be so routine that it'll be almost automatic."

We climbed to sixty-five hundred feet and leveled off. My instructor brought the power back to cruise setting and set cruise pitch on the propeller, then said, "You take it now, Steve, and practice some straight and level flying." Mr. Lattimore pointed out the area of the cockpit windscreen—where the horizon line intersected—that could be used as a rough reference for level pitch, but cautioned that I needed to scan the instrument panel and double check that with the altimeter and vertical speed indicator to maintain level flight. The airplane controls were trimmed perfectly for level flight, and as I curled my hand gently around the control stick, it felt solid and needed no changes on my part to hold level flight. I learned later that it is a matter of flying etiquette to trim the airplane properly before transferring control to another pilot. The primary control surfaces of all airplanes have trim tabs mounted on them so that once positioned properly with the control stick or rudder pedals, the trim tabs can be set to hold the control surface aerodynamically in the desired position. This relieves air pressure forces on the stick and rudder so that the pilot doesn't wear himself out physically holding the airplane in one attitude.

After a minute of me feeling exhilarated at actually controlling a flying machine Mr. Lattimore said, "See that water tower off to our right? Well, turn the airplane toward that tower and maintain this altitude and airspeed." I pushed the stick gently toward the right and was rewarded by the T-34B obediently banking and the earth tilting to the left. I was looking to the right, toward the water tower, when he said, "Now watch your altitude; you're diving." Sure enough, the nose had dropped well below the horizon and the altimeter was unwinding through six thousand feet. I had not pulled back on the stick to increase the pitch attitude to compensate for the reduced lift as the wings banked right away from horizontal. I pulled back on the stick a little and felt an invisible force pushing me down harder into the seat pan. "Easy does it," came the voice from the back seat through the headphones. I looked at the altimeter, which was climbing rapidly back toward sixty-five hundred feet. The water tower was swinging past the nose now, so I rolled the wings level, or tried to. I actually rocked them a little as I overshot wings level. Another gentle reminder to watch my altitude came from the back. Shit! The altimeter was running through seven thousand feet and the airplane was slowing down. I pushed forward on the stick and felt myself become lighter as the nose dropped back toward the horizon. Oops! Not too much; pull back a little. Damn! Now the wing dropped and we were turning. Pull the stick toward level; don't overshoot. That's it now, gently!

"Flying is a constant series of corrections," Mr. Lattimore explained. "The trick is to make your corrections as rapid and small as possible. To do this, you need to anticipate what the airplane is going to do before it happens. This is called 'being ahead of the airplane.' Now, let's try a few more turns right and left, holding constant altitude and airspeed, and really push your eyeballs to make them look at all the instruments and think about what you expect to happen when you make a control input."

After a few more turns I was doing considerably better and had cut my altitude fluctuations to plus or minus two hundred feet. Lattimore then took control of the airplane and said, "OK, Steve, you're getting the picture fine. We need to press on to get everything done today. You will have an opportunity to practice all this on later hops. Next, we are going to do some precision aerobatics. These are the basic maneuvers that all fighter and attack pilots use to accomplish their missions. We teach them here as an exercise in coordinated flying, so that you can experience the feel of the airplane in different regimes of flight. The maneuvers are done precisely to teach you to correct for rapidly changing aerodynamic forces. Anyone can yank an airplane through these exercises, but done properly they resemble a graceful aerial ballet. We will start with the aileron roll."

The aileron roll is a very simple maneuver in which the airplane maintains a constant heading while completing a 360-degree roll about its longitudinal axis. The longitudinal axis is an imaginary line running straight through the airplane from the propeller hub to the tail of the fuselage. Mr. Lattimore pulled the nose up about 15 degrees above the horizon and rolled the airplane smoothly to the right, over, inverted, and up, and continued through to the upright position on the original heading. I was surprised that we ended up at our original altitude because I had noted our rapid climb when he pulled the nose up to begin the maneuver, but a little reflection explained the phenomenon. When the wings rolled through a ninety-degree angle of bank they were not producing any lift, which caused the airplane to fall a little. The altitude gained at the beginning was lost during the roll. Mr. Lattimore said, "Let's do another." The roll was to the left this time, and I watched the earth roll around the canopy. He said, "You try one," then talked me through it. "Pull the nose up fifteen degrees. Now push the stick smoothly all the way over to the right side of the cockpit. Hold it there, now bring it back toward the center to catch the roll at wings level." I overbanked just a little but it wasn't bad, not bad at all. I caught a glimpse of my face in the rearview mirror and I was grinning from ear to ear.

Mr. Lattimore said, "Piece of cake. Next time, though, pay attention to the balance ball and keep the airplane balanced." The balance ball is a device much like a carpenter's level. A little ball floats in a fluid-filled glass tube just under the turn needle. As an airplane banks into a turn, the nose tends to yaw away from the direction of turn. This phenomenon is called adverse yaw and causes the airplane to skid through a turn. To prevent this, the pilot applies the rudder in the direction of turn. Keeping the balance ball centered in its glass tube keeps the airplane balanced so it doesn't skid through the turn.

We worked on the barrel roll next. The barrel roll is a lateral displacement of the airplane with two 90-degree turns while the airplane completes a 360-degree roll. It is more complicated to explain than to do. The easiest way to visualize the maneuver is to picture the airplane flying along the longitudinal axis of an imaginary barrel. It pulls up and at the same time rolls toward the side of the barrel and completes the roll around the side, ending up on the original heading at the original altitude. The barrel roll is a big, swooping maneuver that gives one a sense of exhilarating freedom of movement.

Mr. Lattimore demonstrated one to the right and left, with me following through on the controls during the second one. He gave me the airplane to try one on my own, and I hamburgered through it with my nose much too low on the horizon because I didn't pull up hard enough and rolled much too slowly. Consequently, I dished out the bottom of the roll far too low with excess airspeed. Mr. Lattimore just laughed and said, "No sweat, Steve, you'll get the hang of it after a few more, but since we are going like a rocket, I'll demonstrate the loop next."

The loop maneuver is very simple—just a 360-degree turn in the vertical plane. The airplane starts off on a cardinal heading at a specific altitude, and the pilot pulls the stick back steadily until the airplane is climbing vertically. Maintaining back pressure on the stick causes the nose to continue past vertical until the airplane is flying inverted. As the nose again drops through the horizon, continued back pressure causes the nose to sweep past vertical and begin the pullout, arriving at the original altitude and heading. Although some airplanes have the power to make a perfectly circular loop, the loop in the T-34B resembled a cursive letter L. As the airspeed decreases rapidly during the climb to the top of the loop, the airplane's turning radius becomes much smaller, so that at the top of the loop the airplane nearly swaps ends.

As Mr. Lattimore started the first loop, I became acquainted with what aviators call "Gs." I had been a little aware of feeling that I was being pushed down into the seat, but we hadn't sustained gravity forces (G forces) long enough to really get my attention. The loop changed that. As we started the loop, a giant invisible hand jammed me down into the seat. My neck muscles were fighting suddenly to hold my head up as the hand tried to push my chin into my chest. My flying helmet suddenly weighed a ton and I could hardly move my hands out of my lap. The force relaxed as we floated over the top of the loop, and as we dove inverted down the back side the forces returned when the nose came up from vertical to level off. An involuntary groan escaped as my body fought the G force. I asked Mr. Lattimore how many Gs we pulled. "About three Gs," he said. "You'll get used to them. As a matter of fact, you'll pull twice that many or more in a dogfight."

Mr. Lattimore explained that the next maneuver was designed to recover the airplane from an inadvertent stall/spin situation. As we had done before each maneuver, we performed a quick wing rock and clearing turn to ensure a safe distance from other traffic. As many as thirty or forty airplanes might be in the same area doing the same things we were doing, and the danger of a midair collision was very real. Mr. Lattimore then pulled the nose up sharply while reducing the power to idle and pushing the prop lever to full increase RPM. The little airplane slowed quickly, and it became quieter in the cockpit as the slipstream noise died down. My instructor had to keep increasing back pressure on the stick to keep the nose up as the wings lost lift rapidly and the airplane began to shudder and buffet gently. The wings were no longer producing enough lift to keep the nose up, and the airplane suddenly pitched over into a shallow dive as we began to mush down through the sky. Mr. Lattimore said, "See how nice she stalls? There's plenty of warning buffet, and it is nice and stable in the stall." He then added power and eased forward on the stick and the little craft was flying again with only about five hundred feet of altitude loss.

Next Lattimore said, "Now we'll see how she spins." He again pulled the nose up with power off, and as the T-34B began to buffet, he slapped the stick hard over to the left and fed in full left rudder. The left wing immediately lost its lift, snapping us nearly over on our back, and the rudder input corkscrewed the nose around to the left. We stabilized in a steep, nose-down spiral, rotating counterclockwise. Both wings were fully stalled now, and the airplane gently buffeted as we spiraled down. The spin was not violent, however, and the sensation wasn't even making me dizzy. Mr. Lattimore said, "She spins nice and easy also." We had been told in ground school that the easiest way to recover the T-34B from a spin was to let go of everything and put your feet flat on the floor, because in about three and a half turns the airplane would recover from the spin on its own. For this reason, spins were initiated with the nose pointed at some prominent object on the horizon, and the student was expected to recover the airplane with the nose pointing at that object after two turns. That way the instructor would know that the student had properly initiated the recovery. Mr. Lattimore centered the stick and fed opposite rudder to the direction of rotation, and the little airplane stopped turning and was in a dive with the airspeed rapidly building back to flying speed. We had lost only about two thousand feet so he said "OK, Steve, now you try one. Wait until she's fully stalled before you put the stick over, or you'll just end up making a diving spiral, which isn't really a spin." We were pointing at a large grove of trees on the horizon, and as I felt the first stall buffet, I pushed the stick over to the right, fed in full right rudder, and was rewarded with a very nice spin to the right. "Very nice," Mr. Lattimore said. "Now look for the trees and lead them a little. Now center the stick and left rudder." As I fed in the left rudder, the nose stopped right on the trees and he said, "Good job, Steve. I'll give you an above average for spins on this hop."

Then he said, "Now, as easy as it is to recover from a spin in this airplane, that fact won't help you at all unless you have enough altitude to recover. Next I'll demonstrate the error that kills more new students than any other mistake in primary flight training. It's called a skidded turn stall, and it happens when a student has overshot his turn to final approach in the landing pattern. To correct, he increases his bank angle and really honks the nose around, while helping it with a lot of rudder. All this with the power off, and he's yanking and banking and his speed is being bled off rapidly. Then he stomps in that rudder and watch what happens." While Mr. Lattimore was talking he had been setting up this scenario, and we were in a steep, banked turn to the left with the power off. He added left rudder, and as the nose slid around, without warning we were flipped suddenly to the right on our back, with the nose falling into a steep, inverted dive. As the right wing had begun to skid in the left turn, the airflow had been from the wing tip toward the fuselage, and this spanwise airflow had completely killed the lift on that wing. Because the low wing was still flying, it had the effect of suddenly being without a right wing, and that had caused us to flip over. As he aileron-rolled us upright and recovered, Mr. Lattimore said, "Do that at six hundred feet on final and there just isn't enough sky left for you to recover. Students usually hit inverted, and they die. Remember this well, it will keep you alive. Keep one eye on that airspeed in the landing pattern, and if you overshoot or have a bad approach, wave off and go around. Don't try to salvage it and end up on your back." The swiftness with which a pilot could die by being inattentive impressed me, and this was a lesson I never forgot.

All this stalling and spinning had lost us considerable altitude. We were now down to two thousand feet and not far from the small town of Summerdale, Alabama, as well as the small, triangular auxiliary practice landing field named after the town. Mr. Lattimore lined us up with the runway closest to the direction of the prevailing wind. As he reduced power and began descending into the landing pattern, he called for me to perform the before-landing checklist. I configured us for landing, with landing gear checked down and locked, and flaps set for landing. Mr. Lattimore talked through the first landing as I followed through on the controls. The black asphalt runway seemed to rush up toward us until Mr. Lattimore pulled the nose up gently in a flare, and I could feel the airplane float on a cushion of air as the wheels kissed the runway surface. Mr. Lattimore laughed and said, "Ahh, one of my better ones. Your turn next."

He added power, and after a short ground roll we were airborne. "OK, Steve, give me a thirty-degree-bank turn to the left and we'll climb to eight hundred feet." This altitude corresponded to the pattern altitude at Saufley, so we would practice our touch-and-gos from that altitude. As we climbed, we were turning 180 degrees to the runway heading. Leveling at eight hundred feet, we were on the downwind leg of the landing pattern—a course paralleling the runway off our left wingtip. As the end of the runway passed just behind the left wingtip, Mr. Lattimore had me start a diving left turn toward the runway end. He helped me all the way, adjusting our descent so that we rolled out of the turn lined up with the runway, diving through two hundred feet. "Now, Steve," he said, "start your nose up gently . . . oops, not too much!" I pulled a little hard because it seemed like we would smash into the runway. We ballooned upward and Mr. Lattimore pushed on the stick to get us started down again. "A little more gently this time, Steve. Pull back . . . hold it off . . . hold it off." My flare was more reasonable this time and we were floating a few feet above the runway, but my first yank and recovery had cost us some airspeed, and we dropped the last few feet to the runway.

The landing wasn't hard, though, and I was thrilled with the idea that I had just landed an airplane. "Not bad," my instructor said. "Now let's try again. Add power and climb to eight hundred left downwind." I pushed the power up and felt him correct for the yaw (which I had forgotten to do), pulled the stick back to climb, and we were airborne again. This time I was more used to the closure rate with the runway, but I still tended to flare high, and we floundered along until the wheels finally found the runway in a thumping flop that was a far cry from the gentle kiss of the demo landing. But I hadn't broken anything, and Mr. Lattimore told me I hadn't done badly as we climbed away from Summerdale headed back toward Saufley. Lattimore made me recite the complicated traffic pattern entry procedure that Saufley used, to be sure I had memorized it, and he made the landing, to be sure we remained on our half of the runway. He did let me taxi back into the parking spot and monitored the shutdown and postflight checklists.

The flight line was much too noisy to allow conversation, so we walked in silence to turn in the parachutes, sign off the yellow sheet, and debrief the hop. I wondered what kind of grade I would get. The grading system was simple. The hop itself was either pass or fail—or in our lexicon, either an up or a down. Grades for each event or procedure on a given hop were below average, average, or above average. The grades were all subjective, though, because they necessarily depended on the instructor's opinion of how the student had done.

Mr. Lattimore was much more formal with me on the ground. "Nice first hop, Mr. Gray. I'm giving you an above average for spins and all the rest average. You seemed to know your procedures fairly well for your first hop, and that indicates that you've been studying. I don't see any real problems that we can't correct in your basic flying ability, and as long as you maintain a good attitude, you shouldn't have any real difficulty with primary." He went over the things I should concentrate on for hop two and concluded the session with, "See you tomorrow."

As I walked back to the cadet barracks, I couldn't believe how happy and excited I was. Before, becoming a pilot had been just a means to becoming a naval officer. Now all that had changed—I wanted above all else to become a naval aviator. Never had I experienced such a feeling of freedom, grace, and exhilaration. I had actually rolled, looped, spun, and landed an airplane! All with help, to be sure, but I had done it nonetheless!

Inclement weather canceled the next day's hop, but Wednesday, 28 April, dawned beautifully clear with a gentle high pressure area behind the front. This promised good flying weather for the next several days, and Mr. Lattimore and I were soon airborne on hop two. He demonstrated the "Split S," "Immelman turn," "wingover," and "half Cuban eight" maneuvers. The Split S is simply the second half of a loop, performed by rolling the airplane over on its back and pulling the nose through a vertical dive and back to level flight. It accomplishes a 180-degree turn with a large loss of altitude. The Immelman turn, named after the World War I German aviator who invented it, is the opposite of the Split S. After pulling the nose up over the top of a loop, with the airplane on its back and the nose still 10 degrees above the horizon, the pilot rolls the airplane upright to level flight. This accomplishes a 180-degree turn with a large gain in altitude and loss of airspeed. The wingover is performed by pulling the nose up vertically and then using the rudder to kick the nose toward one wing tip, causing the airplane to reverse course and dive down the same flight path of the climb. The result is a vertical 180-degree turn. This maneuver is used to recover from a vertical climb with insufficient airspeed to level on top, and as a turning tactic in air-combat maneuvering. The half Cuban eight is done by executing a loop, but when the nose is 30 degrees below the horizon coming down the backside of the loop, the airplane is rolled upright and continues the 30-degree dive until leveling at the starting altitude. Mr. Lattimore explained that attack pilots execute this maneuver when using a bomb delivery known as "loft bombing."

We spent the remainder of the hop practicing touch-and-go landings. I was gaining confidence with each one, and even managed a few reasonably smooth touchdowns. Mr. Lattimore was complimentary about my performance in the debriefing, and my elation at learning to fly continued unabated. By hop four I was approaching a state of confidence that bordered on cockiness. The procedures were making much more sense now, and they were indeed becoming second nature. Then, on hop five, Mr. Lattimore brought me back to reality and taught me one of the most valuable lessons in flying.

We were climbing out toward our usual practice area, passing thirty-five hundred feet. Still under the influence of the high pressure area, the weather was gorgeous with smooth, stable air. The little T-34B felt as if it were sliding along on glass, and I was concentrating on trimming the airplane hands-off. I felt great and was thoroughly enjoying the magnificent visibility in the clear, early-morning air. Suddenly the throttle snapped back to the idle stop and the cockpit became much quieter. I was unprepared for this situation and flailed around mentally trying to recall the engine failure procedures. "Shit! Let's see . . . mixture rich, mag switch on both, fuel pump on, fuel tank selector on both, plenty of fuel . . . oh yes, prop full increase. Oh, shit, watch the airspeed. Trim for max range glide about 90 knots . . . where was I? Oh yes . . . carb heat on. . . ."

Mr. Lattimore's voice cut into my frantic mental gymnastics. "Looks like you're not going to get a restart. Where are you going to put it?" I shot a panicky look out the cockpit. We were already descending through fifteen hundred feet; there wouldn't be much choice. There! A field just to my left looked like a good place to shoot a practice emergency landing. "There, Sir, that field at eleven o'clock," I said. This comment was met with silence from the back. As we approached the field it was apparent that we would not have enough altitude to even try a turn into the wind. And I hadn't noticed a fringe of forty-foot-tall trees on the east side of the field that were beginning to loom large in my windscreen. To make matters worse, a deep ravine cut diagonally across the field, decreasing our available landing distance by half. My panic grew as it became obvious to me that we were not going to clear the trees. Instinctively I tried to push the throttle up, but it remained firmly locked at idle. After giving me a few more moments to contemplate the oncoming treetops, Mr. Lattimore said, "I've got the airplane," and he pushed the throttle up to full power.

The T-34B leaped skyward, and as we climbed out, Mr. Lattimore said, "Look back over our right wing." As he banked right, I could see a huge, flat, freshly plowed field covering an area almost as large as Saufley. He said, "You climbed right past that field and it didn't even register that it would make a great emergency landing field. As I told you before, Steve, you must always have a plan in mind to deal with emergencies, and you should always be looking for and aware of potential ditching sites when you are flying a single-engine airplane without an ejection seat. If that engine quits and you can't get a restart, you have to know where you're going to put the airplane. If this had been a real engine failure, we would be picking what was left of you out of those trees, because by the time you decided you had to ditch, you were too low to bail out. You just experienced the most dangerous and insidious enemy of an aviator—complacency. Any time you start to feel comfortable in an airplane, look around quickly to see what you've forgotten or if anything's wrong, because that's when things quit, emergencies happen, or events conspire to do you in. You have to teach yourself to fight complacency and keep on fighting it until constant alertness becomes automatic. Put this into your 'I learned about flying from that' file and remember it; it'll keep you alive."

My complacency cost me two below-average grades for that hop, and I vowed to do better. On the next two hops I got all averages with a few aboves, and on hop eight I got an above average on my engine-out approach emergency. On hop nine I flew with a different instructor. Training command policy required independent evaluation of students on periodic testing hops. Lieutenant Lattimore and Lieutenant Simon had swapped students to get us used to flying with different instructors. The extra apprehension I felt at having to perform for a stranger proved beneficial for me, though, and I flew my best hop so far. Mr. Simon gave me several above averages and told me he enjoyed the hop. I tempered my excitement with the remembrance of my humiliation on hop five, and cautioned myself not to get cocky again.

Mr. Lattimore used hops ten and eleven as practice for the PS-12 check. The "PS" prefix stood for "primary solo," and the twelfth hop was a check ride to make sure the student was safe for solo. Mr. Lattimore told me after hop eleven not to be nervous and to treat the twelve check just like the other hops we had been doing. He wished me luck and said he'd see me on hop fourteen. I checked the schedules board before leaving the hangar and found my PS-12X scheduled for the next morning with a Lieutenant Hill.

Lieutenant Hill met me the next morning, 13 May, at 0800. He briefed me on the maneuvers that I would be required to demonstrate for him and indicated that other than receiving his direction on what to do next, I was to act if he was not even there. He said that if all went well we would make a full-stop landing at one of the outlying fields, and he would get out and watch me make at least three landings. This would be my first actual solo in an airplane, and I felt a thrill of anticipation when he said that. I was surprised when he said that I had better not become so enthralled with flying solo that I forgot to land and pick him up!

Even though he wasn't saying much, I was acutely aware of Mr. Hill's presence in the rear cockpit. As the hop progressed, however, I was concentrating so hard on procedures and on doing everything correctly that I got over what little apprehension I felt. Mr. Hill gave me the simulated engine failure on climb out and I shot an acceptable approach to an open field. After letting me descend to about three hundred feet over the field, he told me to add power and continue the climb out. I demonstrated a loop, barrel roll, aileron roll, and wingover, followed by two spin recoveries. We were over Silverhill practice field, so I made two very nice touch-and-go landings. Mr. Hill then said the words I had been waiting to hear: "Mr. Gray, make your next landing a full stop and taxi back down to the approach end."

After we landed and taxied back, Mr. Hill told me to stop, wait until he was clear of the airplane, then take off and make three touch-and-go landings. "Don't you dare forget to land and pick me up after the last touch and go," he said. I watched as he opened the canopy and climbed off the trailing edge of the left wing. He gave me a thumbs-up from the grassy edge of the runway. I added power after going through the takeoff checklist and was soon airborne. I kept looking in the rearview mirror to convince myself he was really gone and I was flying solo. My landings were quite good and I felt really proud that I had passed my solo check.

En route to Saufley, Mr. Hill said, "Nice job, Steve, how did it feel to fly solo?"

"Aw, great, Sir! I'm prouder of this than anything I've ever done."

He laughed and said, "Yeah, I remember, but just wait until your first carrier landing—that's an even bigger thrill."

The flight back to Saufley was uneventful. Even though I was concentrating hard on making a perfect entry and landing, I couldn't ignore my excitement. I didn't have long to savor it, though, because as soon as Mr. Hill had finished the debriefing, I checked the schedules board and found that I was scheduled for my PS-13 solo next.

It felt a little strange to be checking the yellow sheets and walking out to the flight line by myself. The plane captain greeted me with a big grin and a cheery, "Good afternoon, Sir! Nice day for flying!" I carefully checked all the preflight items and was soon strapped in for my solo hop. I felt confident and not at all nervous. In fact, I was much more relaxed than I had been the first time I was allowed to take the family car out alone. I was ready for takeoff by the time I reached the duty runway, and the pattern was void of landing aircraft. As I climbed out west over Perdido Bay, I again checked the rearview mirror and exulted over the empty rear seat.

The syllabus called for the usual practice aerobatics, which I performed in rapid succession. I had chosen to do my air work over Silverhill practice field, and I did some spins to drop my altitude to pattern entry level. After only four touch-and-gos, I climbed back out to cruise around the area and enjoy flying. There were some distant thunderheads off to the west—too far away to pose any problems—that made a beautiful contrast to the clear blue sky over southern Alabama. My fuel state finally dictated that it was time to return to Saufley, but I could have gone on flying for hours. Indeed, my logbook showed that the PS-13 solo was the longest flight I logged while I was at Saufley.

I was happier that afternoon than I had ever been, and I shared looks of pride and accomplishment with the rest of my classmates who had soloed. Friday afternoon, 14 May, my class assembled in the squad bay of the barracks for the traditional "wetting down" of the new solo students. After a few beers, Mr. Lattimore cut off my tie in the traditional ritual that welcomed me to the ranks of those who had taken flight alone and returned safely to tell about it.

The next week went by in a flash. We had finished ground school and all we had left of the course was flying. Our confidence increased with each hop. With the end of our time at Saufley nearing, the main topic of speculation was whether we would be assigned jets or props for the remainder of training. Most of us wanted jets, of course. Most young flight students had romantic visions of becoming swashbuckling fighter pilots, and at that time an assignment to the jet-training pipeline was the only way to become a fighter pilot. There was an opportunity to request jets after completing carrier qualifications in props, but it was a long shot. I was resigned to getting props because, for the last several weeks, only a few very-top-of-the-class Navy students had been assigned jets. Even though my grades—both academic and flying—had been good, the history of the past several weeks told me that I was nowhere near high enough on the list to be selected for jets.

On Thursday, 20 May, my final solo in the T-34B began with some excitement. I was just retracting the landing gear after takeoff from Saufley when suddenly the prop began surging into fine pitch, causing the engine RPM to exceed the red line. I retarded the throttle as much as I could without losing flying speed, but the surges continued and grew worse. I needed to get the airplane the ground as soon as possible, so I called Saufley Tower: "Saufley Tower, this is Saufley eight-one-eight. Request an immediate downwind turn; I have an overspeeding prop."

The effect of this transmission was galvanic. "All T-34s in the twelve-hundred-foot circle remain at twelve hundred," the tower ordered. "All T-34s in the eight-hundred-foot circle depart the pattern and reenter at twelve hundred. Eight-one-eight, you may turn downwind for landing." I was only at three hundred feet and was anticipating a crash on the field if the engine came apart before I could land. I got the gear back down and did a tight turn to final. As I rolled in I could see the crash trucks rolling toward the duty runway with lights flashing, and I was impressed and a little embarrassed that I had caused all this commotion. I landed just fine and shut the engine down as I rolled clear of the runway. A line tug came out and towed me back to the flight line. The maintenance officer explained that the plane's propeller had been replaced just before my hop, and there must have been some air trapped in the hydraulic pitch mechanism. I was issued a replacement airplane and continued on my hop without further problems.

My last hop with Mr. Lattimore was simply a review and a time to show my instructor how far I had progressed in just eighteen hops. We really wrung that airplane out. We spent most of the hop doing aerobatics and enjoying flying in general. At the debriefing I tried to express to Mr. Lattimore how much I had enjoyed having him as an instructor and how grateful I was for all the flying skills he had taught me. I'm sure that I was just another student to him, but he will always be a special teacher to me.

———•———

Primary was over. On Tuesday, 24 May, our class mustered in the personnel office to receive our basic flight assignments. The beaming personnel officer announced to the class, "Everyone who wanted jets got 'em." There was a moment of stunned silence, and then the room erupted in wild cheers. The powers that determined such things had decided that the jet pipeline had a hole in it and we were needed to fill the gap. The "needs of the service" once again took precedence, but this time they matched our own desires.

Mike Totten was also leaving, having completed his carrier qualifications, and was on his way to NAS Corpus Christi for advanced prop. We wished each other luck and he congratulated me on getting jets. He said, "I was pretty disappointed when I didn't get jets, but I'm really happy now because there's a good chance for me to get jets at advanced, and I really loved flying the big old T-28. See you in the fleet!"

As I drove out the front gate of Saufley Field, I was very much aware of leaving with much more experience than I had brought with me. I was confident but not cocky, and I was clearly focused on my goal of becoming a naval aviator. I had also learned a lot about myself and how I would perform when a situation demanded fast and clear thinking. I had soloed an airplane, passed the first hurdle of the program, and was really looking forward to the next step. I knew that many challenges remained to be conquered, and I felt ready for them.

4

McCain Field

Meridian, Mississippi, seemed an incongruous place to build a naval air station. Located just across the Alabama line in extreme eastern Mississippi, the air station was much closer to the small town of Lauderdale, but Meridian, the closest large town, got the namesake. The explanation I heard for the base's location was a believable rumor that it was located on land owned by the chairman of the Senate Armed Services Committee and leased from him by the Navy. That at least made some sense, because the base was a heck of a long way from the water.

I arrived at the front gate in the wee hours of Sunday, 30 May 1965. I had intended to spend Saturday night en route and give myself most of Sunday to get checked in and settled, but I was eager to get there and drove straight through instead. The gate guard was not a bit surprised or ruffled by my arrival at such an unusual hour, and he had a sheet listing my room assignment. I was given directions to the cadet barracks and a base vehicle parking sticker. My room was on the second deck of a modern brick structure that looked more like a nice motel or college dorm than the military barracks to which I had become accustomed. The rooms opened out onto an exterior walkway that ran around the entire building, and each shared a bathroom in the center of the building with the room on the opposite side of the building. The rooms were very spacious, each side housing a full-size bed, a large desk, and a chest of drawers. The bathroom had two sets of double wash basins, two large mirrors, two commodes, and two showers. I was awestruck; compared with my previous quarters this was opulence indeed. I kept repeating, "Wow!

This is great! I can't believe it!" Finally, my new roommate, whom I had awakened, said, "Well, don't believe it in the morning . . . good night!" Sheepish at having disturbed him, I slipped quietly into the wonderful new bed and decided to finish unpacking in the morning.

Daylight revealed a modern new facility. From the cadet mess to the administration and classroom buildings to the enlisted barracks, it was first-rate. I knew I was going to like it here. The BOQ, a larger version of the cadet barracks, was about a quarter of a mile away across a three-acre lake, doubt-less created by the excavation of fill dirt during the base's construction. But it was a nice architectural touch, complete with a small, wooded island in the center. There was only one problem: the lake had no natural spring or other water source. After nearly four years, only a small amount of rainwater had managed to accumulate in the bottom, creating a dismal, swampy marsh. The lake was named for the wife of the first base commander and was officially known as Lake Hester; the flight students had promptly recommissioned it "Lake Fester."

I have no idea how many acres the naval air station encompassed, but the barracks and administration area were a couple of miles from the opera-tions area known as McCain Field (named in honor of the late Adm. John S. McCain, USN). The airfield was home to two training squadrons, VT-7 and VT-9. Two large hangars, one for each squadron, housed maintenance and administration spaces. The layout of the field centered on a huge, square concrete apron with both hangars on the west side and parking space for each squadron's aircraft, and three eight-thousand-foot-long runways extending from three of the square's corners.

VT-7 and VT-9 each had about fifty T-2A Buckeye jet trainers. The single jet engine, slung under the fuselage, gave the airplane a football shape. The wings were mid-mounted straight wings with extra fuel tanks on the tips. All the T-2s were dual cockpit aircraft with a single clamshell-type canopy. A thick steel tail hook that attached to the tail boom just above the exhaust and extended just aft of the vertical stabilizer was a constant reminder that these would be the kind of aircraft in which we would make our first aircraft carrier landings.

———•—•———

We needed a month of ground school before we could start flying the T-2s. The step up to jets was a giant leap for fledgling aviators like us. We would be flying at altitudes five times higher than those at which the T-34B operated, so we had to learn about the physiology of high-altitude flight. The flight characteristics of the T-2A were quite different from those of the

T-34B, so we needed more aerodynamics classes. The operating envelope of the T-2A would be at speeds up to three times faster than anything we had experienced before, and because the maneuvers we would perform would generate high gravity forces, we needed training in the physiology of high-G flight and the use of G-suits. The higher speeds meant that our operating area would be many miles larger than before, so we needed to learn radio instrument navigation. We would be flying in all kinds of weather—and because of the greater distances covered in our flights, there was a greater danger of being caught in inclement weather on a solo—so we needed to learn instrument flight procedures. The speed of the jets required an ejection seat for bailout, so we needed a session in an ejection seat trainer. In addition to all this, we had to learn the airplane's systems, know normal and emergency operating procedures, and pass another blindfolded cockpit check.

Although we chafed at the prospect of spending an entire month on the ground, we had little time to think about it. The pace of exposure to these new subjects required us to study hard to assimilate everything. The high-altitude physiology classes required a session in the hypobaric chamber to give us firsthand experience with the effects of too little oxygen (hypoxia). Since the symptoms of incipient hypoxia are highly individualistic, we had to experience them for ourselves. This was a dangerous undertaking, and trained medical personnel accompanied and supervised us in the chamber. Except perhaps for a trip to the mountains, most of us had never been close to oxygen-deficient altitudes. The air at sea level contains many more oxygen molecules than our bodies require. Above ten thousand feet, though, the air is much less dense and correspondingly fewer oxygen molecules enter the lungs on each inhalation.

The brain is the first organ to be affected by hypoxia. The lack of oxygen-rich blood interferes with normal thought processes and produces bizarre reactions until one finally loses consciousness. Permanent brain damage can result within minutes, and if the hypoxia continues long enough, death is the final result. In high-speed aircraft, though, loss of consciousness because of hypoxia usually results in the death of the pilot long before the effects of oxygen deprivation cause any damage. The onset of hypoxia can be so gradual that the pilot can easily fail to detect his or her decreasing ability to function until it is too late.

The hypobaric chamber was an iron room with many windows that allowed outside observers to monitor those inside. We entered the antiseptically white-painted interior through an airlock. Arranged along the walls were benches with two sets of oxygen control consoles and oxygen masks between each bench. We were instructed to take a seat, don a mask, and perform the preflight check of the console and mask, checking for proper oxygen flow through the mask. Just as in the airplane, we breathed 100 percent oxygen. After receiving a good test with thumbs up from each station, the pair of monitors in the chamber hooked up their own masks and signaled the run to begin. Air was pumped out of the chamber to simulate increasing altitude, and a surgical glove tied to the ceiling began to inflate as the pressure outside it decreased. An altimeter at each console allowed us to keep track of the chamber's simulated altitude. The chamber "climbed" at about the same rate as the T-2, so we had some time to kill before we reached the chamber's level-off altitude. The instructor outside the chamber lectured us on the various effects we were experiencing as the pressure on our bodies lessened.

Finally, the chamber reached a simulated altitude of twenty-eight thousand feet above sea level and "leveled off." The student on my left was given a deck of cards and a shoebox with a large slot cut in the lid. The instructor told him to remove his mask and begin dropping the cards through the slot one at a time. For the first minute, the student put the cards in the box nicely, one at a time. Toward the end of one minute, however, his movements became slower and less sure. He wrinkled his brow in concentration, and his hand began to waver as he tried to hit his mark. Finally, after about two minutes, he seemed unable to find the slot and simply stopped with the card suspended over the box. We had been told to watch him for signs of hypoxia during this time, and his lips and fingernails had turned dark blue, indicating oxygen-poor blood. The monitor in the chamber quickly hooked the student's mask back over his face, and he continued to put the cards in the box gradually, finally recovering his normal dexterity in less than a minute. "That didn't seem so hard," he said. "What's the big deal?" He was completely unaware that he had had any difficulty putting the cards in the box. It was a graphic demonstration of the effects of hypoxia, and it impressed on us to check our fingernails anytime we felt the least bit strange while flying at high altitudes.

We were all given an opportunity to take off our masks and experience our own symptoms. I immediately sensed difficulty in getting enough air. I was given a pad of paper and a pen and told to write my name again and again until I was told to stop. The next thing I knew, I was sitting with my mask on and writing my name. I was amazed to see that my writing became smaller and smaller as hypoxia manifested, until I was drawing a tiny circle; then I began to write increasingly larger as my blood oxygen rose.

Another pair of students was told to play patty-cake with their masks off. They started off really well, determined to prove their superior coordination over the rest of us, even without oxygen. Soon, though, they were laughing uproariously while slapping each other all over. One sat calmly while the monitor reattached his mask, but the other resisted having his mask replaced. This is another possible side effect of hypoxia: a euphoric feeling that everything is just fine and no one else knows what is best.

————•————

After about two weeks of ground school our class was directed to report to supply for flight gear issue. The only gear we had brought from Saufley was our flight suits and boots. The step up to jets required more sophisticated equipment than the helmet and boom microphone we had used in the T-34B. Each cadet was issued a shiny new white helmet complete with two retractable visors. The visors—one tinted and one clear—slid out of a recess at the front when the wearer pulled down one of two knobs on either side of the helmet. Two oxygen mask clip holders were mounted on either side of the face cutout, and the headphone cord came out of the rear of the helmet.

Next, each of us was issued an oxygen mask, a molded plastic cup with a soft rubber insert that fit over the bridge of the nose and under the chin, completely covering the nose and mouth. The inhalation and exhalation valves and the microphone were inside the mask. A long hose and a microphone cord extended from the base of the mask. Nylon web straps attached the plastic cup to the helmet clips.

Because the parachute used in the T-2's ejection seat system remained in the seat rather than being worn by the pilot, we wore a corset-like affair called a "torso harness" into which the risers of the parachute snapped. The torso harness was just a parachute harness covered with nylon material.

A strange garment called a "G-suit" completed the ensemble. The purpose of the G-suit was to help the aviator maintain consciousness during prolonged exposure to high gravity forces. The G-suit looked somewhat like a pair of cowboy chaps. A wide belt with a rubber bladder fit around the waist, with the bladder over the abdomen. The legs of the G-suit zipped up from ankle to inner thigh, with bladders over each thigh and calf. An air hose extended from the left waist to knee level. Exposure to high G forces tends to pull blood away from the brain and pool it in the lower extremities. Loss of consciousness will occur very rapidly—within a few seconds—if the blood supply to the brain is cut off. The rubber bladders over the abdomen, thighs, and calves were inflated proportionally to the level of gravity forces by a high-pressure air connection in the cockpit. The higher the Gs, the harder the bladders would inflate, squeezing the lower body tightly to force the blood up and increasing the blood pressure to the brain. Pilots were trained to "grunt breathe" at the same time, forcing the diaphragm muscle against the pressure exerted by the abdomen bladder and increasing its effectiveness. A manual inflate button in the cockpit inflated the G-suit immediately to its maximum.

The new flight gear both increased our impatience to begin flying the T-2 and reminded us how much we still had to learn before we could properly begin flying jets. At the first opportunity, though, I donned my new flight gear and modeled it in front of my mirror. With the helmet and oxygen mask completely covering my head and face, and with the tinted visor down and all the cords and hoses dangling, I looked more like a creature from a grade B science fiction movie than a pilot! Although my fashion show occasioned much laughter from my roommate and some other cadets from down the hall, all this gear had a deadly serious purpose, as our training in its proper use emphasized.

The T-2 and most other modern jets were equipped with a rocket-powered ejection seat, unlike older jets, which used an explosive charge to propel the seat hard enough to smash through the canopy and achieve a trajectory high enough to allow the parachute to open. The effect of this explosive charge subjected the pilot to sudden and massive G forces that could cause severe injury if he was not positioned perfectly in the seat when it fired. The rocket seat was a vast improvement over the old ejection system and gave a much gentler push over a longer period to loft the pilot to safety. The improved system also jettisoned the canopy by explosive charges prior to ejection, so it was no longer necessary to blast through the canopy.

Regulations required a visit to the ejection seat trainer to familiarize pilots—or anyone else riding an ejection seat—with the seat's operation. A pilot who had experienced the blast of the seat firing supposedly would be less hesitant to pull the ejection handle in a real emergency. Because it was impossible to simulate the rocket seat's firing, the ejection seat trainer used the explosive charge of the older seats. The trainer itself was a mock-up of a cockpit with two rails extending up and back about thirty feet. The ejection seat was mounted on these rails and traveled about twenty feet vertically. A snubber system to halt the seat's upward travel took up the remaining ten feet of the rails.

The trainee mounted a platform next to the cockpit mock-up and slid into the seat while it was suspended a few feet above the cockpit. After strapping into the seat by hooking the torso harness to the parachute risers and buckling the seat-pan straps to the hip connections on the torso harness, a ratchet-and-chain affair lowered the trainee into position in the cockpit. Unlike Air Force seats, Navy ejection seats could be fired in two ways. The primary mechanism consisted of a rubber ring mounted just above the pilot's headrest on the seat. When the pilot pulled down sharply on the ring, a curtain came down and completely covered his or her head and face. Originally designed to protect the pilot's face from flying pieces of Plexiglas, the curtain also helped protect the face and eyes from the wind blast of a high-speed ejection. Mounted between the pilot's legs on the front of the seat pan was a secondary D ring that could be used to fire the seat if high G forces prevented the pilot from being able to reach the face curtain.

Our class gathered around the base of the ejection-seat trainer, jocularly ribbing the first member to ride the wild seat. Although the trainer used only one 40-mm cartridge, we were still instructed to position ourselves carefully in the seat with back and neck straight and pressed firmly into the backrest, feet flat on the floor in front of the seat, elbows and forearms together in front of the chest, as we grasped the rubber ring of the face curtain. *Whoomph!* The first trainee was kicked up the rails and had stopped before we could register his ascent. "Man that was fast!" I exclaimed. The seat began its slow, ratcheting descent to the boarding position while the first trainee released the face curtain and sat with a dazed smile on his face. "Man, that's a hell of a kick. It wasn't so bad though," was his comment. The bored parachute rigger 2nd class who was helping us strap into the seat called for the next trainee while his supervisor, a parachute rigger 1st class, removed the spent cartridge and reloaded the firing chamber. After several more shots the sight of the seat and occupant popping up the rails had become old hat, and we were standing around chatting and waiting our turn with the same bored air as the operators.

When my turn finally came, I climbed into the seat, strapped in, and was lowered into the cockpit. "OK, Sir, whenever you are ready. Be sure to position properly before you fire the seat," the PR2 said as he stepped back to a safe place on the platform. I slid my butt back into the backrest, straightened my back, looked at the horizon, and with elbows together felt for the ring above my head. Taking a deep breath, I pulled sharply down on the face curtain. Nothing happened. "Misfire! Misfire!" called the now-alert PR2. I peeked sheepishly around the face curtain.

"Don't move, Sir," the PR1 called from below. "It may be a hang-fire."

"Hey, Gray, you broke it!" called one of my classmates. "Jesus, man, you're dead!" he said. Other encouraging remarks ensued.

"Sir," called the PR2, "try using the alternate handle." I again positioned myself and pulled up sharply on the handle between my legs, learning in the process that keeping your elbows away from the canopy rail is difficult when doing this. As before, the cartridge didn't fire.

The PR1 said, "OK, raise the seat up and let him climb out while we wait." There was a prescribed waiting time to ensure that hang-fires didn't go off while being removed.

"Damn, Jerry, this fucking seat won't move!" the PR2 shouted.

"Well, shit . . . the firing sear has jammed in the seat rail. I'll have to clear it. Have him climb out so I can open the firing cap."

The PR2 said, "Sir, go ahead and unstrap, but I'd climb out of there real carefully and try not to jostle the seat."

Great, I thought, if this thing fires while I'm climbing out, I'll get to see what a shot put feels like. I climbed out gingerly. The jammed sear and firing cap were removed, and the misfire was cleared.

"Ready to try again, Sir?" came the cheerful query from the beaming PR2.

"What the hell . . . why not?" I said. I climbed back into the seat while my classmates cheered me on. When I grabbed the face curtain this time I was rewarded with a *whoomph!* and the fastest twenty-foot gain in my life. Although the blast had only half the kick of the real thing, I could easily understand the importance of proper ejection position if one didn't want to be permanently shorter.

———•———

Although the entire class attended ground school together, half of us were assigned to VT-7 and half to VT-9. Cadet Terry Rieder, who had been one of my Indoc roommates back in Preflight, was assigned to VT-7 and was the first of our class to begin flying the T-2. Because we all would have our first flight soon, we listened intently to Terry's impressions of his first flight.

Because the transition to jets was such a big step for fledgling aviators, the first T-2 flight was written in the syllabus as an orientation hop. The student was to ride in the front cockpit and observe while the instructor demonstrated takeoff, area departure, training area orientation, syllabus aerobatics, field reentry procedures, and landing techniques with a couple of touch-and-gos. The student was expected to know the normal and emergency procedures, and how to preflight and run the checklist, but it was to be an ungraded hop with the instructor doing all the flying. It was referred to as the "free" hop or "the dollar ride."

Terry's instructor, a Marine captain, was an old hand at instructing, this being his third year of a four-year tour as an instructor. He was of the opinion that the "dollar ride" was a waste of time, and the student should get to do some flying right off the bat. The captain was in a very good mood when he met Terry in the preflight briefing because he was due to depart on two weeks' leave as soon as he returned from this hop. He immediately put Terry at ease by explaining that he wouldn't put any pressure on him and not to worry about doing well or poorly, just relax and enjoy flying a jet. By the time they had concluded the briefing and walked out to the airplane, Terry was convinced the captain was really a great guy and a super instructor. Things just got better.

After helping Terry pull the ejection seat safety pins and strap in, the captain reviewed him on preflight and engine start procedures and was very complimentary about Terry's fine preparation for the hop. Terry was really impressed with the takeoff. The feeling of speed was incredible, and Terry was feeling great about the prospect of getting to fly this bird. After establishing them on the field departure course, the captain let Terry take the controls, coaching him on what to do next as they zoomed out over the operations area. He even let Terry initiate the first series of aerobatics. Although Terry had no flying experience prior to primary training in the T-34B, he had a natural talent for flying and had done well at Saufley.

The captain was very pleased with Terry's flying skills and complimented him frequently as they roared through the aerobatics syllabus and completed the area checkout. Terry was having the time of his life and was about to burst with pride every time the instructor added another compliment about his flying. Soon it was time to head back to McCain field for the landing demos. The captain told Terry to keep control of the airplane; he would coach him through the entry procedures and even let Terry try a few touch-and-gos. "That'll really get you one step ahead of your classmates," the captain said.

The entry procedure called for the airplane to be flown up the duty runway at an altitude of eight hundred feet and a speed of 250 knots. Terry had the T-2 level at eight hundred feet and trimmed to hold altitude, and the instructor had helped him set the power to hold 250 knots. There were several miles of straight flying before reaching the runway, so the captain told Terry to just concentrate on holding speed and altitude into the "break" at the mid-point of the runway, and he would talk him through the break and downwind turn and help him set up for the landing approach.

Terry was ecstatic. The captain lapsed into silence for the few minutes' ride into the break, just letting Terry enjoy flying straight and level. Perhaps it was thoughts of his impending vacation, and undoubtedly he was lulled by Terry's fine flying skills, but the captain momentarily forgot that he was flying with a neophyte and remained silent as Terry roared into the break. Terry, adrenalin flowing from the exhilaration of the flight, and going a hundred knots faster than he'd ever gone in his life, thought the instructor wanted him to go ahead and break because he wasn't saying anything and the midpoint of the runway was under them. Just as any aviator would do when faced with an unusual situation, Terry fell back on his training. Flop, chop, prop, drop came to mind. This was a little memory ditty we used in primary to memorize the procedure for beginning the break turn. Flop. Terry slapped the stick hard over to the left, but it only took a fraction of the stick movement for a forty-five-degree bank in the T-2 at 250 knots than it had in the T-34B at 150. The agile little T-2 snap-rolled smartly, inverted. Terry was unaware of this because his eyes had wandered involuntarily down into the cockpit to look at the unfamiliar throttle quadrant. Chop. Terry, still influenced by adrenalin, chopped the throttle all the way back past the idle stop to the cutoff position. Prop didn't apply, and neither did the 110 landing-gear speed limit of the T-34B. Hell, the T-2 landed faster than that, so drop. Terry dropped the landing gear.

The effect of all of this on Terry's instructor was electric. "What the . . . ?!" the captain exclaimed, his reverie shattered by his helmet bouncing off the canopy during Terry's snap roll. He awoke from his musings to find himself inverted at eight hundred feet off the runway with the engine shut down and the landing gear extending. He immediately rolled the T-2 upright, came back around the idle stop with the throttle in time to relight the engine, and retracted the landing gear. Terry, eyes back out of the cockpit after dropping the gear, was no less stunned and wondered how he had managed to end up inverted instead of in the downwind turn. The tower, noticing this very novel maneuver in the break, inquired if they were experiencing difficulty. "Negative," was the only response from the shaken instructor, as he flew into the downwind and lined up for landing.

After a silent landing and taxi in, the still-shaken instructor simply mumbled a vague, "Don't worry, son, it'll come in time," and stumbled off to start his much-needed leave. Terry gathered the shattered pieces of his ego and headed for the officers' club to submerge his sorrows in a few beers.

On my first flight in the T-2, my instructor suffered no such delusions about my flying ability. It was the prescribed "dollar ride" and I simply observed, but the differences in jet flying enthralled me nonetheless. The engine indicators, for example, are quite different in a jet. The engine RPM indicator in jet airplanes is calibrated in percentages of the engine's actual revolutions, because a jet engine's RPM are in the five-digit range. The gauge was calibrated from zero to about 105 percent, so at full throttle one would expect to see around 100 percent, depending on atmospheric conditions that could affect the engine's output. An exhaust gas temperature gauge, fuel-flow meter, and engine oil pressure and quantity gauge completed the engine indicators.

While the basic flight instruments in the T-2 functioned exactly like those we were used to in the T-34B, there was a new gauge in the cockpit and a new indicator mounted on the glare shield. These were angle-of-attack indicators. To control the speed of a carrier airplane during carrier landings, the Navy used the angle of attack rather than the airspeed indicator because angle of attack gave a faster and more precise indication of the airspeed than the pilot could get otherwise. It was also a quicker gauge of the airplane's performance abilities in slow-speed flight. The angle-of-attack gauge was round with a needle pointer calibrated in degrees of angle. Angle of attack is defined as the angle that the leading edge of the wing makes with free stream air, depending on the nose attitude of the airplane. The gauge had marks at ten, fifteen, and twenty degrees' angle of attack, with fifteen degrees being the optimum angle for carrier landings. On top of the glare shield to the left sat a vertically mounted rectangular indicator called the angle-of-attack indexer. The rectangle contained three lenses. When lighted, the bottom lens displayed a V, the center an O, and the top an inverted V, or chevron. The V signaled that the angle of attack was too shallow, meaning the plane was traveling too fast; the O, or "donut" symbol, meant that the plane was at fifteen degrees angle of attack and "on speed"; and the chevron meant the angle of attack was too high, or the plane was too slow. Flying with a chevron indication meant that the plane was close to stalling. If the V or the chevron lighted along with the donut, then the plane was traveling slightly too fast or slightly too slow.

My instructor, a Marine captain named Bindrim, helped me through the preflight, start-up, and taxi-out checklists. Captain Bindrim demonstrated the time lag inherent in jet engines, from the time the pilot pushes the throttle forward until the engine accelerates enough to provide sufficient thrust to get the plane moving. Recip engines provide almost instantaneous power, but it took nearly eight seconds for the T-2 engine to go from idle power to full thrust. As we accelerated on takeoff roll, my instructor pointed out the runway-remaining markers, small billboards set at one-thousand-foot intervals along the runway. We calculated from tables—using the existing wind and temperature for that day—the expected takeoff roll distance and the distance it should take for us to reach a speed of 100 knots. We expected to be airborne in slightly less than three thousand feet. We hit the 100-knot speed before reaching the five-thousand-feet-remaining marker, and as the marker flashed by, Captain Bindrim rotated the T-2 and we lifted smoothly off the runway at 120 knots. Everything happened so much faster than it had in the T-34B. The climb rate was fantastic, and there was a feeling of smooth power pushing us along. We leveled at sixteen thousand feet in a much shorter time than it took to climb the T-34B to just six thousand, and we accelerated to a comfortable 300-knot cruising speed. Captain Bindrim flew around the training area, pointing out the boundaries and prominent landmarks and memory hints to help remember the names of the towns that passed below us.

Next Captain Bindrim demonstrated an aerobatics series, explaining that we would always do the aerobatics in a series—one following right after another, starting with the vertical maneuvers (loop, barrel roll, vertical recovery, Split S, and so on). That way, we wasted no time or fuel, and we could use the speed gained from the previous maneuver to start the next. He accelerated the T-2 by adding full power and starting a shallow dive. We quickly accelerated to 450 knots (four times faster than I had ever flown before), which was the safe speed to complete a loop with a good margin above stall speed coming over the top.

The aerobatics in the T-2 were thrilling, and at the same time a little uncomfortable. The higher G forces would take some getting used to! My neck muscles were straining to keep my head up when Captain Bindrim pulled up to four Gs in the overhead maneuvers. I could feel the G-suit inflating and squeezing my legs and abdomen. Then we dropped down to ten thousand for a series of stalls and stall-recovery exercises, both "clean" (gear and flaps up) and "dirty" (gear and flaps in the landing configuration). After the air work, Captain Bindrim demonstrated the procedure for reentering the field traffic pattern, flying us into the break at 800 feet and 250 knots. The touch-and-go landing demonstrations that followed proved beyond doubt that I would be learning an entirely new way to land an airplane.

All Navy and Marine Corps runways have an optical aircraft carrier landing aid on the left side, situated about a thousand feet down the runway from the approach end. This aid consists of five square lenses, arranged vertically. The top four lenses project an amber beam up at an angle of three degrees from the runway. The bottom lens projects a red beam. Extending on either side of the second lens from the top is a horizontal row of green lights called datum lights. When mounted on an aircraft carrier, the entire affair, called a Fresnel lens, is gyro stabilized so the pitch and roll of the ship affect it as little as possible. As he turns onto final approach about a mile and a quarter behind the ship or runway, a pilot on the proper glide path sees an amber blob of light in the center of the row of green lights. If the blob of amber light, called the "meatball," hovers above the green lights, then the pilot knows he is too high on the glide slope. If the blob hovers below the green row of lights, the pilot is too low. A red ball of light indicates that the pilot is dangerously low and will hit short of the flight deck and crash into the back of the ship.

After snapping the T-2 sharply into a forty-five-degree angle-of-bank turn and pulling the power back to idle, Captain Bindrim extended the speed brakes. The speed brakes—another new feature of jet aviation for the former

T-34B students—were flat, square plates that extended hydraulically forty-five degrees out from either side of the aft fuselage. The tremendous drag force they created served two purposes: to help slow airspeed rapidly and to allow the engine to operate at a high power setting on landing approach. A jet engine's power response is much faster if the pilot keeps its RPM spooled up as much as possible while still maintaining the desired airspeed and rate of descent.

As we slowed to gear extend speed, my instructor dropped the landing gear and extended the wing flaps to help slow us to approach speed and configure us for landing. At the 180 position, beginning the turn for final, Captain Bindrim recited the before-landing checklist. "Gear checks down and locked, flaps are down, tail hook up, speed brakes out, brakes pumped and firm, and we have fifteen hundred pounds of fuel remaining," he said over the intercom. He began a nonstop description of what he was doing during the landing approach. "OK, Gray, there's the ball. Slightly high. I'll ease off a little power, hold fifteen units angle of attack . . . see the indexer? Remember, nose controls airspeed or angle of attack, power controls descent rate. You need to get a scan going—head up out of the cockpit, use the indexer—and it's meatball, lineup, and angle of attack; meatball, lineup, and angle of attack."

I could see the donut in the indexer lighted and the ball centered in the datum lights. We were nose-high, descending at about seven hundred feet per minute, with the power between 85 and 90 percent. Captain Bindrim constantly fed in small corrections to keep us lined up with the center of the runway and to keep the ball in the center of the datum lights. I was looking at the ball as we neared the runway, and it appeared to slide off to the left when we touched the runway. Wham! We hit hard. "Oof!" I grunted as Bindrim retracted the speed brakes and added power to take off again.

The T-2 was almost instantly airborne, climbing to eight hundred feet and turning downwind for another pass. Captain Bindrim laughed and said, "Startled you, huh? It's not supposed to be gentle. Some people have described it as a controlled crash, but what you're doing is a very precise descent on a very narrow glide slope." To land even in the wires you have to stay within a ten-foot-thick glide slope, and to get a 3-wire, which is the target wire, you have to stay in the center of that glide slope."

The wires he was referring to were the arresting wires on a carrier deck that drag the airplane to a fast stop in the landing area. "Did you notice how fast we got airborne again?" he added. "At these speeds, you've got flying speed when you touch down. As a matter of fact, you could level off just by pulling the speed brakes in, so when you suck in the boards and add full power you rotate right back into the air."

After two more passes, smashing down in the same spot each time, the first lesson was finished. As we taxied in, Captain Bindrim said, "You will concentrate most on learning to make good carrier-type passes during familiarization stage. We'll rush through the air work as quickly as we can, so that we can get back here with as much fuel as possible to practice landings. You'll have hop T-two next week, so come ready to work and know all your procedures so that we can concentrate on landings."

———•——

Familiarization stage in the T-2 was a lot like primary in the T-34B. It consisted of eleven dual-instruction hops with a safe-for-solo check ride on the twelfth hop and a solo on the thirteenth. After that, there were nine practice hops with more solos than had been the case in T-34B primary. The main purpose for fam stage was to get us used to the jet so we could begin to learn more advanced flying techniques; the only really new thing taught was the constant-angle-of-attack approach and landing and the use of the Fresnel lens. Accordingly, as Captain Bindrim had promised, we spent as little time as possible doing the air work on our hops and concentrated on landings.

The main thing most of us had to overcome during fam stage was our tendency to overcontrol; the T-2 was much more responsive than the T-34B. My instructor constantly admonished me to keep my control corrections small and rapid to reduce the amount of countercorrection that inevitably followed any control input. "Flying is a constant series of corrections," he would say. "Anticipate, scan, and keep them small." But I was getting the picture, and by the fourth hop my air work was really good and I was managing to keep the ball at least somewhere on the lens all the way to touchdown.

"Meatball, lineup, and angle of attack," Bindrim would drone during each approach. "Don't spot the deck, keep your eyes moving." A pilot who became fixated and stared at the touchdown point had an instinctive tendency to pull back on the stick, causing the plane to lose its rate of descent and land long.

Captain Bindrim's instruction took hold, and I sailed through the twelfth hop with no trouble. Soloing the T-2 was the most thrilling thing I had done in flying. Although we were supposed to do only the prescribed maneuvers on solo hops, we sometimes experimented with ways to apply our newfound skills. During the last solo prior to my fam stage final check hop, the training area was full of the vertical columns of clouds that we had learned in meteorology classes to call "towering cumulus" ("towering Q," for short). The bases of these clouds were far below me, down around five or six thousand feet. I was up at fourteen thousand, flying through the spaces between the Qs. There was plenty of room to remain clear of the clouds, but it became a game to fly vertically up one side of the cloud, roll inverted, pull the nose down and top the cloud inverted, then continue the pull and dive down the backside of the column, keeping the canopy as close to the cloud as possible.

I decided to see what it would be like to fly through one. They weren't very thick—only a mile or so at the most—and I would be getting some early practice with instrument flying, which we were due to begin next week. We had been cautioned against going into instrument-required meteorological conditions, but this would be for just a few moments. I bore-sighted a friendly-looking cloud a few miles away and envisioned a cartoonist's drawing of a T-2-shaped hole in the cloud after I passed through it. The top of the cloud towered above me as I approached it at fourteen thousand feet, and I noted that the sides were boiling upward energetically as I entered the cloud. How curious.

Slam! Wham! Buck and jump! No friendly, soft, fleecy cloud this! I was thrown violently about the cockpit. It had gotten quite dark and rain was beating furiously against the canopy. I suddenly recalled lectures about the effects of hail and intense rain on jet engines. I looked frantically at the engine instruments but couldn't read them because the instrument panel was shaking so violently. "Oh, don't flame out on me!" I exhorted the engine. Finally, after what seemed a very long time to travel a mile or so, I was spit out the other side of the cloud back into bright sunlight—two thousand feet higher than when I entered and nearly inverted.

Shaking and shaken, I regained control and checked the engine. All was well. Jesus! I thought. That was dumb! Really, really dumb! I began to notice that the columns were becoming walls. I dived toward the entry point for McCain Field, and as I leveled at the entry altitude beneath the bases of the rapidly forming clouds, I could see some rain shafts off to the east. Suddenly the gloom under the clouds was split by a couple of lightning bolts, and as if on cue the radio came to life. "Recall, recall! This is Navy McCain Tower on guard broadcasting a general weather recall. All Navy McCain aircraft return to base immediately." Rain was already pelting the tarmac as I walked into the hangar to sign off on the yellow sheet, suddenly imbued with a great desire to learn instrument flying.

———•—•———

Instrument stage at Meridian was just an introduction to instrument flying; it wasn't intended to qualify us fully as instrument pilots—that would occur in the advanced course later on. This training was to give us just enough instrument skills to help us out of trouble if we should accidentally find ourselves caught in instrument conditions. The stage consisted of seventeen hops: ten basic instrument hops with a check ride on the eleventh hop, and five radio instrument hops with a check ride on the sixth hop. In the early days of aviation they called instrument flying "flying blind," which is a good description of the process. Controlling the airplane solely by reference to instruments requires a number of gauges to tell the pilot what the body's senses cannot. There must be a means of determining when the airplane is right side up, for instance. In an airplane, turning forces displace the fluid in the inner ear and confuse the body's sense of balance. Many non-instrument-qualified pilots have died because they did not understand these phenomena when flying in instrument conditions; it is easy to control the aircraft into a stall, then spin or fly into the ground inverted.

We had covered all the procedures and maneuvers for instrument flight training in the classroom, so instrument training began without preamble. All the takeoffs would be instrument takeoffs. Technically, a Navy pilot can take off in zero visibility conditions if the mission requires it, but nobody in their right mind would really try this. I was seated in the rear cockpit, which would be my station for the entire instrument training syllabus. An instrument hood—a spring-loaded, canvas-covered bow that matched the canopy contour and slid forward to latch in front of the rear cockpit-glare shield—would obscure the outside world and completely enclose me within the tiny world of the cockpit.

My instructor was a Navy lieutenant named Kuehler. We taxied out to the hold-short point for the duty runway, and Mr. Kuehler said, "OK, Steve, go under the bag." We took the runway while I slid the instrument hood forward and latched it in place. Mr. Kuehler informed me that we were exactly lined up with the runway centerline. "Whenever you are ready, Steve, you have the airplane."

"I have it," I acknowledged, and added power while holding the brakes for the engine run up. At 85 percent power with all the engine instruments reading normal, I released the brakes and pushed the throttle up for full power. The left brake released slower than the right, causing the airplane to lurch to the left. I added a touch of right brake to realign with the runway heading, but I overshot it slightly. As the compass swung too far to the right, I tapped the left brake. We were accelerating through eighty knots and the fishtailing caused by my efforts to get straight down the centerline was growing worse.

"Settle down back there, Steve. Make your corrections small and keep us on the runway," said the voice from the front cockpit. Hurtling down the runway, totally blind, at nearly one hundred miles per hour—even with an instructor in the front cockpit to save you from disaster—was a hair-raising experience. Finally, after what seemed a very long time, we were at takeoff speed and I yanked us off the runway. "Easy, easy! Don't over-rotate. Keep your wings level, watch your airspeed . . . you're turning! Watch your heading, you're getting slow. C'mon Gray, scan, scan, scan! Keep those eyeballs moving . . . watch it! Keep us climbing!"

A constant stream of instruction came from the front cockpit as I struggled to make all the gauges indicate properly. I had thought this would be easy once we were in the air! Instead, I was engaged in a desperate juggling act as I tried to get everything under control. The altimeter was showing us in a steady climb, and my instructor's comments seemed a little less frantic as we got some room between us and the ground.

"Jesus! I hate these B-one hops," he said. "We're still alive, but we get to see some wild rides until you guys get the picture. Steve, you must learn to scan—keep those eyeballs moving and don't spend any more time looking at one instrument than at another. You must learn to interpret what that gauge is telling you with a glance, and then scan on to the next one. We aren't supposed to take the airplane away from you unless we're about to die, so you have a chance to learn from your mistakes, but sometimes it's hard to know how far to let you go."

After finally reaching cruising altitude, we practiced straight and level flight for a while. I finally got the airplane more or less trimmed up at 250 knots, at nine thousand feet on a heading of three-three-zero, or 330 degrees magnetic. Actually, I was fifty feet low, but for the first time this flight I had the airspeed exactly on 250 and the heading was holding steady on 330, and I didn't want to fool with anything! My instructor wasn't about to let me get away with this, though.

"It's just as easy to hold nine thou as it is to hold eighty-nine fifty," he remarked. "Look, Steve, never accept anything less than perfect in your flying. I'll never jump you for not being exactly perfect as long as you are doing something to try to make it perfect. You might not ever get it exactly perfect, but if you ever quit trying, someday you'll get sloppy and it will kill you."

We tried making level turns of 180 degrees at 30 degrees bank angle, and I fought to keep the altitude within one hundred feet of nine thousand and the airspeed within 20 knots of 250. Then Kuehler had me try to hold altitude and heading as we slowed to landing-pattern speed and configured for landing. I quickly learned that the nose attitude pitched down drastically and the airplane tended to balloon upward as the flaps were lowered. I hadn't been so conscious of these attitude changes when I could look out at the horizon, and the extra drag of the landing gear and the resulting loss of airspeed required drastic trim changes to hold the nose up and keep from losing altitude. Mr. Kuehler's debriefing concentrated on highlighting my weaknesses and said very little about me doing anything well, but he ended up by grading the hop average and I mentally vowed to do better the next time.

During the next two weeks my world centered on instrument flying, and I really had to struggle to perform up to standard. On the second basic instrument hop we began flying S patterns, maneuvers designed to develop the instrument scan and coordination of controls and power. I hated them. Flying wasn't fun anymore. Gone was the sense of freedom and grace: this was hard, sweaty drudgery, and I was developing an intense dislike for "the bag."

The S pattern sounded simple enough. While holding a constant heading and trimmed up for 250 knots, I was supposed to punch the elapsed-time clock and begin a thousand-foot-per-minute rate of descent. At the end of one minute I should be 1,000 feet lower, my airspeed should still be 250 knots, and I should still be on the same heading. Then I was supposed to reverse the descent and begin a thousand-foot-per-minute climb, so that after the end of two minutes I should be on the original altitude, at 250 knots, with no change in heading. Of course, when one begins the descent rate one must reduce power to compensate for airplane's tendency to accelerate, so it became necessary to include the engine RPM gauge in the instrument scan. One more task to juggle! Something always seemed to go wrong. I might get behind the clock on the descent and end up ten seconds late; or I could be right on at the thousand-foot low point and get behind the clock when trying to stop the descent and start the climb. I could never relax: as soon as I established the desired descent rate and power reduction, I had to begin anticipating the reversal and lead it so that as the sweep second hand approached the one-minute mark, I added power to stop the descent and begin the climb.

I was struggling with basic instrument flying, but at least I was surviving. Several in my class just threw in the towel and DOR-ed. Most of those who left at this point did not particularly love flying, and their decision to quit had been simmering for some time. More tragic were those who tried hard to stay in the program but just could not get the hang of instruments. The instructors would try to convince them to transfer to the Naval Flight Officer program to become crewmen if they wanted to remain in aviation. But washing out of flight training was a bitter pill for some of them to swallow. Instrument stage, more than anything we had yet encountered in our training, underscored the fact that it takes a special aptitude to become a naval aviator—just wanting it is not enough.

By the fifth or sixth BI hop I was beginning to make all the gauges do what I wanted and stay with the clock, but there was a danger in this. Even though my instrument scan was developing nicely, I was getting so wrapped up in making the needles point the right way that I was totally ignorant of my position in relation to the earth. This wasn't important in basic instrument stage, because we weren't really navigating yet, but the total concentration I was developing in scanning the instruments was making me lose sight of the reasons we were making the instruments do these things.

Our first instrument approaches to McCain Field were ground-controlled approaches because we would be getting ground help if we were caught out in bad weather and needed assistance getting back to the field. We wouldn't be learning to shoot TACAN (tactical air navigation) or ADF (automatic direction finder) approaches until advanced training. The TACAN system consisted of ground radio navigation beacons that emitted an infinite number of radio beams called radials. Receivers in the airplane determined the radial on which the airplane happened to be. They could also measure the slant range to or from the station. ADF was an older, less sophisticated radio beacon that provided magnetic bearings to or from the station. A ground-controlled approach, or GCA, was conducted by radar approach controllers sitting in a radar room underneath the tower. The initial controller used a circular radar scope that depicted a map view of the area within twenty miles of the field, with the control tower in the center of the scope. The initial controller would turn the approaching aircraft toward the runway by giving it heading commands and assigning appropriate altitudes. When the aircraft was in the proper position, the procedure was turned over to the final controller, who gave instructions to the pilot all the way to touchdown. The final controller had two radar scopes: one gave the aircraft position in relation to the centerline of the runway, and the other showed the aircraft position in relation to a three-degree glide slope until it intersected with the runway.

Normally we would land at this point without enough fuel to do more than one approach, because the main focus was on basic instrument coordination. The instructor would say, "OK, I've got it. Pop your bag," and land the airplane. What a relief it was to hear those words! I felt as if I had just dropped a heavy load, and I would sit in the rear cockpit, drained of energy, while he landed the airplane.

Finally, after almost a month of hard work, I passed my BI-eleven check ride. I still had six instrument hops to go, but the end was in sight and I would at least be through with the hated S patterns and could begin to learn practical things. The first radio instrument hop introduced radio instrument navigation and was scheduled at night to provide an introduction to night flying. Because it was fully dark by the time we taxied out for the RI-one, my instructor allowed me to keep the bag stowed and we flew the hop in a more realistic fashion. The instrument takeoff was, of course, much easier with forward visibility reference, but once airborne I had to use the instruments just as much as I did under the bag, because even though it was a clear night, there was no moon and a slight haze obscured the horizon. The RI-one hop dealt with flying a TACAN course to intercept a new course to a different TACAN station, and flying to various fixes as defined by either intersecting radials or by the distance from or to a TACAN station.

On 4 October 1965, I flew my RI-six check and passed with no problems. It was a night hop and I was out from under the bag. I learned from this that I suffered from "bag-itis." I was much better at flying instruments without the claustrophobic influence of the canvas over my head, which proved a famous theorem coined by one of my classmates: "One peek is worth a thousand scans." With instrument flying behind me, I was ready—and really excited—to begin the next stage: formation flying—the fighter pilot's stock in trade.

———

Formation stage consisted of eighteen hops and dealt with two-plane and four-plane formation flying. There are many reasons why military flying formations are necessary: for tactical reasons in combat, for neatness and a military bearing in operations, and to save airspace around the field. The kind of formation we would be learning to fly was called "parade" formation; this is the familiar tucked-in-tight formation seen at air shows. In the two-plane formation, the second pilot, called the wingman, flies a position that puts his cockpit slightly behind and slightly lower than the leader's cockpit, which allows the leader to be able to see him clearly by looking over his shoulder. The proper wing position is flown by lining up some portion of the leader's wing with an easily located mark on the leader's fuselage. In the T-2, we aligned the nose of the wingtip fuel tank with the ground rescue canopy-jettison handle, which was just below the front cockpit and denoted by a red inverted triangle. This put the wingman's airplane on approximately a 30-degree bearing line aft of the lead airplane and slightly below it. The distance between airplanes depends on how "tight" a formation is desired. For students, about twenty feet normally separated the airplanes.

In an effort to keep radio chatter to a minimum, the lead and wingman communicated with hand signals devised to alert the wingman to prepare for maneuvers or change configuration, to ask for fuel state, and so on. Because at a distance of twenty feet or less the wingman's eyes are glued to the leader's airplane and cockpit, the lead merely has to hold up the proper signal for the wingman to see. For example, to ask his wingman how much fuel he had remaining, the leader would hold his fist with thumb outstretched and make a drinking motion. The wingman would hold up fingers for each hundred pounds of fuel he had remaining. The first five hundred pounds were signaled with the fingers above the hand; for numbers above five hundred, the fist was held with thumb on top and fingers extended horizontally; a zero was simply a clenched fist. To signal a configuration change, the lead would make a motion with his hand describing the device to be moved. To extend or retract the landing gear, for instance, the lead would make a cranking motion with his arm and hand. To give the signal to execute, the leader would lean well forward in the cockpit and then snap his head back into the headrest.

The first formation hop was flown with two instructors and two students; one instructor and one student flew lead for half the hop, then switched to wing position for the remainder. A Lieutenant Brown shepherd me on my F-one, and we were wingman for the first half. After climbing to the practice area behind, but in sight of, the lead airplane, Brown told the lead instructor to begin a 30-degree-bank turn to the left. Mr. Brown then cut inside the lead aircraft's turn radius, explaining that by flying across the circle, we would set up a closure rate because we were flying a shorter distance than the lead airplane was. The prebriefed target airspeed was 250 knots, and to expedite our rendezvous, Mr. Brown kicked us up to 270. The dot that had been the lead airplane was growing larger in the canopy as we closed, and when we could make out the wings and tail Mr. Brown explained that it was time to pick up the bearing line and fly it to rendezvous. Indeed, the position of the lead airplane in our canopy hadn't changed; it had just grown larger. We seemed to be sliding up closer, and the tip tank nose was just on the red triangle. The nose of our airplane was on roughly the same heading as the leader's, and Mr. Brown eased the throttle back to bleed off our excess airspeed and momentarily cracked the speed brakes out to stop us smartly twenty feet out and in perfect position. At this point, two airplanes were flying as one, synchronized perfectly in all their motions.

The two instructors flew through a few turns to demonstrate the proper position and technique to remain there. Mr. Brown kept up a running commentary to explain what he was doing to remain in position. "Remember, Gray, angle of bank controls the bearing, power controls the closure rate." He demonstrated by easing off the throttle and correcting the bank slightly, and we slid down the bearing line away from lead. Adding a little power caused us to slide right back up the bearing line and into position. To build my confidence, Mr. Brown slid us in really close; only about three feet separated our canopy from the lead's wingtip. "When you get the hang of it, the proper formation position feels like a kind of notch," he said. "You just feel like you snap into place and it feels really comfortable and you just instinctively do whatever is necessary to stay in the notch."

Finally, it was my turn. As the crowd at an air show thrills to the graceful maneuvers being flown by a formation of airplanes, the announcer makes frequent mention of the high speed of the airplanes as they swoop and roll in unison. "Now ladies and gentlemen, as the Blue Angels come down the back of the loop, their speed is in excess of six hundred miles per hour, with only inches separating their airplanes. . . ." In fact, the speed of the airplanes relative to the ground is completely irrelevant; their speed relative to one another is what is important. I was about to learn the concept of relative motion firsthand.

We had been flying straight and level for a few miles when Mr. Brown gave me the airplane. It was perfectly trimmed up, and for a few seconds nothing happened. We flew on as before, two airplanes perfectly in sync. Then, almost imperceptibly, oscillations began and quickly increased in magnitude. I began to wobble, and I decided instinctively that more room between my airplane and the no-doubt nervous lead airplane was prudent. "Come on, Gray. Settle down, relax, and make your inputs smooth and small," came the voice from the back cockpit. We were bucking up and down, and the wings were wobbling as I fought frantically to keep the tip tank on the triangle. Because I had instinctively eased back on the throttle, we were moving away from lead. "You're drifting out too far," Mr. Brown said. "Add power and close it up." I added a little power and we seemed to leap toward the lead airplane. The tendency in this situation is to bank away from the impending collision, but that is the wrong thing to do because it makes the plane slide out ahead of the leader and go forward of the bearing line (going "acute"). It is also very difficult to keep the lead's airplane in sight if you throw your wing up at him while banking away. The lead's airplane will tend to slide behind you so that you have to look back over your shoulder to keep him in sight. This is a dangerous situation in a formation flight; the lead may try to take evasive action just as you try to correct, and a midair collision could result. Realizing my mistake, I corrected back toward the bearing and yanked the throttle back to idle. We slid away from the leader rapidly and I jammed the throttle back nearly full, causing the engine to chuff as its compressor stalled. "Concentrate on small corrections," said the patient Brown.

After a few more minutes of this, I gradually settled down and was able to maintain a shaky wing position. Far too soon for my liking, the lead airplane gave me the upraised clenched fist, the signal for the wingman to cross under the leader and take up position on the opposite side. As we descended, the lead airplane rose above us and I eased the stick over to nudge the airplane under him. I watched through the top of the canopy as the lead seemed to float over us and to our left. Then I pulled the nose up and added a little power to keep the airplane from sliding behind the bearing line, or "going sucked." Just as I slid into a shaky but passable wing position on the right side of the lead, the student in the front seat of the lead's airplane gave me a circling motion with his right gloved hand and then a "kiss-off" signal, like kissing your fingertips and flinging them outward. This was the signal to break up and rendezvous. The lead airplane broke sharply left while we continued straight ahead for about thirty seconds, then rolled left and pulled our nose through the lead's radius to get on the inside of his turn and begin the rendezvous.

As we passed inside the lead's turn, we hit an invisible bump and the wings began to roll drunkenly. "What the hell!" I muttered. As I fought to regain control, my instructor laughed and explained, "You flew through his jet wash. It's just like crossing a boat's wake. See, we're through it already." Indeed, I regained control as we pulled on through our turn and crossed into undisturbed air. The lead's airplane was about a mile from us as we began to slide up the bearing line to rejoin the formation. Both airplanes were still at 250 knots, but we still had a closure rate by virtue of being on the inside of the lead's turn. "Kick the speed up a little, Gray," Brown said over the interphone. "We need to expedite this as much as we can to get at least four or five done before we swap places." I pushed the power up and we accelerated to 290 knots and seemed to roar up the bearing line. This time I did it all. I banked away, nearly losing sight of the lead and sliding way acute, so I pulled power and popped the speed brakes, which made us go sucked immediately, and I had to struggle back up to formation speed to regain the bearing. Fortunately, my instructor was not a "screamer." He patiently talked me back into position without losing his composure, which was remarkable because we flirted with disaster while I flailed around. Finally, we were more or less stabilized enough to cross under and wobble up to parade position on the lead's right wing. Then I had to do it again. The lead would roll out of the thirty-degree angle-of-bank turn and fly straight and level just long enough to give us the break-up-and-rendezvous signal, and we would began the process again.

Finally, after five or six breakups and rendezvous, it was our turn to assume the lead and let the other student practice flying formation on our airplane. "Relax, Gray, I've got the airplane," Mr. Brown said as he wobbled the stick to show me he had control. "You'll do all the flying on subsequent hops, but I want to give him as stable a platform as I can for his first try, just as Captain Connor did for you." I got to sit and laugh at the other hapless student as he wobbled, pitched, bucked, went acute and sucked, panicked, lost sight of us, and just generally flailed around, exactly as I had done. After we did six or so practice rendezvous, Mr. Brown had me give the fuel state signal. Captain Connor answered because at this point the student was incapable of releasing his grip on the stick or throttle long enough to respond. Our fuel state dictated a return for landing, and we kept the lead into the break at the field. The other student had settled down considerably by the time we flew up the runway, and Mr. Brown muttered, "Good. Gotta look good around the field." I gave them the kiss-off signal and we broke for landing. Mr. Brown gave me the airplane on final so I would get another practice landing. We debriefed as a flight, sharing some chuckles over our first wild attempts to get stable, but Lieutenant Brown and Captain Connor said that it was an average first formation hop and we would soon be as comfortable on somebody's wing as in our own beds.

Indeed, the pace of flying intensified to two hops a day. The next five formation hops were a repeat of the first in format, with interminable break-ups and rendezvous. I repeated to myself again and again, "Angle of bank is the bearing, power is the closure rate," as I slid up the bearing line to join. During these hops, a transition of which we were hardly aware was taking place. We no longer were thinking about how we were moving the controls; we were too busy thinking about staying in formation or positioning for the join-up. Just as one gives no conscious thought to the mechanics of walking, we were not thinking about flying the airplane. Our control movements were becoming natural and instinctive; we thought about where we should be in relation to the other airplane, and our hands and feet responded with the necessary movements to get us there. We also sweated blood to fly as smoothly as possible when it was our turn to fly lead, to give a stable target to our wingman. We were finally beginning to feel and act like aviators.

The seventh form hop was a safe-for-solo check ride. I passed with no problem and flew the next three hops solo on an instructor's wing for the entire hop. I was becoming quite comfortable with two-plane formation flying and was beginning to understand what Mr. Brown meant when he described the parade wing formation as an invisible notch. I felt as if I was locked to the lead airplane by an invisible force. Formation flying was becoming fun! The F-ten hop was a solo check ride with the instructor grading from the lead airplane. I did so well that the instructor flew me through some formation acrobatics. As we did a formation barrel roll, I thrilled to the beauty and graceful feeling as I watched the backdrop of the world in my peripheral vision roll about our two airplanes. I was begging for just one more when our fuel state demanded a return for landing.

A two-plane formation is called a "section." A four-plane formation is called a "division." Four-plane parade formation is flown in a variety of ways, the most common and standard being the "finger four" formation. If you look at the outstretched fingers of your hand, the position of your fingertips roughly resembles the positions of the airplanes in this formation; hence the name. In a division, the lead is called number one, his wingman is number two, and the other two airplanes make up the "second section," with number three leading number four. In a finger four, the lead's wingman is in parade formation on one wing, number three is in parade formation on the other wing, and number four is in parade formation on three's outside wing. The next eight hops were four-plane formation hops, and the next two hops were flown dual with an instructor.

Flying number two in a four-plane formation was no different from what we had been doing in two-plane. Even flying number three in a finger four was easy. The fun began when we were put in echelon and three had to fly parade position on two, and four the same position on three. Any errors for which three corrected were magnified greatly for number four. It was sort of like playing "crack the whip." Until we settled down and learned to scan up the formation and dampen out the oscillations, number four was a wild ride!

Incredibly, we all passed our safe-for-solo checks, and by the final hop—our graduation hop from Meridian—we were looking pretty sharp. All of us had taken turns flying all the positions and leading the formation during the last two hops. Captain Tuttle led us on our final hop, and we had asked him to let us fly a "graduation" break formation on returning to McCain Field at the end of the hop. We had seen a division enter the break in diamond formation from time to time during our training. Normally, students were not allowed to fly this formation, and everyone seeing it knew that it was a graduation group returning from their last hop. Tuttle let us practice the diamond out in the area before we flew back to the field. In the diamond formation, two and three both fly tight parade formation on the lead, while number four flies be-hind and below the lead in parade formation on both two and three. Number four is, of course, the most difficult position to fly because the pilot must keep his eyes roving back and forth between two and three. To get the proper step down so that the formation looks nice and tight, four must stick the top of his vertical stabilizer up into the lead's jet wash and feel it buffeting slightly to know that he is in the correct position.

We entered the break in tight diamond position. I had been given the honor of flying number four and was concentrating on holding as tight as I could, every nerve in my body taut as a bowstring. Out of the diamond, num-ber two on the lead's left wing breaks first, then lead, then four, and finally three, all fanning out in five-second intervals in the downwind turn, hold-ing the interval throughout the final, with each airplane touching down five seconds apart on alternate halves of the runway. It is a beautiful sight, and we executed it perfectly. I was bursting with pride as we taxied in, turned into our parking spaces, and shut down in unison. A new class was just getting their T-2 orientation lecture when we came in, and they watched us taxi in with respect and envy showing on their faces.

———

The next day, 28 October 1965, I packed my gear for the transfer to VT-4 at Forrest Sherman Field, NAS Pensacola, Florida. I was leaving Meridian conscious of having gained stature as a student naval aviator. Only half my original class remained, but I was eager to meet the challenges of the rest of the program. At VT-4, we would be learning skills that would set us apart from other military pilots, and I was confident that I could meet these challenges as well.

5

Forrest Sherman Field

Only six months had passed since I left NAS Pensacola for basic flight training, but I had learned and changed so much that I felt as if I were returning to a school for a reunion. I watched a new company of Indoc poopies drilling behind the battalion as I drove by on my way out the coast road to Forrest Sherman Field. It seemed years ago that I had been on that same drill field, although it had only been a year. I marveled once again at the beauty of the sparkling blue waves of the Gulf of Mexico splashing on the white beaches to my left and the Florida pine forest rolling by on my right. I pulled into the parking lot for VT-4 and parked in the closest slot to the hangar entrance marked "VT-4 Administration." Two rows of T-2s were parked on the apron behind the hangar, and several empty spaces between planes indicated that flights were airborne. The gunnery airplanes caught my eye. A squat, ugly pod hung from each wing with a short, stubby gun barrel protruding from the front. The holes in the air-cooling jacket surrounding each barrel gave them a distinct machine-gun appearance. Another strange bit of equipment was slung under the belly of a couple of airplanes. I guessed that this was the target pod, which contained a reel of cable that pulled the target banner for gunnery flights.

I entered the hangar and walked down a short passageway to the door marked Personnel. A bored-looking personnel man 2nd class took my orders and logged me in to the squadron. I was assigned a temporary room back at the same group of wooden buildings that housed Indoc battalion and the Naval Aviation Officer school (NAO school)—quite a letdown from the opulent quarters of Meridian. The personnel man explained that a new class would be formed in a couple of days, and I would get a permanent room assignment then. So it seemed that I was on my own for a couple of days with no duties or anyone to whom I had to report. For the first time since joining the Navy I was more or less released on my own recognizance. This was the way officers were treated, and I loved it.

A Navy bookkeeping anomaly had created a "good deal" for the students at VT-4. Because we were attached officially to the Advanced Training Command after finishing at NAS Meridian but VT-4 was attached to the Basic Training Command, we were considered to be TDY (temporary duty away) and were therefore eligible for per-diem pay in addition to our normal salary. Furthermore, TDY pay could be drawn up to thirty days in advance! So, with what amounted to two months' additional pay in my wallet, I was flush.

It got better. At our orientation briefing, the VT-4 training officer, Lt. Cdr. "Whitey" Gramlich, explained that VT-4 had a bad-weather backlog of students and it would be about two weeks before my class could begin flying. There was no formal ground school for our training at VT-4—just a series of lectures tailored to the type of flying for each stage—so we would have no duties or assignments for the next two weeks. Anyone who happened to have leave on the books could go on leave if they desired, but most of us were either out of leave or in the hole. NAO cadets in Preflight training would stand all the normal watches because we were considered "senior" cadets while occupying part of their barracks.

Next, Commander Gramlich explained that the base really didn't have room for all of us, so anyone who desired could use his per-diem pay to live ashore, or off the station. This was a huge departure from the norm: we were not supposed to have off-base living privileges until we had finished advanced instrument training and received an official promotion to "senior NAVCAD." Gramlich explained that living ashore would be strictly unofficial, and that if we got into trouble out there we would be on our own; VT-4 would deny encouraging us to live off base. But if we acted responsibly and maintained a low profile, the gate guards didn't know the difference between senior NAO cadets and NAVCADS, and we wouldn't be caught.

This was great; extra money and two weeks off to play! I elected to stay in the NAO barracks. I was somewhat hesitant to live off base, being rather more cautious than some of the men in our class. But open-gate liberty, meaning I could come and go as I pleased, was a tremendous increase in freedom. The two weeks went by in a whirlwind of parties and fun, but then the student backlog cleared out and it was time for us to get back to business.

We started gunnery training on 13 November. The pattern we would be flying was a circular pattern known in the training command as "squirrel cage" gunnery. The stage consisted of ten hops: the first four were flown dual with an instructor, and the remaining six were flown solo. The gunnery training was designed more to teach coordination and energy management than how to shoot down an enemy airplane, but it did give us an introduction to the weapons tactics we would be using in later training.

The gun hops included a target tow airplane and four shooter airplanes. The flight taxied out to an "arming area" with parking lines painted on the surface of the hold-short area for the duty runway. The four shooting airplanes parked parallel to each other, their gun pods pointing in a safe direction. For safety, the guns were never armed in the operations area. A ground arming crew of aviation ordnancemen would open each gun pod and, after cocking the breach block back, place the first round of .50-caliber machinegun belted ammo into the breach of the gun. The gun was ready to be armed after the pilot moved the master arm switch in the cockpit to "arm" and the gun-arming switch to "arm." This sent an electrical signal to the pod, which used compressed air to ram the breach block, which in turn pushed the first round in the belt into the chamber of the gun. The gun was now ready to fire. When finished firing, the pilot would "safe" the guns by moving the gun-arm switch to "safe," which locked the breach block open and ejected any round remaining in the chamber. Moving the master-arm switch to "safe" removed power from the gun trigger and all other weapons stations on the aircraft. The arming switches were never to be armed until the flight was in the gunnery range area over the Gulf of Mexico.

The target tow airplane, called the "tractor," took off while the gun flight was arming because it was a bit slower with the target pod on board. The gun flight took to the runway, two airplanes in front on alternate sides, with the second section similarly spaced behind. After takeoff, the flight did a "running rendezvous" on the way out to the gunnery range, with the lead flying slowly until the rest of the flight caught up. Once in the range, the lead climbed the flight to the starting altitude, which was five thousand feet above the target altitude. On gaining visual contact with the tractor, which by now was streaming the target banner out behind, the lead put the gun flight in line-astern formation: each airplane directly behind and slightly lower than the one ahead of it. The lead set a course perpendicular to the target course. Just as he was about to cross the target's course he commenced a rolling dive toward the target, accelerating to about five hundred knots and leveling off at the target altitude paralleling his course, so as to pass about fifty feet abeam of the tractor up his port side. Each of the other gun airplanes peeled off in ten-second intervals and followed the leader.

The tractor towed the target at two hundred knots, so the gun airplanes had a three-hundred-knot speed advantage on it. As the lead passed the tractor, he commenced a sharp nose-up, rolling right turn to a course ninety degrees off the tractor. On gaining a ninety-degree angle off from the tractor, the lead reversed his turn and roll so as to parallel the target's course again. This turn, called the "high reversal," would place the lead abeam of the tractor on his right about three thousand feet out and five thousand feet above, paralleling his course. This was called the "perch position." The lead announced the beginning of his run by calling in, then rolled and dove toward the target, pulling the gun sight down the tow cable until it reached a point roughly halfway between the banner and the tractor. He then started a turn reversal, called the "low reversal," and began tracking the banner. The lead's dive grew shallower as he approached the banner altitude, and he began pulling more Gs as he banked to keep the banner in the proper position in the gun sight. The firing cone was from forty-five degrees to thirty degrees off the target to keep the bullets well behind the tractor, and the proper firing range was from twelve hundred to nine hundred feet out from the banner.

To hit a moving target it is necessary to "lead" it—to shoot the bullets at the point where the target will be when the bullets arrive. If one simply aims at the target, it will have moved by the time the bullets arrive—unless the target is very slow and the bullets are very fast. The T-2 did not have a lead-computing gun sight, as did the real fighter planes of the day, so we had to improvise. The gun sight on the T-2 was a series of concentric rings with a V-shaped pipper at the center projected on a clear glass screen on the windscreen of the canopy. The gun sight was calibrated in mils, a measure of angular displacement. To lead the target in the T-2, we put the pipper about halfway up the target tow cable, which would place the banner toward the bottom of the gun sight as we tracked it.

The tractor pilot was the instructor in charge of the gun pattern. His job was to ensure that the pattern was flown in a safe manner and that the range was clear of surface vessels before allowing firing runs. If a pilot reversed too soon in his climb to the perch, he would end up too close to the tractor and too far acute, or ahead, to make a safe run. If he commenced a run from this position, he would dive below the tractor's altitude and have to pull so tight a turn after the run that he would get out of position in the pattern and pose a collision hazard to the other airplanes. If he tried to correct by sliding out and waiting until the tractor moved abeam of him, he would be on the perch too long and the trailing airplane might hit him because both pilots would be focusing their attention completely on the target. If a pilot reversed too late, he would end up sucked on the perch, or too far behind; it would also take him longer to get there, and the airplane following him in the pattern might end up in a proper perch at the same time. This was the most dangerous situation because if the two airplanes commenced simultaneous runs, they would be tracking the same point in space and would collide at the low reversal. It was the tractor driver's responsibility to prevent this from occurring by giving the out-of-position airplane a "high wave-off" and making him fly a figure-eight pattern at the perch altitude until he could work himself back into his slot in the proper position.

The target range airspace was off limits to other aircraft while a flight was using the range, but the surface of the Gulf of Mexico belonged to no one, and the tractor pilot had to keep an eye out for surface vessels before clearing live firing runs and declaring the range "hot." If a surface vessel was in the area or a cloud deck between the pattern altitude and the surface prevented surveillance, the range remained "cold," meaning we could still make "dry" runs at the target without firing.

The .50-caliber bullets in the ammunition belts were colored blue, indicating that they were just slugs of lead and contained no explosive or incendiary charge. The bullets' noses were painted with different colors of greasepaint—usually red, yellow, black, or white—so the students' runs could be scored. When a bullet passed through the thick nylon mesh of the target banner it left a residue of greasepaint, with the color indicating which airplane's bullet had struck there.

———————

Although I did all the flying on my first gun hop, my instructor kept up a running commentary, coaching me around the pattern. Each pilot was able to make only about ten runs at the target because of fuel constraints. The engine was operating at nearly full power the entire time, so fuel consumption was prodigious. After three or four runs, I felt that I could track the banner well enough to shoot, and we were cleared in "hot." As I reached the low reversal, looking at the target through the gun sight, I began to squeeze on the trigger. The rattle and chatter of the two fifties was not as dramatic as I had pictured it in my mind—and as I had seen in so many World War II aviation movies—but it was still a thrill because these were the first machine guns I had ever fired. "Nah, Steve," came from the rear cockpit, "you're way too far out; and don't John Wayne your bursts—you'll be out of bullets before you finish the runs." I had fired much too soon and for too long a burst. The guns were set so that their streams of bullets would converge about a thousand feet in front of the airplane. If one fired too far out, one missed both left and right of the target.

As I started the next run my instructor said, "Now wait until I tell you to shoot this time. I'll get you in the proper range, and you'll get the picture." The banner was approaching at a magnificent rate, growing larger and larger in the gun sight, and still he was chanting, "wait." Finally, when I was about to break off the run, he said "Shoot!" I gritted my teeth and jerked the trigger for a very short burst before I yanked up and over the banner, convinced I had collided with it. "Yeah, that's the way; we probably got some hits that time," came my instructor's voice. "You have got to get in really close to hit it." My eyes were wide and my heart was in my mouth as we zipped through the high reversal back to the perch. My burst had been only about one second long, which meant that I had fired probably ten rounds per gun. At that close distance, I couldn't see how any of them could have missed; it felt as if the banner was right over the muzzles.

For the remainder of the runs I gritted my teeth each time and waited until I was sure that I would collide with the banner before shooting. My instructor had beer bets with the other instructors on each of their students' hits, and he kept telling me, "That's great, Steve, I won't be buying any beers tonight!" At the end of the hop, though, I was amazed and chagrined to find that I had gotten only ten hits. Out of two hundred rounds, only ten hits! I had visions of a banner riddled with holes. My instructor said, "That's not bad, Steve. This will give you some idea of how hard it is to shoot another airplane down with guns. Remember, that banner is just flying along, not jinking or trying to get on your six to shoot at you, and those ten hits would have to hit something vital to bring him down. Some of your runs were a little too steep, or you were a little acute on the perch and had to pull too many Gs in the firing run—all that will affect your accuracy, but that will come with practice. Overall, not a bad first guns hop." I felt better after the debriefing, and I came away with a renewed respect for the skill of the fighter aces of our previous wars. I had the most hits on that hop, and indeed my instructor got to collect on the beers that night.

On completion of our fourth gun hop we were certified safe for solo in the gun pattern. The solo hops were flown with an instructor leading three students. Hops five and six were "dry," though; we were not allowed to shoot solo until hop seven, and gun stage drew to a close rapidly with live firing on hops seven, eight, nine, and ten. I never did equal my hit total of hop one—mostly getting just three or four hits a hop—but the object had not been to make gun aces out of us; it was to teach coordination, and my flying skills had increased apace. Next we would be learning the skill that sets Navy pilots apart from the rest of the flying world: aircraft carrier landings.

Carrier qualification stage, or "car quals," began with a series of classroom lectures. The first period dealt with the structure of the training: the syllabus called for ten practice hops called FCLP hops for "field carrier landing practice." The eleventh hop would be our first trip out to the USS *Lexington*, the carrier assigned to the training command to train new pilots, for our first carrier operations. To qualify we had to make three arrested landings and three catapult takeoffs, called "cat shots." But there would be much to learn before that day came.

The instructors for CQ stage had all earned a special title that set them apart from the rest of the Navy carrier operations pilots: all were landing signal officers, or LSOs. To qualify as an LSO and become a carrier landing expert, a pilot had to undergo a lengthy apprenticeship. He had to watch thousands of approaches in the FCLP pattern and at the ship as well as fly many practice hops himself. The title LSO was a reference to the time when someone literally guided each airplane down to a landing by signaling the pilot's lineup and height above the deck with a set of brightly colored flags that resembled oversized ping-pong paddles. In fact, the LSO nickname was "Paddles" for that very reason. The advent of jet aircraft with much higher landing speeds and different aerodynamic characteristics had rendered the old "Paddles" obsolete. The modern Navy pilot is simply too far away and is approaching the deck too fast to be able to see and respond to paddle signals. The optical landing system had replaced the paddles, and now the LSO communicated with the pilot by radio.

Because of his tremendous experience and training in carrier landings, the LSO could detect trends in the airplane's approach speed by changes in its attitude even before the pilot was aware of a need to correct the trend. The LSO transmitted these correction instructions to the pilot. During routine carrier operations in good weather, with an experienced air wing aboard, the LSO simply monitored the approaches and landings; few if any correction transmissions were needed. But in bad weather and at night, the landing pilot's life was literally in the LSO's hands. If the mission demanded flying when the carrier was encountering rough seas, the pitching of the flight deck made landings especially difficult and dangerous. The LSO could sense the pitch up and down of the flight deck and give the pilot verbal instructions for corrections long before the pilot could respond to the conditions visually. If the deck pitched up while the airplane was on a normal glide slope, the force with which the airplane struck the deck would be multiplied and might even break the landing gear off the plane; or it could make the airplane danger-ously low on the approach, with the possibility of crashing into the back of the ship.

The next lecture consisted mainly of two movies. The first was an hour-long compilation of footage of horrendous and spectacular carrier-landing crashes, most the result of the airplane flying in too low and striking the aft edge of the flight deck, called the "round-down" or "ramp." Some of the crash-es were the result of the pilot deciding to reject the landing, or "go around," and then over-rotating the airplane too close to the flight deck and snagging the tail hook on an arresting wire. This was called an "in-flight arrestment," and it slammed the airplane violently onto the deck, breaking the gear off and injuring or killing the pilot.

One crash even had comical aspects. A two-seat TF-9J trainer—which we would fly in the advanced training program—came in way too low and had a terrible ramp strike. The point of impact was just behind the rear cockpit, about where the wings joined the fuselage. The entire airplane disappeared in a huge, fiery explosion, and most of us in the audience gasped. Then the cigar shape of the cockpit part of the fuselage came rolling out of the fireball up the flight deck and came to rest with the canopy facing the bow of the ship. A very lucky and thoroughly frightened student crawled out and scrambled up the flight deck to safety.

While that incident ended well for the student, most of the crashes on the film captured images of the last few seconds of men's lives. We were a sober bunch when the reel ended, and I suppose that was the purpose of the film—to impress on us that this was no easy or light undertaking we had set for ourselves, and to weed out any who lacked the stomach to face these risks.

The second movie was the famous *Sabre Dance*, a film shown at one time or another to every Navy and Air Force jet flight-training class. The movie is a real-life demonstration of the immutable aerodynamic law of power available versus power required to sustain flight. An unfortunate aerodynamic fact of life is that after a wing is configured to provide maximum lift with extend-ing flaps, the only way to produce any more lift from that wing at the same speed is to increase its angle of attack. As the angle of attack is increased to produce more lift, the induced drag increases dramatically. Now, it requires much more power to overcome the increase in induced drag. When the equa-tions for maximum lift over drag, speed versus angle of attack, and power available versus power required are combined into one graph, the power line is represented by a curve. The slower the speed on the graph, the higher the power curve goes, until there is no more power available. In short, it takes more power to go slower. By adding just a few knots to the graph, the power curve drops dramatically as the speed of the wing produces more lift without nearly as much induced drag. The area just behind the peak of the power curve is where fifteen units angle of attack, our carrier-landing speed, placed us on the graph. This area was known as "the backside of the power curve," or "the region of reverse command."

Sabre Dance is a film clip of an Air Force pilot attempting to make an emergency landing in an F-100 Super Sabre fighter; because it was a test flight, the entire sequence was captured on film. A hydraulic problem caused the emergency landing. On short final, the airplane suddenly pitched high nose-up. Because the pilot was too slow and low to eject, he went into full afterburner— maximum power—in an attempt to go around. But the sudden pitch up had slowed the airplane far into the region of reverse command, and full power was required just to remain in the air. So the airplane proceeded down the runway, almost vertical, with the tail about eight feet off the runway surface, seemingly held aloft by the plume of white fire from the afterburner. The airplane began a slow wobble from side to side that gradually increased in magnitude, and the pilot struggled to maintain directional control as first one wing and then the other stalled and dropped. Finally, the oscillations became too great and the macabre "dance" ended with one wingtip digging into the runway and the airplane cartwheeling and dissolving into a huge fireball. The point so graphically made to us was that since we were already operating on the backside of the power curve in our carrier-landing attitude, we could never accept a "slow" indication. A "slow" required an immediate and positive power addition, otherwise we could end up low and unable to clear the sixty-foot obstacle posed by the back of the ship.

The LSO's commands were given in succinct prose so that there could be no misunderstanding about the intent of the instruction. If the LSO said something like, "Little power, don't climb," he meant that he had detected a slow trend and a small power addition was required to correct, but be careful not to add too much and balloon above the glide slope. If he simply said, "Power!" that meant a healthy shot on the order of 5 percent RPM. If he said, "Power, power!" that meant full throttle and, depending on how close the airplane was to the flight deck at the time, probably meant missing the arresting wires. A call of, "Power, power, power!" meant abandon the approach and escape. Only in an extreme case when the airplane had become excessively low or slow would the LSO issue such a command, and if the pilot wanted to live, he would heed it!

Each carrier pass, whether FCLP or at the ship, was graded. An enlisted assistant stood beside the LSO and copied, in a special shorthand, the remarks he made about the pass during the approach, and the LSO used these to debrief the pilots. Landings were graded in the fleet as well as during car qual training, because maintaining carrier-landing proficiency required the pilot to mentally review every detail of each pass he made at the deck to understand the reasons for any errors he made and the corrections required.

If the pass were picture perfect, the cryptic notation would simply say, "OK, 3 wire." If the pilot got fast or high and the tail hook touched down beyond the last arresting wire, he was said to have "boltered," in which case he added power and went around for another pass. That notation would probably read something like: "OK start, slow in the middle, power to a fast, pulled nose up in close, bolter." The classic ramp-strike scenario would be recorded as: "High start, settle in the middle, low at the ramp, power, power, 1 wire, FNKUA." This would earn that hapless pilot an ass chewing from the LSO—usually publicly—at the debriefing in the ready room and a bad grade for that pass. FNKUA was an abbreviation for "fucking near killed us all."

The original aircraft carriers had straight flight decks. There was no going around after a certain point, and if the airplane failed to catch one of the fourteen arresting wires, a specially designed barrier made of heavy nylon webbing and steel cable caught it, usually causing some damage to the craft. The advent of the much larger, heavier, and faster jets demanded a better system. The Royal Navy is credited with the design of the angled-deck carrier, which allows the pilot to simply go around if he lands long or his tail hook skips over the arresting wires. The modern angled-deck aircraft carrier has four of these wires. The third, counting from aft to forward, is the target wire. On the smaller *Essex*-class carriers such as the USS *Lexington*, there was only about twenty feet between arresting wires, and the entire landing area was only sixty feet long. The LSO platform was located just before the first wire on the port side of the deck. There was a net slung below the deck edge for the occupants of the LSO platform to dive into if a crash on the deck sent debris hurtling at the platform. The entire innovation had made carrier operations much safer, but because of the speeds involved and the small area of operation, carrier flying was still the most hazardous type of flying in the history of aviation.

Ironically, we learned how to make carrier landings at an Air Force base. Eglin Air Force Base, a giant, sprawling reservation, was located about thirty miles east of NAS Pensacola. There were a number of outlying airfields on the reservation, and the Navy had borrowed Eglin Field Six, an inactive base left over from World War II, for FCLP training. The first four FCLP hops were dual so that the LSO instructors could fine-tune our approaches and at least get us into the envelope before we began to work with the LSO on the ball.

We joined up and flew over to Field Six and entered the pattern normally. My first look at the field revealed a white box painted on the left half of the runway just short of the Fresnel lens. The box was about sixty feet long by fifty feet wide and represented the touchdown area on an *Essex*-class carrier. The main wheels of the airplane had to touch down within this box to count as an "arrested landing." I had thought my landings were pretty accurate—after all, we had been landing on the meatball since we started flying the T-2—but now I was learning what real precision meant! My instructor harped at me on every pass. He would not allow even one knot fast or slow from fifteen units' angle of attack. "Come on, Gray, work at it! Don't get lazy on me. You boltered that last pass 'cause you overcorrected in close." But the old, familiar message was coming through loud and clear: "Never accept less than perfect." Meatball, lineup, angle of attack, scan, scan, scan; it was hard work, but we were beginning to achieve the level of precision required for a good carrier pass. The practice was gradually building an instinct for how much power to add or subtract to correct an off-speed condition. The process that separates naval aviators from mere pilots had begun. After ten FCLP hops and one refresher—seventy-eight passes at the box on the runway—on 8 January 1965 I was judged to be ready for my first carrier qualifications.

———

The tenth of January was a perfect day for flying. Cloudless skies and calm winds made the Gulf of Mexico a smooth mirror of the sky above. Our period was scheduled early in the afternoon since the "Lex" had been hosting T-28s from Saufley Field all morning. We launched as a three-student flight led by an instructor, and I was in the first launch. It was a short flight out to the ship, which was only about twenty miles offshore from the air station. After a short time orbiting overhead we were given "signal charlie," which meant the Lex was ready for us. The instructor led us into the break up the starboard side of the ship, and then departed the pattern to hold overhead in case any of us had difficulty or were banished from the pattern and had to return to the field.

The downwind leg was my first look at the ship, since I had not been able to get much more than a glance while flying formation. I was the second airplane in the pattern and heard my classmate calling the ball as I started my turn off the 180 position. The first couple of passes would be touch-and-gos with the tail hook up to let the LSO see how we were doing before allowing us to attempt our first arrestment. The first thing I noticed as I rolled into the groove after passing the green wake of the ship was the slow closure rate. The ship was making nearly thirty knots to get the proper wind across the deck, because the winds were very light in the Gulf that day. This gave us an effective closure rate with the ship of only one hundred knots. This was thirty knots slower than our closure rate with the box in FCLPs, and everything seemed in slow motion in comparison. It seemed as if we had all day to make corrections. This was going to be a piece of cake! We hadn't been told about this beforehand, I guess so that when we experienced the slower closure rate it would bolster our confidence.

I slammed down in perfect position with my main wheels just beyond the third wire, and boards in, power full, I was airborne by the time I reached the end of the angled deck. Our call sign was Plank Flight—a bit of grim humor from our instructor, as he likened our trip to the ship as walking the plank. Because I had flown to the ship as number three in the formation, I was Plank Three. "OK pass, Plank Three, do it again," the LSO said over the radio, and I could feel myself grinning behind my oxygen mask as I turned downwind. My next pass was also right on the money, and as I turned downwind the LSO called, "OK, Plank Three, drop your hook, the next pass is for real." I reached up and lowered the black-and-white-striped handle in the cockpit that lowered the tail hook.

I was a little keyed up with adrenalin as I called, "Plank Three, ball, twenty-three hundred."

"Roger ball," said the LSO. "Looking good, Three, ease gun a little," he called as my indexer showed a donut and V, indicating a little fast. I eased off a little power and brought the nose up to a donut. The ball drifted slightly high so I eased off a smidgen more, and then caught it with a slight addition of power as the ball settled down in the center of the datum lights. Lineup needed a little left but I was on centerline as I crossed the round down. The ball slid into the left datum lights as the wheels pounded down, and I was pushing the speed brakes in when a giant, invisible hand grabbed the airplane from behind and yanked it to a stop. My head snapped forward and the shoulder harness bit into my shoulders. "Damn," I thought, as I retarded the throttle. "That was harder than I expected." The airplane rolled backward a little as the arresting wire retracted, and I became aware of a yellow-shirted flight deck crewman giving me a signal with his right hand, thumb up, sweeping into his outstretched left hand, palm down—the signal to raise tail hook. As he watched my tail hook retract and drop the arresting cable, he began taxiing me out of the landing area and into line for the starboard "cat," as the catapult was called, just forward of the ship's superstructure, or "island."

As I taxied forward I could see small tendrils of steam rising from the cat track on the deck. At the end of the track was a large lump of shiny steel shaped like a mushroom cap with a nose jutting out of the forward end. This was the shuttle that was attached to the steam piston just under the flight deck. A thick nylon hawser called the "bridle" with loops on each end was slid under the nose of the shuttle, and each loop was hung on a hook just forward of the left and right main landing gear. A bungee cord attached the bridle to the shuttle to help pull the loops free of the airplane after the end of the cat stroke and to keep the bridle from being flung overboard. The yellow-shirted flight deck crewman motioned me carefully forward until the nose of my plane rose up sharply over the shuttle. As the nose wheel rolled off the front of the shuttle, the crewman suddenly gave the "hold brakes" signal by crossing his arms over his chest with clenched fists. I pressed hard on the brake pedals to stop the airplane. This was to prevent being yanked to a stop by the "holdback," which was attached as I taxied over the shuttle. The holdback was a frangible link of metal resembling a barbell. A chain was attached to one end of the cylinder and anchored to a special track in the deck. The other end of the cylinder was slipped into a fitting mounted to the tail hook's attach point. The purpose of the holdback was to allow the airplane on the cat to go to full power without moving. The holdback was designed to break when the cat fired, but it was possible to break it by not jumping on the brakes soon enough after crossing the shuttle.

Of course, I couldn't see all of the activity taking place below and behind me. While the holdback was being installed, other crewmen were attaching the bridle to the launch hooks on the landing gear. After the yellow shirt gave the hold brakes signal, he passed control by sweeping his hand toward another man standing forward and to the left of the nose. This was the cat officer, whose title was stenciled on his white jersey in black letters. The cat officer made a sweeping motion below his waist with his left hand while he raised his right hand over his head with two fingers extended in a circling motion. His below-the-waist signal was to the catapult crew, who were standing on a platform beneath the starboard side of the flight deck with their heads just above the level of the deck. The signal told them to take tension on the catapult. I felt the airplane squat on its struts as they did this. The process was just like cocking a pistol; it required only the push of a button to fire the cat after tension was applied. The two fingers over his head was the signal to me to go to full power. The pilot wanted to be at takeoff power in case the cat fired inadvertently, because nothing could stop the airplane from being launched at that point!

I flipped the catapult hold handle down as I pushed the throttle full forward. The cat hold handle was to prevent the force of the cat shot from dragging my left hand back and inadvertently pulling the power off during acceleration. The T-2 trembled and strained against the holdback as I scanned the engine instruments. Satisfied that everything was in order, I saluted the cat officer, positioned my head firmly into the headrest, and grasped the stick. Seconds passed and nothing happened. Curious, I looked left to see if the cat officer was suspending the launch. Big mistake! The cat fired at that moment and I made my first cat shot with my head firmly locked over my left shoulder. There was no way to move your head during the cat stroke because of the twenty or more transverse Gs pulled during acceleration. The stroke was only about two hundred feet long, and the plane was accelerated from 0 to 150 knots in that two hundred feet! The stroke was a lot longer on the newer and much larger "supercarriers" being built at that time, and on those ships it ended far enough short of the bow that pilots rotated to takeoff attitude while the wheels were still rolling on the deck. Not so on the *Essex*-class carriers. The cat stroke ended at the bow of the ship and you were flung out into space, ready or not. The force of the acceleration had pulled my right hand holding the control stick back into my belly, so I rotated and climbed sharply off the cat. Even though I had made the shot looking to the side, it was still a great feeling!

My next pass was also a good one, and I caught the third wire again. This time the trap wasn't so much of a surprise, but it still seemed more violent than I thought it would. I could easily see why checking the shoulder harness to see if it was locked was so important—at least if the pilot didn't want to wear the gun sight for a face! This time I made sure to look straight ahead as the cat fired, and I exulted in the great feeling of speed and acceleration. "Just one more trap and I'm car qualed," I thought, as I turned off the 180 for the final. But this time a late correction for a slow caused me to float a little, and the ball rose up above the datum lights as I slammed down. I was hoping for the fourth wire, but no such luck. I sucked in the speed brakes and went to full power as the main wheels rolled off the angle deck, and I heard "Bolter, bolter, bolter," in my headset as the LSO announced my miss.

Mentally chastising myself as I turned downwind, I performed the landing checklist again and turned final. This time the pass was near perfect, with the ball sliding off into the datum lights. The main wheels smashed down and I braced for the sudden stop, but this time no giant hand snatched me. Startled, I slammed the throttle up as the mains rolled off the deck and settled a little off the angle. "Bolter, bolter, bolter! Pull up!" came the voice over the radio. Confused now, I climbed to the downwind thinking, "What the hell? That pass was OK."

The LSO called and said, "Plank Three, you had a hook skip bolter." This meant that my tail hook had bounced over the third and fourth wires. "Don't anticipate the trap; you were late getting the power on." The next pass was good also, but this time I got the power up and boards in at touchdown. Sure enough, "Bolter, bolter, bolter," as I again flew off the angle. "Damn!" I thought; now I was getting concerned. I had only eighteen hundred pounds of fuel left, and fifteen hundred was a mandatory bingo back to the field. I would have to come back and do this all over if I failed to qualify, not to mention the huge disappointment I would feel.

The LSO called and said, "Steve, that was another hook skip. Write up the tail hook snubber as weak when you get back to the field. This pass, I want you to hold one ball low, if you can, to give you a shot at all the wires." I rolled into the groove slightly low and he began talking. "Looking good, Steve. Hold what you have . . . real little power now . . . don't climb . . . ease off just a little. That's it, keep her coming . . . OK, OK. . . ." The round-down slid under me in my peripheral vision, and I slammed down with the ball sliding out the bottom of the lens and the giant hand yanked me to a stop. "Nice pass, Plank Three. You skipped the two and grabbed the three; be sure and gripe that snubber, it's getting worse," said the LSO as I, grinning hugely, taxied clear of the wires and up to the jet blast deflector, a large, square steel portion of the flight deck raised by hydraulic actuators to shield airplanes waiting in line for the catapult from the jet blast of the airplane about to be launched ahead of them.

As I climbed out after my final cat shot, Primary Flight Control, or "prifly"—which performed the same function on the ship as the control tower at the field—called on the radio with my steer back to Forrest Sherman Field. "Plank Three, your signal bingo, steer three-five-zero for twenty-five miles, angels fifteen." This meant that I should climb to fifteen thousand feet to clear any inbound traffic to the ship, and Forrest Sherman Field should be on a magnetic heading of 350 degrees at twenty-five miles. I was elated. I had joined a very exclusive and elite group in aviation; I was now a carrier-qualified aviator.

The other guys in my flight were waiting on the tarmac as I taxied in and shut down. We held a little celebration right on the flight line, with back slaps and handshakes and congratulations all around. As each member of the class returned, the ceremony was repeated. The entire class had qualified, and with the sun low on the horizon, we headed off to the ACRAC club to "wet down" our carrier qualification and graduation from primary training.

6

Chase Field

The headquarters of the Chief of Naval Air Advanced Training (CINAVANTRA) was at NAS Corpus Christi, Texas. The Training Command was feeling a sense of urgency as our military operations in Southeast Asia were growing and the air strikes against North Vietnam increased steadily. For that reason, the day after our car quals on Friday, my class checked out of VT-4 and was ordered to report to CINAVANTRA HQ on the following Monday morning for assignment to our advanced training squadrons. After driving late into the night Saturday in a pounding rainstorm and finally finding a motel with a vacancy south of Houston, I checked into the transient BOQ at NAS Corpus Christi on Sunday. Corpus had been my first duty assignment out of enlisted boot camp, and returning as an officer candidate gave me a sense of accomplishment.

Monday morning, I was standing in line abreast with four other cadets from my class in the CINAVANTRA personnel office. A staff lieutenant commander, arbitrarily starting at one end of the line, said, "You three are going to VT-21, -22, and -23 at NAS Kingsville; and you two [pointing to me last] will go to VT-24 and -25 at Navy Chase in Beeville." I had been hoping for NAS Kingsville because the word was that Kingsville (home to Texas A&I University and closer to Corpus Christi) was much better liberty than Beeville, which was stuck out in the middle of the mesquite and prickly pear cactus flats of south Texas about halfway between Corpus and San Antonio. He softened the assignment to Beeville by saying, "Kingsville might be better liberty, but you guys will get to fly the F-11." He was referring to the Grumman F-11 Tiger, a supersonic, afterburner-equipped fighter. The last remaining F-11 squadron in the Navy was located at NAS Beeville, and the students flew their last few syllabus hops before graduation in the F-11. The Kingsville students flew the Grumman F-9 Cougar for their entire training.

NAS Chase was home to three training squadrons. VT-24 and VT-25 flew the Grumman F-9, and VT-26 flew the last of the Grumman F-11s. The F-9 was a true fighter plane that the Navy had pressed into service as an advanced trainer. Although the airplanes were very old by aviation standards—my instructor's instructors had flown these same airplanes when they were students—they were still capable of performing any mission the Navy decided it needed. Indeed, during the Cuban missile crisis in 1962, some of the F-9s had been pressed into service as defensive fighters with new Sidewinder infrared-tracking, air-to-air missiles installed, and the instructors had stood ready alert duty as part of the nation's Air Defense Command until the crisis was resolved.

The original version of the F-9 was a straight-wing model called the Panther. The Cougar was a newer, swept-wing version introduced into fleet service just after the Korean War. For several years the Cougar was the Navy's hottest and most potent carrier-based fighter plane. There were even a few squadrons of F-9s still on active duty, mostly with Marine Corps photographic reconnaissance units, when I reported to NAS Chase, although they were being replaced rapidly with newer aircraft. The F-9 was said to have been built by the "Grumman Iron Works" because it was such a sturdy airplane. A pilot could do lasting damage to himself before overstressing the airplane by pulling Gs, and the airplane had no maximum airspeed limits—as fast as you could get it to go was fine with the F-9.

Visually, the F-9 managed to look both sturdy and sleek at the same time. The swept wings suggested high speed, but the thickness of the fuselage spoke of stocky muscle. The wings joined the fuselage just behind the cockpit and were faired into the fuselage with diamond-shaped fairings, which made the jet engine intakes diamond-shaped as well. The trailing edge of the wing curved back into the fuselage gradually, ending just slightly forward of the tail section. Four 20-mm cannon mounted in the nose provided the F-9's bite. In addition, each wing carried two ordnance stations on which external bomb racks or missile launcher rails could be mounted. All in all, even by more modern fighter standards, the F-9 packed a respectable punch.

Just as the transition to jets from the T-34B had been a big step for us, entering advanced training required expanding our knowledge before we could begin flying. We began with six weeks of ground school, with classes in advanced aerodynamics and high-speed flight, engineering classes dealing with the design and systems of the F-9, high-altitude meteorology, and radio instrument navigation classes covering the Federal Aviation Regulations for instrument flight in the United States.

Nearly eight weeks would pass before I began syllabus training in the F-9. Just to get to fly a little, during February I cadged a ride in the backseat of a TF-9J on a formation hop. The instructor let me fly a bit during the hop, and I was amazed at how much trouble I had flying smoothly. The airplane was incredibly sensitive, and I didn't notice actually moving the stick for control inputs at all. It was almost as if I merely thought "bank" and the airplane would roll that way. As usual, and especially after that ride, I could hardly wait to return to flying to break up the monotony of classroom and study.

In Beeville that year, there was a group of five young, single, female schoolteachers who were engaged in a noble effort to provide a place for lonely and bored flight students to spend their liberty hours in town. These young ladies, in their first years of teaching and therefore on the bottom of the pay scale, had banded together to rent a large garage apartment. The bottom story included a double garage, large living room, and dining room. The upstairs contained the bedrooms. The landlord had painted the entire exterior of the apartment bright lime green, so the apartment was known to all the flight students as "the Green House." Now, given our youth and single status, it might be inferred that some salacious enterprise was afoot in the Green House. This was not the case. These were nice young ladies of decent moral character, and even though two of the girls eventually married flight students, dating was mostly of a casual, platonic nature. Given the scrutiny applied to single female schoolteachers in a small town, it could not have been otherwise. The girls hosted a sort of unofficial USO club. The flight students would bring food over from the local market and would have cookouts and the like, and we could lounge around in the large living room and watch TV and listen to records. The girls were mostly anti–Vietnam War, but they were very supportive of the Navy flight students, and what they were doing for us was a very nice thing.

I was introduced to the girls and the Green House during my first week at Beeville, and for a month or so I enjoyed their hospitality whenever I was on liberty in town. I was watching TV one night when two young ladies from out of town dropped by to visit one of the Green House girls with whom they had attended college. Also schoolteachers, they were from Sinton, Texas, another small town about twenty miles south of Beeville. The girl they had come to visit was out on her bowling league night, and I volunteered to drive them to the bowling alley. Something about one of these young women interested me, and I asked her for a date. She was somewhat reluctant to date a Navy man, but she agreed to a double date with her friend, who happened to be dating a cadet from Beeville. She was Miss Alma Mae Thumann, a graduate of Texas Lutheran College, a high school business teacher, and a country girl raised on a farm eight miles southeast of Weimar, Texas. Soon, I was spending all of my liberty hours in her company.

Advanced flight training began with a seven-hop familiarization stage in the TF-9J. The first six hops were dual; the seventh was a solo. The fam stage was much shorter than previous fam stages because there wasn't much new in the mechanics of flying the airplane. During the dual hops we learned the peculiarities of the F-9, the procedures for that airplane, the course rules for operating in the Navy Chase region, and the visual landmarks of the training area. Like many airplanes designed for aircraft carrier use, the F-9 had folding wings to save space in the confines of the hangar deck. We practiced folding the wings using a lever in the cockpit, and we learned the importance of making sure the little red tabs located in the wing-root hinge were not visible on preflight. If these tabs popped up into view, the wings were unlocked and could fold; in flight, this would be disastrous.

There was also a high-speed flight demonstration during the dual hops in fam stage, and the instructors used this as an excuse to try to get the TF-9J supersonic. Flying the F-9 through the sound barrier required skill and finesse. It was necessary to climb the airplane as high as it would go, which was about thirty-eight thousand feet, and accelerate to its maximum level speed, which was about seven-tenths of the speed of sound, or Mach 0.7 at that altitude. Then the airplane had to be completely "unloaded," which meant pushing forward on the control stick to achieve zero G, until the nose was absolutely vertical in a dive toward the earth. Of course, the throttle had to be pushed all the way forward, commanding maximum thrust from the engine throughout the maneuver. If all these things were done precisely, as the airplane screamed down through thirty thousand feet the airspeed needle would creep slightly past the "Mach meter" on the inside of the airspeed indicator. There was a very slight buffet and tendency for the nose to tuck under a little as the Mach shock wave (sound barrier) traveled back to the trailing edge of the wing. By twenty-five thousand feet, the air was becoming denser and the speed of sound was increasing, so the Mach meter crept back above the airspeed needle and the airplane was subsonic again. If the airplane was not completely unloaded or the dive wasn't perfectly vertical, it would never make it through Mach 1. It was quite a challenge and worth bragging about if a pilot could get the Cougar supersonic.

Fam stage went smoothly for me; I was getting used to the responsiveness of the F-9 and was improving my control inputs. Because of the swept wing the airplane was much more challenging to hold on the ball at optimum angle of attack and wasn't nearly as stable on approach as the T-2 had been. The fam hops began with a climb to the training area for the series of acrobatics and high air work, then a return to the field for touch-and-go practice until the airplane was low on fuel and we had to land. I could see that carrier qualifications in the F-9 would be more difficult than in the T-2, but there were more immediate challenges to meet.

After soloing the TF-9J on the last fam stage hop, I immediately began what was to be the most difficult—for me—phase of flight training, advanced instruments. Instrument stage consisted of six basic instrument hops ("B" stage)—mostly practice flying the airplane on instruments—and eighteen radio instrument navigation hops ("C" stage) using the nation's air traffic control system and the Federal Aviation Regulations. The last hop in advanced instruments was the "C-eighteen check," the final instrument check ride. On successful completion of this hop, the student was given his military instrument rating and was rated to fly in any instrument conditions allowed by his command. C stage was the last big hurdle to clear in flight training and the last real washout stage. Most students who completed C stage would have no trouble graduating and getting their wings. I wasn't looking forward to instruments, and remembering my difficulties in basic, I viewed advanced instruments as something to be dreaded.

B stage began with a new wrinkle. The primary attitude instrument in the cockpit is the attitude gyro. It indicates the airplane's pitch and bank. Other instruments will provide bits of this same information, but several have to be viewed and interpreted together to understand what the airplane is doing, while the attitude indicator provides this information at a glance. Accordingly, we watched it primarily in our scan of the panel, and we used the other instruments to back up and verify what the attitude indicator was telling us. The instructor in the front cockpit had a switch that caused the attitude instrument to fail with no indication, no "off flag"; it just froze in its last position and therefore provided false information. Flying instruments with a failed attitude gyro was called being on "partial panel," and the attitude gyro was failed on takeoff roll on the B-one hop and was never used again in advanced instrument stage.

The instrument hood in the TF-9J was chartreuse, and I hated it from the moment I pulled the "green overcast" over my head, shutting out the outside world. Just like basic, we began with an instrument takeoff, and I immediately noticed that the attitude indicator wasn't working. When I rotated for takeoff, it was still indicating level pitch. Jesus! I thought instruments stage was hard in the T-2; this was impossible! I struggled to keep the airplane climbing and the wings level as my eyes darted frantically about the instrument panel. Vertical speed, altimeter, airspeed, turn needle, and compass all had to be interpreted together to understand what the airplane was doing.

"This will really strengthen your scan," came my instructor's voice over the intercom from the front cockpit. "Now turn left to three-two-zero," he said as we climbed through five hundred feet. I could feel his hand on the stick until I had got us safely above the mesquite trees. "Watch your bank," he said. As the compass began to spin rapidly toward 320 degrees, the altimeter began to indicate a descent and the turn needle was pegged hard left. I yanked the stick back to the right and then neutral, but the turn needle just bounced back and forth on either side of neutral. "Easy does it, you've got to be gentle partial panel."

I swallowed my frustration and tried to resume a controlled turn toward the assigned heading. I finally figured out that if I left the turn and bank indicator about a half-needle-width shy of the left edge of the full rate turn mark, that would give me about twenty-eight degrees of bank. If I put the turn needle all the way on top of the full standard rate turn mark, I couldn't tell if I was overbanking because the needle would be pegged full deflection. Oh, man! I'm going to just love this, I thought. After reaching the operating area, we began the hated S and Y patterns again, only they were much harder on partial panel. I hamburgered my way through them, and by the end of the hop I was able to come close to the clock on the S pattern. The Y pattern was still pretty ragged, though.

Hop B-four called for "unusual attitude recovery" training. My instructor, Lieutenant Ingham, joked in the briefing that these should be easy for me because I had already done some self-induced unusual attitude recoveries. The point was to induce vertigo so that the student would be forced to use the instruments to recover the airplane. So-called seat-of-the-pants flying would get a pilot killed in instrument flying conditions; pilots had to learn to ignore their senses and believe their instruments. The student was told to close his eyes and put his head down on one shoulder while the instructor flew through some wild acrobatics, rolling and pulling Gs. Then, with the airplane in some really unusual attitude, like nose-up inverted, he would say "You got it," and the student had to figure out from the instruments what the airplane's attitude was and make the appropriate control inputs to bring it back to level, controlled flight. Of course, the student would be completely disoriented and would be forced to ignore his scrambled senses while he recovered.

The first step was to determine from looking at the altimeter and airspeed indicator if the plane was climbing or descending. The pilot either pulled power if the plane was in a dive or added power if it was climbing. Next, the pilot had to try to determine if the plane was upside down or not. If the turn needle deflected the opposite direction from the control input, the airplane was on its back and would have to be rolled upright. Then the pilot either pushed or pulled the nose to level flight. The most difficult attitudes to determine were inverted either nearly straight up or straight down because the student had a very hard time determining when the wings were level to start recovering the nose. Surprisingly, given my aversion to partial panel flight, I did very well with unusual attitude recoveries, earning high marks for that portion of the hop. This was extremely valuable and important knowledge for survival when flying in bad weather, and it would save my life one day. Although I didn't enjoy it much, I did OK in B stage; my troubles wouldn't become apparent until C stage.

Most of the hops in C stage used a canned flight plan called a "round robin" because it started and ended at the same field. The air route traffic control center, which was Houston Center for our area, had copies of these flight plans, and the students and instructors would file them with Center at Base Operations about thirty minutes before manning their airplanes. After completing all the checklists, the student called clearance delivery on the radio. "ATC clears Navy NJ345 to the Navy Chase airport via the Red One canned flight plan. Climb and maintain ten thousand; expect clearance to flight level three-one-zero ten minutes after departure. Contact departure control on three forty-five point three, squawk one-five-zero-zero." The student read the clearance back to ensure that he had understood it correctly and proceeded to fly it.

A typical canned flight plan headed out west of Chase Field to George West VORTAC, then up to San Antonio, over to Houston, down to Palacios, and finally back to Navy Chase for practice approaches. Some of the hops called for "out and in" flights, which were actual cross-country flights to other military fields—with a stop for lunch or supper—and a return to Chase Field. These hops were more fun than the canned flight plans because the students were able to visit new bases and see other parts of the military establishment.

By C-ten it was becoming increasingly apparent that I was struggling. My old problem of getting so wrapped up in just flying the airplane that I lost track of what was coming next on the flight plan was causing me to miss course changes and altitude restrictions. It was easy to get lost in the gauges and lose track of where I was in relation to the outside world. The only gauge in the cockpit that indicated the airplane's position was the RMI compass, with its two needles, and the DME window. The abstract information presented by the TACAN needle and DME had to be translated to the plane's position on the map. If it was left or right of course inbound to the station, it had to be turned toward the head of the needle pointing to the station, but if it was outbound from the station, it had to be turned away from the tail of the needle to correct the course. Another problem was "point-to-point" navigation. If the plane was on the 150-degree radial at thirty miles from a station and the pilot was commanded to fly point-to-point to the 270 degree radial at forty miles from the station, he had to pick out a course to fly from looking at a gauge that was about two inches in diameter. Shipboard navigators had plotting boards on which to work these problems; we had to eyeball the course using a pencil to lay a parallel line across the face of this small instrument while flying with the other hand. I just wasn't getting it.

The C-eleven hop was an in-stage check ride to gauge our progress, and it was flown with a different instructor. I amply demonstrated to the check instructor that I was not up to speed, and he gave me a down on the ride. I knew it was coming but it stung nonetheless. I was trying so hard! I had memorized the instrument flying guide and knew all the FARs; I meticulously planned every hop with pages of kneeboard paper that detailed courses to fly back to the TACAN fixes for Chase Field. I flew each approach mentally, again and again, at night in my room in the cadet barracks, and my new girlfriend, Alma, was beginning to learn my procedures by heart because I asked her to quiz me on them routinely. I couldn't know then that part of the problem was that I was getting no instruction. Every hop was a check ride. My instructor would tell me when I had done something wrong, but he failed to tell me why I had made the mistake. In the briefing for the extra time hop that was required before continuing in stage after a down, he suggested that it might help if I requested a new instructor. I was crushed! My problems couldn't possibly be his fault. After all, he was a god, a rated naval aviator—and therefore omniscient in all things concerning flying. And he had given up on me and wanted to wash his hands of me. I was despondent, and the possibility that I might bilge out of flight training haunted me. Grimly, I hung on and tried harder.

In the briefing for C-sixteen my instructor told me that by this time there was nothing new to be presented in C stage and asked what I thought would be the most beneficial practice. I answered that holding patterns would be the most useful. A holding pattern is a racetrack-shaped pattern flown inbound to a fix in space—usually a TACAN DME fix—that is used as a parking orbit for airplanes when air traffic control becomes saturated. Practice entering and flying holding patterns contained all the elements of radio instruments in which I needed review: turning the proper direction, tracking courses both out- and inbound, timing, and point-to-point. Mr. Ingham drew a series of holding patterns around the Chase TACAN. I was to enter each one, then fly one turn around the pattern and depart and fly a point-to-point to the next. I got all screwed up trying to enter the third pattern, and the hop went downhill from there.

In the debriefing, Mr. Ingham told me that I was in no way ready for the C-eighteen check and said that he would have to give me another down just to buy some more practice time. I had to agree with him because I was just as frustrated with my performance as he was. At least a down now would give me an extra time hop and a re-fly of C-sixteen, a total of three more hops before the C-eighteen check. He asked if I could think of anything in particular that would help me get the picture. I answered no, that I would just keep plugging. My morale was at a low point and I was really afraid of failing. I was determined not to quit, though—they would have to throw me out!

My performance on the extra time hop showed some improvement. Encouraged, I was glad we had C-sixteen scheduled for the same day. During C-sixteen, something clicked in my mind and it all fell into place. All the study, all the worry, all the time spent thinking only about flying radio instruments suddenly paid off, and I flew a damn near perfect hop. My instructor was cautious with his praise during the debriefing, fearing that it was just a fluke. But on C-seventeen I proved to him that I really had the picture and flew a flawless instrument hop. I hit all the checkpoints on the money and flew perfect approaches and missed-approach procedures. The C-seventeen hop was designed to be a full-scale rehearsal for the C-eighteen check, and it really put the student through the wringer.

After my last GCA, which was right on the money at minimums, Lieutenant Ingham said, "I got it; pop your bag." He added power and cleaned up the gear, and we departed the pattern for half an hour of wild, exuberant, celebratory flying. We went down to Lake Mathias and beat it up, rolling, diving, yanking and banking, and putting on quite an air show for the fishing boats. Mr. Ingham was ecstatic to see me finally get through C stage. My love for flying was rejuvenated when I was reminded how much fun flying was out from under the hated bag.

The sun was low on the horizon as we hit the break for landing. My instructor said, "Steve, I don't want to worry you about your eighteen check tomorrow, but you got the first launch with Major Bannigan." Major Bannigan was the instrument standardization officer, and he was in charge of all the instrument training in VT-25. He had a reputation for being a real hard-ass and the toughest check pilot in the squadron. My instructor continued, "Now, don't let that rattle you. If you fly as good as the last two hops, you will pass with no sweat." I was really confident now and figured that I could hack even the toughest instrument check ride in the training command.

The C-eighteen check hop used a canned flight plan that allowed the instructor to depart from the airways navigation portion and return to Chase for approaches when he decided he had seen enough of the student's navigating. The student planned the hop, with times between checkpoints and fuel burned per leg, on a kneeboard card with a copy for the instructor. I met Major Bannigan at Base Operations, filed the flight plan with Air Route Traffic Control, and we were soon launched on the check ride. South Texas was not under radar positive control in those days, and Houston Center had to keep traffic separated by time and position reporting. Houston Center immediately began to screw up by not clearing us to the points on the flight plan. I guess Navy student training traffic was given low priority on airspace usage, because we got vectored all over the sky and cleared direct to points that skipped much of our flight plan.

Major Bannigan, irritated by all the center vectors, finally canceled our flight plan and directed me to proceed back to the TACAN fix for the first of our approaches. This was fine with me; I was relaxed and confident and had done well up to this point in the hop. "How are you doing on fuel according to your fuel plan?" Major Bannigan asked. We had been flying so far off the flight plan that there was no way to directly correlate the fuel, but at that point I had three thousand pounds showing on the gauge. For our time of flight I had figured we would have about thirty-two hundred, so three thousand was close enough. "Pretty close, Sir," I answered. "We should have had thirty-two hundred at the TACAN fix and we've got three grand now." He answered, "OK."

The hop was a repeat of C-seventeen in performance. I flew all the approaches and misses perfectly, and after the last GCA, Major Bannigan had me pop the bag and landed out of the approach. I felt great! C stage was over, and I had done it. Because I had no postflight duties to perform on taxi, I beat the major out of the airplane and was standing on the ramp watching him climb down. I was feeling just fine, it was a beautiful morning, and I had passed the dreaded eighteen check.

Major Bannigan headed back toward the hangar and I fell into step beside him. "Well, Gray, that was a pretty good hop, but I'm going to have to give you a down."

"What!" I bleated. "Why?"

"I failed your fuel gauge back there and you didn't catch it. When I gave the fuel gauge back to you, you were down to twenty-eight hundred."

I didn't even try to argue how chickenshit it was to gig me for a lousy two hundred pounds of fuel, considering how Houston Center had screwed up our flight plan. Instead, I tried to appeal to his sense of fairness. "Gee, Major," I said, "let me appeal my case. I've already had two downs in C stage, and a down now is an automatic speedy board. Do you think the hop was so bad that I should go before a speedy board?"

"Naw, naw, man. You flew a good hop; you won't have a speedy board, I'll just recommend a re-fly tomorrow. You just needed a reminder to check that fuel more closely. I'll bet you never forget to check it again."

Disappointment, anger, anguish—I felt all these emotions as I hung around the student ready room to see when they would reschedule my C-eighteen re-fly. Two hours later, the student training officer came through the room. "Gray, your speedy board is at fourteen hundred tomorrow," he said without preamble and with a slight sneer. My worst nightmare: I might get bounced out of flight training after all.

"Speedy board" was student slang for Student Pilot Disposition Board. The board was made up of senior instructors and chaired by the executive officer of the squadron, or the squadron training officer. It was the board's function to determine if the Navy ought to invest any more time and money trying to teach a failing student to fly. If the board decided to drop a student from the program, its recommendation would be forwarded to CINAVAN-TRA for approval, and it was rare indeed for the admiral to overrule the board's decision. My future as a naval aviator hung in the balance.

I was thirty minutes early for the meeting, spiffy in highly starched khaki with a mirror-gloss spit shine on my shoes. I had spent the previous evening with the ever-patient Alma at her apartment in Sinton, shining my shoes and practicing what I would say to the board. I received an occasional appraising glance from the board members as they arrived, which was in my plan. I wanted them to know that I was very concerned with the outcome of this proceeding.

Finally, the board convened and called me in to hear my appeal. I faced five officers seated behind a long table. The executive officer chaired the board and asked me to tell them how I felt about continuing in the flight program. In what I hoped was a strong and eloquent voice, I told the board that I desired to be a naval aviator above all else in life. Although I had difficulty in C stage, I told them, I had mastered the problems and had flown a very good eighteen check, and I didn't feel that my presence was warranted at a speedy board. The spontaneity of my answer surprised me, and I wondered fleetingly if I hadn't committed a grave error. Here I was, questioning the actions of an instructor in giving me a down. But I truly believed he was just being a typical Marine by nitpicking my fuel plan. The XO asked me to step out of the room while they heard from my instructors, Lieutenant Ingham and Major Bannigan. After what seemed a very long time, but was actually only about fifteen minutes, I was summoned back before the board. "Good news, Gray. The board has decided to let you remain in training," said the XO. "You'll get two extra time hops and a re-fly of the C-eighteen check."

"Sir, I don't want that," I heard myself saying. "I've lived with C stage long enough. I know I can pass the check ride now; I just want to get this over with. I request just a re-fly of C-eighteen."

The board members looked at one another and a lieutenant commander spoke up. "You really ought to take the extra time hops. Don't you realize that if you bust another C-eighteen check, we'll have no choice but to drop you from the program?"

"I know, Sir," I answered. "I just feel that a re-fly is the best thing for me."

"Very well, Gray," the XO said. "You'll re-fly C-eighteen tomorrow, and best of luck. Board dismissed."

Lieutenant Ingham clapped me on the shoulder and said, "Don't worry, Steve. If you fly your recheck just like you flew the last three hops, you'll do OK. Major Bannigan just doesn't think a cadet should pass his instrument rating check the first time around."

The next morning, I was relieved to find that I had been scheduled with a Navy instructor, a Lieutenant Commander McKean. Commander McKean was known as a really nice guy and a forgiving instructor. But because I was fully aware of what was riding on this hop, I was scared anyway. On the first leg I was so nervous that I couldn't keep my hand from shaking on the stick, and the airplane flew in little jerks from side to side. My nerves affected my flying a little, and the hop wasn't as flawless as the previous ones had been, but it was good enough—I got two below average grades, but I got an up for the hop. It had been, without a doubt, the toughest exam I had ever taken. On 22 April 1966 I became a fully instrument rated student naval aviator and a senior NAVCAD.

7

Cougars and Tigers

N ow that C stage was behind me, I began to believe that I really would graduate and become a naval aviator. A large display board in the foyer of the officers' mess contained rows of gold naval aviator's wings with all the students' names under their wings. I was not overly superstitious, but until I made it through C stage I avoided looking at my name under a set of wings. Now, though, I sometimes lingered for a few seconds visualizing those wings on my uniform.

D stage involved a very short series of hops designed to introduce the student to the AF-9J, the single-seat fighter version of the Cougar. But first we were scheduled to fly a dual hop to get us back to VFR flying from the front cockpit and to brush up on our landings with touch-and-go practice. Nearly eight weeks had gone by since we had flown any landings, and the training command wanted to be sure we were proficient before turning us loose in the AF-9J.

It was great to be out from under the bag and in the front seat again. Flying the AF-9J was a real kick. It seemed to perform better than the T model, and having only one cockpit, was lighter as well. Finally, I felt like a real fighter pilot. The AF-9J was the first single-seat airplane I had ever flown and the first not designed to be a trainer. For the rest of our training, whenever the syllabus called for a solo hop we would fly either the AF-9 or the TF-9—whichever was available.

Our training accelerated after we completed C stage. Our ground school classes were complete except for a few lectures, and the remaining five stages of training in VT-25 could be flown in any order since none was a prerequisite for the others. Also, now that ground school was over we could be scheduled for two hops a day. The weather wasn't cooperating, however; for the last week of April and the first week of May, a slow-moving cold front north of us funneled tropical moisture over south Texas, and our operating area was solidly IFR. Since practically all the remaining hops the senior cadets had to fly required VFR conditions, training came to a standstill. Two enterprising instructors submitted a plan for a cross-country flight to the western United States, where the weather is nearly always good, that would allow us to complete some low-level navigation hops and cross-country hops. It would also allow some great liberty in Las Vegas at government expense. Since I needed to complete these hops, another NAVCAD and I were grabbed to provide the students necessary to justify the mission.

The trip was great fun—like playing hooky from school. We launched as a two-plane formation on 4 May en route to Kirkland Air Force Base in Albuquerque, New Mexico. The cloud cover extended from the surface all the way to thirty thousand feet, confirming that it would probably be several days before the weather at Navy Chase improved enough for VFR training flights. After refueling at Kirkland, we launched on a low-level navigation hop to the Grand Canyon in northern Arizona. I was in the front seat on this leg and got to fly down the Colorado River about three hundred feet above the canyon floor making knife-edge turns with the canyon walls sometimes less than a hundred feet from the canopy. What a great way to see the Grand Canyon! We landed at Nellis Air Force Base just a few miles north of Las Vegas. The plan called for an overnight at Nellis, giving us a night of liberty in fabled Las Vegas. Having only recently attained the minimum age required to participate in the adult activities abounding in the city of sin, I had never been in a casino and was looking forward to the experience with great anticipation.

One of the opening salvos in the so-called sexual revolution of the mid-1960s was the phenomenon of women going topless. Somehow, probably because my focus had been entirely on learning to fly, I had missed the news coverage of the topless phenomenon. Las Vegas, the logical place to implement this latest wrinkle in social evolution, had gone whole hog, enthusiastically topless. Our first requirement before assaulting the casinos was sustenance; it had been a while since breakfast, so we stopped at a restaurant on the famous Las Vegas Strip. I had my head buried in the menu when the waitress arrived at our table to take our orders. She was young, pretty, short, extremely busty, and topless. Hearing her voice, I turned from the menu and found two rosy pink nipples inches from my nose. The shock was immediate, and total. Much to the amusement of the other three pilots, I was rendered speechless and had to wait for her return to place my order. In truth, none of us was used to the sight of acres of topless women, and for a while our thoughts were more on gamboling than gambling. It was great fun to watch all the action at the gaming tables, but I had little to gamble with. I came away without much cash but with a desire to spend more time in Las Vegas in the future.

Upon returning to Beeville, even before calling Alma to tell her of my return, I made a fast trip to a jewelry store in Corpus Christi to pick up an engagement ring. Alma and I had been discussing marriage, and now that I had completed C stage, my future looked brighter. We had been shopping for the engagement ring, but I wanted the actual presentation to be a surprise and was looking for the proper time to formalize my proposal. On our date that night, I regaled Alma with stories of fabulous Las Vegas, including the topless phenomenon. I put on a morose face and admitted that I had gambled away all the money I had saved for the down payment on the engagement ring. I was joking, of course, but that joke nearly terminated our relationship! I hastily explained, but Alma was not amused. Just to make her wonder, though, I waited until much later that evening to give her the ring.

The remaining five stages to be flown in VT-25—E, F, G, H, and I—consisted of an introduction to tactics, a refresher on formation flying with an introduction to night formation flying, carrier qualification in the F-9, low-level and cross-country navigation, and an introduction to bombing and strafing. The weather improved at Chase after a late-spring cold front passed through, and our training progressed at high speed. After returning from the cross-country, I began flying E-stage hops, which introduced me to the world of the fighter pilot and air combat maneuvering (ACM).

ACM is the fighter pilot's one-on-one, the modern aviation equivalent of the medieval joust. It is the ultimate test of a pilot's skills, the definitive determination of who is better. Although head-on shoot-down capability was in the process of being developed, most weapon systems still required the pilot to be behind the opponent's airplane. Basic fighter tactics introduced the rudiments of ACM. It is not possible to teach a pilot how to win at ACM. The ability to best another equally well-trained pilot in an airplane of equal capabilities is largely a matter of instincts, skill, guts, and the determination to do whatever is necessary with your airplane to get behind your opponent, bring your weapons to bear, and kill him. The basic maneuvers can be taught and common mistakes can be demonstrated, but the ability to put it all together at the right time and make all the right moves must be developed.

The first few tactics lessons were two-plane hops that were set-piece affairs with the airplanes positioned to demonstrate various basic fighter maneuvers. One of these hops demonstrated a maneuver known as a "high yo-yo." Let's say that you are in perfect position to shoot down your opponent—that is, directly behind him with no angle off. All you should have to do is close to within range, put your gun sight pipper on him, and shoot him down. But suppose he is a good fighter pilot, constantly keeping his head on a swivel and checking his six o'clock position (his "six"), and he sees you coming. He waits until you are almost within gun range and then suddenly snap-rolls into a high-G turn, ninety degrees' angle of bank, to your left. To get him in your gun sight now, you have to turn inside his turn radius and get your nose up ahead of him because you must lead the target if your bullets are going to arrive at the same place he will be. Since you were already going faster than he was because you were closing on him, he has a smaller radius of turn. If you try too tight a turn and pull too many Gs, you either overstress your airplane or accelerate stall and lose control of it. As his turn continues, he slows even more because of the G loading on his wings, and this makes his turn radius smaller still. He is hoping that you will try to turn inside him because he knows that you will overshoot. As soon as he sees your airplane slide outside his turn radius, he will reverse his turn and snap-roll back to the right, putting your plane and his canopy to canopy in a scissors maneuver. If he can force you to make a few more overshoots, he will gradually work the scissors until he is behind you and in position to shoot. The high yo-yo is the countermove for this tactic.

The high yo-yo involves sharply pulling your nose up into a steep climb as soon as your opponent does his break turn. You decelerate as you climb, and this gives you a turn radius as small as his. As he gets about a ninety-degree angle off your heading, you do a wingover turn toward him. You still have the advantage because you are above and behind him and can work your way down on him as he frantically twists and turns trying to get you to overshoot. Each time he tries, you repeat the yo-yo, controlling your speed differential by using the vertical plane. His only hope now is to Split S away from you and try to get vertical separation before you get into firing position, because with each turn he loses airspeed—and therefore his ability to maneuver—and eventually he won't be able to pull enough Gs to keep you off his six.

The two instructors who briefed me and another student on one of the basic fighter maneuver (BFM) hops were good friends who had a constant running ACM competition. The hop was planned so that the students would fly the attacking runs and one of the instructors would fly the defensive maneuvers. The other instructor would ride in the backseat and coach the attacking student to try to keep the advantage and close for the shot. As usual, they had beers bet on the outcome. I was allowed to begin the first attack. As expected, the instructor in the target airplane broke sharply left before I was in gun range. I countered by pulling my nose up into the high yo-yo. As I did so, the instructor in the target airplane reversed his turn. He expected me to follow by rolling right, which would cause me momentarily to lose sight of him as his airplane slid beneath mine. His plan was to reverse his turn again while under my airplane and out of my sight, catching me banking away from him. He could then pull his nose up and yo-yo back on me, causing me to overshoot in the vertical plane and lose my advantage. I remembered the oft-repeated admonition in the tactics lectures and the tactics manual to *never lose sight of your enemy in ACM*, though, and I didn't make that mistake. As he reversed his break turn, I snap-rolled inverted out of my yo-yo, mainly to be able to keep him in sight through the top of the canopy, and saw him make his roll back to the left. When he pulled his nose up to yo-yo back on me I already had my nose up higher than his, inside his turn radius. He had bled so much energy off in his transition to the vertical that he could not maintain the maneuver, and his bid to make me overshoot failed. He was in trouble now. I had the altitude advantage to be able to keep enough speed to pull a tighter turn by diving slightly each time I started to get slow as I worked him into my gun sight. Eventually he ran out of airspeed, and as his airplane mushed out of the sky on the ragged edge of a full stall, I was able to lock on and track him with the gun sight. My instructor had been going ape all this time, yelling over the intercom, "Yeah, yeah, good! Keep on him! Watch his turn, now. Take him! Shoot! Shoot!" He transmitted to the other airplane, "That's it, Flash [his buddy's call sign], you're dead meat, we win."

In the debriefing he was still ribbing his buddy as the other instructor gallantly complimented me on the victory. I got all "above averages" on that hop. A few later hops, though, I was to learn the sickening feeling of having my opponent firmly established on my six and bringing his guns to bear as I, unable to shake him, ran out of airspeed and ideas, knowing that if this had been real combat I would most likely be dead.

Interspersed with tactics and formation hops we began flying FCLP hops early in May to prepare us for carrier quals in the F-9. The Navy had leased an airfield at Alice Orange, Texas, a few air minutes southwest of Navy Chase, for FCLP training. FCLPs were easier for us than they had been in the T-2 because we were more experienced now and we had been practicing landings on the "ball" since the first flight in the F-9. The F-9 was a little harder to hold on the ball, but FCLP was a good deal easier than the real thing in the F-9, as we were soon to discover.

After ten FCLP hops we were scheduled for car quals on the USS *Lexington* on 25 May. The Lex had been working with Kingsville squadrons all morning, and the Beeville flights were scheduled for ramp times early that afternoon. The weather forecast was uncertain, with a cold front to the north causing possible thundershowers all around the operating area and strong, gusty southwest winds. Now that we were instrument qualified, we were given more latitude with regard to the weather minimums, and the decision was made to launch us to the Lex in spite of possible poor weather.

We launched in flights of four, with an instructor leading three students for the thirty-minute flight out in the Gulf of Mexico. The *Lexington*, operating about fifty miles northeast of Corpus Christi, had a problem, though. The strong southwest winds had caused the Lex to move too close inshore while the Kingsville squadrons were finishing their car qual session, and she needed to run cross-wind for a while to get more sea room before turning back into the wind for our recovery. Accordingly, the Navy Chase flights flew holding patterns above the ship while she maneuvered back out to sea. But the weather forecast was proving accurate, and thunderstorms were beginning to pop up back at Navy Chase. Our primary divert field was changed to Navy Corpus in an attempt to buy time, but the thunderstorms were beginning to threaten Corpus Christi as well. I was struck by the contrast between this day and the near-perfect conditions that had accompanied our initial car quals in the T-2. Today a high, dark overcast caused by blow-off from the thunderstorms to the west darkened the sky, angry-looking whitecaps and streaks of foam marred the surface of the Gulf, and the *Lexington* was kicking up quite a bow wave as she plowed through the mounting seas. We were already below bingo (i.e., divert) fuel for Navy Chase and were rapidly approaching low fuel state for a divert to Navy Corpus. The decision was made to take us aboard, refuel us, and hold us until the Lex got more sea room and the weather at Corpus improved.

The procedure that day was supposed to be the same as it had been on our initial car quals: we were to make a couple of touch-and-gos with the tail hook retracted while the LSO determined if we were ready for arrested landings. But our low fuel states and the worsening weather at Corpus precluded that, and we were told to drop the hook; our first pass would be for real. I could feel my adrenalin level rising; my first look at the deck in the F-9 would be the real thing. My flight was to be the first to land, and since I was flying in the number two position, I would be the first student to land. The instructor led us into the break and then left the pattern to wait until all his charges were safe aboard before landing himself. I rolled onto final, completing the landing checklist, and saw the "meatball" right in the center of the datum lights. I called the ball, and our senior LSO instructor, Lieutenant Teboe, began talking me down. "The deck is pitching a bit, Gray. Don't chase the ball. I'll call your power." I wasn't having much trouble keeping the ball centered. The trouble was the lineup. I kept drifting left of the centerline.

I didn't know it at the time, but the Lex's skipper was responsible. He was trying to have it both ways, regaining sea room while recovering us at the same time. This created a stiff crosswind on the deck. It is impossible to fly the precise glide path required for carrier landings with a cross-controlled, wing-down, top rudder crosswind correction. Consequently, we had not been trained for crosswind carrier landings; the wind was supposed to be right down the deck, splitting the angle. I concentrated less and less on the lineup as the distance to touchdown decreased and the glide slope narrowed, and more on the meatball. I slammed down hard on the deck and felt the violent grab of the arresting wire, but the airplane was rolling out too far to the left and the deck edge was rushing toward me. The airplane came to a halt with the left main landing gear inches from the deck edge. I was looking straight down at the angry waters of the Gulf sixty feet below. Luckily, I had caught the 3-wire, and it had a short enough run-out to stop me before I went over the side. I had landed with a bad right-to-left drift. The *Lexington* didn't have centering arresting gear like the newer carriers have, and any drift a pilot had at touchdown remained throughout the arresting wire's run-out. I was afraid to move the airplane because I was so close to the deck edge, so a flight deck crew member ran under the nose and attached a tiller bar to the nose wheel to steer me out of the landing area.

I was taxied over next to the "island," the *Lexington's* superstructure, just short of the starboard catapult blast deflector, and given the shutdown signal as the flight deck crew scurried under me to chain the airplane to the deck. My heart was pounding with fear and excitement. Jesus! I thought. That was hairy. I had just opened the canopy and felt the warm rush of moist Gulf air when the flight deck crash alarm sounded. "Crash, crash, crash, crash on the flight deck, port side," blared the ship's PA. I quickly looked left and was amazed to see the 4-wire hanging over the port side and a thin geyser of water shooting about fifty feet into the air over the flight deck. I hurriedly unstrapped and scrambled down the side of my airplane, running to join the flight deck crew lining up on the port flight deck edge. An F-9 was hanging by its tail hook from the 4-wire, with its nose underwater just about up to the canopy. The engine was still screaming at full power and, with the intakes just a few feet above the surface, was sucking a fair amount of seawater into and through it. There wasn't enough water going into the intakes to flame out the sturdy centrifugal flow engine, and the ship's tower radioed the pilot to shut the engine down.

The F-9 was making rapid figure eights as the drag of the ship's forward motion through the waves pulled at it. The hapless pilot, NAVCAD Ron Burton, had to wait until the gyrations stopped before he could safely exit. Ron had landed right after I did and had experienced the same bad right-to-left drift, only he had caught the 4-wire and the run-out had put his left main wheel over the side. Ron suddenly found himself vertical with his nose in the water wondering, What the *hell* do I do now? What was a comical situation now could easily have been tragic. Had the 4-wire or the tail hook broken—and they were taking much more stress than they were designed to take—Ron would most likely have become a permanent resident of Davy Jones's Locker.

After about ten minutes the ship had slowed enough to allow Ron to swim out of his cockpit without danger of the ship running over him as he swam clear. The plane guard helicopter, which was hovering right alongside, promptly lowered the rescue sling and deposited Ron, shaken and soggy, on the flight deck. Ron was hustled off to sick bay for a checkup as Tillie, a giant yellow crane, chugged into position to try to drag Ron's airplane back aboard. Of course, the flight deck had to be closed until the wreckage was cleared, and the flights holding overhead were forced to divert, thunderstorms or no thunderstorms. Everyone landed safely, but hairy divert stories rebounded around the happy hour bar for weeks afterward.

It took Tillie all night to drag Ron's airplane back aboard, so we spent the night on the *Lexington*. The cold front passed during the night, the *Lexington* spent the night maneuvering farther out to sea, and by morning the weather was much improved and the ship could again turn into the wind. As soon as enough airplanes were aboard, Ron and I were given airplanes to resume our qualifications. Ron wasn't blamed for the mishap, which really wasn't his fault. We both finished our quals without further excitement, getting our traps quickly without even a bolter.

The syllabus at Navy Beeville called for students to transfer to VT-26 and fly their final twenty-two hops in the F-11 Grumman Tiger fighter. But VT-26 was running out of F-11s, and this was creating a bottleneck in the training pipeline. Far more F-9s had been built for the Navy than F-11s because the latter had not been a very successful fleet fighter. The Kingsville students had been graduating in the F-9 for several years, and CINAVAN-TRA had directed VT-24 and VT-25 to develop the "150-Hour Syllabus" for the F-9 to start graduating students in the Cougar. This was a simple matter; it required only the addition of air-to-air gunnery and expanding the tactics hops because gunnery and tactics were the final hops anyway. The problem was that the Blue Angels, the Navy's flight demonstration team, also flew F-11s and had first priority on them. When they lost one due to high time on the airframe or in an accident, they took one from VT-26. The airplanes were old, having been around longer than some of the F-9s, and were due to be phased out of the training command eventually anyway. So my group was given a choice. If a student's flight grades were good enough, and if he volunteered, he would go to VT-26 and complete the final two stages there. Otherwise, he would remain in VT-24 or 25 to graduate. In spite of my travails with C stage, my flight grades were quite good, and I had a burning desire to fly an afterburner-equipped supersonic fighter, so I volunteered for the F-11. It was a serious mistake.

Despite its good looks, the F-11 was not a very good fighter. It was a transition airplane with a few new technology design changes at the expense of performance. The airplane's main drawback was its limited fuel capacity, and this was the principal reason why it didn't see much fleet service. Built before air refueling techniques had been developed and before the era of the supercarrier, the F-11 must have played havoc with the launch-and-recovery cycles of the carriers of its day. Its main job had been to protect the fleet against high-altitude Russian bombers, so the F-11 was designed to launch, climb rapidly to thirty thousand or forty thousand feet, shoot down a Russian Bear or Badger bomber with missiles or guns, and return to the carrier. It had no fuel reserves for any contingency that might delay its landing. The airplane's drag-reducing design was responsible for its limited fuel capacity. The thin wings had no room for wing fuel cells, and the area rule fuselage couldn't accommodate large fuel tanks. The designers had tried to cope with this problem by sticking fuel tanks wherever they could find empty space on the airplane. The main tanks were in the fuselage, but the vertical stabilizer was also a fuel tank, called "fin fuel." There were small fuel cells in the wing roots, and even the voids in the engine intake bulges were fuel tanks, called "cheek tanks." A row of flip-flop gauges along the bottom of the instrument panel showed the pilot which tanks had fuel, which tank was transferring, and which was empty. Even with all those extra tanks the airplane carried only about fifty-six hundred pounds of fuel. If the pilot lit the afterburner on takeoff roll and just left it on, the engine would flame out from fuel starvation fifteen minutes later.

The other major drawback to the F-11's fighter performance was also related to its design for supersonic flight. The extremely thin wing allowed the airplane to accelerate more easily and rapidly through the drag and turbulence caused by the sonic shock wave that builds on the wing's surface as the airflow over the wing approaches the speed of sound. The extremely thin wing didn't produce much lift, though, and as a consequence was very subject to accelerated stall when suddenly pulled into a high angle of attack during high-G turns. The accelerated stall and the tremendous drag and loss of lift that it produced caused the airplane to bleed off energy at a high rate. At thirty thousand feet going Mach 1 (the speed of sound), the pilot had about 6 Gs available in a forty-five-degree angle-of-bank turn. If he pulled 6 Gs, though, after about ninety degrees of turn the airspeed would have bled off to about Mach 0.8. At that speed he would have only 1.3 Gs available before encountering accelerated stall. If this maneuver were plotted out on a graph using airspeed and Gs available as the coordinates, these points would fall within the extreme upper-right-hand corner of the outline of the aerodynamic operating limits of the airplane. This corner, which fighter pilots called the "coffin corner," was where most air combat occurred in the F-11, indicating a very small range of maneuvering capability in a fight.

VT-26 personnel had an "attitude." The instructors considered themselves an elite bunch because theirs was the last F-11 squadron in the Navy and because the Blue Angels also flew the F-11. I suppose they were trying to engender aggressive confidence in their students, whom they treated with aloof, cool disdain. Some considered this "best of the best" attitude an essential part of the fighter pilot psyche; others thought it made VT-26 pilots an insufferable pain in the ass. At happy hour in the officers' club bar, the VT-26 instructors would sometimes unfurl a large banner that depicted a very male Bengal tiger mounted atop and furiously fornicating with a distressed-looking and very female cougar. This display didn't win them many friends among the Cougar instructors, and they and the Tiger instructors mixed it up in heated ACM whenever the opportunity presented.

Students in VT-26 were made to feel damned lucky to be there and were led to believe that they were just barely hanging on to their position, which, given the difficulty of flying the Tiger, was not entirely inaccurate. Students in VT-26 were not called students; they were "wingmen," because all the takeoffs except one in the syllabus were formation takeoffs in section. That is, two airplanes on opposite halves of the runway began their takeoff roll together and lifted off the runway in parade formation. There were no two-seat versions of the F-11; it was never intended to be a trainer. Your first hop in the airplane was also your solo.

The syllabus called for an instructor to chase the first hop. The student was to take off in section, with the instructor leading until departing the pattern. Then the student was to take the lead out over the Gulf of Mexico to the gunnery range, light the afterburner, begin a shallow dive, and take the airplane supersonic. This hop was meant to allow the novice to experience the pitch changes that occur as the airplane transits the so-called sound barrier, which is merely the Mach shock wave. The airplane's nose would try to tuck under as the plane passed through the speed of sound, and conversely would pitch upward as the speed slowed below Mach 1. This hop would satisfy the young pilot's curiosity about going supersonic so that he wouldn't be tempted to try it on his only solo hop, because going supersonic over land was strictly forbidden.

When an airplane goes supersonic, it is traveling through the air faster than the air molecules can move. This creates a thin area of compressed air that is the Mach shock wave. As this shock wave passes people on the ground, they experience a sharp sound like thunder. Generally they hear two distinct booms, one created by the shock wave passing over the nose, and another as the tail passes through it and the airflow behind the airplane slows to subsonic again. This sharp double boom can be quite startling, and the pressure wave can cause windowpanes to crack, livestock to stampede, and chickens to quit laying. The "sonic boom" was a touchy subject for the military and the FAA when I arrived at VT-26. A year or so earlier, the FAA and the military had decided to conduct a test to gauge civilians' reaction to sonic booms. A variety of airplanes flew supersonic over Oklahoma City and its environs. After about a year of this intense sonic booming, the press somehow found out and informed an outraged citizenry of their guinea pig status. The military and the FAA were besieged with complaints of jangled nerves, stampeded livestock, and a drop in egg production. So the Word was passed: "Thou shalt not go supersonic over land."

I was already beginning to doubt the wisdom of volunteering for the F-11 when I discovered that some of my classmates who had elected to remain in the F-9 would be finishing ahead of me. I had flown my last F-9 hop on 31 May, but my first hop in the Tiger was delayed until 9 June because I had to go to school to learn the new airplane's systems, have the inevitable blindfolded cockpit check, and attend lectures on the flight characteristics of the F-11. The men who had remained in VT-24 and 25 were happy and relaxed for their last few hops before graduation, flying an airplane in which they were comfortable, and the hops were all fun hops—tactics and aerial gunnery. I would see them at happy hour laughing with their instructors. Those of us who had gone to VT-26 were having to learn an entirely new airplane, were anything but comfortable with it, and were being treated like shit by our instructors.

My third hop in the F-11 started the gunnery syllabus with two other students. Lieutenant Tyler, our instructor, had a reputation of being a hard-ass.

VT-26 also introduced us to the practice of calling the pilots by their tactical call sign rather than their names. Lieutenant Tyler's call sign was "Raider." We launched on the first gun hop with Lieutenant Tyler flying the tractor, one student escorting the banner, and the other instructor with the other two students taking off last to catch the tractor in the gunnery range. A student was assigned to escort the banner because the banner tow would cross a couple of designated airways on the way to the gunnery range and the FAA required an escort. While escorting the banner, the student was to fly formation about thirty feet abeam of it. The tractor had to climb in afterburner because of the extreme drag the banner created. The escort couldn't keep up with the banner in basic engine and was too fast in afterburner, so he had to select afterburner, slowly pulling ahead of the banner, then come out of afterburner and slowly fall behind until selecting afterburner again. When afterburner was selected, there was always a puff of white, unburned fuel until the afterburner lit, so it was possible to watch the banner escort from a great distance on clear days because a string of evenly spaced burner puffs marked his progress.

Upon arriving in the gunnery range and climbing to thirty thousand feet, the banner escort joined the gun flight, and the other instructor, "Raider One," put us in line astern and rolled in behind the tractor for the initial spacing pass. I was "Raider Two," NAVCAD Terry Rieder was "Raider Three," and the banner escort, whose name I cannot recall, was "Raider Four." We started at thirty-one thousand feet. As each of us rolled in on the tractor at ten-second intervals, we lit the afterburner and accelerated through Mach 1 before passing it. The tractor was a blur as I zipped up his left side and pitched up and rolled right toward the perch. Just before reaching the high reversal, my airplane slowed to subsonic again and I had to counter the tendency for the nose to pitch up sharply to keep it from bleeding too much energy and making the perch too high and too close to the tractor. I really had my hands full; the airplane was so new to me that I had no feel for it yet and the speed was awesome. I felt as if I were hanging onto some wild beast instead of flying the airplane. As I turned to parallel the tractor's course and leveled on the perch, I heard Raider One call "in" on his first run and glimpsed his airplane diving toward the tractor, his afterburner glow visible in his tailpipe even in the bright sunlight. I was lucky on the first pass to be able to see the tractor because I was able to follow Raider One's run visually. I lit the burner, pulled the nose through about halfway down the distance between the tractor and the banner, and commenced the low reversal. As I went supersonic, I again had to counter the nose's tendency to tuck under and make my dive too steep. As I came out of afterburner, the banner just leaped at me! I didn't have time to look for it through the gun sight, much less track it. The firing range was less than a second long! A mere flick of the stick at that speed flashed me up and over the banner, and then the snap to a ninety-degree angle-of-bank turn to parallel the tractor for an instant, then snap wings level as I flashed past the tractor, and pitch and snap-roll to start the climb back toward the perch. With heart racing and adrenalin level peaking I thought, Gawdamighty, I'll never hold that thing still enough in the gun sight to shoot it! I somehow managed to hang on and at least stay in the pattern, but I never had a run good enough to track the banner.

We began flying a gun hop or a tactics hop each day, and sometimes two or even three hops a day as we rushed toward completion. Our skills in the gun pattern increased as we became accustomed to the high speeds involved, but tracking the banner was still almost more than I could handle. The tactics hops were fun, and sometimes comical. After showing the students all the basic maneuvers, the instructors would sometimes let two students have at one another and then critique the outcome. Most of the students' ACM ended with both students having bled off all their energy and the two airplanes locked in a slow-speed scissors, neither having the advantage, until one airplane finally stalled and fell out of the fight. As the student fought to regain flying speed and avoid a spin, the other student whose stalling nose happened to fall toward the first would claim victory. Toward the end of training, the syllabus called for us to engage our instructors in a no-advantage, head-on attack.

———•———

One day in mid-June, with only a few hops remaining before graduation, I was scheduled for a tactics hop with Raider. We had completed the usual section takeoff, and Raider had just signaled me "gear up" by making a rotating motion with his hand, then leaning forward in his seat and snapping his head back to signal execution. This ensured that both of us would retract our landing gear at the same time, making it easier to stay in formation as the airplanes accelerated while the gear came up. The afterburner was to be selected just after brake release on the takeoff roll to help get the heavy fighters airborne, and we would come out of burner as soon as we had climbed through twelve hundred feet.

A VT-24 instructor named Ditto, a Marine captain, was the recognized "ace of the base" in ACM. Captain Ditto's favorite pastime when flying solo on an F-9 test hop was to lurk above Chase Field until he saw a section of F-11s taking off. He would commence a diving attack on the formation, catching them just about the time they got their gear up, and would make machine-gun sounds over the radio and snigger, "Gotcha!" as he zoomed past. Ditto bounced Raider and me in this fashion just as we finished cleanup and came out of burner. The gauntlet thus flung, Raider called, "Raider flight, burner," his fury evident even over the radio. Raider wanted a piece of Ditto bad. Delighted, I answered, "Rog, burner," and pushed the throttle outboard into the afterburner detent, tickled at the prospect of a nonsyllabus fight. Unfortunately, these instructors knew what they were doing, and I didn't. No one had shown me what a wingman should do in a dogfight. Instead of hanging out wide enough to have time to react to the wild maneuvering of the combatants, I tried to fly too tight on Raider. Had I known what I was doing, Ditto would have been in deep trouble. I could have sandwiched him between Raider's airplane and mine, blocking his ability to maneuver without turning into one of our gun sights, until Raider could close for the kill. Instead, trying to hold position on Raider, I was caught unprepared when Raider snapped upright in an Immelman-type maneuver while I was still inverted coming down the backside of some vertical yo-yo. I found myself upside down, in tight parade position but sliding forward of Raider's wing, totally disoriented and without the slightest clue how to regain upright flight without running over my leader. Raider had to break off the fight and allow Captain Ditto to escape while he talked me out of my predicament.

The abortive fight with Captain Ditto had cut into the fuel available for the syllabus demonstrations, so Raider had to rush me through them. We returned to Chase Field and landed with minimum fuel. Students were forbidden to unstrap or perform any after-landing checklist items until safely parked in the chocks with the engine shut down. The instructors, on the other hand, would taxi in with straps flying off and shut down their engines while still yards away from the parking spot, allowing the airplane to coast silently into the chocks, so they always beat the students into the hangar. We didn't leave the parachutes in the ejection seat in the F-11; we carried them back into the hangar and checked them into the parachute locker at the end of the hop. I was walking across the tarmac, parachute over my shoulder with the straps hanging down my back and the steel connectors on the ends jingling as they slapped against my legs, when I saw Raider standing in the hangar door. I must have been a hundred feet from him when he began to scream at me. "Gray, you miserable shit, you better show me more tomorrow! You ain't ever gonna be a fighter pilot in my Navy until you learn to fight this airplane! You better be able to show me some fight tomorrow or you're out of here!" Sailors on the ramp stopped what they were doing and stared at us in open-mouthed astonishment. Raider turned on his heel and disappeared into the dark recesses of the hangar. That was the debriefing.

I was mortified and frightened because I believed him. I really thought that I could still wash out of the program this close to graduation. That night

I devoured the tactics manual, convinced that my future as a naval aviator hinged on my fighting ability tomorrow. The next morning, after flying on the early gun hop, Raider and I launched again on the next tactics hop. We climbed up to thirty thousand feet, and true to his word, Raider had us split sixty degrees off each other, fly about five miles apart, turn head-on, light the burner, and pass one another level with a twelve-hundred-knot closure rate for a no-advantage, head-on attack. As soon as our noses passed, the fight was on! I had maybe sixteen hours in the F-11 and about three hundred hours' total pilot time. Raider had probably five or six hundred hours in the F-11 and close to two thousand hours' total time. It was, of course, no contest. Within a very few passes and turns I was in the familiar predicament: all my energy bled off, in a slow-speed buffet, with Raider firmly established in firing position on my six.

At this point, the instructor was supposed to break off his attack, call "resume," and as the flight repositioned for another run enumerate the student's mistakes so he could avoid making them in the next engagement; not so for Raider. Enjoying my plight, Raider called over the radio, "OK, Gray, you pussy, now I'm moving my [gun sight] pipper onto your canopy, and as my 20-mm shells smash through your cockpit, I see you dissolving into pink foam." I wasn't concerned about any "pink foam," but I was afraid of washing out of the program. When I read the tactics manual the night before, I had come across a last-ditch maneuver, to be used only in extremis, called a "high-G barrel roll." The first priority was to destroy the opponent's firing solution and regain maneuvering airspeed, so the maneuver called for pushing zero G and lighting the afterburner to cause very rapid acceleration. After reaching a speed of about three hundred knots, the pilot was to level the wings and pull up sharply. As the nose came above the horizon, the pilot stomped full rudder, corkscrewing the airplane over on its back, causing an extremely rapid loss of airspeed, and popped out the speed brakes. If the opponent tried to follow the pilot through the maneuver, he would overshoot, and the pilot could suck in the speed brakes and roll into the opponent's six. If the opponent countered correctly by pulling up into a high yo-yo, the pilot could suck in the speed brakes and Split S away from him, at least gaining vertical separation that would allow the pilot to try to scissor back up into him. At least that was the way it was supposed to work.

I certainly believed that this situation qualified as in extremis. My airplane was in a slow-speed buffet on the ragged edge of a stall in a forty-five-degree bank turn. So I tried the maneuver. My push to zero G and simultaneously selecting afterburner certainly destroyed Raider's firing solution. I felt the tremendous push of the burner lighting and suddenly found myself cranked around almost backward in the seat trying to keep him in sight. After a couple of seconds, I was just turning to look at my airspeed to see when to start the pull-up when Raider screamed over the radio, "What's your airspeed?" My eyeballs snapped back into the cockpit and I was horrified to see the airplane in a vertical dive, the altimeter needle a blur as it spun through twenty thousand feet, the airspeed well over the speed of sound, and the runways of Navy Chase Field etched in my windscreen. I yanked into a six-G pullout and pulled the throttle out of burner and back to idle just as Raider called again, "What's your airspeed?" The high-G pullout had bled off some speed, but the airspeed needle still hovered around Mach 1. "Unh . . . unh . . . Mach 1," I stammered over the radio. "Aw, Jesus, right over the field," came Raider's disgusted reply.

The last few hops before graduation were flown in flights of three students, so groups of three to nine students finished the program each day. Accordingly, there was an intimate graduation ceremony and presentation of wings and commissions every day or so. These ceremonies were held in the base commanding officer's office, which was located on the upper deck of the administration building. The CO's large office had windows looking out over the entire base, and from his vantage point as the tallest building on the base, he could survey his command at will. The windows were equipped with Venetian blinds to block out noise, and these were closed during the graduation ceremony.

The graduation groups were small; each student would usually have his parents, his sweetheart, or both there to witness the ceremony. There is a tradition that one's mother pins the wings on her son's chest and one's sweetheart puts on one officer shoulder board (in the case of a NAVCAD receiving his commission as an ensign) or second lieutenant's gold bar (for a MARCAD). This intimate, dignified ceremony was in progress when my focused, extremely powerful sonic boom arrived. *Ba . . . boom!* reverberated through the countryside. The assembled ladies gave startled squeals as dust jarred loose from the ceiling sifted down into their hair. The Venetian blinds jumped, and one window gave way with a crack. It was the most severe sonic boom ever recorded at Navy Chase. The base CO excused himself, dialed the skipper of VT-26, and demanded an explanation. Since the F-11 was the only airplane on the base capable of creating a boom this severe, it was obvious that one of his pilots was responsible.

Once again, Raider was waiting in the hangar doorway as I walked across the tarmac. He didn't shout at me this time, simply saying as I walked within earshot, "We have to go see the skipper." My heart sank. I already knew I was in trouble; this confirmed it. I figured that I was probably history as far as flight training was concerned. We walked up to the second deck of the hangar, where Commander Pritchard's office was located, and I was told to wait outside while Raider went in to make his report. I cooled my heels for thirty minutes or more in the passageway outside the skipper's office waiting for Raider to reemerge. He said not a word to me when he did, but turned on his heel and marched away. I was called into the office by the duty yeoman. I stopped the regulation thirty-six inches from the skipper's desk, came to rigid attention, and announced "NAVCAD S. R. Gray reporting to the commanding officer as ordered, Sir!" Commander Pritchard looked up and said, "Mr. Gray, I understand that you went supersonic over the field this morning, and I'd like to know why." I explained about being in extremis and attempting the high-G barrel roll and becoming disoriented and inadvertently diving supersonic over the field. Commander Pritchard nodded and said, "I can understand that, but we are trying to be good neighbors to the civilian community here." Whereupon he delivered a short speech about community relations and how upsetting sonic booms could be to the area, told me to try not to let it happen again, and dismissed me. Relief washed over me like a cool breeze, and I left the office grateful that the skipper was such a nice guy.

I never saw Raider again. I was assigned a new instructor, took a huge amount of ribbing from the other students and instructors in VT-26, and was famous for a few days. Finally, on 25 June 1966, I came to my final hop before graduation. The last hop was supposed to be no-advantage head-on attacks with our instructor, but Commander Pritchard had asked to fly against me for the final hop. He had me demonstrate the high-G barrel roll to him just to prove that I did know how to execute the maneuver correctly, and then we split up for the fights. I was anything but aggressive during the following ACM; my only concern was not doing anything wrong. Commander Pritchard was winning all the engagements and was enjoying himself hugely. As a result, we stayed a little beyond bingo fuel. We weren't worried because the weather was good and the field was almost directly beneath us. When we switched over to Navy Chase tower frequency for landing instructions, though, pandemonium reigned!

An F-11 had experienced a burner flameout with the afterburner nozzle stuck open on takeoff and the pilot had to abort at very high speed. He dropped the tail hook to engage the cross-deck wire, which was attached to heavy battleship anchor chain, to help him stop. When the tail hook engaged the wire, the airplane's momentum yanked the tail, engine and all, out of the F-11 and covered the runway with debris. The runway had to be closed until the debris could be cleared. The other long runway at Chase was closed for resurfacing. Only the short north-south runway was available. This runway was too short for jets, but the Navy had installed mobile arresting gear (MO-REST) at midfield so that the runway could be used in case of emergency. The MO-REST was essentially a shipboard arresting system. There was a problem with it, though; it had to be reset after each trap. As luck would have it, a large number of student solos had returned at the same time, and the extra landing time involved was running some of them short on fuel. A solo instructor who had waved off to let low-state students land ahead of him had just flamed out abeam the runway and had to eject.

This was the situation as Commander Pritchard and I arrived in the Chase Field traffic pattern. We were below bingo fuel for Navy Corpus, and we didn't have enough fuel to wait for the MO-REST on the short runway. Commander Pritchard called me and said, "Steve, We don't have a choice, land behind me on the taxiway." The taxiway, which ran the entire length of the long runway, was narrower than the runway but perfectly usable, so I made my final landing before graduation on the taxiway at Chase Field.

The next day, 26 June, in the base CO's office, with one window still taped, six of us were designated U.S. naval aviators and I was commissioned an ensign, USNR. My mother, father, and fiancée, Alma, were there to share the moment with me. Mother pinned the gold naval aviator's wings on my chest, and Alma slid one ensign's shoulder board on my dress whites while my father installed the other. It was the proudest moment of my life. A Navy chief yeoman positioned himself outside the administration building to render the first salute to the newly minted officers and to collect the traditional silver dollar for receiving the first return salute given by a new officer. Life was sweet. I wouldn't have traded positions with anyone in the world on that day. I had thirty days' leave and travel time before reporting to Replacement Air Group training, and I checked out of NAS Beeville and departed on leave the next day.

On 24 July 1966, in a small, wood-frame, un-air-conditioned Lutheran church in Columbus, Texas, Miss Alma Mae Thumann and I plighted our troths and were married. The wedding reception was held in the Columbus VFW hall, and I discovered with a shock that Alma was related to a large chunk of Colorado County. Some two hundred people crowded into the traditional Texas barbecue reception. After spending our wedding night in a posh Houston hotel, we swung back by the farm to pick up our belongings and headed for my next duty station, NAS Lemoore, California. We would honeymoon en route.

Our departure was traumatic for everyone involved. Adolf and Hulda Thumann were devastated that their only child was going to, what was to them, the ends of the earth with this stranger, and I felt like a real shit for taking her away from them. Alma had hardly been out of Texas before, and even though she had been teaching in another town for two years, she had made frequent trips to the farm. We hitched my little Rambler to Alma's 1965 Chevy Impala and left for California, leaving Adolf and Hulda in tears. Alma had a teaching job waiting in the fall at Tulare, California, and I, due to the longevity of my enlisted service, was making maximum pay for an ensign. We had one thousand dollars cash in our pockets and the world by the tail as we headed west.

8

The Replacement Air Group

My orders directed me "to proceed and report to the commanding officer, Attack Squadron VA-127, for training, for further transfer to the commanding officer, Attack Squadron VA-125, for training, for further transfer to the commanding officer, Attack Squadron VA-212, for duty involving flying." I had received this set of orders several weeks before graduating from flight training, but their significance was not apparent to me at the time. Most of my flight mates got an "open-ended" set of orders to the Replacement Air Group (RAG) and would be assigned to a squadron just returning from a cruise after they had completed the RAG training. The RAG trained pilots in the aircraft flown by the fleet squadron to which they would be assigned, in the process giving them weapons familiarity training and qualifying them for carrier duty. When a squadron returned from a deployment aboard an aircraft carrier, typically half its pilots and enlisted men were due for rotation out of the squadron. The squadron used the turn-around time before the next deployment to train its new complement of personnel.

The training normally consisted first of a deployment to a weapons training center like NAS Fallon, Nevada, or Marine Corps Air Station Yuma, Arizona, for two to three weeks of intensive weapons training. This was followed by two to four weeks of deployment aboard the aircraft carrier to which the squadron was attached for both day and night carrier qualification training. Thus, a new pilot fresh from RAG training would get another entire training cycle before he deployed with his fleet squadron. But I was assigned to a squadron due to deploy about the time I would finish the RAG training. There would be no additional training for me. I was destined for combat in Vietnam with only half the training most new aviators, or "nuggets," got before they deployed. Obviously, some detailer in the Pentagon had made a mistake, but it was a mistake never rectified.

VA-127's training officer assigned me to a class scheduled for Survival, Escape, Resistance, and Evasion (SERE) school, which would convene at NAS North Island, San Diego, on Monday. Our group from Lemoore would travel by chartered bus, leaving the base on Sunday afternoon. So after only two weeks of marriage, the honeymoon was over. I would be away at school for a week. Welcome to Navy life, Alma.

All naval personnel bound for duty in Southeast Asia were required to attend SERE school. The final part of SERE school was training to help us survive in case we were captured and became POWs. Some word of what this training entailed had filtered back down to us from acquaintances who had completed the school, but we didn't know much about it except that we would be placed in a POW environment for about twenty-four hours to get a taste of what POW life would be like. I didn't understand how this training could be very effective. We knew going in that we would be in the POW compound for only one day. What could be so difficult about that? When the time came, the effectiveness of the training would be made very clear to me.

SERE school began with an all-day session in the classroom. The first portion dealt with survival, learning how to acquire the basics of life: water, food, and shelter. The breakfast we ate before the class commenced was the last civilized meal we would have for nearly a week. Since there was no require-ment for a lunch break, the lectures continued all through the day until about 1700 or 1800 that evening. The first survival lectures and films taught us how easy it is to survive on a seashore in a warm climate. To experience the ease of seashore survival firsthand, the class adjourned to buses that took us to a jetty on the southwest side of North Island directly across San Diego Sound from Point Loma.

The class comprised one hundred men—twenty-five officers and sev-enty-five enlisted. Tepees made of parachute canopies had already been set up to shelter us for the night, and we had strips of parachute canopy for each man to use as a crude bedroll. The camp was on beach sand, so it was possible to gouge out hip and shoulder holes to make sleeping on the ground more comfortable. Several of our class had never been camping before and found the prospect of sleeping on the ground without a bed somewhat distressing. I was thankful for the camping skills I had learned as a Boy Scout and settled down to enjoy the campout. We organized the class into teams, with an officer assigned to each team, to gather food for the evening meal. The lectures proved correct; in fairly short order we were able to gather plenty of food to make a seafood chowder. A large kettle had been provided, and we scavenged enough driftwood to make a good cooking fire. The ingredients for the chowder included crabs, clams, snails, and even some small fish that had been caught using some of the parachute cloth as a seine. The chowder wasn't as tasty as restaurant chow, since it lacked seasoning, but it wasn't bad, and most of us ate our fill. All in all, the seashore survival course was fun.

The next phase of training, "mountain survival," took place in the arid mountains east of San Diego at a place called Warner Springs, California. The bulk of the second day's classes dealt with the POW compound phase. POW training was conceived after the dismal survival record of our POWs in the Korean conflict. Many of the Korean War POWs failed to survive simply because they lost all hope of rescue, repatriation, or escape. Contrary to popular belief, it wasn't "brainwashing" or intense torture that caused many to defect or die; it was simply giving up in despair and losing the will to live. So a "code of conduct" for POWs had been formulated to give American POWs a guideline to follow while in captivity.

The class taught us how to resist coercion by the enemy without endangering our own survival. It is the military duty of a POW to resist to the point where his personal survival is threatened, we learned, and then to give in as slowly as possible to the enemy while protecting his well-being. It is OK for a POW to give information to the enemy or sign "confessions" as long as the POW has resisted the torture or coercion to the best of his ability. It is also the military duty of the POW to attempt escape by any means possible. Establishing a military chain of command in a POW situation is imperative if the prisoners are to be able to help and support each other. We heard detailed lectures on the Geneva Convention agreements on the treatment of POWs because, if captured, knowledge of the terms of the Geneva Convention might well be our only shield against our captors.

The POW compound phase of our training had certain ground rules. The "POW" camp guards were Navy and Marine personnel, officers and enlisted, who had received special training in imitating Asian communist military prison guards. To make the training more realistic, physical abuse of the student prisoners was allowed, but only in the form of "insult slaps" and physical exertion punishment. The students were prohibited from attempting physical retribution or making physical attacks in escape attempts. Not only might such behavior result in execution in a real POW situation, but the guards were healthy, in excellent physical condition, and had been eating three meals a day. The students, who had not been given much to eat all week, were run down and debilitated, and would be unlikely to prevail in a physical confrontation. The classroom lectures stressed escape attempts. Prisoners who were successful in escaping would earn a reward of milk, sandwiches, and cookies. If the student was in the company of a prison guard and wanted to attempt an escape, he was to announce to the guard, "I have an escape attempt." The guard would suspend the training environment and evaluate the plan. If he considered it to have merit, he would turn the other way and allow the student to try it. If he thought it likely to fail, he was to explain the flaws to the student and return to the training environment. Thus equipped with all this knowledge, late Tuesday afternoon we boarded buses for the ride to Warner Springs. Our seafood chowder was fading into a fond memory.

Although the bulk of the second day's classroom lectures had involved POW training, we still had three days and two nights to practice our mountain survival skills. After constructing tepee-like shelters out of parachute cloth, we were free to scour the area for whatever food we could find. Dehydration and heat stroke were a real possibility in the hot, extremely dry mountains, so we were given a plentiful supply of water. The previous day's lectures had taught us that in a survival situation, anything that creeps, crawls, flies, or walks has food value. The mountain survival area had been used for training for about two years, though, and anything of food value had long since been devoured by starving trainees. We weren't desperate enough yet to sample spiders or scorpions, but a lizard or snake would have been a delicacy. By Wednesday morning, we were beginning to feel real hunger.

On Wednesday, the mountain survival instructors gave us a number of lectures, which included some hands-on training with the survival gear we would likely be using. We had been split up into groups of about eight men each. The first lecture began shortly after reveille with the instructors issuing each group a large, white, pink-eyed, cuddly rabbit. While the issue was going on, we all petted and fondled our rabbits, looking into the cute pink eyes and stroking the soft, white fur. The ensuing lecture dealt with methods of quietly dispatching, cleaning, and cooking rabbits. After the lecture, it was our task to kill the pretty white rabbits and prepare them for the pot. Growing up in Oklahoma I had spent a good deal of time hunting and fishing, and had killed, cleaned, and cooked many wild rabbits. The rest of my group seemed to be city boys who wanted no part of cleaning the rabbit. After having petted and cuddled the rabbit, it was a bit embarrassing to have to kill it, but I apologetically and, I hoped, humanely broke the critter's neck.

While I cleaned the rabbit, the rest of the group received instructions on how to make a small, nearly smokeless fire in a cooking pit. Now, while the rabbit would have been a feast for one and even a meal for four, it was not adequate food for eight men. To gain as much as we could out of it, we were instructed to cut it up into very small pieces and boil it all day in a covered gallon tin. We placed the tin in the cooking pit surrounded by hot stones and the remaining coals from the fire, covered it with dirt, and let it simmer all day. It was difficult to concentrate on the lectures that followed. Our minds kept wandering back to the delicious meal waiting for evening, and the sound of rumbling stomachs filled the air.

Late that evening, we uncovered the tin and discovered that the rabbit had cooked into a rich broth. We each got a little less than a pint of broth with a few morsels of stringy meat. It was delicious and went a long way toward satisfying our growing hunger. It also lifted our morale, and we boarded trucks for a night evasion exercise in high spirits.

The night escape and evasion (E&E) course was a hoot. The course was a corridor bounded by roads that was about two miles long by a half-mile wide. Several obstacles representing border-crossing barricades blocked the corridor in spots. The objective was to make it across all the obstacles in the allotted time without being caught by the "border guards." Most of us completed the course successfully and stood laughing and filthy, swapping stories of our trek while waiting for the others to finish. We were not yet aware that we had burned far more energy than our rabbit broth had provided and would feel increased physical exhaustion in the morning.

We arose tired and sore Thursday morning despite a full night's sleep. All of us felt the effects of our exertions on the previous night. Thursday called for a fifteen-mile hike over rugged, hilly terrain. It was billed as a cross-country navigation hike, but its real purpose was to further drain us of energy and to weaken us physically and mentally. We began about 0800, each of us carrying two canteens of water. The temperature rapidly climbed above 100 degrees as we struggled up the arid hills. About noon, we reached a small spring in a rocky valley and stopped to rest and cool off in the small, shallow stream. A few pools in the streambed were nearly waist deep, and most of us climbed in and rolled about in the cool water. Reinvigorated by the dip, we continued to hike to a campsite where we would stay overnight. We reached the campsite about 1600, very near exhaustion. The campsite was just a grove of trees on a small hill shaded by the trees and a much larger hill to the west. There were no shelters at this camp; we simply sank onto the ground to sleep.

Reveille came early on Friday, and we were told to drink all the water we could hold and turn in our canteens. We were then led up to the top of the larger hill to the west to begin the day E&E course. The day course was larger than the night course—about three miles long by one mile wide—and covered a long valley that lay at the foot of our hill. Thick manzanita brush, more than six feet tall in spots, covered the hill. The rules called for the E&E course to last until noon, at which time everyone who had not already been captured would be taken into custody for the POW compound phase of the training. Those captured early would have to spend more time in the POW camp, a definite incentive to avoid capture. Also, anyone who managed to reach Freedom Village at the end of the course would be able to feast on sandwiches, milk, and cookies until noon. Our hundred-man group was spread out across the hilltop and told to get going. It was about 0730, and we had a ten-minute head start.

It took most of the morning to reach the foot of the hill and get out of the brush. My watch showed 1130 and I could see Freedom Village ahead through the trees. If I didn't hurry I wouldn't have time to eat. All had been quiet, and there had been no sign of enemy activity for the last half hour, so I began running toward the little stone house that was sanctuary. Big mistake! Rounding a clump of trees, I ran right out in front of a squad of "enemy" troops. Their squad leader, a big guy about six four or five, exclaimed, "Ah! Insect, where you go in such hurry?" I was quickly herded into a group with four other captives and marched to a waiting truck. I had come within two hundred yards of Freedom Village, but it may as well have been two miles.

The POW compound looked much like the prison camps in all the old World War II POW pictures. A double barbed wire fence at least ten feet tall surrounded the compound, and concertinas of barbed wire were coiled along the base of the inner fence. I could see one prominent guard tower on the far side of the camp as I was pushed out of the truck into a holding area off the main compound. We were in one of the last trucks to arrive, and I took some pride in being among the last to be captured. There were about twenty of us in the last group, and we were forced to strip completely naked and give our clothes over to the guards for inspection. This was accomplished with much screaming and invective from the guards. When the guards finished rummaging through our clothes, they flung them back at us and told us to bundle them in our right hand. Next we had to give the requisite name, rank, and serial number to a clipboard-toting guard who registered us into the camp. After this processing, we were forced into a tunnel with a dirt floor, board sides, and a barbed-wire top. Still naked, we had to crawl about fifty feet; the barbed wire just above was a reminder to keep your ass down while crawling. The guards laughed, taunted, and jeered as they poked us with sticks to hurry us through the tunnel. We emerged into a large compound that probably measured one hundred feet by seventy feet. The ground was bare rock and sand with a small hill on the far side. There was no shade, and a merciless afternoon sun beat down on the yard. Three bunkers—each about twenty feet deep and twenty wide—had been dug into the small hill. Sleeping racks mounted to iron poles formed rows three bunks high from front to back. The roofs of the bunkers were corrugated iron with a layer of sand and gravel covering them. A guard tower on the opposite side, complete with machine gun, looked out over the entire yard. It looked like a serious, no-nonsense prison compound.

After we had milled about in the yard for a few minutes, the guards began to scream for us to fall into a military formation. Our senior officers began circulating, encouraging us to fall in so that they could begin to negotiate for our well-being, just as we had been taught to do in the classroom. Our senior officer was a navy commander slated to take command of one of the A-4 squadrons at NAS Lemoore upon completion of SERE school. We had a few lieutenant commanders and lieutenants in the group, but most of the officers were nuggets like me. As soon as we had all formed up, large gates at the end of the compound swung open and the camp commandant walked in with two platoons of guards. We were called to attention, the guard's order being echoed by our own chain of command, and the camp commandant began to lay out the rules of behavior for prisoners. He informed us that we were all criminal prisoners and had no military rank. All prisoners would be treated equally, as were all people in their "classless society." Infractions of the camp rules would be severely punished. By now it was close to 1300 and the temperature in the yard was well over 100 degrees. We had drunk no water since starting the day E&E course at about 0700 that morning, and we were becoming seriously dehydrated.

Our senior officer spoke up to request water for his men and was immediately attacked by three of the guards, who slapped him three or four times and forced him to his knees. The guard detail leader screamed at him that prisoners were not allowed to address the commandant directly. All requests had to go up the guard chain of command. I was shocked at their treatment of him. The classroom lectures had said that the prison guards would try to break up the POWs' chain of command by trying to humiliate the senior officers in front of the men, but I had no idea that it would be this brutal. The guards backed off, and our second in command helped our senior officer to his feet. The commander then requested permission from the guard leader to have a conference with the camp commandant.

We had been standing in formation for almost an hour in the broiling sun. Finally, after much shouting and slapping around of our senior officers, the camp commandant announced that we would be issued all the water we cared to drink just as soon as our "personnel inspection" was complete. We formed up in three platoons of about thirty men each in front of the three bunkers. I was in the second rank, at the head of the squad making up that rank, standing perfectly still and waiting for the exercise to be over. I didn't see the guard who walked up and delivered a slap that nearly knocked me down. Ears ringing and head swimming, I recalled the classroom lecture where we had been told that any blows we received would be "insult slaps" designed to make us lose our temper. Jesus! I thought. That was a hell of an insult slap! The guard was screaming at me for moving in ranks, although I was certain that I had not.

About this time a siren mounted in the guard tower began to wail. "*Air raid, air raid!*" screamed the guards. "*Everyone into bunkers! Quick! Quick!*" The guards began pushing and kicking us into the bunkers. It was like running into an oven. The temperature inside the bunker must have been 130 degrees. Our dash inside stirred up clouds of thin, talcum-like dust that coated our dry throats and made us choke and cough. Sounds of high-speed aircraft and engines soon signaled the "attack." The machine gun on the guard tower began firing, adding its staccato roar to the sounds of battle. We all cheered. "Our guys" were attacking the camp!

When the siren signaled "all clear," the guards screamed at us to fall back in. Gratefully we piled out of the hot, dusty bunkers and began forming up again. It took only a minute this time to form up and dress right in ranks. We were really parched by now, and our time inside the bunkers had made our need for water acute. The camp commandant and his entourage had just begun the tedious process of walking the ranks, supposedly inspecting us, when the air raid siren began wailing again. Crap! Back in the cursed bunkers again, more choking dust, and this time the air raid was met with much less enthusiasm. Once again we fell into ranks at the all clear, beginning to get desperate for water. As before, the commandant had just begun the farcical inspection when yet another air raid began. This time, the attacking planes were viewed with outright hostility. "Goddammit, we need water! We don't have time to put up with all this air raid shit!"

Finally, weak with thirst and with some of us very near heat stroke, the camp commandant relented and allowed us to be issued water. As we shuffled through a long, single-file line past a lone faucet on the edge of the yard, the hastily appointed "water detail" handed each of us a canteen cup full of water—which was scalding hot! We could only take small sips, like drinking hot coffee, while we cursed the sadism of our captors. Even so, the water helped restore our morale, and soon we began to organize our escape committee just as we had learned to do in the classroom.

While all this was going on, the guards kept up their continual harassment, assigning us to work details and physical punishment for real or fictitious infractions of camp rules. Amazingly, considering our dehydrated state, one of our men decided that he needed to relieve his bladder. There were no latrine facilities in evidence, so he complied with the camp rules and presented himself at the foot of the guard tower and requested permission to relieve himself. The guard in the tower beamed at the prisoner and said, "Oh, yes, yes, Yankee boy, you need whiz, you whiz." The prisoner began to unzip his trousers. "No, no," called the guard. "I not say whip it out. You go in pants." Our guy stopped in disbelief, then looked around at the yard, shrugged, and let it rip. As the wet stain spread down his trouser front, the guard shrieked with laughter and said, "Yankee pig, you piss in pants, you stink now, go jump in people's pool."

The "people's pool" was a shoulder-deep pit about seven or eight feet long by five feet wide filled with muddy, scummy water. Our guy jumped in and crawled out the far side, dripping wet. "Hey!" The thought struck us all at the same time. Jumping into the people's pool would sure feel good in the 110-degree heat of the yard. Soon all of us were lined up for a trip through the people's pool, which undoubtedly saved some of us from heat stroke. The evaporative cooling of our wet clothes lowered our body temperature and really improved our morale.

With thirst and heat solved for the time being, our escape committee swung into action. Small groups of prisoners were being taken back into the smaller compound for "interrogation." The walls of a couple of buildings and a tall board gate hid the compound from our view. When their interrogation was finished, they were led into another large yard we could see beyond the double fence. They were too far away to talk with and remained isolated from those still awaiting their time with the interrogator. Our senior officer, the navy commander, whom the guards had begun calling "Senior One" derisively, had disappeared. We figured that he had been removed so the enemy could see how well our chain-of-command structure would deal with it. No problem; in his absence, our second in command headed the escape committee.

Although we couldn't see into the entry holding area, none of the guards seemed to be watching the tunnel we had crawled through when we first entered the yard; they all seemed to be occupied in the yard or with interrogations. The two men who had noticed this and proposed the escape attempt were tagged to be the escapees; the rest of us would create a diversionary "fight" over by the gate into the interrogation compound. We surreptitiously passed the word to our comrades, and everyone began to get into position. At the signal from our leader, we began the mock fight with much shouting and shoving. The guards came running, blowing whistles and screaming for us to fall in. In the confusion, our two escapees scooted into the tunnel and scurried out into the holding pen. They were met by grinning camp guards toting AK-47s. "Ah, little Yankee rabbits, where you going?" asked one of the guards. "You go to interrogation now."

In the classroom lectures, our instructors had stressed the part of the POW code of conduct that described the duty of an American POW to attempt escape. They didn't tell us that for each escape attempt, successful or not, the rest of the camp would be severely punished. The punishment consisted of physical exertion exercises punctuated by verbal abuse and slaps from the guards. Our two would-be escapees caught hell while the guards tried to break them and force them to reveal the identity of the escape committee. Several more escape attempts were tried that afternoon, and one was even successful, but by evening, escape attempts were being viewed with a jaundiced eye. They just didn't seem to be worth the punishment we were getting.

With the onset of evening, shadows from the hills began to shade part of the yard and the heat began to abate. The guards seemed to be slacking off somewhat, and we began to think that the worst was over. Then the shift changed and fresh guards replaced the tired ones. The harassment began anew with vigor. Only about half of us remained in the yard; the other half had already been to interrogation. The interrogated ones over in the other compound didn't seem to be getting harassed as much as we were. I wondered why it was taking the guards so long to get around to me. I had eased over by the large board gate to try to get a peek into the small compound where the interrogations were being conducted. Suddenly, the gate swung open to reveal "Senior One" standing with the second-shift camp commandant. The camp commandant beamed at me and said, "Insect [their term for an ensign], come here." As I walked toward them, I noticed that my commanding officer was wearing one of the camp guard garrison caps with the red star on the front. "Your senior one has a duty for you," said the commandant. The naval commander, who didn't seem to be in complete control of his faculties, mumbled, "You need to pick up this area." I noticed that a quantity of scrap paper lay strewn about the small compound. What the camp commandant was getting the commander to do was a violation of the Geneva Convention Accords; officers were not to be assigned manual labor. But I wasn't about to question or disobey an order from my senior officer. I gave him a snappy, "Aye, aye, Sir," and started picking up the paper, thinking that this must be part of the training. How would we cope if our senior officer defected to the enemy?

I had only just begun picking up the mess when the camp commandant interrupted me and said, "Go tell your senior one that you have finished your task." I had only had time to pick up a few pieces of paper, of course, and the area was still littered with it. Wording my report carefully, I said to the commander, "Sir, the camp commandant told me to tell you that I had finished my task." The commander didn't catch the nuance of my report. "But there is still paper on the ground," he said. "*Ah, hah!*" the camp commandant shouted. "Your man disobeyed his orders; now you must punish him."

For my commanding officer to punish me at the behest of the enemy would be an egregious violation of both the Geneva Convention and the POW code of conduct—and would be outright collusion with the enemy. The commander looked unhappy and stammered plaintively, "Uh, what should I do?" The camp commandant said, "Show him your displeasure. Slap him." In addition to the other violations, doing this would also violate the Uniform Code of Military Justice, which prohibits physically striking a subordinate. In a real POW situation, it would be grounds for court-martial upon repatriation.

The commander clearly did not want to slap me, but he complied with the commandant's demand by gently touching my face with his fingertips. "That not how you slap," laughed the commandant. "Here, I show you." He delivered a resounding, ear-ringing slap. "Now you try," the commandant said, grinning. Jesus! I thought. They're making this awfully realistic. The commander grimaced and gave my cheek a slightly firmer tap. "No, no, not light tap. Like this," the commandant said. He double slapped me this time, catching the opposite cheek on the backswing with the back of his hand. Cheeks burning and eyes watering, I thought, Go ahead and hit me, Sir. Let's get this over with!

This time the commander gave me an audible slap that seemed to satisfy the commandant. "That fine. Now punish him." The commander, looking distressed, thought desperately for an easy punishment. His befuddled brain recalled the enthusiasm we had shown for the people's pool earlier. "Go jump in the people's pool," he beamed. Ah, shit, no, Commander, I thought. But I gave another "Aye, aye, Sir" and proceeded to the pit. It was fully dark now, and the temperature in the extremely dry desert atmosphere had dropped into the low sixties. The last thing I wanted to be was wet. But having no choice, I jumped in and emerged, dripping, into the cold night air.

Our group was quite small now. Only about thirty of us remained to be interrogated. We still had no idea what went on in the interrogation area. Earlier, a big, strapping, blond ensign in our class whom we had nicknamed "Swede" had been called into the small compound for interrogation. We later learned that the first stage, designed to soften up the prisoners, involved a type of torture known as the "claustrophobia box." The prisoner was crammed into a black box that was barely large enough to hold him. The box was hinged to unfold on all four sides, and the prisoner was required to kneel on the floor of the box while crossing his ankles, and then, bending double, to place his elbows on either side of his knees. The sides of the box were then closed, squeezing him tightly, and the lid forced closed over his back and latched. This position forces your chest down on your thighs, restricting your ability to breathe and adding to the panicky feeling of suffocation experienced by people with claustrophobia. Most of us were able to suffer the experience in silence, but for a few more claustrophobic members of the class, it was a hellish experience that could not be endured long. It must have been worse for Swede. He was larger enough than the average student that two guards had to sit on the lid of the box to force it closed. As soon as the lid was latched Swede began to howl and scream to be let out. Would he sign a germ warfare "confession" if they let him out? inquired the guards. "Yes, yes, just let me out," answered Swede. The guards opened the lid and dropped the sides, and Swede stood up gasping for air. The guards said, "Here, sign this," thrusting a piece of paper at him. "Fuck you," Swede responded. "If you not sign, you go back in box," the guards told him. "Fuck you," the articulate Swede reiterated. When one of the guards grabbed him to put him back into the box, Swede smashed him between his running lights, dropping him like a pole-axed steer. Swede was immediately removed from training and sent back to NAS Lemoore to be rescheduled for training at a later date. He was eventually sent to the other West Coast E&E school at Whidbey Island, Washington. He returned to us a visibly bruised, subdued, and properly POW-trained young man. Back in the yard, though, we were told that Swede had been executed for crimes against the Democratic People's Republic.

Finally, close to midnight, when only a handful of prisoners remained in our yard, I was called for interrogation. The guards led me into the small compound and over to the claustrophobia boxes. I was thoroughly chilled by now, lips blue and body shaking almost uncontrollably from the effects of my dip in the people's pool. As the lid of the box was forced shut, the claustrophobic effect was offset by the fact that it was quite warm in the box. I found myself actually enjoying the experience! This was the first time I had been alone in a week. No one was hassling me, I was warm, and it was quiet. I promptly fell asleep. The guards were outraged to find me dozing when they opened the box. "Lazy American pig," they screamed. "Get into interrogation room!" And they shoved and kicked me across the compound into a building.

Stumbling in the door, I was blinded by a circle of bright spotlights mounted between myself and the interviewer. We had been told in the classroom to resist, as much as possible, answering questions in a room, because it was easy to record our answers, clip words out of the tape, and splice them together to make it sound as if we were confessing to something or giving information to the enemy. The interrogator began asking me questions in a reasonable tone, starting with name, rank, and serial number. I stood mute, refusing to answer. Soon he was screaming at me for the answers and three guards began slapping me and shaking me. They made me sit in the "captain's chair," a form of physical exertion torture in which you assume a sitting position (without a chair, of course), arms extended, and maintain a half deep-knee-bend posture, held up only by your thigh muscles. Unable to hold this for more than a few minutes, I would sink to the floor, only to be yanked up the guards, slammed into the wall, and forced to resume the position. After doing this several times, I was confused, mentally and physically exhausted, and filled with determination not to tell these bastards a thing. Finally, the interrogator asked me if I was willing to give my life for my country. The realization that I was indeed willing to die for my country if the need arose caused an emotional dam to burst within me and I began to bawl uncontrollably. The POW camp guards were obviously affected by this display. After all, they were American servicemen too, about our own age, and, we were told, found it extremely difficult to administer this brutal training to their own guys. In fact, even though tours of duty as camp guards were short, many of them asked for transfers before finishing the tour because they found it too difficult to be so hard on their service brethren. My interrogator obviously felt bad about making me cry, and at the end of the interrogation had me sit on a stool until I regained control so that the other men wouldn't see me crying when I returned to the yard. I appreciated that, but I still left the building without uttering a single word.

Since I was in the last group to be interrogated, all the prisoners had been returned to the yard by the time I was finished. We were finally allowed to turn in for the night, and I happily fell into one of the cots in the bunker. The bunkers retained some of the heat from the day, and I was deliciously warm. We were awakened about 0530 the next morning and told to fall in. Informed that we had been "rescued" by American forces during the night, we had an emotional flag ceremony as the Stars and Stripes was hoisted above the compound. Then we loaded into buses and were taken to a cafeteria-style restaurant for breakfast. The POW phase instructors debriefed us after breakfast, apologizing for being so rough on us. They told us that the defection of our senior officer, the Navy commander, was not a planned part of the training. He had in fact folded completely and had defected for real, and he had been taken back to NAS Lemoore for further administrative action. This was quite a shock to us. They ended the debriefing by expressing the hope that we had found the training enlightening and would never have to use it, and with good wishes to us on our upcoming tours to Southeast Asia. Years later, after the release of the American POWs at the end of the U.S. involvement in the Vietnam War, many of them said that they had relied heavily on things learned during their POW compound training at E&E school. I felt that the only thing I got out of the POW training was a deep desire never to be captured!

VA-125 was located in a huge, cantilevered hangar just across the street from VA-127. Learning to fly the A-4 Skyhawk began, as usual, with about two weeks of ground school lectures about the airplane, its weapons systems, weapons we would be learning to use, and the syllabus while at VA-125. At last I was learning about the equipment and weapons I would be using in my fleet squadron. The ground school instructors were fleet aviators, and many had recently returned from combat in Vietnam. Their observations based on their experiences in combat made some of the lectures riveting. It was exciting and exhilarating. I was embarking on a relationship with an airplane that I would come to love.

The A-4 Skyhawk was designed by Edward Heinemann of the Douglas Aircraft Corporation. Its small size, agility, and speed earned it the nickname "Heinemann's Hot Rod" during the flight test phase. Built originally to be a nuclear weapons delivery vehicle, the little airplane proved to be extremely versatile and was assigned a variety of tasks, which led to follow-on models incorporating design changes to accommodate the wider mission profile. The key to the A-4's success was the beautiful simplicity of its design. The airplane was very small, only about 40 feet long from nose to tail, with a wingspan of only 27 feet. Even the Navy's smaller, older aircraft carriers could carry three full squadrons of ten to twelve Skyhawks each. The short wingspan eliminated the need for the bulky and heavy wing-fold mechanisms necessary on larger carrier airplanes. The flight controls were hydraulic, but there was a manual cable system for backup if the hydraulic systems failed. There was no battery for electrical power. If the engine-driven generator failed, a small ram-air-driven turbine, which folded under the right side of the fuselage beneath the cockpit, could be deployed for emergency backup electrical power. The landing gear, hinged at the rearmost point of the wheel wells, retracted forward. If hydraulics failed, the gear could be unlocked and would freefall down to be locked in place by air loads.

The A-4's tiny wing, only 260 square feet in area, was designed to cut through turbulence during low-altitude, high-speed flight. The wing's low-speed lift performance was enhanced by leading-edge slats deployed by aerodynamic loads. Heinemann's ingenious design didn't depend on a complicated hydraulic mechanism to activate the slats. Mounted on sliding tracks, they dropped automatically to their fully extended position at airspeeds of 150 knots and below. This helped solve the problem faced by other jets, which had difficulty flying at slow enough speeds on their final approach to carrier landings. The result of Edward Heinemann's genius was a small, lightweight, simple airplane that could perform a variety of missions well while packing a hell of a wallop.

My first two flights in the A-4 were in the brand-new T model, a two-seat version that had been designated the TA-4F. The TA-4F was destined to become the Navy's advanced trainer, replacing the venerable F-9. I was a little disappointed that I had to fly with an instructor rather than jumping straight into the single-seat A-4, but I did get the benefit of the instructor's insights on the handling characteristics of the airplane as we put the little craft through its paces in the familiarization stage. The tiny A-4 cockpit gave me the feeling that I was strapping the airplane on my back rather than strapping myself into it. The little airplane's agility and easy handling delighted me; it truly became an extension of my own hands and feet. Just as you don't consciously think of moving your feet when you are walking, we didn't think about moving the controls in the A-4 when we were flying, we simply thought of where we wanted to be or what we wanted to do, and our hands and feet automatically moved the controls to make it so.

My next series of familiarization flights was in the A-4C model. The first noticeable difference between the C and the T was in the power available. The T model was powered by a J52-P8 engine that was much more powerful than the old J65 that powered the C. The C was still fun to fly, though, and I was thrilled finally to be flying an airplane from the fleet. Fuel capacity was another of the C's drawbacks. It had only three external stores stations: one on each wing and one on the centerline under the fuselage. The standard configuration for the A-4C was two three-hundred-gallon fuel tanks slung under the wings on stations one and three, giving the airplane a fuel capacity of ninety-six hundred pounds—fifty-six hundred internal and four thousand in the external tanks. This was enough for a little over three hours' flying time at normal mission fuel consumption. Most of the fam stage missions lasted only an hour and a half to an hour and three quarters. We would generally climb into the operating area and do acrobatics until the external tanks were dry before starting touch-and-gos, because the attach points of the wing stations were not designed to bear the stress of landing with external tanks full of fuel. This gave us plenty of time to explore the flight characteristics of the airplane, and as "idle time is ripe for the devil's work," we would occasionally engage in air combat maneuvering if an opponent could be found.

Designed primarily for carrier use, the A-4 had long, spindly landing gear to allow room under the wings to hang external stores. This characteristic made the little airplane difficult to handle during a long rollout on a runway in a crosswind. If the wind got under the "into the wind" wing and lifted the landing gear off the runway, the pilot could lose control and scoot off the runway or even flip over. Every A-4 pilot quickly learned "stick full forward and into the wind" on every landing.

Our flying quickly progressed into day and night formation flying and learning a new skill: air refueling. Air refueling was a way of life in the fleet squadrons; indeed, many missions required air refueling. Most Navy carrier airplanes had a refueling probe installed, some retractable, some fixed. The A-4 had a fixed refueling probe that extended along the right side of the nose. The tanker would extend a cone-shaped refueling receptacle on the end of a hose called the "basket." The receiving pilot would simply fly formation on the basket and slide his probe into the basket with a slight closure rate until over-center latches in the refueling receptacle locked over the head of the probe, allowing fuel to flow into the probe.

A-4s often flew tanker missions. A refueling package called a "buddy store"—basically a four-hundred-gallon external fuel tank with a hose reel and basket—was hung on the centerline external store station. A tanker con-trol console that plugged into a space on the side console panel in the A-4's cockpit extended and retracted the hose and controlled the transfer of fuel. All but a small amount of internal fuel could be transferred from the tanker to the receiver. We took turns flying both receiver and tanker in this phase of training.

Air refueling wasn't really difficult, but it required developing a tech-nique, which only experience could provide. We flew the practice refueling hops as flights of five. An instructor flew with three students, and a fourth student would be the tanker pilot flying an A-4 equipped with a buddy store. Our first attempts at air refueling were comical. The procedure was to stabi-lize the probe a few feet behind the basket, then goose on a little power to drive the probe into the basket. Once contact was made inside the basket, the pilot ensured a good mating with the receptacle by adding power to push a few feet of hose back into the reel before fuel flow began. An amber light on the store would change to green as fueling began. The J-52 engine in the A-4E, TA-4, and later the A-4F was very sensitive to ingested fuel and had been known to explode if raw fuel was ingested down the intakes. For this rea-son, the receiving pilot had to be prepared to disengage quickly if fuel began leaking around the probe and into the engine intake. To further complicate matters, the basket would not remain docilely stable while we approached. It would bob and weave on the end of its hose like a nervous virgin in response to slight air turbulence or rough movements by the tanker pilot.

My early training flights went as follows. Thinking I was perfectly lined up, I would goose it with a little power only to have the basket dodge away at the last second and plop ignobly onto the nose, or bang on the cockpit, or try to go down the right engine intake. I would back away and try again. It would get frustrating after the third or fourth attempt while my classmates hung off to the side waiting their turn, especially if the man ahead of me lucked out and nailed it on the first pass. Success required small corrections of pitch, roll, and yaw, sometimes simultaneously. Wild stabs simply didn't work, as emphasized by the instructor's comments over the radio, "Easy, easy, Four, this is a gentle seduction, not a rape!" But gradually we developed a feel for the technique; it was sort of like learning to ride a bicycle—once you got the picture it wasn't all that hard.

Night air refueling was harder but entailed the same technique. A refueling probe light on the starboard intake illuminated the probe and basket, and the basket was illuminated by rows of tiny white lights. If the probe light wasn't working and the basket lights were out, and the basket was lit only by the occasional sweeps of the anticollision beacon, it became very difficult indeed. The odds were good, though, that some dark, stormy night at sea, our ability to refuel in midair under adverse conditions would save our lives. So we practiced diligently until we were good at it, and we kept our skills current.

Even though the primary focus of carrier air wings in the Pacific at that time was flying air strikes in the Vietnam theater, the primary focus of our training in the RAG was still for nuclear war. After all, the nuclear strike capability of aircraft carriers as part of the nation's strategic nuclear deterrence plan was the main justification for funding a large carrier navy. Accordingly, the bulk of weapons training and tactics in the RAG syllabus were for nuclear delivery. It was pretty much left up to our operational squadrons to train us in conventional weapons and tactics. All junior attack pilots were required to become certified nuclear weapons delivery pilots, and much of our RAG training prepared us to meet that qualification. To meet proficiency standards, the fleet attack squadrons and their carrier had to conduct periodic nuclear weapons loading drills, and all junior attack pilots had to become nuclear weapons loading officers. Accordingly, there was a two-week hiatus in our flying while we attended nuclear weapons loading school.

Once we had become nuclear weapons loading officers, our flying resumed in late October with nuclear weapons mission profiles. This proved to be some of the most exhilarating and fun flying I have ever done. The nuclear weapons attack mission planners envisioned a long-range mission in the event of nuclear war. To achieve the maximum possible range for the A-4, the mission profile called for a climb to the highest altitude possible for that airplane's weight. The attack airplane would fly at that altitude until reaching a predetermined descent point, then descend to a very low altitude before reaching enemy radar coverage. After that, the airplane would maintain the low altitude, remaining beneath radar detection while navigating to the target, delivering the weapon, and then escaping.

The RAG syllabus called for the students to plan and fly simulated mission profiles, and we were given simulated targets out in the high desert in the Edwards Air Force Base and Nellis Air Force Base test and bombing ranges. Planning one of these practice missions required several hours of preparation. We would draw out the profile and plot the course to the target on aeronautical maps called world aeronautical charts (WACs) that showed terrain elevations and features.

The route we selected to fly was supposed to take advantage of terrain features to help us avoid detection, like flying down inside valleys and canyons, and to avoid areas of simulated enemy activity. Since a straight-line course to the target was impossible, we had to plot course changes and checkpoints based on "dead reckoning" navigation, accomplished by timing marks based on flying at a constant speed over the ground, and magnetic headings to the next checkpoint.

The best speed for us to fly was close to 450 miles per hour. In order to mask our airplanes from enemy radar we had to fly low enough to hide in the ground return caused by radar signals bouncing back from the ground. The lower you could fly the better, but at altitudes lower than three hundred feet above the ground the pilot had to spend too much time concentrating on not flying into the ground to navigate accurately. Consequently, three hundred feet above ground level was selected as the optimum altitude en route to the target.

After plotting all the times on a kneeboard card and making corresponding tick marks on the chart, we would cut a continuous strip about three inches wide with our course line in the middle for the entire low-level portion of our flight. The three-inch-wide strip represented about a half mile on either side of our course line. We would fold the strip so that it would fit on our knee clipboard, which was strapped to our left leg, and could be unfolded as we flew up our course line, keeping track of our position and how the time was going. Our flight planning had indicated a time over target, and we were expected to hit it within two minutes of the planned time. It was demanding, dangerous flying, but at the same time exciting, fun, and rewarding.

We didn't fly weapons delivery profiles on these missions; that would come later, so flying directly over the simulated target was considered a hit. At three hundred feet above ground level (AGL) we didn't have much time to correct if we were right or left of the course line, so precision flying was a must. After all that planning and difficult flying, it was very disappointing to be a quarter-mile off the course and fly past the target rather than over it, which was considered a miss.

I was the happiest human on earth. During the drive to the base each morning after kissing my new bride goodbye, I would reflect that I was doing exactly what I wanted in life and wouldn't trade places with anyone. In a few hours I would be provided with one of the finest airplanes our nation could build and told to go fly it and develop my skills. Never before had I experienced such a feeling of belonging and clear sense of purpose. That I was taking my place in the ranks of naval aviators was the proudest accomplishment of my life to date, and I wondered if my warrior ancestors, perhaps watching me from some Valhalla, were pleased.

9

Weapons and Fleet Training

The time had come for us to begin learning the tools of our trade. In early November my class launched for a two-week weapons training deployment to the Marine Corps Air Station (MCAS) at Yuma, Arizona. VA-125 maintained a permanent detachment at MCAS Yuma to handle the continuous stream of RAG classes, and the station had all the equipment and spares needed to support the deployment. The students flew the aircraft down from Navy Lemoore in six four-plane division formations. At Yuma, we would be flying three hops a day, practicing both nuclear and conventional weapons deliveries on the several target complexes scattered around the area. The desert climate ensured the good weather we needed for the hops. There was a live ordnance area in the Chocolate Mountains just north of the air station where we would be dropping our first real bombs and firing our first live rockets. Several of the target ranges had been designed specifically for the nuclear weapons delivery profiles and were instrumented to track our deliveries as well as record our hits. The target ranges had outlandish code names whose origins were never explained: Kitty Baggage, Rakish Litter, Inky Barley, and Loom Lobby.

The first of the four targets we would use for practice bombing, Loom Lobby, was located about ten minutes' flying time west of Yuma across the Imperial Valley in California in the unirrigated—and therefore uncultivated—desert just southwest of the Salton Sea. A ten-mile-long strip of sand carved into the desert provided a run-in line to the target. The target was marked by three concentric rings of white-painted tires: a one-hundred-foot-diameter circle in the center, then a five-hundred-foot ring, and finally a twelve-hundred-foot ring for the outer edge of the target. Located east of the target were three range towers that housed the spotting and tracking crews. The run-in line resembled an absolutely straight road running north to south and ending at the outer target ring. Billboards every ten thousand feet provided distance reference points during the target runs.

Our first hops—and indeed most of our bombing hops at Yuma—were nuclear delivery hops. We had to log a certain number of practice hops and achieve a required score to become certified nuclear weapons delivery pilots, so the emphasis was on getting us qualified. The nuclear delivery profile required flying down the run-in line at an altitude of one hundred feet and a ground speed of five hundred knots. The weapons delivery system was designed to toss the bomb in a ballistic arc to the center of the target. We flew low-angle-, medium-angle-, and high-angle-loft profiles. The LABS, the airplane's low-altitude bombing system, directed the profile and timed the release. On a low-angle loft, for instance, we would calculate from tables the proper point to begin a four-G pull-up with an onset of two and a half Gs per second. At approximately forty-five degrees into the pull-up, the LABS would release the bomb, which would be lofted toward the target. We would continue the pull into a half Cuban eight maneuver, rolling upright when the nose was below the horizon on the back side of the loop, and then break toward the downwind leg to roll in for another pass. The theory was that running away from the blast at top speed would put sufficient distance between the A-4 and the nuclear detonation to allow it to escape. Since an A-4 had never dropped a real nuke, this survival maneuver was purely theoretical.

We used one of the billboards as our initial point (IP). When passing the proper billboard, we pressed the "pickle"—the bomb-release button on the stick. This would start the LABS timer counting the time from IP to pull-up point, which we had calculated from tables in feet per second at the airplane speed of five hundred knots. At the pull-up point, the airplane's attitude gyro—the AJB3A, which we dubbed the "abba jabba"—would go into bombing mode and a set of crosshair needles would appear. The horizontal needle would go up the face of the gyro at a two-and-a-half-Gs-per-second rate, and it required a 4-G pull to center it. Our job during the pull-up was simple: keep the needles centered. A slow onset of G would put the airplane outside the optimum profile and cause the bomb to hit long. A too-rapid onset of G or pulling more than 4 Gs would put the airplane inside the profile and cause the bomb to hit short. If the wings were not kept level, a side error would be introduced causing the bomb to hit left or right of the bull's-eye. The delivery was exactly the same whether we used a low, medium, or high angle, and was strictly an instrument maneuver. It required finesse and skill to keep the needles centered and the wings level throughout the maneuver as the airspeed rapidly dropped and the slats tried to extend. The target crew would track each pass with an optical tracking device and debrief us on the downwind leg. "Two, you were on at the pull-up, inside fifty feet at the ninety degree, outside twenty feet at the hundred twenty," for example, then call our hit: "Two, you hit two hundred feet at seven o'clock."

The high-angle-loft maneuver, also called "over the shoulder," was the most difficult because it required the most precise flying for a longer period. Because it was also the least accurate method, the high-angle loft was used primarily as a backup. If the initial point was missed or nonexistent, the pilot switched the LABS to O/S for the high-angle loft and flew over the center of the target, hitting the bomb pickle and beginning his pull-up. The LABS would release the bomb at approximately the 120-degree position in the pull-up just before the airplane completed the top of the loop. The bomb would be thrown very high before turning over and falling back down onto the target, giving the delivery airplane time to escape the blast effects—or so we hoped.

The practice bombs were the Mark-76, an inert chunk of steel weighing twenty-five pounds. The cigar-shaped nose was about six inches in diameter at the thickest point and about two feet long. A hollow steel boom about two feet long extended behind the nose with four fins enclosed in a box to give the bomb stability. A hole in the center of the nose contained a pyrotechnic charge that resembled a large shotgun shell; it provided a bright flash at night and a dense puff of white smoke in daylight to mark the bomb's hit. I was impressed with the accuracy of the system. On low-angle-loft missions we tossed these twenty-five-pound bundles of steel some five miles, and many of our hits were bull's-eyes, inside the one-hundred-foot circle. It was rare to miss the five-hundred-foot circle, which was considered an OK hit.

We were flying the A-4C model configured with a centerline four-hundred-gallon tank and a practice multiple bomb rack (PMBR) on a wing station. The PMBR carried six Mark-76 practice bombs. On a typical day we would fly three hops, each about an hour long, totaling eighteen delivery profiles. Flying at one hundred feet and five hundred knots was very demanding—we were less than an eyeblink away from the ground—but it was great fun. There were no RAG instructors with us on these hops. We would launch in sections, join up, and fly to the target as a division, alternating positions on each hop so that we flew all parts of the division. As time went by, we began to feel that we were really taking our places as full-fledged naval aviators. We quickly established a routine. The briefing for the first bomb hop was early in the morning and the first launch was at dawn. The third hop would recover early in the afternoon. After the debriefing and stopping by the BOQ to shower and change into civvies we would reassemble in the Yuma "O club" bar for happy hour.

Once we had flown the required nuclear qualification hops, the remaining hops in the weapons training syllabus were devoted to conventional weapons and tactics. This included a live ordnance hop during which each pilot dropped two Mark-81 general purpose bombs. The Mark-80 series of general purpose bombs consisted of the Mark-81, a 250-pound bomb; the Mark-82, at 500 pounds; the Mark-83, at 1,000 pounds; and the Mark-84, a 2,000 pound bomb, the largest single bomb the A-4 could carry. The weight of the bombs included explosive, bomb case, fins, and fuse. The 250s were called "Lady Fingers," a reference to a very small firecracker, but they were by far the biggest explosion I had ever made.

The Mark-81s were loaded on the outboard wing stations on the A-4C while I did my walk-around preflight inspection. The bomb racks had two sets of hooks that were latched open for loading the bombs. When lugs on the bomb case were lifted up to contact the middle of the open hooks and push them over center, the spring-loaded hooks snapped shut. Sway braces curved to match the contour of the bomb stabilized it and kept it from wobbling in the slipstream.

This mission was intended to simulate a division attack on a convoy of vehicles. The target was in the Chocolate Mountains live firing range about ten minutes' flying time from Yuma. We launched as a flight of four in two sections, joining up in a combat spread formation en route to the target. I was leading the second section; a lieutenant commander from our class led the division. We split up on divergent headings as we approached the target, intending to have each section make a bombing run perpendicular to the other's course to practice confusing antiaircraft defenses. The convoy was harder to spot than I thought it would be, but I finally made out the shapes of the trucks parked alongside a simulated runway bulldozed out of the desert. I called the target to my wingman and positioned for the roll-in. We separated enough for each plane to make an individual run. As I rolled in for a thirty-degree dive-bombing attack, I could see the other section making their run, the lead airplane crossing my nose as I crossed his wingman's nose. Placing the gun sight pipper short of the middle of the convoy, I allowed it to move up to the target as the altimeter spun down to release height. The pipper touched the target when the airplane reached release height, and I pressed the bomb pickle. *Whump!* I was startled by the jolt as the bombs left the airplane. The A-4 jumped as I pulled up out of the dive, straining against my G-suit to keep my vision clear. I rolled back to look at the hits. My bomb and the other section leader's bomb detonated almost together, dark red flashes producing dense black smoke. My section had the south half of the target and the other had the north half. The wingmen's bombs went off just a second after ours, and smoke blanketed the entire convoy. It looked as if we had really creamed the target. As the smoke cleared, the only damage visible from our altitude was black smudges on the desert floor. The bombs didn't leave craters because they detonated a few feet above the ground, set off by their shock waves. That way the target could be used many times without becoming pocked with bomb craters. The black smudges were all along the convoy, indicating that we would have seriously damaged a real target. Elated, we returned to Yuma in a tight diamond formation to look sharp at the field.

We finished our weapons deployment with some rocket and strafe hops and five night bombing hops. The targets for the night bombing hops were illuminated with parachute flares dropped by a Marine C-130 cargo plane. The C-130, a turboprop four-engine transport, could hold hundreds of flares and could orbit the target for several hours, allowing many four-plane bombing hops to use the target during its on-station time. These airplanes were used extensively in Vietnam and Laos to patrol all night and continuously light up enemy supply routes, so bombing with a C-130 flare ship was something we were likely to do in real combat. We would orbit the target in a racetrack pattern at eight thousand feet. The C-130 would make a light-up run dropping four flares at thirty-five hundred feet. Each parachute flare consisted of a candle of powdered magnesium and a four-foot parachute folded inside an aluminum tube about five feet long. When the flare was dropped, its arming wire was pulled out. After a short delay, a small charge would blow the covering tube off the candle, allowing the parachute to deploy and igniting the candle. The target would be bathed in brilliant white light, with terrain features standing out in stark relief. Shadows would dance crazily across the target as wind currents caused the flares to swing under their little parachute canopies.

We were making thirty-degree dive-bombing runs, releasing at three thousand feet and pulling up sharply to keep from diving beneath the flares, which would illuminate our planes and provide a target for antiaircraft gunners. Bombing at night was much more difficult and dangerous than daylight bombing. We constantly fought vertigo as we rolled and pulled with only the lighted target as a reference. It was easy to become disoriented or to fixate on the target. The flare drop usually allowed each airplane to make two runs before we had to pull up overhead and allow the flare ship to reilluminate the target. As difficult as night bombing was at Yuma, it was nothing compared with the real thing in the stygian blackness over the jungles and karst ridges of Laos and Vietnam. The short training we received at Yuma would be all we could rely on when we did it for real the first time.

The night flying at Yuma finished our training there, and on 19 November we returned to Navy Lemoore. After a one-day break we began FCLP training for our initial carrier qualifications in the A-4. This car qual period would include our first night carrier landings, so the majority of our FCLP hops would be at night. The night FCLP hops were designed to condition us to the different look of the lighted landing area at night, but it was impossible to duplicate the near-total darkness that exists at night at sea. Light scatter from background lights at the base and from the surrounding towns always provided a dim reflection from the ground, and the night hops did not entirely prepare us for the difficulty of night carrier landings.

The night FCLP hops were flown to a darkened runway with a lighted outline of a carrier landing area set up on the end abeam the Fresnel lens. The rules required RAG students to fly car quals in the airplane used by the fleet squadron to which they would be reporting, which in my case was the A-4E. I needed the practice. The A-4E had a more powerful engine than the A-4C, and the power response was much different in the two airplanes. This requirement would have extra implications for me when we went to the ship for initial quals.

We began intensive flying—two to three hops a night, sometimes ending the last hop well into the wee hours of the next morning. Finally, on Pearl Harbor Day, 7 December 1966, my class departed for our training carrier. Normally, the initial RAG car quals took place on an attack aircraft carrier that was on a turn-around training cycle between cruises to the western Pacific. For some reason no attack carrier was available when my class was ready for the ship, so the USS *Yorktown*, one of the older World War II–era carriers, provided the deck for our qualifying flights. Although she was an *Essex*-class carrier, she had been performing an antisubmarine-warfare (ASW) mission for the last several years and carried the designation CVS rather than the CVA of the attack carriers. The *Yorktown*'s aircraft complement consisted of ASW helicopters and propeller-driven ASW patrol airplanes, and none of the ship's company had been training with jet aircraft. As a consequence, our car quals had a less than smooth beginning.

My RAG class included a number of lieutenant commanders who had never flown the A-4 before, and in some cases were new to jets as well. All were returning to flight duty from primarily nonflying assignments such as staff duty. Their seniority in rank gave them first priority for their car quals. Accordingly, they flew the airplanes out to the ship while I and the rest of the junior officers rode out in the COD (the acronym for carrier onboard delivery), a version of the prop-driven S-2 ASW patrol airplane that had been converted to carry passengers, spare parts, and mail out to the fleet carriers. This was my first carrier landing as a passenger, and I didn't like it one bit! My classmates shared this sentiment, and we were a nervous bunch as the COD pilot cut his power for landing. Although I was scheduled to spend no more than three days on the *Yorktown*, I didn't leave for a week.

The rules for initial night car quals required the student to have two successful day landings, or day traps, on the same day before looking at the deck at night. Accordingly, the senior officers got their two day traps first, and then the junior officers got their chance. Then we all waited for the sun to set. Because the senior officers had the highest priority, they were launched for their night traps just as soon as the sun went down. A depressing pattern developed. The senior officers, particularly the lieutenant commanders, who had not been flying much on their previous assignments, would get airborne and then would be unable to make all their required traps. They would have to bingo to the beach, taking all the A-4Es with them and leaving many of us with no airplanes to fly. The next day, the hapless "bingoees" would fly back out to the ship at first light, get their two day traps, and turn the airplanes over to the rest of us for our two traps. Then we would all wait for the sun to go down and the pattern would repeat. Because I was a former NAVCAD, I held the lowest rank militarily and had the lowest priority for an airplane. I didn't get a chance at the deck at night until the last night the *Yorktown* was scheduled to be at sea for car quals.

There was another problem with using the *Yorktown* for car quals: she had hydraulic catapults. All the other carriers in the *Essex* class—with the possible exception of the *Essex* herself—had steam catapults. The main difference was in the way the power of the catapult was transferred to the airplane during the cat shot. The steam cats provided a smoother, more linear, power application throughout the catapult stroke. The hydraulic cat stroke seemed to give all the thrust at the beginning of the stroke. The effect was rather like being booted off the ship rather than slung off. Our launching weight for car quals was around sixteen thousand pounds, much lighter than the weight for an operational mission. This gave the A-4 a minimum flying speed off the cat of about 150 knots.

My first cat shot off the *Yorktown* was a shock. I felt as if I had literally been kicked in the behind! We had been told that we should concentrate on making an instrument catapult shot to prepare for the sudden transition to night flying on instruments. That was impossible because the instrument panel was shaking so violently that all the instruments were an unreadable blur.

Finally, on the last night of the car qual period, after a frustrating week of waiting my turn for a night try at the deck, I got an airplane. The *Yorktown* was operating in the Santa Barbara Channel off the coast of Los Angeles. We were far enough at sea that the lights of the LA basin were just a glow on the eastern horizon.

At night, the pilot indicates his readiness to launch by flipping on his exterior aircraft lights. After bracing for the cat shot, I flipped the exterior lights switch, which was located on the outboard side of the throttle handle, with my little finger. I had already double-checked the gooseneck flashlight shoved into the harness of my survival vest to make sure it was on and now focused on the instrument panel. If the aircraft's electrical system should fail during the cat shot, I would lose all the cockpit lights, and on a dark night at sea without reference to the airplane's instruments, I would probably fly into the water off the cat. A thin, high overcast obscured the stars, and there was absolutely no visible horizon. It was like being launched into an inkwell.

Nothing in our night FCLP training had prepared us for the reality of night carrier operations. At the field, even though the runway was blacked out except for the simulated carrier deck, there was still enough background light to provide dim visual cues of the horizon and ground. Out at sea, the entire visible world consisted of the backlit red glow of the instruments in the cockpit and the lighted outline of the landing area on the carrier deck. A single vertical line of lights, called "drop lights," extended down the fantail from the centerline of the landing area to help the pilot get a vertical perspective of the deck, but even this didn't prevent the feeling of vertigo I got when banking and turning for my final approach. I suppose it was the fact that the lighted landing area looked so short in the absence of any other visual cues that I got the feeling that I was in a steep dive for the deck rather than in a normal fifteen-degree-angle-of-attack, stabilized approach. I had to grit my teeth and ignore what my senses were screaming at me and believe what the meatball and my angle-of-attack indexer were indicating. I realized now why the other pilots had so much trouble getting aboard. This was much harder that I had thought it would be! My first pass was a bolter because I carried a little too much power and landed long. I settled down on the next pass and got a 2-wire trap. I was becoming accustomed to the environment, and the vertigo after the cat shot wasn't as bad for the next pass. Concentrating hard and shoving the vertigo into the back of my mind, I got a good 3-wire trap on the next pass. OK, I said to myself; two down and two to go (I needed four traps to qualify). I was strapped to the port catapult for my third launch when the ship steamed into a fog bank. The visibility on deck dropped to near zero, trapping many of the airplanes airborne. The only thing left for them to do was bingo to the divert field, and the rest of the operation was canceled. The *Yorktown* pulled into Long Beach Naval Station the next morning, and those of my class who hadn't bingoed to the beach the night before were picked up and flown back to Navy Lemoore. Five of us, all former NAVCADS, had failed to qualify, so we joined the next class for another round of FCLPs. I was really ticked off at not getting to qualify, but the further training would be good for me.

In the winter months, from late November until March, the San Joaquin Valley resembles an elongated bowl of cream from an altitude of about six thousand feet. Nearly surrounded by mountains, the valley fills up with thick ground fog that only infrequently burns off. We used to refer to the visibility as being a "one-pole fog" or a "two-pole fog," meaning the number of power poles we could see down the road. The VFR weather conditions we needed for FCLP training simply didn't exist for weeks at Navy Lemoore. Consequently, two days after Christmas, my new car qual class launched for a hop over the High Sierra to NAS China Lake, California, for ten days of day and night FCLP training.

Alma's school was closed for the Christmas holidays, so she drove over to stay with me, which made the deployment much more enjoyable. Several of the other married students' wives also made the trek to China Lake, which is in the Owens Valley desert at the foot of the eastern slope of the Sierra Nevada, and we had some social life when we weren't flying. On New Year's Eve, our instructors gave the married men the first bounce period after dark, and we all got together after flying for a New Year's Eve party. The single guys ushered in the New Year by calling the ball in the FCLP pattern. We finished up at China Lake on 5 January 1967. On the ninth, the USS *Yorktown* was back on station in the Santa Barbara Channel for car quals.

Suddenly, I was a "must pump," meaning that for some reason the powers controlling the RAG had decided it was essential that I be qualified and transferred to VA-212 ASAP. Accordingly, I got first priority at the deck. On 9 January I flew out to the *Yorktown*, got the two required day traps, launched after sundown, and got the four required night traps, boom, boom, boom, boom. After the last trap, I launched back to Navy Lemoore and was home at my apartment in Hanford by midnight. What a contrast to the first car qual period!

During this at-sea period for the *Yorktown*, an operational accident cost the life of the commanding officer of VA-125, a superbly trained and highly experienced carrier pilot. He was making a routine day landing in good weather with a calm sea. After a picture-perfect approach and touchdown, he caught the 3-wire. During the deceleration of the arresting wire's run-out, the tail-hook spade snapped off and the airplane rolled off the deck edge. The airplane had slowed well below flying speed but was still doing nearly one hundred miles an hour as it dove off the deck. There simply wasn't time to eject as the airplane nosed over and hit the water nearly inverted. There was also no way to keep the ship from running over the crash spot at nearly thirty knots. No debris surfaced to mark the crash site, and only a brief spot of foam marked the final resting place of this fine naval officer and aviator. It was a sobering reminder that there is a certain element of luck or fate—or whatever you want to call it—in surviving carrier flying.

I had to pass one final examination before graduating from the RAG and transferring to VA-212. To qualify as a nuclear weapons delivery pilot, I had to plan and fly a simulated low-level nuclear attack mission culminating in dropping a dummy nuclear weapon on one of the targets at Navy Fallon, Nevada. To qualify, I had to be at the target within two minutes of the time planned and deliver the weapon within twelve hundred feet of the bull's-eye. The "weapon," a two-thousand-pound practice bomb case filled with concrete called a "shape," was the same size and weight as one of the nuclear weapons carried by the A-4. To help the target crew mark the weapon's trajectory after launch, a piece of angle iron had been welded to the rear end of the shape, and four red smoke grenades had been taped to it. An arming wire had been run through the safety pins on the grenades. On release from the airplane, the pins would be pulled and the red smoke would allow the tracking crew to see the weapon's flight. I hit the target right on time and delivered the shape in an over-the-shoulder loft. Releasing two thousand pounds while pulling four Gs with the airplane's nose 120 degrees above the horizon gave me quite a jolt. It felt more like the weapon had jettisoned me than vice versa. The mission profile demanded an immediate pop-up to high altitude for the return to Navy Lemoore to allow for instrument flying condition fuel reserves, and I never did get a report on my hit from the target crew. Presumably the shape hit within twelve hundred feet of the bull's-eye, because I was designated a nuclear weapons delivery pilot. On 19 January the training officer of VA-125 signed off on my logbook with the cryptic comment, "No further flights this command," and I was transferred to Attack Squadron 212.

Reporting with me was Ens. Terry Rieder. Terry had been one of my roommates in Indoc battalion in preflight, and we had paralleled one another all the way through flight training. We even ended up in the same flight in VT-26, graduated together, and both finished RAG training at the same time. Like most of the nugget RAG students, Terry had been issued an open-ended set of orders and got his assignment to VA-212 late in the RAG syllabus. Being ex-NAVCADS made us the lowest military rank of all the pilots, and it was comforting to have someone I knew reporting with me.

Attack Squadron 212 was located in the last hangar on the left in the operations area. The fleet squadrons divided their time between deployments aboard an aircraft carrier and residence at Navy Lemoore. The squadron was to leave the next day for embarkation aboard the USS *Bon Homme Richard* (CVA-31). The squadron spaces at Lemoore included a large squadron ready room with smaller offices adjoining it. Not much was happening in the squadron area when we arrived. Most of the squadron's airplanes were off on some training mission, and the rest of the officers were with their divisions packing cruise boxes to be loaded aboard trucks for transport to NAS North Island, where they would be loaded aboard the ship.

Terry and I presented ourselves and our orders to the squadron duty officer (SDO), Lt. (jg) Billy Putnam, who was delighted to see us. He explained that until our arrival he had been the junior officer in the squadron and had therefore been the recipient of all the unwanted, pain-in-the-ass collateral duties that came up. Now that we had finally shown up, he could happily transfer those duties to us. After logging our arrival in the squadron logbook, he called the commanding officer to report us aboard. The CO directed the SDO to have us see him in his office, separately, in about ten minutes. Although we were both ensigns, Terry technically outranked me. A NAVCAD's date of rank was the day he made his initial car quals, and Terry had "hit the boat" a day earlier than I had, making him senior, so he would meet the skipper first.

Cdr. Homer Leroy Smith, U.S. Naval Academy class of 1949, was the commanding officer of VA-212. Terry rolled his eyes at me after leaving Commander Smith's office, indicating that it was my turn and good luck! My knock was answered with a single word, "Come," and I marched into the office at attention and stopped about three feet from his desk. "Ensign Stephen Gray reporting for duty, Sir!" I announced, keeping my eyes fixed on the wall over the skipper's head. "Welcome to the Rampant Raiders, Mr. Gray," he said as he rose to shake my hand. "Be seated." Commander Smith was an imposing figure, a handsome man about six feet tall with curly black hair. Billy Putnam had given him the copy of my service record that now lay open on his desk. The interview was brief and brusque. With the myriad details involved in getting the squadron ready to deploy for a nine-month cruise, he clearly had more important matters to attend to than a brand-new carrier pilot. He was concerned with the lack of experience and training Terry and I had received, and said that he would have much preferred it if we had reported at the beginning of the squadron's training cycle rather than just days before deployment. We would have to try and overcome this deficit in training as best we could. He expected us to work hard and get ourselves up to speed quickly so that we could be contributing members of what he considered the best attack squadron in the world. He intended that it remain so and didn't want a couple of nuggets degrading the squadron's performance. Accordingly, he intended to get as much training into us as he could before we entered combat. Collateral duties would be assigned to us sometime after we deployed; for now, he wanted us to devote our energies to learning the squadron's mission and tactics. He turned his attention to another matter, indicating that the interview was concluded. I snapped back to attention and departed with, "Aye, aye, Sir," and "Thank you, Sir!"

Terry had already left when I got back to the SDO's desk. Lieutenant Putnam directed me to go to one of the spaces below and draw a cruise box, go home, and get all my gear packed and have it back to the squadron by 1600. "And by the way," he said, "don't pack your flight gear. You're going to fly one of the airplanes down to San Diego tomorrow, brief at 0800." Well, damn, I thought as I hurried home to pack my gear. Welcome to VA-212!

The briefing the next day was short—just the necessary formation assignments, IFR flight plan clearance, NAV-AID, radio frequencies, and emergency procedures for the flights of squadron aircraft to NAS North Island, San Diego. The squadron had a complement of fourteen aircraft, and we would fly three divisions of four airplanes and one two-plane section. As I did my preflight walk-around, I stopped to admire the squadron symbol painted on the side of the fuselage. It was a navy-blue two-tailed lion rampant on a shield with a gold background, with the squadron name on an unfurled banner underneath. It was indeed a proud symbol, and, remembering Commander Smith's admonition, I vowed to do my best to become a member of the Rampant Raiders' team. I flew number two position in the first division on the flight to San Diego, and Terry flew number two in the second. During the uneventful flight, I reveled in the fact that my training was finally over and I was finally a professional naval aviator contributing my skills to the mission of naval aviation.

The *Bon Homme Richard* was docked at the carrier pier on the north side of the air station. I was concentrating on flying a tight parade formation during the breakup for landing and caught only a glimpse of her as I rolled in on final approach. After landing, we exited the runway on a taxiway that led down to the dock alongside the ship. After watching one of the huge dockside cranes hoist my airplane aboard, I went up the gangway to explore my home for the next nine months. The greatest adventure of my life was beginning.

10

En Route to War

The USS *Bon Homme Richard* (Capt. Charles K. Ruiz, USNA class of 1949, commanding) had a bone in her teeth. Captain Ruiz wanted to waste no time transiting to Hawaii, where we were to undergo an operational readiness inspection, so he was pushing the Bonnie Dick along at a constant twenty knots. The pace caused the ship to pitch up and down as she met the long swells of the Pacific, and even though I had been on two previous cruises on the USS *Essex*, I was conscious of the motion and knew it would take me a couple of days to get used to it. The pitching motion of the ship gave the sensation of riding an elevator, up and down, that never stopped. The ship was more than one thousand feet long, and the bow made vertical movements of one hundred feet or more with each wave. As I lay in my bunk, I felt as if I were pulling about a G and a half on the way up, and half a G on the down trip.

With the trauma of departure day behind us, the ship's company and Air Wing 21 were settling into the routines that would be our way of life for the next several months. My quarters were in a space directly aft of the bow, just behind the area where the huge anchor chains came into the hull. This space was officially designated the junior officers' bunkroom, but it was known to one and all as the "JO Jungle." The compartment ran the beam of the ship and was about ten feet deep fore and aft. Part of the compartment contained permanent beds in double bunk style, one atop the other, with two closets forming a partition wall. About twenty of these beds were available. Twenty-five JOs slept in the bunkroom, however, and extra bunks had been bolted to standpipes in the port side of the compartment to accommodate the extra five. These were intended originally to be battle casualty hospital bunks, as this area had been designated a combat casualty center. I sincerely hoped this wasn't an omen.

Over the next few days, I learned my way around the ship and familiarized myself with shipboard and air operations. The Bonnie Dick's main battery—Navy lingo for a warship's largest guns—was its aircraft. Air Wing 21 consisted of two F-8 Crusader fighter squadrons, VF-24 and VF-211; and three attack squadrons: VA-76 flying the A-4C, VA-212 flying the A-4E, and VA-215 flying the venerable A-1H Skyraider propeller-driven attack bomber affectionately nicknamed the "Spad." A number of smaller detachments of other squadrons provided support aircraft for the ship and the air wing. These detachments consisted of VFP-63, flying the RF-8 photo-recon version of the Crusader, which was armed with cameras instead of guns and missiles; VAH-4, or Heavy Attack Squadron 4, flying the two big KA-3B tankers; and VAW-11 ("Det Lima"), the Radar Early Warning squadron, flying E-1B Tracers, S-2s with a large radar antenna dome mounted above the fuselage. The HC-1 detachment was considered part of the ship's company because they provided all manner of utility missions in addition to flying plane guard duty and rescue for the air wing. Flying UH-2B Sea Sprite turbine-powered helicopters, they were known as the pickup and delivery guys.

We entered Pearl Harbor on 29 January 1967, with all available air wing and ship's company personnel lining the edges of the flight deck. Scanning the mountainous terrain of Oahu, I easily picked out the valley to the north from which the first wave of Japanese bombers had attacked the anchorage on 7 December 1941. I joined the ranks of sailors on the port side to see the USS *Arizona* memorial as we steamed slowly past the area off Ford Island known as "Battleship Row." The ship's PA called us to attention and ordered "Present arms" as we rendered a salute to honor those sailors still entombed in the flooded hull of the *Arizona* and the other servicemen who fell in the Pearl Harbor attack. I had studied the history of the attack extensively, and as I stood in salute I felt the thrill of anticipation at the thought of going to war myself.

The Bonnie Dick would be in port for only a day and night while we picked up the operational readiness team and refueled our oil bunkers for the two days of operation connected with the inspection and the transit to Japan. I was among the lucky ones who didn't pull the duty in port, so I was able to go on liberty for the time we were in Pearl. I tagged along with some of the other VA-212 JOs who had been to Hawaii on their previous cruise. After making a phone call to Alma, I joined them at the U.S. Army–run R&R (rest and relaxation) center at Fort DeRussy on Waikiki Beach. After a quick swim—where I discovered that the Pacific is surprisingly cool, even in Hawaii—we repaired to the center's bar to quench the thirst we had worked up in the 85-degree heat. It was here that I was introduced to the mai-tai, a blend of tropical fruit juices and rum—three types of rum, in fact. Thinking that the fruity drinks couldn't possibly be very potent, I swilled three of them in quick succession . . . then discovered that I couldn't walk when we tried to get up to leave. My similarly disabled companions and I began to giggle over the fact that we had gotten shit-faced accidentally. Fortunately, the R&R center had a room where we could crash and sleep it off before we had to return to the ship.

Flight operations began as soon as the Bonnie Dick got far enough away from the harbor to have sea room, and they continued for the rest of the day and into the night. This was my first real operation with the "Flying Eagles" of VA-212, and I had butterflies in my stomach as we briefed for the hop because I wanted to perform well. The ORI team was observing shipboard operations, so there was an added incentive not to screw up. For some reason, the Navy had a tradition that the most junior pilot in the squadron flew wing on the most senior pilot. Accordingly, I was always assigned as the wingman for the air wing commander when he flew with our squadron, the skipper, the squadron executive officer (XO), the administration officer, or the operations officer. This day I was number two in a four-plane division led by the XO, Cdr. Marvin Quaid. During RAG training I was occasionally asked which squadron I had been assigned to join. When I answered VA-212, the response was nearly always, "Boy, you're going to a squadron with a hell of a fine XO!" I was looking forward to getting to know this officer who was spoken of in such terms of affection and respect. I was not disappointed. Over the next year and a half I came to respect and genuinely like Commander Quaid as much as any man I have known.

The mission that day was a training hop to practice a coordinated bombing strike with a division from VA-76, the other A-4 squadron on board. We were to drop two Mark-82 five-hundred-pound bombs per airplane on Kahoolawe, an island off the southwestern coast of Maui. Actually part of the rim of a mostly submerged volcanic cone, the target island was a barren lump of volcanic rock resembling a loaf of bread about half a mile long by a quarter of a mile wide with sheer cliffs that extended about one hundred feet above the dark blue Pacific. It had been used as a bombing target since before World War II. Occasionally a group of native Hawaiians would paddle outrigger canoes to the outcrop to protest the bombing of what they considered a sacred rock in the islands' religion, so it was necessary to make sure the rock was indeed uninhabited before commencing the attack.

Having been briefed on all this, we manned our airplanes. The flight deck was a swarm of activity and color as crewmen scurried about readying for the launch. So their functions would be easily identified, all flight deck personnel wore jerseys color-coded to designate their tasks. Ordnance personnel wore red, plane captains and mechanics wore brown, fueling personnel wore purple, taxi signal directors wore yellow, catapult officers wore white, and catapult and arresting crew wore blue. Because voice communication was virtually impossible during flight operations, visual identification and hand signals were essential to conducting business.

The flight deck of an aircraft carrier during launch and recovery is the noisiest and most dangerous workplace in the world. Flight deck personnel had to keep their heads moving on a swivel to avoid being run over by airplanes, and their eyes were their only warning of impending harm because it was impossible to hear anything. They had to operate within feet of spinning propellers and jet engines spewing 400°C exhaust streams. At high power settings, the intake of an F-8 Crusader fighter is a gaping maw that can literally suck a person off the deck and slice him to ribbons with the compressor blades. If an arresting cable broke during a trap, the heavy cable could snap like a bullwhip and amputate someone's legs in an eyeblink. And to make it worse, these people were working in a thirty-knot gale on a deck made slippery by spilled jet fuel, hydraulic fluid, and engine oil.

The *Bon Homme Richard* was an *Essex*-class carrier known as a "twenty-seven charlie." This referred to the name of the engineering order that converted the old World War II carriers to the angled deck and gave them the so-called hurricane bow, which closed in what had been a weather deck under the overhanging flight deck. These aircraft carriers were the smallest attack carriers in the Navy and were unable to launch and recover aircraft simultaneously.

The Bonnie Dick carried about seventy airplanes during a cruise, and careful planning was required to get all of them launched. Aircraft were positioned for the launch on the aft part of the flight deck, leaving the bow catapults clear. As they were launched, the planes positioned farther back in the "pack" had room to move up to the catapults for their turn. Not all the aircraft positioned on the flight deck would be scheduled for launch at any given time. Those that remained on the deck had to be moved, or "spotted," forward on the bow to clear the landing area for recovery. Three huge elevators moved the airplanes between the hangar deck and the flight deck. One was located on the starboard side aft of the island; and one was amidships on the port side, its surface making up part of the landing area on the angled deck; a third was in the center of the bow between the catapults.

Airplanes were launched as they reached the head of their respective queue rather than according to their position in formation. If only a few planes were being launched, each could simply circle above the ship and wait for the rest of its formation. This wasn't feasible if a lot of airplanes were to be launched, because the airspace over the ship would quickly become congested. Accordingly, each squadron was assigned a rendezvous fix off the ship's TACAN (tactical air navigation) system at a designated altitude. For example, VA-212's division was assigned the 240-degree radial at the thirty-mile DME (distance measuring equipment) fix for rendezvous. The first airplane to launch turned to intercept and flew out the 240-degree radial to the thirty-mile fix, then started a 30-degree angle-of-bank turn to the left. As subsequent aircraft arrived at the fix, they simply had to look left to spot the formation, then cut across the rendezvous circle to join up. After the entire division was in the air, we sorted the formation out into proper positions and proceeded on the mission.

On this day, my airplane happened to be the first VA-212 A-4 to be launched, so I would be leading the formation rendezvous. The steam–cat shot was a smooth pleasure after the harsh kick of the *Yorktown*'s hydraulic catapults, and I quickly raised the landing gear to clean up and accelerate to flap-retract speed and climb speed for the trip out to the rendezvous fix. Reaching the thirty-mile fix on the 240 radial, I began a left rendezvous turn and was happy to see another A-4 below and behind me. As the other airplane joined me, I could see that it was Commander Quaid, so I passed the lead to him and slid back into a comfortable parade position on his right wing. The other two airplanes joined us before we had made a complete circle, and the XO turned us to join up with the four VA-76 planes. From my position on the outside of the formation I was able to see the other seven airplanes and marvel at the powerful image of force we represented. The A-4s looked businesslike with olive drab five-hundred-pounders hanging underneath. VA-76 flew the A-4C, which had only three external stores stations and was thus configured with two three-hundred-gallon fuel tanks on its wing stations and an MER (multiple ejector rack) hung on the centerline station. The MER held two sets of three bomb stations arranged in tandem. The Mark-82s were hung nose to tail on the center station. Our A-4Es, having five external stores stations, were configured with a single four-hundred-gallon centerline fuel tank and a TER (triple ejector rack) on stations two and four, which were located approximately under the center of each wing. This would be our standard bombing configuration.

The attack on Kahoolawe was an exercise in coordination and timing rather than bombing accuracy. The entire rock was the target, and it was impossible to miss so large an area. Commander Quaid brought us down to thirty-five hundred feet, accelerating to 450 knots for the run in to the target. This altitude was judged to be optimum because it was thought to be at the maximum effective range of small arms and light antiaircraft artillery while still keeping us below radar-guided surface-to-air missile coverage. (The air wing would learn later, painfully, that these assumptions were erroneous.) The plan was to pop up to seventy-five hundred feet for a thirty-degree dive-bombing run, with release at four thousand feet and 450 knots, and recovery by three thousand feet. The divisions split a minute out to allow sixty-degree divergent run-in headings. Quaid pumped the second section into right echelon and we began our pop-up to the roll-in altitude. As he began his roll-in, I counted two seconds, rolled seventy degrees left, and dropped my nose toward the reddish brown volcanic rock. As I centered my bomb-sight pipper on the target, I could see Commander Quaid's bombs leave his airplane and white streaks of condensation trailing off his wing tips as he began his pullout. Two seconds later I punched the bomb pickle and felt the jolt of the release. Suddenly a thousand pounds lighter, the airplane leaped into the pullout and I had to relax my pull on the stick a little to keep from blacking out with the onset of about six Gs. My left hand stabbed the max inflate button on the G-suit control, and I felt the hard squeeze on my legs and abdomen. As the Gs pulled blood away from my head, I steadily lost peripheral vision until I had a spot of vision about the size of a quarter surrounded by white-speckled blackness. Just a tiny increase of back pressure on the stick at this point would cause my remaining vision to shrink to nothing, and soon after that, unconsciousness.

As my nose passed above the horizon and I relaxed my pullout, the Gs decreased. My vision rapidly returned as my laboring heart pumped blood back into my brain. I had only a second to roll back to see the hits before joining up on the XO, and I saw the last two bombs explode. I was struck by the fact that I couldn't hear the sound of the explosions. The shock waves flashing outward from the blast formed a white ring of condensation in the humid tropical air. Kahoolawe was shrouded in smoke and volcanic dust, and I thought that the sound of eight thousand pounds of bombs going off must have been incredible.

The two divisions returned independently to the ship after the attack. Quaid joined us with another VA-212 airplane, this one configured as a buddy tanker. Although we had plenty of fuel, it was necessary to make sure that the refueling packages were operating properly. The practice plugs would also help us sharpen our skills for a time when we might have to do it right the first time. We took turns plugging the tanker, pushing the hose back into the store a few feet and receiving a few hundred pounds of fuel. After a couple of plugs apiece, it was time for the recovery.

Quaid led us into the break in a tight echelon and we kept a tight interval in the pattern. My pass was a good one, and I caught a 3-wire. After being taxied out of the wires and parked at the bow in a line of A-4s, I shut down and watched the next two planes land while I waited for my plane captain to attach the ladder to the side of the cockpit. The tropical breeze cooled my face and evaporated the sweat from my flight suit, and it was pleasantly quiet up on the bow because the noise of flight operations was carried aft by the thirty-knot wind.

In the debriefing, Commander Quaid complimented us for a good mission and then turned to me and said, "Good job, Steve; you did great on your first time out. I'll give you an 'attaboy' for today." One of the other pilots laughed and said, "Just remember, it takes six attaboys to make up for one dumbshit." The day's performance boosted my confidence and made me feel that I was becoming a part of the Rampant Raiders team.

That night the first tragic loss of the cruise occurred. A young airman, a flight deck blue-shirt in the V-1 division of the ship's company, was lost overboard during flight operations. One of the two KA-3B Skywarrior tankers attached to the air wing had just landed and was being spotted just aft of the island. The KA-3s were always parked there because the two-engine bombers were the largest airplanes on board and it was the only place where they wouldn't block a major portion of the flight deck. The big Skywarriors also required more tie-down chains than the smaller airplanes, and the young blue-shirt had been sent below to gather as many more tie-downs as he could carry. The chains were heavy, with quarter-inch-thick steel links and heavy steel hooks on each end. A tensioner close to one end added several pounds to the six-foot-long chains, which weighed probably twenty pounds apiece. The young airman had draped two chains over his shoulders and carried four more in his arms, so he was laden with about 120 pounds of chain as he made his way up the ladders from the hangar deck to the flight deck. During his absence, the second KA-3 was readied for flight. No doubt fatigued from his climb, the airman was probably in a hurry to get rid of his burden as he stepped up from a catwalk onto the flight deck.

Unaware that the second KA3 was about to leave its parking spot, he stepped into the exhaust stream of the port engine just as the pilot added power to taxi up the flight deck. The three-hundred-mile-per-hour blast lifted him like a leaf in a gale and flung him far over the side into the dark water sixty feet below. Several crewmen saw the tie-down chains flailing around his body as he plummeted toward the water. Life jackets and smoke lights—wooden floats with a saltwater-activated pyrotechnic charge that burn with a bright white light and dense white smoke—were flung immediately over the side to mark the place, because it would take the Bonnie Dick several miles to slow her twenty-five-knot momentum and turn back. The "man overboard" alarm sounded almost immediately and the plane-guard helicopter sped into position, bathing the area in intense light from onboard spotlights. Flight operations were suspended, and airborne planes were diverted to NAS Barbers Point on Oahu. We searched all the rest of that night and into the next day, hoping against hope that we would find him in the light of day. Daylight revealed the burnt-out husks of hundreds of smoke lights and dozens of life preservers floating in a knot on the gentle ocean swells. The young airman was gone from us, claimed by the deep. The words of the Navy Hymn took on new poignancy to me as we abandoned the search: "O hear us when we cry to Thee for those in peril on the sea."

———

With the ORI completed and the inspection team returned to Pearl Harbor, Captain Ruiz set our course for the two-week transit to Japan. After we crossed the International Date Line we began encountering rough seas, the result of a storm far to our west. The ship's PA advised nonessential personnel to avoid the weather decks, and extra tie-downs were ordered for all aircraft. The ship occasionally shuddered as the bow smashed into large waves, and the TV monitor in the ready room showed white spray flying over the bow onto the flight deck. Flying weather was good, with only a few low clouds scudding by, but we were too far out to sea and too far away from any shore-based airfields to launch any airplanes. The ship was pitching way out of the limits of the gyro stabilizing mechanism for the Fresnel lens, and it was just too rough to fly safely. The Soviet air force chose this time—on purpose, I suspect—to play a Cold War cat-and-mouse game with us. The Soviets scheduled reconnaissance flights over all American aircraft carriers en route to the western Pacific, using their large turboprop-powered Tupelov TU-95 strategic bombers. Nicknamed "Bear" by U.S. intelligence, these Soviet bombers patrolled at high altitude, using their powerful radar to search for carriers. On spotting one, they tried to sneak in undetected and make a few low-altitude runs over the ship, taking propaganda and intelligence photos and electronically sampling radar signals and radio frequencies to gain knowledge of U.S. detection and weapons systems. The carriers would launch fighters to intercept the Bear at least a hundred miles out and "escort" it. The fighters took pains to keep at least one U.S. fighter between the Bear and the ship—clearly visible in any photos the Soviets might take—the inference being that they would have been shot down long before reaching the ship had this been a "hot" war.

Only the most experienced pilots were picked for this launch. VF-24 and VF-211 launched two aircraft each, VAW-11 sent the radar-equipped E-1B to provide the intercept information for the fighters, and VA-212 provided the tanker. I went up to the LSO platform to watch. As a "nugget" I was encouraged to visit the LSO platform to observe landings and thereby help develop my proficiency at carrier operations. The catapult launch officer had to time his cat shots carefully when the bow was in the trough of a wave so that the bow would be coming up as the plane was launched. If the cat fired with the bow coming down, it might well launch the airplane into the water. The launch was completed without mishap, and we settled down to await the Bear's arrival. The F-8s headed out on a vector provided by the Tracer and we monitored their radio calls over the radio on the LSO platform. The fighters made the intercept easily, still miles outside the hundred-mile buffer zone desired by the ship. Both sections took up station on either side of the Bear with their wingmen riding above and behind the Soviet bomber so as to be immediately able to drop into firing position. Of course, in a real combat situation the Bear would be no match for the F-8s. It could fly neither as fast nor as high as the fighters, and their AIM-9D Sidewinder missiles would make short work of the big plane. Its ability to record information was the Soviet plane's only threat. But this airplane represented the enemy of our country, and when it came within visual range of the Bonnie Dick, the ship's PA announced its position. Every member of the ships crew who was not required to be on duty elsewhere crowded the flight deck to watch the fly-bys. For many of us, this Soviet plane was our first look at our nation's enemy. The Bear made four passes over us at about a thousand feet, the huge airplane dwarfing the F-8 fighters tucked in close on either side. The red star, symbol of communism, was prominent on the wings and tail, and the airplane seemed to radiate hostility. The tension was eased somewhat by a report from the fighters that a Soviet crewman in one of the observation bubbles on the side of the fuselage had been displaying the latest *Playboy* magazine centerfold picture to the escorting fighter pilots!

After the Bear retired to its base in Vladivostok, we began the really tough part of this mission of getting our airplanes safely back on board. The Fresnel lens was useless because the deck was pitching and rolling far out of its gyro-stabilized limits, so the LSO dragged out the "manual meatball," a cross-shaped stand with green datum lights on the horizontal bar and amber lights on the vertical bar, and placed it in front of the Fresnel lens. He positioned the amber light where he wanted the approaching airplane to fly—high, low, or centered—without regard to the constantly shifting glide slope. The trick was to get the approaching pilot to average out the pitching of the deck and arrive over the round-down on a proper glide slope with an appropriate rate of descent to touch down in the wires without smashing down so hard that the landing gear broke off or having the deck drop out from under the airplane at the last critical second and causing a bolter. I was awed by the LSO's skill as he correctly anticipated the motion of the deck and kept the incoming airplanes on a proper glide slope. I was equally impressed by the pilots' airmanship. Each instantly and correctly responded to the LSO's commands and landed safely. When I expressed my admiration to one of the pilots, he answered that "stark terror really speeds up your reflexes."

A few days later we steamed into winter. A subtropical warm front had masked the fact that we were steaming steadily into higher latitudes, and we awoke to find snow falling on the flight deck. We were just a day out of Tokyo Bay and our next port of call, Yokosuka, Japan, where we would remain for about a week while the ship and air wing relieved the off-going carrier. The process consisted of conferences and cross-briefings on the state of the war and the transferring of the "Yankee team assets"—things like electronic countermeasure sets and missile control modules for the combat airplanes. These electronic "black boxes" were in short supply and were very expensive, so they had to be passed to the incoming air wing. I was excited to talk to pilots who had just returned from combat. I wish I had attached more value to what they had to say; they had learned some important lessons the hard way. But each air wing had developed its own set of tactics and had preconceived notions of how to prosecute the war. We had to learn the bitter lessons for ourselves.

To get as many of our airplanes as we could into corrosion control facilities ashore we had flown most of the squadron airplanes to Atsugi Naval Air Station just outside Tokyo. We flew proficiency missions from the air station because we hadn't had much opportunity to fly since Hawaii and we were feeling rusty. I was on the fly-on when the ship left Japan en route to the Philippines so that I could get another carrier landing under my belt.

The ship would take a week to steam to Subic Bay, the main base of operations for the Seventh Fleet's activities in Vietnam. On the west coast of

Luzon just north of the entrance to Manila Bay, Subic Bay is a large natural port ringed by mountains with a narrow mouth out into the Pacific. The naval air station was located on the south side of the bay. The airfield had only one runway, aligned roughly east to west, at the foot of a very steep hill that rose some eleven hundred feet above the runway. The air station was only a small part of the sprawling naval station, which stretched around the bay.

The air wing was to get the maximum flight time possible during this period because this would be our last opportunity to train before beginning combat operations. I flew four day missions and two night hops, adding steadily to my meager store of carrier experience. One mission was a training hop in the use of the AGM-45, an air-to-ground missile called the "Bullpup." The Bullpup came in two sizes, the B model, which was launched off a rail after its rocket motor ignited, and the much larger C model, which had such a large rocket motor that it had to be dropped like a bomb; its rocket ignited after it had fallen a safe distance clear of the airplane. The pilot of the launching airplane literally flew the Bullpup into the target. The concept was simple. After the missile's rocket motor fired, a bright white flare in the missile's tail ignited. The pilot put his zero-depressed gun sight pipper on the target, flew the flare into his line of sight to the target, and kept it there until the missile struck it. A small guidance panel with a little joystick plugged into the left console of the A-4's cockpit and sent radio guidance signals to the missile. The pilot flew his airplane with his right hand and controlled the missile with his left, a feat that required more than a bit of ambidextrous ability. The Bullpup was a perfect example of a weapon that worked well on the desert target ranges of Nellis Air Force Reservation or NAS China Lake, but wasn't much good in real combat. The pilot had to fly his airplane perfectly steady in a shallow dive toward the target while he carefully maintained the missile's flight path down his line of sight. This required nerves of steel when anti-aircraft shells were bursting all around the airplane and tracers were coming through the 100-mil ring of the gun sight! The other problem was determining the missile's distance from the target during its final few seconds of flight. The pilot saw only a bright dot of light superimposed on the target. If the dot of light drifted off target, there was a tendency for the pilot to panic and overcontrol the missile while trying to correct its flight track. During the latter stages of its flight, the Bullpup would be hypersonic, and what seemed like small corrections could cause huge and erratic changes in its flight path.

The target for my first experience with the Bullpup was a deserted chunk of volcanic rock barely jutting above the surface of the Pacific far to the east of Okinawa. Only about a half mile long and completely bare of vegetation, the islet had served some now-unknown purpose during World War II. All that remained of human occupation was the skeleton of a dilapidated pier that extended about three hundred feet off the island's south shore. This was the target. We were all carrying the small Bullpups, and each of us made an individual run while the rest of the flight hung off and watched. Only one of us hit the pier. My missile whooshed off the rail, and after initially losing sight of it in the rocket's exhaust smoke I managed to visually acquire it and fly it up into my line of sight with the target. I lost radio control about halfway to the target, though, and the missile began a graceful ballistic arc down to the water and exploded three miles short of the target. One of the other pilots never did get his missile to respond, and the remaining pilot overcontrolled his to a near miss. I was grossly unimpressed with this introduction to the Bullpup.

A few nights later we conducted night carrier operations to give the air wing some night landing practice. We were only a day out of Subic Bay, and this would be our last opportunity to practice before arriving in the Tonkin Gulf and beginning combat flying. The prospect of night carrier operations made me nervous. Even though I had qualified without any problems on the *Yorktown*, I hadn't forgotten how difficult it seemed.

Of particular concern was the bad vertigo I had experienced on my landing approaches. This optical illusion didn't exist for me during daylight landings, but at night, when configured for landing and flying the meatball on final approach, I couldn't get over the feeling that I was in a thirty-degree dive for the deck. It was probably because the landing area was outlined in amber lights, making the shortness of the landing area apparent. I really had to grit my teeth, believe my angle-of-attack indicator, and fight the tendency to pull my nose up as I came aboard the ship. I knew that I had to overcome this fear, and I certainly wasn't going to admit my fright to any of the other pilots because of the even larger fear that they would find me unsuitable to be a carrier pilot. So I kept my misgivings to myself and with rapid heartbeat and sweaty palms I prepared for my first night launch from the Bonnie Dick.

To my immense relief the weather couldn't have been prettier! A calm Pacific Ocean sparkled with phosphorescent marine life under brilliantly clear skies and a full moon. Normally the sea air contains enough moisture to diffuse the light of a full moon into a soft glow that obscures the horizon. This night was unusually clear, though, because a dry cool front had lowered the humidity, and the horizon was sharply defined. My fear drained away as I sat in the darkened cockpit awaiting the signal to start engines.

The briefing called for two plane sections to join after launch and get some night formation flying, then enter the marshal pattern for the recovery.

At night and in bad weather each airplane is assigned a holding pattern, a racetrack-shaped flight pattern, using a radial and DME fix off the ship's TACAN. Other airplanes are assigned fixes that place them a thousand feet above the airplane ahead of them and a few miles farther out, creating a "stair-stepped" stack of airplanes. The airplanes are assigned approach times generally one minute apart, and it is a matter of professional pride for a pilot to hit the approach fix exactly as the sweep secondhand of the cockpit clock hits the zero of the approach time. So each pilot times his turns in the holding pattern so as to arrive at the fix and call "commencing" at the proper second.

When commencing the approach, the pilot flies a three-hundred-knot descent with speed brakes extended, giving about a four- to six-thousand-foot-per-minute rate of descent down to a point ten miles astern of the carrier on the recovery course and twelve hundred feet above the water. At ten miles the airplane is slowed and dirtied up into the landing configuration so as to be established on the recovery course. By six miles out the gear, flaps, and tail hook are down and the airplane is slowed to fifteen units angle of attack. Normally, night and bad-weather operations are conducted using precision approach radar that gives approach controllers on the ship lineup and glide slope information on the airplanes in the pattern. This type of pattern is flown level at twelve hundred feet until the airplane intercepts a three-and-a-half-degree glide slope to the deck. The controller instructs the pilot to begin his descent, giving him constant lineup and glide slope corrections until, at six hundred feet and a mile and a quarter from the ship, he instructs the pilot to "check for the ball." At this point the pilot glances up from his red, backlit instrument panel and acquires the meatball visually and flies it down to landing.

Inevitably, the ship's precision approach radar was out of service on this night and we had to make "surveillance" approaches to the ship. This meant that we dirtied up and descended to six hundred feet above the water with the ship's controller giving us lineup information only until we acquired the ball at a mile and a quarter out from the ship. My marshal pattern was twenty thousand feet above and some twenty miles behind the ship. In the beautiful bright moonlight I could clearly see the outline of the carrier and the plane guard destroyer five miles astern, their wakes highlighted by the twinkling phosphorescence in the water. Piece of cake! My fear completely gone now, I was enjoying the beauty of this night and exulting in having overcome my fear. I commenced right on time and arrived in line to land number four at ten miles behind the ship. After completing the landing configuration change and the before-landing checklist, I settled down to fly into the glide slope. I was completely relaxed and could clearly see the drop lights down the fantail of the Bonnie Dick. I was just about to learn a nearly fatal lesson about complacency.

It was a classic setup. Complacency strikes a pilot when a fear has been alleviated and he lets his guard down. At six hundred feet over the water at night, even with a sharply defined horizon, peripheral cues for altitude reference are not enough to allow proper altitude management without constant monitoring of the altimeters. I was happily looking at the back of the ship and the other airplanes without realizing that I wasn't cross-checking my altitude by scanning the barometric and radar altimeters in the cockpit. The first indication that anything was wrong came when the carrier-controlled approach (CCA) controllers, who were fiddling with the precision radar, called the LSO to say that number four in the groove looked low. They weren't more assertive because the precision approach radar (PAR) had been down and hadn't yet been recalibrated. The LSO, whose attention was focused on the airplane about to land, simply transmitted, "Four, check your altitude!" I glanced into the cockpit and noticed that I was at four hundred feet instead of six hundred. This should have alerted me to the danger, but I was firmly in the grip of complacency and simply added a little power, climbed back to six hundred feet, and began looking at the back of the ship again.

A few minutes later, now number three in the groove, my airplane's descending lights caught the attention of the LSO and he screamed over the radio, "*Three, you're low!*" Startled out of my reverie, I looked at the instruments and this time understood my peril. I was descending through three hundred feet with a fifteen-hundred-foot-per-minute rate of descent! Shaken, I applied a healthy shot of power and jerked back up to six hundred feet. I didn't take my eyes off the instruments until CCA called mile and a quarter and I could see the meatball. The pass was OK, but after my airplane was parked and chained down, I sat in the darkened cockpit stunned by the realization that if the LSO hadn't called me in time to recover, I probably would have flown into the water two miles behind the ship. The LSO in the debriefing simply said, "Gray, I hope you learned something tonight. If not, you'll end up being fish food."

"Thou shalt not take thine altitude for granted, for the earth may rise up and smite thee." I learned about flying from that.

The next day the *Bon Homme Richard* steamed into Subic Bay and docked at the carrier pier on the Cubi Point Naval Air Station side of the bay. We would be in Subic this time only long enough to load the ship's bomb bays with weapons and top off the fuel and water tanks before departing for our first period on the firing line in Vietnam.

Ready for war, on 26 February the Bonnie Dick left Subic Bay for the Gulf of Tonkin. Steaming time to the Gulf was about a day and a half, and we arrived on Yankee Station during the night of the twenty-seventh. Finally now heading for war, we were made aware of an uncomfortable reality of carrier life. The Bonnie Dick's steam catapults required an enormous amount of fresh water for each cat shot. The ship manufactured its own fresh water by distilling seawater. The evaporators on the Bonnie Dick were old, though, and the ship's officers were afraid that the ship wouldn't be able to keep up with the demand for fresh water that the upcoming flight operations would require. Therefore we went on water conservation practices just as soon as we uncoupled the freshwater supply from the dock. This meant that no fresh water was available for showers and we would have to take seawater showers for the duration of the line period. Even in the tropical climate of the South China Sea, the water temperature in February was several degrees colder than most of us prefer our showers to be. We would shortly all become "salts."

11

On the Firing Line

"Yankee Station" described a geographical fix in the Gulf of Tonkin north of the Vietnam DMZ latitude line and roughly thirty miles off the coast of North Vietnam. Three U.S. aircraft carriers performed an intricate ballet of launch and recovery here while maneuvering to keep out of one another's way and maintain their proper station about Point Yankee. Depending on the prevailing wind, this could pose a formidable challenge. Since the ships had to accelerate to get thirty knots of wind across the deck in order to launch aircraft, maintaining station and separation from the other ships in the area could give navigators ulcers.

We arrived on Yankee Station sometime during the night of 25 February 1967. It was the night before the war for many of the pilots of Air Wing 21, and few of us were able to sleep. Air operations against North Vietnam were scheduled to begin at 0600, at first light. The air wing briefing was to begin at 0400 to give us time to get the overall picture of air strikes and where the Bonnie Dick's air wing fit into the big picture as well as the latest intelligence information, code words, squadron rendezvous points, tanker locations, and weather for Southeast Asia. After the air wing briefing we would return to our individual squadron ready rooms, where our flight leader would brief us on our part of the mission.

After futile attempts at sleep, I was dressed in my flight suit and wandering the hangar deck by 0200. I was not alone. Many other shadowy figures were likewise roaming the deck or staring out into the blackness of the hangar deck sponsons, listening to the gentle hiss of the Gulf waters sliding past the hull. We didn't congregate, preferring to deal with our anxieties alone. I was more keyed up than ever before in my life. It was not an easily definable anxiety, less fear of combat than fear of not performing well. The feeling was much like that experienced by athletes just before an important contest—part stage fright, part self-doubt, and part having to acknowledge the impending reality of what had until now been only an abstract possibility. In a few hours, I would be trying to inflict death and destruction on other human beings, who would be trying equally hard to kill me. One other figure emerged from the darkness and engaged me in conversation. He was the Catholic chaplain, a much older man than I, probably nearly forty, who was walking among us keeping an eye on the spiritual needs of his "boys." Now, I was raised a Methodist, and I wasn't even particularly religious at this point in my life, but I found conversation with this priest easy and comforting. The Protestant chaplains on the ship seemed a soft, milquetoast group, like most preachers I had known. The Catholic priest was a Jesuit, a hard charger, and he had the tremendous advantage of being able to go drinking with the men on liberty. Also, he was unquestioningly supportive of our military duties.

"Good morning, unh, Ensign Gray—ahh, Steve, isn't it?"

"Yes, Sir," I said, snapping to attention. He was, after all, a U.S. Navy commander.

"Relax, Steve. You having trouble sleeping too?" he asked.

"Yessir, I guess I am," I answered.

"Well you're certainly not alone. Want to talk?" he asked.

"Aw, I don't know, Father. I guess I'm just keyed up."

"You're flying this morning?" he asked.

"Yessir, first launch," I responded.

"Well, son, I think you'll do just fine. Just rely on your training and remember that you are the best pilots in the world. If you need to talk about anything or just want to shoot the breeze, come see me. Good luck today, and good hunting!"

"Thank you, Father, I appreciate it." Nothing had changed, but I felt better just having exchanged a few words with him. I turned toward the air wing's intelligence spaces for the air wing briefing.

———•———

During the month-long cruise to Yankee Station I had attended many lectures and briefings about the array of enemy antiaircraft defenses possessed by the Asian Communists. Antiaircraft artillery ranged from 12.75-mm heavy machine guns, 23-mm track-vehicle-mounted guns, and venerable old 37-mm World War II antiaircraft guns to modern radar-directed 57-mm and 85-mm guns and 100- and 120-mm heavy stuff. The bulk of the North Vietnamese air force fighters consisted of Soviet MiG-17s, an old but still potent airplane, and first-line MiG-21 fighters that were rumored to be superior to any of the U.S. fighters. In addition, the North Vietnamese had been supplied with SA-2 Guideline surface-to-air missiles, which we called simply SAMs. We would come to learn that much of our intelligence on these weapons was inaccurate or incomplete. But in early 1967 we still had much to learn about our enemy. Lectures and training were over now; it was time for the real thing.

The air wing intelligence spaces were crowded when all the first-launch pilots assembled for the air wing briefing. Each squadron had been assigned an individual mission. The Barn Owls of VA-215 would launch six A-1H Skyraiders to act as spotters for Navy destroyers and cruisers that were shelling targets on Highway One, the main coastal highway in North Vietnam. VF-211 and VF-24 would provide F-8 fighters for combat air patrol to protect the Seventh Fleet ships in the Gulf from any possible attack from the North Vietnamese air force and to provide fighter cover for the attack planes on their missions. The two A-4 squadrons had been assigned strike targets along Highway One. I was to be number two in a four-plane division. Our target was a bridge. The bridge had been bombed and rebuilt several times since 1964, when operations against the North began. It was still listed as "down," but photo reconnaissance indicated construction on the bridge abutments, and the Seventh Fleet Target Planning Staff believed that temporary pontoon-type bridges were being strung across the river at night. Our division was to bomb and destroy the approaches to the bridge area.

VA-76 would launch their division of A-4s against a "suspected POL area," a storage site for petroleum oil lubricants such as gasoline and diesel fuel used to refuel the trucks that supplied the Viet Cong in the South. Such areas were targeted randomly to deny their use to the enemy. The map showed several antiaircraft positions around the target areas, indicating that antiaircraft fire had been observed there in the past. The North Vietnamese had many, many prepared gun emplacements scattered around every target site in the North, but these might or might not be active. The guns and missiles were moved frequently, so unless we had very recent photo recon of the area, we could never be certain which site would be firing at us.

These targets were considered "milk runs" because they were in the lower part of North Vietnam where the antiaircraft defenses were not as intense as they were farther north. It was a way to ease us into combat. The U.S. military had divided North Vietnam into six "route packages" reflecting the air power mission to prevent supplies from the North reaching the guerillas in the South. In early 1967, the DMZ, or Demilitarized Zone—the buffer zone established by the Geneva Accords that had divided Vietnam into North and South—and northward was Route Package 1, a joint strike zone where Navy, Air Force, and Marine aircraft operated. Route Packages 2, 3, 4, and 6A, from the coast inland to the border with Laos, were Navy areas of operation. North Vietnam was shaped roughly like a pork chop. Route Packages 1–4 encompassed the lower leg of the pork chop, while Route Packages 5 and 6B, which belonged to the Air Force, covered the wide part of the pork chop. Aircraft operating in Route Package 1 were always under positive control; that is, they were directed either by airborne forward air controllers (FACs) or by the airborne command post. Friendly ground forces sometimes operated behind enemy lines in Package 1, so it was not a free fire zone. All of our target assignments were in Package 2 this morning, but the weather forecast did not bode well.

The air intelligence officers who conducted the air wing briefing began with the overall tactical picture for that day: which targets the other two carriers on Yankee Station (USS *Enterprise* and USS *Ticonderoga*) were hitting, our individual squadron assignments, the MiG and SAM warning code words for the day, strike operations and search-and-rescue radio frequencies, tanker frequencies, launch and recovery times, and rendezvous points for each squadron. This morning the primary divert field in an emergency was Da Nang, South Vietnam. The Marine air base at Chu Li was the divert field for offloading hung or unused bombs.

Next came the weather brief giving the overall weather picture for Southeast Asia and specific weather for our target areas. The weather forecast for our targets indicated weather minimums far below what we needed to operate. Dive bombing required at least an eight-thousand-foot ceiling and ten miles' visibility. This day the target weather, provided by a Marine A-6 Intruder weather recon mission, showed ceilings of less than five hundred feet with visibility less than two miles in rain and fog. The decision to divert to secondary targets in South Vietnam would be made after launch, but it seemed certain that we would divert. After the anticipation of the night before, I felt a pang of disappointment at not being able to go after our bridge target.

The meteorological officer explained that bad weather was normal for North Vietnam at this time of year. From about October until March, North Vietnam experienced a winter monsoon characterized by constant fog, low ceilings, and drizzle broken occasionally by periods of torrential rain. South Vietnam was on the opposite side of the calendar and was having its dry season at this time of year, so the weather dramatically improved the farther south one went.

The weather briefing concluded, the air intelligence officer went over the procedures for diverting to the South. Since all air operations in South Vietnam, Laos, and Route Package 1 were conducted under positive control, our flights would contact an airborne command post for assignments. The airborne command post was an Air Force C-130 Hercules orbiting over Da Nang airfield that had been fitted with a number of radio stations. During daylight hours, the command post's call sign was "Hillsborough"; at night it was "Moonbeam." The controllers in the command post assigned strike aircraft to missions called in by airborne FACs or ground FACs, or to radar bombing missions called "combat sky spots." We were to contact Hillsborough with our flight call sign, number of aircraft, type of ordnance, and on-station time. The latter was limited by our need to be on time for recovery. The Bonnie Dick had a launch schedule to keep. This information concluded the air wing briefing, and we trooped out to our various squadron ready rooms for the individual briefings.

Appropriately, the skipper, Cdr. Homer Smith, was leading the first combat mission of VA-212 on the 1967 cruise. As the most junior pilot, I would fly as his wingman, as I did for the senior pilot—whoever he was—whenever we flew. Terry Rieder, the other nugget, flew for the most senior pilot on alternating launches. I was secretly tickled that I was scheduled for launch on the first go, thereby becoming a combat-experienced pilot before Terry, whose baptism in combat would come later in the day. We briefed bomb loads, launch weights, rendezvous point, lost radio procedures, emergency divert information, search-and-rescue duties, and instrument recovery procedures on return to the ship. After that, we had about half an hour to kill before being called to man airplanes. I used this time to get dressed in torso harness, G-suit, survival vest, and life preserver. I checked my signal devices—mirror, flare pen, hand-held smoke, and flare—and my .38 snub-nosed pistol. If I should happen to go down over land, though, only the smoke stick might be of some use. If I flashed sunlight with the mirror, the search-and-rescue planes would most likely think it was muzzle flashes from ground fire; the same would be true for the flare pen and tracer shells from the gun.

The only thing likely to get a pilot rescued from the ground was a small radio with a five-foot steel-tape folding antenna designated the PRC-10, or "prick 10" as we called it. I carefully checked it on the test stand provided for that purpose to ensure that the batteries were fully charged and that it was transmitting properly. The radio would transmit a continuous distress signal on the emergency, or guard, frequency. The signal was an intermittent tone starting high and decreasing in pitch; or selecting "voice" on the transmitter key made it possible to send and receive voice communications. If a pilot had to bail out over land in the combat zone, the PRC-10 was his only hope of rescue. After these preparations I stood around talking to the other pilots for a few minutes until the overhead screen that projected teletype messages to the ready rooms clattered into life: PLTEOS, MAN YOUR PLAQUNS, it proclaimed on the first attempt, then PILOTS MAN YOUR PLQUWS, and finally PILOTS MAN YOUR PLANWS. "Well, I guess that means us," laughed the skipper, and we followed him out to the escalator to the flight deck. My logbook showed four hundred hours' total pilot time.

The existence of an escalator on an aircraft carrier always surprised visitors. The flight deck was three full decks above the bottom of the escalator, though, and for pilots loaded down with flight gear it would have been quite a climb. We sometimes had to make the climb when the escalator was out of service, and on those occasions we missed it sorely. The top of the escalator disgorged us into a small compartment in the island, and we exited through a steel hatch onto the flight deck.

It was a forbidding day. Low clouds scudded by overhead, and shafts of rain dotted the seascape. The *Bon Homme Richard* had already turned into the wind and was accelerating to get thirty knots of wind down the deck. The stiff breeze blowing down the deck felt uncomfortably cold even though the temperature was in the low sixties. The A-1s were parked in the center of the flight deck aft of the island and their plane captains had already started their engines to get them warmed up before the launch. We gingerly threaded our way to our airplanes through a forest of spinning propellers. A misstep into one of those shimmering prop arcs would result in instant death, or at the very least loss of a body part.

I reached my aircraft and began the walk-around preflight inspection. We were carrying the standard A-4E bomb load of six Mark-82s (500 pounders) and two Mark-81s (250 pounders). The Mark-81s were loaded on stations one and five, the outermost stations on the wings, on the parent bomb racks. The Mark-82s were mounted three each on triple ejector racks on stations two and four. A four-hundred-gallon external fuel tank hung from the centerline bomb rack. I inspected each bomb carefully to ensure that it was loaded properly: lugs firmly engaged by the hooks in the rack; sway braces tightened properly; arming wires attached to the racks properly and threaded through the holes in the arming propeller on the fuse screwed into the nose of the bomb, and secured by at least two fawnstock clips.

The bombs were called "Snakeyes," after the type of tail fin they carried. These fins were held closed by a band that could be jerked free by an arming wire when the bomb was released. If the bomb was dropped in this fashion, the fins would spring out from the body, making the falling bomb resemble a miniature palm tree with four fronds. This was called a retarded drop because the extended fins slowed the bomb's fall considerably. The "snakeye" method of bomb delivery was an extremely accurate way to drop bombs, but it required a shallow, ten-degree bombing run and release of the bombs about nine hundred feet above the ground. The small arms and light antiaircraft fire around most targets in the North was too heavy and too accurate to make this type of delivery effective. Instead we used steeper dive-bombing runs with higher release altitudes that precluded the use of the snakeye delivery. When the fins were folded along the bomb's body, raised ridges along the edge of each fin acted as stabilizers for the bomb, allowing it to be dropped in conventional dive-bombing fashion.

After completing the preflight, I climbed the eight-foot ladder fitted into the left side of the fuselage and swung my leg down into the cockpit, taking care not to step on the seat pan or hit the alternate ejection handle on the front of the seat pan. After stowing the "head knocker," a handle that when extended out from the headrest safetied the ejection seat firing pin, I settled down into the seat, pushing my feet down into the rudder pedal tunnels under the instrument panel. I hooked my G-suit hose into the fitting on the left side of the cockpit and connected the hip fittings to my torso harness. The assistant plane captain, or "second mech," had followed me up the ladder and was fumbling with my parachute straps, trying to fit them into the quick-release fittings on the shoulders of my torso harness.

"S-s-sorry, S-sir," he stammered. "This is the f-f-first time I've done this."

I realized that he was more scared than I was. "No sweat, man, relax, it's a piece of cake," I said as I grinned up at him.

"OK, Sir," he said, relieved as he managed to snap the second shoulder strap into its fitting. "Good luck out there."

I gave him a thumbs-up as he climbed down the ladder and removed it from the airplane. The prestart checklist completed, I looked out to see the plane captain giving me the start signal. The A-4 had no battery, so it depended on external power and high-pressure air to start. After start, when the engine had stabilized at idle and the aircraft generator was supplying power, I signaled to pull power and air. "Rocket Tower, Eagle two-two-three, radio check, over," I transmitted. "Rocket" was the *Bon Homme Richard*'s call sign. There was no answer. In fact, I realized that I wasn't hearing any radio transmissions at all. I tried again, "Rocket Tower, Eagle two-two-three, over." Still nothing. I dialed the frequency in manually; still no joy. The radio was dead. No luck on squadron common or strike frequency either. "Damn,

damn, damn," I cursed as I pounded the canopy in frustration. I couldn't believe this was happening. Reluctantly I signaled the skipper, parked next to me, that my radio was dead, and he gave me the cut signal indicating that I was scrubbed from the launch. I could imagine the spare pilot's grin behind his oxygen mask as he moved into my place.

After the launch was complete, I rode the brakes for the respot crew as they pushed my airplane onto the number three elevator to be struck below for repairs. When the plane was safely chained down on the hangar deck, I climbed down from the cockpit and walked dejectedly toward the ready room. My nervous anticipation had turned into a crushing letdown. I wasn't scheduled for another launch that day, so my baptism by fire would have to wait. The weather worsened. My flight the next day was canceled after earlier flights had to be diverted to the big Chu Li air base in South Vietnam because weather was below landing minimums at the ship. I was beginning to fret because Terry Rieder had already flown two combat missions and was getting ahead of me.

A tragic accident on 27 February made me forget my personal concerns. One of our two HC-1 detachment helos was landing on the bow after a mail run to some of the escort destroyers on Yankee Station. The *Bon Homme Richard* was steaming with just enough forward motion to keep steering ability on a crosswind course. The crosswind posed no problem for the helo. The pilot simply headed into the wind in a hover and matched the speed of the ship before settling down onto the flight deck. TV cameras sent a live picture of the helo's landing to all the ready rooms, and I happened to be watching when the accident occurred. The helo was making an approach to the bow with its nose pointing toward the starboard side. It had stabilized in a hover with its wheels only a few feet above the flight deck when suddenly it lurched forward, nosed over the side of the ship, and crashed upside down into the water sixty feet below. The motion on the TV screen had caught the attention of several of the VA-212 pilots in the ready room.

"Holy shit!" someone screamed. "The helo crashed starboard!" The ship's crash alarm was sounding as we raced up the escalator to the flight deck. A crowd was gathering on the starboard catapult, everyone anxious to help rescue the downed helo's crew. A patch of white foam moving slowly down the starboard side as the ship's momentum drove her past the crash site was the only indicator that anything had happened. No debris marked the spot where four men had just disappeared into the gray waters of the Tonkin Gulf. A search effort failed to find even a trace of them. In just a few seconds, four men had died. No one ever knew for sure what caused the helo to nose over suddenly and crash. The most likely explanation was a severe mechanical failure of the rotor head causing an unrecoverable loss of control, but without any wreckage to inspect there was no way to prove that. I knew only one of the pilots on the helo, and him only slightly, but their deaths had cast a pall over the ship as if all of us had experienced a death in the family. Once again we were reminded how fragile existence could be in carrier aviation.

Finally, on the last day of February 1967, I was airborne on my first combat mission. The weather over North Vietnam was still stinko, so we would be heading directly for Da Nang to make ourselves available for whatever Hillsborough could find for us to do. The XO, Commander Quaid, would be leading our division, but because I happened to be first in line for the launch, I would lead the rendezvous. All airplane systems seemed to be working perfectly as I taxied up to the starboard cat. The weight man showed me 24,500 pounds on his weight board, which was max takeoff weight for the A-4E. I gave him the thumbs-up indicating that the weight was correct and taxied onto the cat. I felt the nose go up and over the shuttle and slammed on the brakes to keep from hitting the holdback too hard. The catapult officer gave the tension sign to the cat crew while signaling me with his other hand to turn up for launch. I shoved the throttle up to the stop and flipped the catapult hold handle down, grasping it with my fingers, and squeezed the throttle into my palm. A quick scan showed the gauges all in the green, so I saluted the cat officer as I pushed my helmet firmly into the headrest.

An invisible steel hand slammed me back into the seat when the cat fired. There was no need to rotate the airplane; the force of the cat shot had shoved the stick all the way aft into my gut. I even had to push the stick forward to keep from over-rotating. Damn! That liked to have knocked the breath out of me, I thought as I flipped the landing gear handle up and turned away from the launch heading. The A-4 at max combat weight may have been the smallest and lightest airplane on the ship, but it took the hardest catapult shot. With the weight of all the bombs and fuel tank suspended from its tiny wings its minimum flying speed was 174 knots, attained in about 120 feet of cat stroke. This was my first max combat weight takeoff, but I would get so used to the force of this cat shot that launches at a lighter weight would scare me into thinking that I was getting a cold cat and wouldn't have sufficient speed to become airborne.

The clouds ended at ten thousand feet, and I popped up out of the overcast into brilliant sunlight. Squinting against the sudden glare, I reached up and flipped the shaded visor of my helmet down into place over the nose bridge of the oxygen mask. It was a beautiful day on top with clear, deep blue skies. The rendezvous point was sixteen thousand feet on the 180-degree radial off Rocket TACAN for twenty miles. As I reached the fix and began the orbit turn, I could see the other three airplanes in my division far below and behind me in trail, three dots leaving thin black smoke trails against the pure white of the undercast. "Eagles, go tactical," the XO's voice came over the radio. I reached down and selected channel 20, the squadron's tactical frequency, on the channel selector dial. "Eagle check," transmitted the XO. "Eagle Two," I responded, and "Eagle Three" and "Eagle Four" came in quick succession as the second section checked in. "Eagle Two, head two-two-zero and fly two-fifty; we'll do a running rendezvous. I'll join on your port side." A few minutes later, Commander Quaid called, "Push it up to three-fifty and check seven o'clock, Eagle Two." Glancing over my left shoulder, I could see the XO's airplane closing rapidly, speed brakes out as he slowed from four hundred knots to keep from overrunning me too far. As he slid up my port side the XO's helmeted and visored visage turned toward me. He tapped his helmet with two gloved fingers and pointed at himself, signaling that he was taking the lead. As I settled into position on his right wing, the second section, having already joined, slid into position on his left side. We had already traveled half the distance to Da Nang, and the XO signaled us to switch to Hillsborough radio.

"Hillsborough, Hillsborough, Flying Eagle, over," the XO called.

"Flying Eagle, Hillsborough, go ahead, over."

"Hillsborough, Flying Eagle Leader with four A-4s, twenty-four Mark-82s, eight Mark-81s, banded Snakeyes, limited twenty mike-mike, one hour station time, over."

The XO had just told Hillsborough what we were, what ordnance we could deliver, and how much time we had for whatever target assignment Hillsborough could give us. The reference to "limited twenty mike-mike" described the internal machine guns the A-4 carried. We were indeed limited in 20-mm capability, because the radar-guided surface-to-air missiles and antiaircraft artillery used by the enemy required electronic countermeasures (ECM) equipment. The only place to install such equipment in the A-4C and A-4E was in the gun ammunition bays. The ECM "black boxes" were so large that they left no room for the ammo cans, which normally held two hundred rounds per gun. So that we wouldn't completely lose 20-mm capability, chutes that held about forty rounds per gun were installed on either side of the gun bay. This gave us about two short bursts or one medium burst before we fired dry, but it was better than nothing.

"Flying Eagle Lead, Hillsborough, orbit the Da Nang zero-eight-zero for twenty-five. We have nothing for you at present. Will keep you informed, over." Apparently it was a slow day in I Corps—the military designation for the northern part of South Vietnam and the southern part of Laos. The bad weather extended south as far as we could see; we were still flying on top of a solid undercast.

Other flights were also checking in for target assignments. Soon a number and variety of airplanes were flying holding patterns all around the Da Nang TACAN. After about thirty minutes of holding, Hillsborough called: "Eagle Lead, Hillsborough, fly to the Da Nang two-nine-zero for sixty miles and contact Spotlight for a combat sky spot mission. You will be joined by all available Hillsborough control flights, over." Commander Quaid acknowledged and headed us for the Spotlight vector. Spotlight was a ground-controlled intercept radar site whose mission of directing fighters to intercept hostile aircraft had been modified to direct radar-controlled bomb drops. They claimed a one-hundred-foot circular error probable accuracy, meaning that at least 50 percent of the bombs they directed would hit within one hundred feet of the intended target. Spotlight normally controlled the big B-52 bombers on their high-altitude "Arc Light" bombing missions. Essentially we would be performing an Arc Light mission today.

The DMZ between North and South Vietnam was anything but demilitarized in 1967. North Vietnam had long used the DMZ as a route for supplies intended for the Viet Cong and NVA forces in the South. So the U.S. Military Assistance Command (MACV) divided the zone into grids, and each grid was systematically carpet bombed until the area resembled the back side of the moon. Enemy forces or matériel that tried to infiltrate the DMZ were likely to be caught by this random bombing. Anyone on the ground in Spotlight's selected target grid would receive no warning. The thick blanket of clouds would block the sound of the airplanes twenty thousand feet overhead. The ground would just suddenly begin to erupt in bomb explosions.

Other flights joined us as Commander Quaid led us to the Spotlight vector. By the time we contacted Spotlight we were a formation of five divisions. VA-76's division of four A-4Cs, the "Spirits," had joined first, being very close to us in the holding pattern. A division of A-6 Intruders from the USS *Enterprise* joined on our right, and a division of Marine F-4Bs from Da Nang joined on the left. The last four-plane division to join was a flight of F-105 Thunderchiefs from their base in Thailand. I was struck by the novelty of flying in a formation of so many different airplanes as I glanced around the flight.

Spotlight began giving Commander Quaid small heading corrections and transmitting distance-to-drop information. A few thousand meters from the release point, Spotlight gave us the command to arm our switches. I reached down, flipped the station select switches to the armed position, and turned the master arm switch to "arm." The bomb release button on the stick was now "hot"—bombs would fall if I pressed it—so I made sure to keep my thumb clear of it until the right time. A bombing sequencer device was supposed to control the bomb release, and I selected "ripple pairs" on the sequencer. I dropped the bombs in pairs from opposite stations to keep the airplane balanced; the two Mark-81s first, then the Mark-82s, one from each TER, until all were dropped. Theoretically, the pilot need only press and hold the bomb pickle and the sequencer would do the rest, but the devices were notoriously unreliable. I usually punched the bomb pickle four times just to make sure all the bombs had been dropped.

As we approached the radar-calculated point in space to drop our loads, Spotlight gave one final course correction to the XO and then transmitted: "Eagle Flight, stand by . . . stand by . . . stand by . . . hack, hack, hack." My airplane jumped as the bombs rippled off my wings. "Bombs away," called the XO as the flights peeled away from the formation to return to their various bases. Glancing back and down I could see the last of the dark bomb shapes disappearing into the clouds below. "Thank you for your assistance, Eagle Leader, and have a nice day," Spotlight bade us farewell. We didn't even get to see the bombs explode.

Back aboard the Bonnie Dick, I pondered the anticlimax of my introduction to war. The instrument approach and landing were the most exciting part of the whole experience. I had been expecting maximum SAMs, MiGs, and antiaircraft fire, and not a shot had been fired at us. Such is war—full of surprises and never quite what you expect. My second mission would prove to be a bit more exciting.

<hr />

The weather improved over the South during the night, but it was still no go over any of the targets in the North. I was scheduled to fly as number two in a four-plane division with CAG, Cdr. Jack Monger, leading. CAG, the acronym for "commander, air group," was an obsolete term because air groups were now called "carrier air wings," but it sounded better than CAW. The air wing commander flew with all the squadrons in the air wing and was therefore qualified in all the different types of aircraft in the air wing. I was a little awed by CAG, but he seemed like a nice guy in the briefing. We launched in sunshine at the ship, but thick monsoon clouds began just off the coast and covered North Vietnam as far as we could see. I was the last airplane to rendezvous, and I concentrated on making a snappy join-up to look sharp for

CAG. All joined, we headed directly for Dong Ha TACAN, which was only ten miles south of the DMZ.

This time we got an immediate assignment when CAG checked in with Hillsborough. "Eagle Lead, Hillsborough. Meet Covey Three-one at the Dong Ha two-six-zero for fifty on two-fifty-six point four." As CAG rogered the assignment my pulse quickened; this time we would be working with an airborne FAC. The "Covey" and "Nail" FACs flew light, unarmored observation airplanes designated O-2s by the Air Force. These Cessna 336 high-wing, propeller-driven aircraft were called "push, pull" planes because they had two engines, one mounted in the nose and a pusher mounted behind the cabin. The only weapons the O-2s carried were two wing-mounted rocket pods, one slung under each wing. Each pod carried seven 2.75-inch-diameter high-velocity ballistic rockets (HVARs). The HVARs had a twenty-pound warhead filled with white phosphorus explosive that detonated with a dense white smoke cloud that the FACs used to mark the targets they wanted the fighter bombers to hit. Patrolling the supply trails that the North Vietnamese and Viet Cong used for resupply was a dicey mission. The relatively slow little Cessnas were easy targets for light-machine-gun fire. The FACs relied on surprise and agility for survival, and the pilots who survived became quite adept at darting in to mark a target and then directing the fighters waiting overhead to plaster it.

"Covey Three-one, Flying Eagle, over," CAG Monger called as we approached the fifty-mile fix on the Dong HA 260-degree radial.

"Roger, Flying Eagle, Covey Three-one. Go ahead, over," the FAC answered right away.

CAG gave him our lineup by side number, our weapons load, and time available on target.

"Rog, Eagle, talley ho your flight. The target is some bunkers I suspect the Gomers are using. There's fresh tracks leading into this grove of trees, possible trucks parked in there. The target is ten miles west in the vicinity of the old plantation airfield at Tchepone. No ground fire observed, but there could be ZPU or ZSU in the area as well as twelve point seven-five stuff, so watch it. Suggest left-hand racetrack eight thousand overhead with east to west run-in and left pullout, multiple runs, correcting between, over." Covey gave us the target info as we approached the Laotian border.

Tchepone was an abandoned jungle airstrip that had once been used by French rubber planters in the area. It was located on a major intersection in the North Vietnamese supply route the American forces called the Ho Chi Minh Trail after the leader of North Vietnam. Tchepone was a jumping-off place for infiltration across the South Vietnam border. Red dots on our maps indicated that antiaircraft fire had been seen there in the past, but there were no recent reports of it. The ZPU and ZSU that Covey cautioned us about referred to tracked vehicles resembling small tanks. The ZPU mounted twin-barrel 23-mm machine guns, and the ZSU had a quad mount of four barrels. The guns were sometimes radar guided. These tracked guns often escorted North Vietnamese truck convoys as they traveled south to drop-off points where the Viet Cong picked up their loads. Orbiting the target area at eight thousand feet would keep us well above the maximum effective range of these guns, and if we observed any ground fire we would be in a position to attack and suppress it.

"Eagle, check eleven low," Covey called as we approached Tchepone.

"Tally, Covey," CAG Monger called when he saw the little Cessna orbiting below us.

"Eagle, give me a ten-second interval, fly right over me, I'm rolling in to mark with Willie Pete."

CAG had us in right echelon and gave me the kiss-off signal. Ten seconds later on my elapsed time clock I kissed off the second section and broke left to follow CAG on the downwind leg. "Check switches, Eagles," CAG called as I rolled wings level behind him. I reached down and flipped the master arm switch to "arm" and turned all the station select switches to "arm" except for the number three station, which was my centerline fuel tank. I caught a flash of sunlight off the canopy of the tiny Cessna far below and to my left as he pulled up from his smoke rocket pass.

"Oops, there's some wind down there. I hit a little short, Eagle. Put your first two bombs a half klick west of my smoke," Covey called as CAG started his roll-in. I watched CAG diving on the small white puff of smoke, timing my run for ten seconds behind him. As I reached the roll-in point, CAG's first two bombs, the two Mark-81s that were on the outboard wing stations, which we always dropped first, exploded in the jungle with dark red flashes and black smoke.

"Good hits, Eagle Lead. Two, put your first two about fifty meters south of Lead's," Covey called as I began my run while CAG pulled up sharply, rolling left for the downwind leg. I tried to guess how much was fifty meters in the dark green jungle canopy below. I settled on a bit more than a pipper width and concentrated on holding a good thirty-degree dive, scanning my airspeed needle as it climbed toward 450 knots and the altimeter spun down toward thirty-five hundred feet, the planned release altitude. My thumb pressed the bomb pickle as the desired speed and altitude came together. The cockpit got a sharp jolt as the A-4 suddenly became five hundred pounds lighter. I felt a *thump . . . thump!* as the bombs released. Thump, thump? I thought as I began pulling out in the recovery. Did I drop three bombs instead of two? I wondered as I checked my switches.

"That was an airburst," someone transmitted. "He's hit," somebody else said. "Who's hit?" I asked. "You're hit, Eagle Two," came the reply. Me . . . hit? How? That was damn good shooting if they hit me that fast, went through my mind as I quickly scanned the cockpit gauges for trouble. The fuel gauge, decreasing rapidly, caught my eye. "Everything looks OK except that I'm losing fuel pretty bad," I transmitted.

Suddenly, CAG Monger slid into parade position on my left wing. "Hold your heading, Steve. I'm going to look you over," he transmitted. I felt my airplane shoved gently up as CAG's airplane slid beneath me. Sliding back into position on my left, CAG tapped his helmet and pointed to himself, indicating that he was taking the lead. "Are we cleared to jettison here, Covey?" CAG called the FAC. "Yeah, Eagle Lead, that's a clear area. Go ahead and dump," Covey responded. I began thumbing the bomb pickle switch as I watched CAG's bombs rippling off his wings. We dropped the bombs armed to keep the enemy from recovering the duds and making them into land mines or booby traps.

CAG looked at me and gave me a drinking motion with his thumb pointing toward his mouth, signaling for my fuel state. The fuel gauge had stopped unwinding at eleven hundred pounds, about thirty minutes' flying time, which was the capacity of the fuselage fuel tank. This meant that I had lost all my wing fuel and my external tank fuel, but the fuselage tank was undamaged. From this point on, I was referred to in the third person.

"Eagle Three, you take the section and continue to work with Covey. I'm going to take Eagle Two to NKP," CAG transmitted. NKP was the identifier for Nakhon Phanom, a small U.S. air base on the Thailand-Laos border.

"How about Da Nang?" someone asked.

"Nah, the weather's too bad at Da Nang, and he only has about a thousand pounds of fuel," CAG answered.

"How about a tanker?" Covey asked.

"I don't think he can tank. He's got a hole in his refueling probe," CAG responded. I glanced quickly out at the refueling probe and saw jagged metal surrounding a four-inch gash about halfway to the nozzle.

"Ah, Eagle Lead, Naked Fanny only has five thousand feet of PSP," came from Covey, who had staged out of there from time to time. PSP, or "pierced steel planking," described the steel planks that could be hooked together to build a temporary road or runway. In other words, the runway at Nakhon Phanom was too short for my airplane.

CAG answered, "That's OK, Covey. I think he's going to have to make a wheels-up landing. He's got a lot of holes in his undercarriage and I don't think he'll be able to get his gear down."

Oh, dear Jesus, I thought as my anal sphincter spasmed. I was beginning to be scared as the seriousness of my plight unfolded. The prospect of sliding to a stop on my belly tank on a short, steel-planked runway was not encouraging.

CAG had been steadily climbing us to the west while these exchanges took place. Passing through twenty-five thousand feet I lost my communication and navigation radios. The electronic equipment bay had been holed, and the gear wouldn't work unpressurized. We finally leveled at thirty-five thousand feet, and CAG looked over and again signaled for my fuel state. "Five hundred pounds," I signaled back. We had long since flown off any maps I had of the area, so I had no idea where we were. The weather had improved from scattered clouds below us to clear skies, and I glimpsed a large river far below that I later learned was the Mekong, the border between Laos and Thailand. Finally, CAG signaled that we were starting down and I gratefully pulled the throttle back to idle for the descent. The J52-P8A engine used very little fuel during an idle descent, so I would have a little fuel left for the landing.

When the gauge showed a little less than three hundred pounds, CAG pointed down and I saw to my delight a huge concrete runway, at least ten thousand feet long, shining white against the green and brown ground. Descending through twenty thousand feet I got my radios back and discovered that we were talking to approach control at Udorn air base in Thailand. They were giving me a ground-radar-controlled approach even though the weather was good and I had the runway in sight. It felt good to have the controller talking me down even though I didn't need it. Reaching short final, I put the gear handle down to see if the gear would come down. Sure enough, all the gear functioned normally and I got "three down and locked" indications. I was breathing easy now. The landing was normal. The fuel gauge showed two hundred pounds, about five minutes' flying time. Piece of cake.

A jeep with a Follow Me sign led me to a parking ramp. I climbed out of the cockpit onto a work stand—Udorn didn't have a ladder that fit the A-4—and examined the damage to my airplane. The A-4 looked like it was bleeding to death. Fuel and hydraulic fluid leaked from dozens of holes. A large piece of shrapnel, about four inches in diameter, had imbedded itself in the wall of the starboard engine intake. But it wasn't from ground fire; it was a chunk of the nose of one of my bombs, which somehow had exploded just after release. A subsequent investigation found a faulty lot of fuses that had to be pulled from inventories Navy-wide. As I examined the damage I refused to let myself think how close I had just come to death. I could have died several different ways. If the shrapnel in the intake had penetrated the second metal wall into the engine, I would have had to jump out of the airplane right in the target area. If its trajectory had been just a little forward, it could have easily come through the cockpit, killing me instantly. If the shock wave had been close enough to detonate one of the five-hundred-pounders, I would have come to a very spectacular end. But it didn't and I didn't, so there was no sense dwelling on it.

CAG landed after me and decided to remain overnight (RON). He would have had a hard time making the last recovery at the ship, and he didn't want to upset the cycle. He also wanted to see that I was taken care of and make arrangements for the repair of the airplane, arrangements that would be difficult for a green ensign on an Air Force base to accomplish.

Our arrival caused quite a stir among the Air Force contingent, which was an advance element sent to prepare for a massive buildup of the base. The ten-thousand-foot runway I had been so delighted to see was a very recent addition. Prior to its construction, the base at Udorn had been a small Air America operation with a small asphalt runway. The U.S. military buildup in Southeast Asia had destined it to become one of the major fighter bomber bases for the U.S. Air Force, and frenetic construction was under way all over the operations area. Air Force Base Operations didn't quite know what to do with us. There was only one naval officer assigned to the base, a commander who was naval liaison to the Air Force general commanding the base, so logically we were given to him to host. Commander Buck arranged for us to stay in downtown Udorn at the Udon Tani Hotel. The troops at the base were sleeping in tents because barracks construction had not yet begun.

CAG would be flying his A-4 back to the ship in the morning, but I would have to wait nearly a week to catch the weekly C-130 shuttle airplane to Da Nang, where I could catch the mail helicopter back to the ship. Meanwhile, Commander Buck promised CAG that he would look after me. Actually, I presented quite a few problems to Commander Buck. All of the A-4s in our squadron were equipped with a "special weapons"—meaning nuclear—control cable installed in the centerline bomb rack. This cable was classified Secret, as was the ECM gear installed in the gun bay. Provisions had to be made for the security of this gear until I could escort it back to the ship. Also, the local citizens of Udorn might be uncomfortable if I wore my .38 pistol to town, so we needed storage for it as well.

After dining at an excellent local restaurant where I had my first taste of incendiary Thai food, CAG and I were taken to the hotel. It was something straight out of an old Peter Lorre spy movie, with rattan furniture and old, slowly turning ceiling fans. I wouldn't have been surprised to see a cobra on the veranda. CAG departed early the next day, and Commander Buck helped me secure some funds to buy a change of clothes. We had been trained to "sterilize" ourselves before combat missions, carrying only our military ID and Geneva Convention cards. No wallet, no pictures of family, no wedding ring—nothing the enemy could use against us should we be captured. So I had no money and just the Nomex flight suit and boots I was wearing. Commander Buck guaranteed a counter check for me to cash at the O club so that I could get a civilian shirt and trousers and a few changes of skivvies.

The commander's main job was to read message releases and prepare a briefing for the general on the Navy's actions on the previous day. This task took only a few hours of the day, so Commander Buck had a lot of free time. He had a friend, a retired Navy commander, who was a contract pilot for Air America. Commander Buck took me over to this man's "pad," a very nice house in the Air America compound in town.

Air America, the CIA's airline, had been operating out of the Udorn airport for several years, dating back to the early days of U.S. involvement in Southeast Asia. They flew a wide variety of missions, from mundane transport of people and supplies to clandestine insertion and retrieval of Special Forces agents deep into communist Pathet Lao– and Viet Cong–controlled areas. Accordingly, they operated a wide range of airplanes, many specially modified for their particular missions. The entire Air America operations area was enclosed in a twelve-foot-high corrugated iron fence with a huge double gate that swung open on the taxiway to allow their airplanes onto the airfield. Most of their operations took place at night, and many of their airplanes were painted flat black. I happened to glimpse some of the exotic aircraft parked in their area one day when the gate was partially open while we were driving by, and I was very intrigued.

The Air America housing compound in Udorn was surrounded by a high stone wall topped with broken bottles and glass shards imbedded in concrete. Anyone who tried to scale that wall without special protection would have their hands and arms cut to shreds. A Thai guard toting a sawed-off double-barreled shotgun and sporting a bandolier stuffed with double-ought buckshot shells patrolled the entrance. Air America was very serious about security. Commander Buck introduced me to his Air America pilot friend, who welcomed us to his home. The house was very large by Asian standards, having a large living room downstairs and several bedrooms upstairs. The downstairs sported a large and well-stocked bar, a state-of-the-art stereo system, and teak furniture. Two stunningly beautiful Thai girls about nineteen years old, whom the pilot called his "housekeepers," silently padded about serving delicious hors d'oeuvres and authentic Thai sticky rice snacks and freshening drinks.

Commander Buck took me to several parties there, and the guests included Special Forces Green Berets who were in town on R&R from "in-country," their euphemism for enemy-held country. They were young, about my age, and some were younger than I. They were sent alone into remote areas to enlist the aid of Montagnard tribesmen to form counterinsurgency forces against the Communists, whom the tribesmen hated. I sat enthralled, listening to them casually discuss operations against the enemy. These men didn't brag, and they exchanged ideas and told of actions as casually as I would discuss flying with my squadron mates. I couldn't imagine myself doing what these men did, and I wondered if I would have the courage to do the things they so casually described. I felt as if I had fallen into a *Terry and the Pirates* comic strip.

On Friday, 6 March, Commander Buck helped me load the two ECM black boxes and the special weapons cable onto the C-130 shuttle that would take me to Da Nang. I thanked him again for taking such good care of me and promised to write, which I always meant to do but never did. I never saw him again, but I wished him good fortune in my mind. The several-hour flight to Da Nang on the lumbering C-130 gave me ample time to think on the surprising fortunes of war. I had been in the combat theater for two weeks, and all I had managed to do, as far as I could tell, was to bomb some clouds and blow myself out of the sky. Combat was turning out to be nothing like I had expected.

Brave smiles for the camera hide the pain of imminent departure. (Author's Collection)

506

30 OCT 1962
CO. COMD'R.   L. JACK SHI
                AND
        PETTY OFFICERS
U.S. NAV. TRA. CEN.   SAN DIEGO, CALIF.

U.S. NTC SAN DIEGO

The author, just left of company flag, learning boot camp leadership. (U.S. Navy)

Newly minted petty officers 3rd class. The author is front-row center. (U.S. Navy)

U.S. Naval School, Pre-Flight Class 39-64. (U.S. Navy)

The author in the T-2 "Buckeye" primary jet trainer. (Author's Collection)

The author's mother pins "wings of gold" on her son. (U.S. Navy)

Overhead view of USS *Bon Homme Richard* (CVA-31) showing the angled flight deck.
(Naval Historical Center)

Surface view of "Bonnie Dick" showing the hurricane bow.
(Naval Historical Center)

Rampant Raider pilots after an awards ceremony in the Tonkin Gulf. (U.S. Navy)

VA-212 junior officers of the IB&T (Iron Bombers & Tankers)—pilots too junior to fly the more glamorous "Walleye" Missions. From left: Terry Rieder, Mark Daniels, Al Crebo, Charlie Ohrenschall, Wiley Decarli, Joe Gatewood, Chuck Laskey (on wing), Davey Wolf, Steve Gray, Billy Putnam. (Author's Collection)

The author posing for his cruise book photo. (U.S. Navy)

The author just prior to the Zuni rocket strike on the barge in Cape Buton, resting his hand on one of the two rocket pods loaded on the triple ejector rack. (Author's Collection)

Centerline bomb rack camera captures bomb hits on the Phu Ly bridge complex. Note the smoke rising from prior hits on antiaircraft gun site at lower center. (U.S. Navy)

Cdr. Homer Smith, right, and Lt. Tom Taylor just prior to the first "Walleye" drop on the Sam Song barracks. Note the "Walleye" loaded under the wing. (Courtesy of Peter Mersky)

"Walleye" strike aircraft manned and ready. (Courtesy Peter of Mersky)

Tom Taylor taxis out for "Walleye" launch. Note Walleye under the right wing.
(Courtesy of Peter Mersky)

Lt. (jg) Al Crebo mans plane number 225 before the fateful April 25 strike on
the Cat Bi ammo storage area. (Courtesy of Peter Mersky)

Al's stricken Skyhawk, with fuel streaming from holes in the left wing. (Taken by Lt. Tom Taylor)

Massive damage to Al Crebo's A-4 caused by a direct hit from a North Vietnamese SA-2 "Guideline" surface-to-air missile. Note the access panels popped open from the force of the concussion. (Taken by Lt. Tom Taylor)

Al Crebo struggles to keep his Skyhawk flying. Note the missing rudder and damage to the vertical stabilizer. The main landing gear wouldn't extend due to buckled wing plates. (Taken by Lt. Tom Taylor)

LSO platform. Al Crebo, standing behind the duty LSO, talks to "Pri Fly" via telephone. (Courtesy of Peter Mersky)

Bomb rack camera records hits and secondary explosions in the Luu Trong "suspected" POL storage area. This is where the author marked the aim point for the strike group by bombing the river. (U.S. Navy)

More hits. Note the A-4s recovering from their bomb runs in the foreground. (U.S. Navy)

Air Wing 21 strikes oil. (U.S. Navy)

"Shrike" antiradar missile used in "Iron Hand" missions. (Courtesy of Rich Mylar)

MK 109 fuse installed in MK 81 general-purpose bomb. Note the fawnstock clips securing the arming wire through the fuse's propeller. (Courtesy of Rich Mylar)

Ordnanceman loads 20-mm cannon belted rounds. (Courtesy of Rich Mylar)

Bomb damage assessment photo showing the runway north of Vinh cratered by bomb hits. This runway was sometimes used by North Vietnamese MiG fighters. (U.S. Navy)

Rampant Raider preparing for launch. (Courtesy of Peter Mersky)

Catapult launch. (Naval Historical Center)

12

Baptism by Flak

The day after I returned to the ship from Udorn I was back on the
flight schedule. During my absence, the weather in the lower route
packages of North Vietnam had improved enough to allow several
sorties to bomb their primary targets. This day, though, we headed for Hillsborough because the weather over Route Package 2 was socko again. Route
Package 1 was fairly clear, and this time Hillsborough assigned us to a "Fast
FAC" in North Vietnam. The Fast FACs were Air Force F-100 Super Sabre
fighter bombers used in Route Package 1 because the antiaircraft concentrated there was far too potent for the slow Cessnas to survive. ZPU and ZSU fire
was common in Pack 1, as was heavier stuff such as 37-mm and even some
57-mm guns. The Fast FACs' call sign was "Misty," and the Flying Eagles
would work with them a lot and develop a good rapport.

This day we bombed a suspected truck and troop concentration area, but
all I saw were some badly blasted trees and bomb craters on the jungle floor.
Misty wanted to hit this area with all he could get, so he must have seen activity of some kind. He even asked us to strafe with our 20-mm guns in the hope
that we might inflict further damage. We didn't racetrack this target because
Misty had reported some light antiaircraft fire earlier. Instead we split into
two sections and made runs from alternating directions. We didn't see any
return fire, but there could have been some. This was the first time I had fired
my guns in a war zone, and I thrilled at the opportunity to do some shooting.
All of us fired out our forty rounds in one pass. Pilots are not supposed to
observe their strafe hits because a ricochet might bounce high enough to

reach the airplane, but everyone wants to see how well they shot, and I held the run until I could see my shells hitting the ground. We alternated high-explosive incendiary (HEI) bullets with armor-piercing incendiary (API) bullets. One out of every five shells was a tracer round, so I saw only eight of my rounds in flight, but they sparkled and twinkled among the blasted tree trunks as they detonated. We were moving far too fast to see much on the ground, and I sure didn't see any evidence of the enemy down there.

The skipper, Cdr. Homer Smith, was leading the division this day, and when we had expended all our ordnance with Misty he split the division, giving the second section leader directions to return to the ship while his section did a little road reconnaissance. Right about then I really began to question the wisdom of having the junior pilot—me—protecting the senior man's wing. We split off due north, flying ever deeper into North Vietnam completely unarmed while the skipper checked out some targets we had been unable to hit earlier due to the bad weather. I felt as if we were poking a grizzly bear's den with a stick! The farther north we flew the more marginal the weather became. We were flying about three thousand feet above the ground, jinking side to side and vertically to make fire control tracking as difficult as possible, while we scanned the roads below searching for signs of activity. Reluctantly, the skipper finally called it off due to the worsening weather and we headed out to sea to return to the ship. I felt a great sense of relief as I saw the coastline slide under us and we called "feet wet" to Strike Control on the ship. I boltered my first pass at the ship and had to go around again, much to Commander Smith's disgust. He chewed on me a little in the debriefing, stating that he wanted the Flying Eagles to look better than that at the ship. The skipper hardly ever boltered because he used a little go-for-it maneuver of cutting power and dipping the nose when he passed the ramp. It gave the LSOs heartburn, but it generally snagged him the 2-wire.

The CAG LSO, who had been on the platform and graded the passes, heard the reproof and gave the skipper an OK pass in the debriefing, then took me aside. "Your skipper has been getting away with that shit for a lot of years," he said, "but don't you try that or you'll bust your ass. You just keep making those power-on passes, and don't mind a bolter once in a while. Your first pass was a piece of shit, you were up and down through the glide path all the way down, and you pulled your nose up to correct for the fast [speed] you were carrying at the ramp, and that caused you to float over the wires. The second pass was a lot better. You settled down and flew an OK three. I agree with your skipper that the Flying Eagles look better than that, and you better try harder if you want to shine with this bunch." Properly chastened, I headed for the wardroom and chow. I had just gone from an intrepid unarmed recon of North Vietnam to getting my ass chewed for screwing up a carrier landing. Such is the life of an ensign.

A few nights later, one of the destroyers patrolling off the coast of North Vietnam caught a large, motorized junk towing a big barge. The junk was hugging the coast, hoping that the radar clutter from the coastal mountains would hide it from U.S. radar. The destroyer spotted it, though, and took the junk under 5-inch gunnery fire. The junk cut loose the barge and fled for cover up a small river whose mouth formed a small bay and a peninsula known as Cape Bouton. The barge ran aground on a sandbar in the middle of the bay and was a sitting duck. The destroyer lobbed a few rounds of 5-inch fire into the area from time to time to keep the North Vietnamese from sending small boats out to unload the barge but couldn't destroy the barge because the terrain around the bay shielded it. The Flying Eagles were given that task.

Because the weather in the area was still up and down, our airplanes were loaded with 5-inch Zuni ballistic air-to-ground rockets. We could make a much shallower delivery with the Zunis than with bombs, which required a thirty-degree dive maneuver and therefore a much higher ceiling. The Zuni was a big rocket with a hundred-pound warhead. We carried them in four-shot pods and normally fired them one at a time. This day each airplane carried twenty-four Zunis, three pods per side, one on each outboard station and two on each TER. The pods were all set on "pairs," meaning that we would fire two rockets from each pod with each shot, and thus twelve Zunis with each squeeze of the trigger! When fired, the Zuni left the airplane with a *whoosh* and a roar and a lot of smoke. I couldn't imagine firing them twelve at a time! The skipper was leading the division with me in my usual spot as number two. We expected that the North Vietnamese had moved mobile antiaircraft artillery around the bay knowing we would send planes to attack the barge, so we briefed for one run, expending all our rockets by firing twice in the run. A sharp 250-foot karst hill sat right on the tip of the peninsula, and we decided to split the sections, with the skipper and me rolling in from the northeast side of the hill on a southwest run-in and the second section attacking from the south side of the hill on a north run-in. Both sections would break toward the Gulf during the pullout. The second section planes would give us thirty seconds to clear the target and to allow the smoke from our hits to begin to dissipate before beginning their runs.

We were the second launch of the day, and all the Spads and the "Willie Fudd," a radar surveillance E-1B with a large radar dish mounted on top, were already airborne. These airplanes normally remained aloft four to six hours at a time, so the deck had a lot more room to spot us for a fast launch. This allowed an overhead rendezvous, and within a few minutes the Flying Eagles were joined and en route to the target, which was only about ten minutes' flying time away. About twenty miles out Commander Smith kissed off the second section for their split and dropped us to about two hundred feet off the water for our run in. Streaking over the water at five hundred knots, the skipper began a sharp pull-up for our twenty-degree dive just before we reached the line of breakers rolling up on the pretty white beach.

On reaching the top of the pull-up, the skipper rolled his belly toward me as he began his target run. I delayed my roll-in slightly so that I would approach from a slightly different direction and make my own tracking pass. As I delayed at the top of the roll-in, I could see all of Cape Bouton Bay and the barge aground in the center. It was a pretty sight, and I thought the spot would be a great setting for a resort. I began my roll-in, banking sharply left and dropping my nose as I pulled the gun sight pipper to the barge. Below me and to my left, a tremendous flash of fire followed by a second flash marked the skipper's shots. The first of his rockets were exploding on the barge when I squeezed the trigger. *Whoom!* The airplane jumped and the outside world was completely obscured by the smoke from my first shot.

Emerging from the smoke, I had to push negative Gs to reestablish a tracking run. Flashes of exploding rockets, smoke, and huge gouts of water from near misses completely hid the barge. I put the pipper in the middle of the maelstrom and fired again. Another *whoom*, again obscured by smoke, but this time I continued the positive G onset to help pull out of the dive. Jinking left, I rolled up to watch my hits and was disappointed to see the barge still there after the smoke and water spray cleared. I had hoped that the barge was loaded with fuel or ammunition and we would see it detonate in massive secondary explosions. No such luck. Whatever the barge was carrying was not explosive or flammable. We would have to be content with having riddled the barge with holes and making it unusable.

I located the skipper's airplane and used the excess speed gained in the rocket run to cut inside his jinking turns and slide into position on his wing. Safely out over the Gulf once again, we performed a ritual "look-over" of each other's airplane, alternating the lead to allow each of us to slide beneath the other and examine it for damage. Neither of us saw any holes, so we loitered to allow the second section to join us. Their luck had been no better; they had simply added to the holes we had put in the barge. The entire attack had lasted only five minutes from start to finish. This was the farthest into North

Vietnam I had yet been, and I still had seen no return fire. I was slightly disappointed that all my missions so far had been unopposed. This would not be my final experience with the barge, though, and the next one would be different.

Two mornings later, on 9 March, events began to unfold that would expand to involve me. What occurred turned out to be one of the strangest capture episodes in the entire war—and one of a very few escapes of an American aviator captured by the North Vietnamese. The details were related to me second- or third-hand from several sources, so my description of what transpired is probably inaccurate in some of the details, but the gist of what happened is as close to the truth as memory allows it to be.

An RA-5C Vigilante medium bomber converted to photo reconnaissance was trying to acquire new intelligence on several new targets in Route Package 4. At this time—March 1967—President Lyndon B. Johnson had designated an area thirty miles in diameter around Hanoi and fifteen miles in diameter around Haiphong as no-fly zones. Indeed, most of the targets identified by the various services' target planning staffs in the northern route packages required specific approval from the president before they could be hit. It was part of his gradual escalation of pressure on the North Vietnamese government. The bad weather had prevented recent recon flights over these targets, and the Vigilante was trying, still in very bad weather, to get photos by flying very low. The Vigilante carried a crew of two: a pilot and a radar navigator. They were hit hard by ground fire over one of their last targets, very close to the coast, and the pilot immediately zoom-climbed them up into the thick cloud cover. Things got very bad very fast in the airplane because of massive systems losses. They had time only for a couple of quick maydays before they were forced to eject. The pilot, Cdr. Charles L. Putnam, was never heard from again. His remains were returned by the Vietnamese in 1988. The radar navigator's parachute opened in the clouds, and as he drifted down he prayed that he was coming down over the waters of the Gulf.

Swinging gently in his parachute harness, the radar navigator, Lt. (jg) Francis S. Prendergast descended through the cloud base about three hundred feet from the surface. He felt a rush of relief as he saw nothing but water below. His relief was short-lived as he realized the danger of drowning attendant with parachuting into the water. He released his seat pan, which contained a one-man life raft, and quickly did a mental review of water survival procedures. All set to release his parachute canopy as soon as he hit the water, to prevent becoming entangled in the shrouds and having a submerged canopy drag him under,

Prendergast splashed down. He was shocked when his feet thudded into the mud bottom slightly less than waist deep. His parachute canopy, still inflated by a ten-knot surface wind, was threatening to pull him off his feet, so he released the Koch fittings that attached the risers to his torso harness and allowed the canopy to collapse. His second shock came when he looked toward the shoreline and discovered that he was only about forty yards off the coast of North Vietnam. Turning the other way, he stepped clear of the lanyard securing the now inflated one-man life raft to his seat pan top. The raft was tugging at the lanyard, which had wrapped around his knees. He took off his helmet and saw a small sandbar about two hundred yards farther out in the Gulf. He decided to make for the sandbar for pickup by the rescue helo and checked his PRC-10 survival radio to make sure it was broadcasting its locator beeper signal. Having decided to keep the life raft with him in case the water was deeper toward the sandbar, he was trying to secure its lanyard to his torso harness when he heard a shout from the shoreline.

Prendergast's third shock hit as he looked toward the shout and saw three North Vietnamese men standing at the water's edge. They were clad in the ubiquitous black pajamas worn all over Indochina. One of the men, probably part of some local militia, was armed with an AK-47 rifle and was pointing it roughly in the center of his chest. He really had no choice. There was no sign of rescue, and the AK-47 made it plain that resistance was not a good idea. Prendergast meekly put his hands up. The man with the rifle and a companion waded out to apprehend him, leaving the third man on the shore. Gesturing for him to keep his hands over his head, the North Vietnamese talked excitedly. The unarmed one reached out and relieved Prendergast of his .38 service revolver. Aiming the revolver at him with one hand, the Vietnamese frisked him with the other, discovering the wallet that contained Prendergast's ID and Geneva Convention card. These he handed to the man with the AK-47, who motioned for Prendergast to start walking toward shore.

The *Bon Homme Richard* was in the process of launching a sortie when the mayday from the RA-5C came over the guard channel in Strike Ops. Four Spads from VA-215, the Barn Owls, were given the mission of providing rescue combat air patrol (RESCAP) for the rescue helicopter that was being launched from the north search-and-rescue (SAR) destroyer. It was the Spads' job to locate downed airmen by homing on their survival radio beacon and ascertain if it was safe for the rescue helo to come in for the pickup. If ground fire became a threat to the rescue, the Spads carried eight Mark-82s plus four 20-mm cannons each to suppress the ground fire. Homing on Prendergast's radio beacon, flying low over the water to stay under the three-hundred-foot overcast, the Barn Owls' skipper, Cdr. George A. Carlton, led his flight of four Spads right over the little tableau of three stick figures in the muddy water below.

The roar from the R-2800 engines in the four Spads thundered by directly over Prendergast's head, so close that he felt as if he could reach out and touch them. The effect frightened the man with the AK-47 and he dived underwater, rifle and all. The other militiaman still held the .38 on him, but he was watching the Spads in obvious fear. Prendergast knew that he hadn't loaded the .38 before launching on the mission. On impulse, encouraged by the sudden appearance of the RESCAP, he performed the most desperate act of his life. Reaching under his survival vest, he pulled a tiny two-barreled .22 derringer from its concealed holster, stuck it right in the face of the man covering him with the unloaded .38, and shot him dead, right between the eyes. About this time, the Viet with the rifle came up from his submerged hiding place. Somewhat dazed by what he had just done, Prendergast hit him hard on the top of the head with the butt of the derringer and struck out for the sandbar. Now waist deep in the water, he couldn't move very fast and had put only about ten yards between himself and his would-be captor when the man recovered from the blow to his head and began raising the AK-47. Prendergast had been fumbling with the tiny pistol, trying to reload it as he struggled through the water. He had just succeeded in inserting another .22 bullet in the fired barrel of the break-open pistol and snapping it shut when he saw the AK-47 coming to bear on him. He stopped and fired both barrels at the Viet. The barrels of a derringer are only about an inch long and have no sights, so its maximum accurate range isn't much over a foot. But the sight of it succeeded in scaring the man enough that he again dived for safety under the muddy Gulf water.

Prendergast began trying to run again and gained a few more yards toward the sandbar. The Viet was just surfacing again when the Barn Owls made another low pass trying to contact the downed pilot and see what was going on down there. The North Vietnamese submerged once more, allowing Prendergast to progress a few more precious yards toward the sandbar. The water had deepened to chest high, and he was half swimming, half wading. He had given up trying to load the derringer and was concentrating all his effort on making it to the sandbar. The sound of the Spad engines receded into the distance and he heard the Vietnamese shout once more. He turned and the militiaman had the AK-47 leveled at him again; why he never fired is still a mystery. Prendergast again had no choice; he stopped in the chest-deep water about fifty yards from his would-be captor and raised his hands. Barn Owl Leader, finally understanding what was going on, fired a short burst of 20-mm shells a few yards in front of the Vietnamese. It was a tenet of combat rescue efforts to try to avoid killing hostiles on the ground if possible. If it wasn't possible to prevent the capture, at least the prisoner wouldn't be facing someone whose brother or father or son had just been killed.

This burst of fire was the clincher for the would-be captor. The capture of the downed American had seemed so simple a few minutes earlier, but with one of his company dead and the one who had remained ashore having fled when the Spads showed up, the capture suddenly wasn't worth it anymore. The North Vietnamese exercised the better part of valor and departed too. The rescue helo swooped in and plucked Prendergast, who was by this time standing on the dry surface of the sandbar.

The war was now over for him. He couldn't be sent back into combat, for he was now officially a war criminal. The Geneva Convention clearly proscribes the killing of an enemy guard during an escape attempt, calling it murder and therefore subjecting the escapee to the laws of the country in which he was being held and removing him from the status of POW. Presumably, the fleeing North Vietnamese militiaman had retained his ID and Geneva Convention cards, and technically he could be termed an escaping prisoner. Should he ever be recaptured he could be tried as a war criminal with all the attendant propaganda that would entail. But before the Navy Department reassigned him to duty outside the Vietnam theater of operations, he was sent to tour the carriers on Yankee Station to brief all the combat pilots on his experience. Of course, the question most frequently asked of him was why he didn't also shoot the guy with the AK-47 as he came above the surface within arm's reach. His answer was, "Look, gentlemen, I am just like the rest of you, raised in comfortable surroundings eating my mom's good cooking. I have never before killed anyone, much less shooting someone between the eyes at close range. I was somewhat stunned, aware that I had done a terrible thing, but I didn't have time to think about it. When he came up, I just reacted, slugging him. Thinking about it, yeah, I should have shot him too, and I guess I'm just lucky he didn't shoot me." Prendergast received the Navy Cross for his courageous escape.

Someone in the rescue helo or in the Barn Owl flight had reported that the tail of Prendergast's RA-5C was sticking out of the water close to the shore. The downed Vigilante was loaded with all sorts of classified gear that the Navy didn't want to fall into enemy hands, so the Flying Eagles were sent to destroy its remains. The three-hundred-foot ceiling made a retarded drop necessary, so we were loaded with Snakeye bombs. We were to break up into sections to search for the Vigilante, and the wingmen were to fly a tight parade position, dropping their bombs when the leader pickled his. Commander Smith was leading, and I was in my usual number two position. We searched for more than an hour, skimming the water under worsening weather, sometimes getting as low as a hundred feet in a futile attempt to find anything resembling the tail of an RA-5C. A conical channel buoy marked the river channel through the sandbars, and the skipper assumed that the RESCAP had mistaken it for the tail of the Vigilante.

Disappointed, we headed down the coast. Not being the type to simply jettison bombs and return to the ship, Commander Smith decided that we would drop them on the remains of the barge still aground in Cape Bouton Bay. We would make individual section runs again, at about one-minute intervals, with the wingmen flying tight on the leader and dropping when he dropped. It would still be a very shallow bomb run because the ceiling was around a thousand feet in the Cape Bouton area. The skipper was using the A-4's crude onboard navigation radar to paint the coastline and the 250-foot hill on Cape Bouton. We popped up and entered the cloud deck. I was flying as tight on the skipper as I dared, with our wing tips nearly overlapping. His airplane was just a dim shape in the clouds, and I strained to see the formation visual cues on his A-4. We popped suddenly out of the clouds, and almost immediately the sky was filled with little glowing red balls. How pretty, I thought, as the balls drifted past in the space between our airplanes; and then I realized that this was antiaircraft fire and it was close! The skipper gave me an urgent hand signal to move forward on the bearing line because he was afraid that his number five Snakeye would hit my wing tip when we dropped. I had just banked away slightly to make the correction when the bottom of the skipper's airplane seemed to blow apart. It was the Snakeyes coming off and the tail fins extending. I punched my bomb pickle eight times to make sure that all my bombs released, and we did a tight, hard left turn toward the open sea. The antiaircraft fire stopped suddenly as we flew beyond the guns' range. I looked back and was astonished to see that the barge had totally disintegrated! All that remained was a column of black smoke surrounded by the small splashes of falling debris. The second section had to drop on the spot where the barge had been because there was simply nothing left.

Flying back to the ship, I thought about having finally seen hostile fire directed at me and realized with a slight chill that there were probably four bullets between each tracer that I had seen. Some of the tracers had been within a foot of our airplanes. Antiaircraft fire would become the rule rather than the exception on our missions, though, and I would soon come to view this encounter as nothing very significant.

The weather continued its steady improvement, with the worst weather retreating slowly northward as the winter monsoons abated. Going south to Hillsborough was becoming the exception as more and more of our targets in the lower route package areas of North Vietnam opened up. Our mission was defined as the interdiction of supplies flowing into South Vietnam to support the Viet Cong insurgency. Along with strikes on hard targets, we were assigned armed reconnaissance missions that we called "road reccies." The road rekies were target-of-opportunity hops; we would fly up a designated road segment looking for something to hit. These missions were not very effective in 1967 both because our range of acceptable targets was heavily constrained by the rules of engagement that controlled what we could attack and because the road segments were much too long for the extremely close scrutiny necessary to spot camouflaged truck parks or fuel dumps.

The Johnson administration was extremely sensitive to adverse press reports generated by the propaganda released by the North Vietnamese. Accordingly, many White House press releases publicized our restraint in North Vietnam. For example, they stressed that all our targets were strictly military. We were forbidden to attack villages, elephants, water buffaloes, or any other domestic animals unless they were "directly engaged in logistics support of the enemy." Our attacks had to be conducted to eliminate the possibility of inadvertently hitting a civilian area if our ordnance missed the designated target. Now, the North Vietnamese were not stupid, and they took full advantage of this widely reported tactical restraint. We subjected ourselves to increased hazard by planning our attacks so that any misses would not hit undesired areas. The North Vietnamese would position their antiaircraft guns along likely attack paths based on this knowledge, and sometimes villages would conceal gun or missile sites.

The amount of hard physical labor required to support our operations was amazing. We were conducting flight operations twelve hours a day, flying from noon to midnight for a week, then switching to midnight to noon. This meant that flight quarters lasted about fourteen hours a day. After each day's flight operations, the ship's stores needed either an ammunition or a commissary restock. These underway replenishments, or "unreps," were conducted while the ship was steaming on station. A supply ship would come alongside, lines would be passed, and the line handlers on each ship would haul trolleys loaded with pallets of either ammo or commissary stores from the supply ship to the carrier. Unreps lasted three to four hours each day. Once the supplies had been unloaded on the hangar deck, other working parties had to stow the bombs in the magazines or carry the food stores to the galleys. This required a few more hours of hard work. Throw in a four-hour watch, and it was routine for a sailor to perform hard labor for twenty-four hours straight and get only a few hours of sleep before his next on-duty period.

Most of the work performed on the flight deck during flight operations was physically hard as well. Pushing airplanes into position, tying them down, carrying chocks or tie-down chains, scurrying under moving aircraft to attach a catapult bridal, and connecting firing leads to ordnance were only a few of the jobs flight operations required. But by far the most physical of all the hard work was performed by the various squadrons' ordnance men. There was no room on the flight deck for the hydraulic bomb-loading trucks that the Air Force and Marine Corps used ashore. With the exception of a two-thousand-pound-bomb, which was so heavy that a bomb dolly had to be used to load it, all ordnance was loaded by hand, even the thousand-pound Mark-83s. Some of these bombs had to be hoisted shoulder high to fit the bomb lugs into the bomb rack hooks. Threaded iron bars would be screwed into the nose and tail fuse receptacles in the bomb, six to ten men would lift and strain to get the bomb up into position, and one would guide the lugs into the hooks in the bomb rack. This operation was repeated eight times per airplane, for four to six airplanes per squadron per launch, for eight to ten launches per day. By the end of the line period, the ordnance men were beginning to look like Mr. Universe contestants!

Attack Squadron 212 had been given a plum assignment during the training period before this cruise: to conduct the combat operational evaluation of a new weapon code-named "Walleye." The Walleye was the first of the so-called smart bombs. A fire-and-forget weapon, it guided itself to the target. The pilot could release the weapon and go on to other things. Once launched, the Walleye was on its own. I think the term "smart bomb" was coined by one of VA-212's pilots, Charlie Ohrenschall, who used to delight us with a characterization of the admiral upon hearing of the Walleye. "What? A bomb ... that can see?" The Walleye was a television-guided glide bomb with the television camera mounted in the nose. The large glass lens of the camera made up the nose of the bomb and gave the weapon its apt name. The bomb was about five feet long with four highly swept back wings that had control tabs mounted on their trailing edges. A ram-air turbine whose propeller was mounted in the tail of the bomb provided internal electrical power. Inside the cockpit, the pilot viewed the image produced by the camera in the bomb's nose on a small TV screen that replaced the terrain radar. The bomb was designed to see only a tiny portion of the picture within a four-mil gate formed by the intersection of a double set of crosshairs. The bomb's guidance system was designed to lock on the area of the target with the highest contrast.

James Reed, a civilian technical representative from the Walleye's manufacturer, had been assigned to VA-212 to provide support during the operational evaluation. Himself a civilian pilot, Reed fit in well with the squadron
pilots and was considered a member of the squadron. Jim had been fussing
with the Walleyes since the beginning of the cruise, waiting for the weather
to improve enough to begin the tests. The weapons selected for the operation
evaluation had been fitted with data link transmitters to allow transmission
of the image seen by the bomb all the way to impact. The data link transmissions would be recorded by a videotape recorder installed in an empty drop
tank carried by a chase airplane. This was new technology back then; video
recording was still in its infancy. The videotape was three inches wide, and the
recorder was the size of a console TV. Jim had set up one of the video record-
ers in the ready room with its own TV set so interested observers could watch
the Walleye test drops.

A fortunate break in the weather on 10 March allowed the first of the
Walleye combat operation evaluation drops to be scheduled against a military
barracks near the village of Sam Son. The barracks was a three-story concrete
building resembling an apartment complex. Located on the coast of North
Vietnam just south of the mouth of the Song Ma River, Sam Son was chosen
as the first target because the run could be made from seaward and would
allow time for any needed adjustments in the delivery or with the data link
without harassment by enemy antiaircraft fire.

The Walleye camera was gyro stabilized but would bob and weave in
response to changes in the aircraft's flight path. A steady, smooth delivery run
was thus necessary to lock the camera on the target. To avoid lineup corrections once the delivery run was begun, the Walleye airplane would slide in
trail behind another airplane on the way to the target and carefully lock the
camera on the tailpipe of the leading airplane, then note the position of the
tailpipe in the gun sight and mark the spot with a grease pencil. In the initial
stages of the roll-in, the pilot would place the grease pencil dot on the target,
then shift his scan to the television picture and make very minor corrections
to lock the camera on the target. Flying a stable run and mustering the concentration required to lock the camera on the target while under fire required
nerves of steel.

Weapon acceptance tests by the Navy had shown that while a very
accurate weapon, the Walleye did not have the standoff range that the manufacturer had advertised. This was because the weapon was designed to search
for the highest area of contrast on the target, and sometimes it would shift
its lock-on point during its flight. For instance, when a bridge was the target,
the weapon was apt to lock onto the shadow the bridge cast on the riverbank

because that presented a higher contrast than the bridge structure itself did. The result was a near miss. The only way to keep the weapon from seeing areas of higher contrast was to bore in closer to the target until the four-mil target gate showed only the desired impact area. Delivered in this fashion, the Walleye was a 100 percent bull's-eye weapon.

The skipper and his chase pilot with the recorder pod returned from the Sam Son mission reporting success with the first combat drop. The Walleye had hit the target and collapsed most of the building. We all crowded into the ready room to see the data link videotape recording as Jim Reed hurriedly threaded it into the recorder. The picture, though somewhat grainy, was very clear. At weapon release, the barracks building, made of whitish concrete, was clearly visible; the weapon was locked on a black area surrounded by a whiter background. As the weapon flew closer to the target, the black area became more distinct and proved to be a window opening shaded by an overhanging ledge. The Walleye flew right through the window. The picture disappeared as the camera smashed into the structure a few nanoseconds before the weapon exploded. The effect of the Walleye's 750-pound warhead exploding inside a concrete building was devastating. The first Walleye strike was an unqualified success.

—————

The weather continued its slow improvement, although we still had to divert to Hillsborough for target assignments in Laos or South Vietnam from time to time. When we were able to get into North Vietnam, the Bonnie Dick was frequently only five to ten minutes from the target, and we would hit the target and be back overhead in as little as half an hour. The ship couldn't recover us until the next launch was complete, so we sometimes had an hour or more to kill before we could land. We utilized this time to sharpen our flying skills. Sometimes we would split into two sections and meet head-to-head in mock combat, or sometimes the fighters would jump us or vice versa and the fight would be on! When fuel or lack of opponents was a factor, the division leader would put us into diamond formation and we would fly formation acrobatics. Looping and barrel rolling in formation is exhilarating. Watching the world roll around the formation out of your peripheral vision while maintaining your precise formation position demands skill and concentration. It was a beautiful and satisfying exercise in excellence.

The end of our first line period came finally on 25 March, thirty days after beginning combat operations. It was high time for a break from the frenetic pace of operations on the line. We were all very tired, and some of the men—especially the flight deck crews—were getting the "thousand yard stare" of cumulative fatigue. Stumbling around the flight deck in a stupor was certain to get a man killed sooner or later, and the crew needed a break. Coupled with the relief from the heavy demands of operations on the line was excitement in anticipation of the upcoming in-port period. Several days in Sasebo, Japan, would be followed by a four-day cruise to legendary Hong Kong. I had been hearing stories of the fantastic bargains available in Hong Kong since the RAG, and Alma had provided me with a "wish list." Before we could enjoy the exotic atmosphere of foreign ports, though, we still had work to do.

Constant exposure to salt spray and ocean flying conditions made corrosion control on our airplanes an ongoing battle. All the squadrons maintained a beach detachment at Cubi Point NAS in the Philippines, and the first order of business on leaving the line was to set up a schedule to rotate all our airplanes through the corrosion control facility ashore. Some of the men would miss Sasebo, but a schedule had been arranged to rotate the Cubi beach detachment back aboard so that all hands would get to enjoy Hong Kong. After launching the airplanes to Cubi Point, though, another difficult and odious task remained.

Air Wing 21 was an integral part of the nation's Strategic Integrated Operational Plan (SIOP) in the event of nuclear war. Because the requirements for maintaining nuclear war readiness were incompatible with conventional war efforts on the line, each carrier was relieved of its nuclear responsibility while on the line. But as soon as the ship left the line, it resumed its SIOP duties. All carriers were required to conduct a certain number of nuclear weapon loading drills. Because of our line period, the Bonnie Dick was way behind in those drills, so we had to spend the next two days catching up. All the attack junior officer pilots had been sent to nuclear weapon loading school as part of our RAG training, and we were all designated loading officers for the drills, which were a huge pain in the ass.

A detachment of U.S. Marines provided security for the ship's nuclear weapons, and they performed their duty with typical Marine Corps dedication. Marine armed guards were posted on the flight deck and hangar deck for the loading drills, and they denied access to anyone who did not have a nuclear weapons loading badge. It made no difference to them that none of the thirty-five hundred sailors on board posed a threat to the security of the nuclear weapons; orders were orders, and it became nearly impossible to leave the forecastle without a loading badge because that required crossing the hangar deck. A great many weapon loads had to be performed to meet the requirements, and loading occurred nearly nonstop for two days.

The ship had two dummy weapons on board for loading drills, real weapons except for the absence of a nuclear warhead. The dummies had to be treated as if they were the real thing, and heaven help any loading crew that dropped one or scratched one or botched the electrical hookups. If a dummy weapon was damaged in any way, it had to be sent for repairs to Sandia Corporation, the manufacturer of all the Navy's nukes, and the hapless loading crew could stand by for a court martial. Two dummy weapons weren't nearly enough to conduct all the loads required, so we used real weapons for most of them. Everyone was uptight during the drills, and it was a huge relief when they were concluded with no mishaps.

The Sasebo in-port period dragged a bit for me after the first couple of days. The huge, sprawling port not only had U.S. Navy facilities, it was also one of the main bases for the Japanese self-defense force navy. Across the bay was a large maritime port facility. Although the in-port period provided a much-needed break from the pace of line operations, young bodies and minds recover quickly, and after the first two days we began to get restless. We quickly developed a pattern of shopping or sightseeing during the day, then repairing to the O club bar and drinking far too much every night. We collapsed into our bunks in the wee hours to recover through sleep from the damage we had inflicted on our bodies so that we could repeat the process the next day. Even though we had made port in Japan on our way to Vietnam, I still found it exotic and wonderful. I enjoyed mingling with Japanese society and browsing through the quaint little shops. I found the Japanese people delightful with their culturally ingrained politeness, civility, and industriousness.

Money presented a problem, however. In an effort to prevent U.S. currency from flooding the local economy and replacing the local money as the preferred medium of exchange, U.S. military facilities accepted only military scrip as currency. These military payment certificates (MPCs) were worthless off the base because at random intervals the military would declare the current MPC invalid and issue new scrip. It was impossible for Japanese citizens to exchange MPCs for yen. So to have spending money on the base, we had to convert U.S. dollars to MPCs, and to have money to spend ashore we had to convert dollars or MPCs to yen. This could be done only at the base's disbursement office during very limited hours on odd Tuesdays—or some scheme equally inconvenient—so we all tried to estimate our expenses ashore and converted only that much money.

Fabled Hong Kong was to be the high point of the cruise. Forty-eight hours after leaving Sasebo the *Bon Homme Richard* dropped anchor in Hong

Kong Harbor—well, almost in Hong Kong Harbor. We were a good five miles out from the waterfront because the inner harbor was much too congested, cramped, and shallow to accommodate a vessel the size of the Bonnie Dick. The steep terrain of the Hong Kong skyline gave the impression that we were much closer, but it was a forty-five-minute boat ride to the docks. Because I had the duty when we dropped anchor, I would have to wait a day before sampling the pleasures of Hong Kong.

I had stood the squadron duty officer (SDO) watch only a few times before. Basically a glorified telephone watch while in port, the SDO represented the commanding officer and handled any problems or assignments that came the squadron's way. At sea during flight operations, and especially in combat, the SDO's job was much more involved and required experience and good judgment. During flight and combat operations the SDO had to coordinate the use of the squadron's airplanes with Flight Deck Control and Strike Operations, notifying them of changes in the launch lineup. He made sure that the ordnance chief was aware of the load orders from Strike Operations and that the ordnance loads were proper for launch, and he informed the pilots what they would be carrying and where it would be loaded on the airplane. I was much too green to be doing that. Terry and I had been told that we would be added to the SDO watch bill now that we had one line period under our belts because that made us "veterans."

The water taxi service began at 0845 the next morning, and I was aboard for my first look at Hong Kong in a light drizzle. Fog and rain obscured the skyline, and the passengers had only the dark gray water of the harbor to look at until we were within a mile of shore. The much smaller British aircraft carrier HMS *Victorious* was anchored much closer in than the Bonnie Dick, and her men had only a twenty-minute boat ride ashore.

Hong Kong was all the things I had been told to expect—exotic, mysterious, and dangerous. Many areas of the city were off limits to U.S. military personnel, and I heeded the warnings. But the shopping was fabulous! Clothes, dinnerware and fine china, silverware, wooden goods, exquisite handicrafts and art, silks, cashmere sweaters, shoes, cameras, just about everything anyone could imagine could be bought for one-third to one-half its cost in the United States. Consumer goods indigenous to China such as ivory, teak, and jade required a certificate of origin to prove that they had not come from Communist China. We didn't want to give the Communists the money to buy antiaircraft shells to be shot back at us!

All the squadrons in the air wing had rented hotel rooms that we called "admin rooms" where we could freshen up and leave our purchases until we were ready to return to the ship. VA-212's admin room was in the prestigious

Hong Kong Hilton. The one-bedroom suite had only two beds and a small sitting room and cost the princely sum of forty-five U.S. dollars per night. All the officers chipped in to rent the room, and although few of us slept there, it was very nice to have a place to rest up and stash goodies between shopping forays and while waiting for the water taxi to the ship.

Ens. Terry Rieder had spent a hard day shopping, diligently filling wish lists for friends and relatives and having several of the famous "Hong Kong suits" tailor-made for himself. Terry was determined to finish as much of his shopping as he could this day because the word was out that a typhoon was in the offing for Hong Kong and we might be pulled out of port early. He left his purchases in the admin room and joined several shipmates in the bar to quaff a few before the water taxi arrived. While satisfying the powerful thirst he had developed during his arduous shopping trip and enjoying the camaraderie of his shipmates, Terry lingered a bit too long in the Hong Kong Hilton bar and arrived on the quay about two hundred yards too late to catch the water taxi to the Bonnie Dick. Unwilling to wait ninety minutes for the next taxi, Terry inquired in pidgin English among the various craft bobbing along side the quay and discovered a sampan skipper who would take him to the ship for a fee not much higher than the regular water taxi fee.

Terry made himself comfortable in the stern sheets of the sampan after directing the boatman to "take me to the aircraft carrier." The bobbing motion of the sampan coupled with the fatigue of shopping and the several beers hastily downed in the bar made Terry sleepy, and he suddenly found himself awakened by the boatman shaking his shoulder. The sampan was banging against the steel side of the ship. Terry groggily thrust a handful of Hong Kong dollar notes into the boatman's hand, gathered his packages, and made the jump to the gangway. He had to concentrate on climbing the slippery, steep ladder to the quarterdeck holding his packages in one hand and the chain rail of the ladder in the other. As his eyes cleared the level of the quarterdeck, he became aware that something seemed amiss. The OOD was wearing shorts! A thick British accent asking, "Good afternoon, mate, and what might we be able to do for you?" confirmed Terry's horrified realization that this was not the Bonnie Dick at all; it was HMS *Victorious*! His instructions to the sampan boatman had not specified which aircraft carrier, and the boatman had simply taken him to the nearest one.

Terry's fears that arriving on the quarterdeck of a vessel of a foreign power, in civilian clothes and half in the bag, would cause some kind of an international incident were quickly relieved when the British OOD turned him over to some *Victorious* pilots who were delighted to have a U.S. Navy flier visit. They took him to the wardroom, which had a bar! (alcoholic beverages are forbidden on U.S. naval vessels) and for three hours treated him to all the alcohol he could pour down his throat before arranging for a boat to deliver him to the Bonnie Dick. A message sent later to our skipper that Ensign Rieder was a "delightful chap" and had contributed to the continued good relations between Great Britain and the United States prevented any disciplinary actions. This was not the last time that Terry's unfortunate waif act would return benefits.

The Bonnie Dick weighed anchor early on 12 April and set course for Subic Bay. Throughout the off-line period a niggling thought in the back of our minds told us that along with the steady improvement in the weather over North Vietnam as the winter monsoon retreated northward would come increasingly intense combat. We had mixed emotions about this, realizing that with increasingly important targets we would face much tougher enemy defenses. But now it was time to return to war.

We spent a short, busy two days docked at the carrier pier at the Cubi Point Naval Air Station replenishing stores and loading ammunition for the coming line period. Three new officers joined the ship when we docked at Cubi Point: Cdr. Fred Whittemore, who would become the new XO when Skipper Smith left and our current XO, Commander Quaid, became the new CO; Lt. Cdr. Pete Yonkey, who was already assigned to VA-212 but had missed the beginning of the cruise due to back surgery; and Lt. (jg) Bernie Smith, U.S. Naval Academy class of 1964, a new pilot.

The ship departed for Yankee Station on 16 April. I was detailed to fly an airplane that had just completed corrosion control at Cubi Point out to the ship after she had cleared harbor. It was the first time I had flown in twenty-one days, and I was amazed at how rusty I felt in the landing pattern. The Navy required a FCLP period if a pilot had not made a carrier landing within the last thirty days, and I fully understood the wisdom of that as I made my pass at the deck. I was acutely uncomfortable but I landed safely, and I soon regained my proficiency. The Bonnie Dick arrived on the line the night of 17 April and resumed strikes against the People's Republic of North Vietnam the next morning.

13

Alpha Strikes

The improvement in the weather meant that most of our strikes were in North Vietnam, with only a few diverts to Laos or South Vietnam. The Johnson administration had been opening up previously restricted targets for us to hit. These targets, ever closer to Hanoi and Haiphong, were much more heavily defended than the truck parks, highway bridges, and suspected POL storage areas that had made up the bulk of our targets until now. Indeed, many of our earlier targets had been undefended or offered only light resistance. The more important, and therefore more fortified, targets required a more concentrated effort, and the entire air wing would work in concert against these targets, attacking in "alpha strikes."

In an effort to punish the North Vietnamese and force them into peace talks, the Johnson administration had decided to attack the industrial capacity of North Vietnam by depriving it of electrical power. One of the first such missions was an attack on the Thanh Hoa thermal power plant located in Thanh Hoa, just south of the Song Ma River. VA-212 was assigned the bombing role in the attack and would target six bombers on the power plant. VA-76, VF-211, and VF-24 would provide the flak suppressors; and VA-212 and VA-76 would provide two aircraft each for the antiradar mission, designated "Iron Hand." The fighter squadrons would provide a section each for purely fighter combat air patrol (CAP), which could be enhanced by the flak suppressor F-8s if the need arose. We didn't expect much in the way of MiG opposition, but this strike was farther up into North Vietnam than we had been going and we were not certain what we might face. Heavy Four (i.e.,

VAH-4) would have a KA-3 Whale for SAR refueling just off the coast, and the A-4 squadrons would have a tanker each overhead the ship.

The Air Wing 21 pilots assigned to the alpha strike assembled in the air wing briefing room two hours before the scheduled launch. With the entire alpha strike force assembled, it was standing room only as the CAG intelligence officer began the brief with the latest intelligence on which flak and SAM sites could be expected to be active, the most recent assessment of possible MiG deployments around Hanoi, and the deployment of available SAR forces. We received mission cards with the SAM and MiG code words of the day and copied down the mission radio frequencies on them. The meteorological officer briefed us on the weather expected at the target: nearly cloudless with a southeast wind at ten knots. Commander Quaid would be leading this strike, and he took over the briefing to discuss the strategy of the attack. The Iron Hand airplanes would fly two racetrack orbits at high altitude southwest and northeast of the target area pointing at the most likely SAM threat. They were to time their orbits so that one airplane would always be pointed at the threat area. The fighter CAP would take station on the Iron Handers, one section above them and the other below and in position to handle any MiG intrusion. The flak suppressors would split off and begin their runs on the suspected flak sites ahead of the bombers so that their ordnance would be exploding on the flak sites as the bombers started their roll-in. After a short question-and-answer session we adjourned to the various squadron ready rooms to brief our individual flights.

The XO, Commander Quaid, was leading the first division of six bombers; I would fly in my usual position as his number two. We looked at reconnaissance photos of the power plant to determine our aim points. The rectangular main building of the power plant housed the steam boilers and electrical generators and had two tall smokestacks at the south end. The XO and I would drop on the south half of the building, two airplanes would drop on the other half of the building; and the remaining two airplanes would hit the transformer distribution field next to the main building. Each airplane would carry three Mark-83 thousand-pounders, one each on stations two, three, and four. Because we carried a Mark-83 on the centerline rather than a four-hundred-gallon drop tank, we would have to refuel after the strike to have normal fuel reserves for landing.

After the briefing we had about thirty minutes before manning airplanes. Those thirty minutes were the worst time of the mission for me. This was the biggest effort we had made so far, and I was keyed up. We could expect much stiffer resistance than we had seen on previous missions. We had been very lucky until now, having not lost a single pilot in combat, and I wondered if our luck would hold. I spent the time checking out my personal gear—pistol loaded, PRC-10 survival radio working, survival vest and survival sheath knife checked—and then settled down to wait.

The launch went smoothly, with Commander Quaid leading the alpha strike formation on a large circle above the ship until everyone had joined. I was excited to be part of this great armada. We held the air wing formation for about fifteen minutes, until it was time for the various components to break off and start their runs. Elements continued to split off until our six bombers were alone. We could see the mouth of the Song Ma River on the coast as Commander Quaid dropped us low for our pop-up to the bombing roll-in.

We crossed the coast at thirty-five hundred feet over the river mouth and began jinking in formation. Quaid called, "Eagles, arm switches," as we crossed the coast, and I flipped the master arm and station switches on. So far, so good, I thought as we reached the pop-up point without seeing any flak. I watched Quaid's airplane turn belly up as he began his run. As I continued to wheel and climb to reach my own roll-in point, I was alone for a few seconds with an eagle's-eye view of the target area. Flashes of exploding weapons dotted the ground as the flak suppressors completed their runs, and smoke was rising from distant fires as I pulled the nose down and shifted my scan to the gun sight.

Picking up the outline of the power plant main building, I noted that the rising smoke indicated nearly calm wind, so no wind correction would be necessary. I put the pipper on the south half of the building and scanned the instruments for bomb release altitude, thirty-degree dive angle, and 450 knots air speed. At four thousand feet I punched the bomb pickle switch three times and felt the little plane buck and jump as the bombs came off the wings. As I pulled out of the dive, the rising Gs started the familiar restriction of vision as gravity pulled the blood supply away from my brain. I jabbed full down on the G-suit's inflation button and grunted against my diaphragm to try to keep as much blood as possible in my head. I had about a fourth of my normal field of view left as blackness surrounded my peripheral vision. I moved my head to keep the XO's airplane in my remaining field of view. My vision cleared immediately when I relaxed the G forces and pulled inside the XO's turn to join on him. I looked back at the target and saw that the power plant building was completely obscured by smoke and the last section's bombs were exploding in the transformer field. A few black puffs of flak burst to our right but were too far away to pose a hazard. I joined the XO's airplane and slid under him for the look-over. He was clean. He passed me the lead and gave me the look-over. I was elated! Either we had caught the North Viets napping or the flak suppressors had been really effective, because the few puffs of flak had been the only visible signs of resistance.

The recovery went smoothly, and I flew a good pass to a 3-wire. When we all assembled in the ready room we were ricocheting off the walls. Our adrenalin levels were still very high, and we were all regaling one another with details of our flights. The air wing flight surgeon entered the ready room with a tray of "lollypops," little brandy bottles the size of airline liquor bottles to be passed out to the strike pilots to help settle us down. This exercise and our elation would become a quaint memory later on when we were flying three alpha strikes a day. After debriefing with the air intelligence officers we were shown the results of the strike. A VFP-63 RF-8 photo pilot had made a supersonic photo recon run over the target about five minutes after the strike group retired. His photos showed the main power plant building to be cratered rubble, completely destroyed. One of the steam boilers had been blasted several yards outside the confines of the power plant yard, and huge craters pocked the transformer field. It would be a long time before Thanh Hoa had any electricity.

The Walleye operational evaluation strikes were going well, and the testing program was almost completed. The data link recordings of the Walleyes flying unerringly into their targets were enthralling. The weapon's star-shaped warhead had been predicted to be very effective in cutting the steel support girders on bridges, and the tests had so far borne this out. Walleyes had taken down several bridges, and the weapon was proving itself to be a very potent addition to our arsenal. The skipper decided to use the first purely operational weapons against the most famous bridge in North Vietnam, the Thanh Hoa Bridge.

The Song Ma River winding its way to the Tonkin Gulf had cut a 50-foot-deep chasm through the plateau on which the city of Thanh Hoa sat. A steel suspension bridge constructed by the French to bridge the gap was a critical point on Highway One, the main road linking North and South Vietnam. Many attempts had been made to drop the Thanh Hoa Bridge, but the bridge was immensely strong and had sustained several direct hits, some from two-thousand-pound bombs, with only superficial damage that the North Vietnamese had been able to repair. The bridge supports had been sunk deep into the rock of the chasm, and only a direct hit on these supports was likely to be effective. A miss of even inches would send the bomb to explode harmlessly in the deep chasm below. The pilots of the unit that succeeded in dropping the famous "Thanh Whore Bridge," as we called it, would gain fame and glory.

Cdr. Homer Smith, a U.S. Naval Academy graduate engineer, was determined to prove that a surgical strike against critical structural support points in the network of steel girders that supported the bridge would cause the bridge to collapse of its own weight. He had even constructed a scale model to help him analyze the strength of the structure. He had determined that if three sets of girders were cut nearly simultaneously, the bridge would fall. He assigned himself and two of the most experienced Walleye pilots to make the attack on the Thanh Whore Bridge. Of course, the attempt would require an alpha strike with emphasis on flak suppression since the approaches to the bridge were extremely well protected by antiaircraft gun sites. The Walleye delivery planes would be very vulnerable to antiaircraft fire during their runs because they had to maintain a very stable dive to lock their weapons on the precise areas of the bridge that had to be hit. This would be my first flak suppression mission.

We had recently been supplied with a new weapon to help in our flak suppression efforts—the container bomb unit (CBU). The CBU, which was about the size of a 750-pound bomb, contained three hundred hand grenade–sized bomblets. At about a thousand feet above the ground, the outer shell would split around its longitudinal hemisphere and open like a pea pod, distributing its load of bomblets. The bomblets were aluminum spheres with raised spiral ridges that caused them to spin during their fall. The spinning motion armed the bomblets, which would explode on impact. A layer of thirty-caliber-sized steel balls was tightly packed around the explosive in each bomblet. The exploding bomblets would unleash a lethal hailstorm of steel balls that would literally shred anyone or anything unlucky enough to be caught inside the CBU's football field–sized effect area. Some CBUs contained delayed action bomblets that would lie on the ground and explode randomly or when disturbed to hamper cleanup efforts after the strike.

In many ways this alpha strike was similar to the Thanh Hoa power plant strike we had made several days earlier except there were many more flak suppressors. I was in my usual position as number two in the lead flak suppression element of six A-4s. My target was a hard-riveted 37-mm gun site containing six guns that was south of the bridge and a little east of the road. We had recent photographs showing which gun sites were occupied, and my site was relatively easy to spot. I had six CBU bombs, three on each TER, slung under my wings.

The flak suppressors broke away from the Walleye group and began our run-in to the pop-up point. We were at thirty-five hundred feet, and I could see the outline of the Thanh Whore Bridge up ahead as we crossed the coast and armed our switches. Heart pounding and mouth dry, I could see the bridge clearly as we arced up and over to the bombing altitude. The lead pilot split off to begin his attack on his flak site, and I frantically scanned the area south of the bridge for my target. There! There it is, I thought as the first muzzle flashes from the guns outlined the site. The target was directly ahead of me at twelve o'clock, so I had to execute a roll-ahead maneuver, rolling upside down with the nose high and pulling the nose down until the target touched the top of the canopy bow, then rolling upright and finding the target in the gun sight. The site was winking with muzzle flashes as the guns poured out rapid fire. The flak gunners could figure out an attacker's intent just as soon as the airplane's nose aimed at them in the dive. At that point it became a them or you situation, and they would shift their fire to concentrate on the incoming plane. The easiest moving target to shoot at is a no-deflection shot. All the gunners have to do is aim straight at the diving plane. The flashes seemed to grow and merged into one continuous flicker as I got closer. White streaks of tracer flashed through the gun sight, and I could hear a staccato *pop, pop, pop* even through my helmet as the supersonic shock wave from near-miss bullets struck the canopy. On reaching release altitude, I punched the bomb pickle and felt the plane jump as the bombs came off the wings. I jammed the stick back and rolled hard left as soon as the nose came above the horizon, then hard right for a few seconds, then hard left again to try to destroy their tracking. Rolling left, I looked back to see my hits. I had missed seeing the bomblets explode, but little puffs of smoke and dust dotted the flak site, and the guns were silent. I never saw a flak site keep shooting after a CBU attack.

I was streaking toward the safety of the Gulf to rejoin the other flak suppressors when an ear-piercing, drawn-out, gurgling scream lanced through my headset. Jesus! I thought. Somebody caught one in the throat and is dying over the air. So chilling was that sound that I almost pissed my pants. The memory of the scream and the certainty that somebody had died lasted until the debriefing when the screamer was revealed to be none other than the skipper, Commander Smith, venting his rage and frustration at the Thanh Whore Bridge. The three Walleyes had struck almost simultaneously in the exact spots he had designated, but the bridge remained standing. Three black smudges on its girders showed where the Walleyes had hit. The good news was that everyone had once again made it safely back to the ship.

Charles Schulz's famous Peanuts cartoon character Snoopy was very popular at the time, and the next day a cartoon showing Snoopy flying his bullet-riddled doghouse away from the Thanh Hoa Bridge was hanging in the ready room. Snoopy was shaking his fist at the bridge, and the word balloon read, "ARRRRG, if there's one thing I hate more than a kite eating tree, it's a Walleye eating bridge!"

The intensity of combat operations continued to grow as the good weather allowed us to go after previously unavailable targets. We all knew that our good fortune in having no combat casualties couldn't continue, and on 24 April a harbinger of things to come occurred when Terry Rieder was hit by 37-mm antiaircraft fire. Terry's airplane was not damaged seriously, just a few holes, but it was some of the first battle damage we had incurred. Terry was a stocky man, and some squadron wag had nicknamed him the "Water Buffalo," or "Buff" for short. Terry didn't seem to mind the nickname until we found out that Buff was also the Air Force nickname for the B-52, and it stood for "Big Ugly Fat Fucker." After that, Terry tried to discourage the use of his new nickname, but of course it stuck. He had been over a small bay on the coast when he was hit, and we promptly renamed Cu Nham Bay "Buffalo Bay."

Later that same day, during an alpha strike, Lt. Cdr. Edwin B. Tucker from VF-24 took a hard hit from an 85-mm antiaircraft shell. His F-8C Crusader exploded, and he was forced to eject in a bad area. He had a good parachute but landed in the middle of a village and was immediately taken prisoner. Commander Tucker was Air Wing 21's first POW. The reality of one of our own being shot down and taken prisoner struck deep in our guts, because we all knew that it could be any of us at any time on any mission.

Although Congress had lifted the restriction on bombing the area around Haiphong at the request of the Johnson administration, the shipping in Haiphong Harbor and the dock areas remained closed to U.S. attacks. On 25 April the biggest show of the war so far was laid on. A plethora of new targets around Haiphong was to be hit throughout the day by all three aircraft carriers in the Tonkin Gulf. These would be the first strikes around Haiphong since the oil refinery strike during the 1966 cruise, and in the meantime the North Vietnamese had greatly strengthened the air defenses around the city. The morning strike was heavily contested. As Air Wing 21 approached the target, which was very close to a MiG base at Cat Bi airfield, a MiG-17 lifted off the runway and bored right up through the strike formation, squirting off an Atoll heat-seeking missile on his way through. The missile flew right up the tailpipe of an A-4 from VA-76 and blew the entire tail section off the airplane. No one in the alpha strike formation saw the pilot, Lt.

(jg) Charles Stackhouse, eject from the burning jet as it spun out of control into the ground. "Charlie Stackgas," as he was affectionately nicknamed by his squadron mates, was presumed to have died in the crash. Another long-awaited and much-dreaded threat materialized for the first time in Air Wing 21 experience: the SA-2 Guideline surface-to-air missile. VA-212 pilot Lt. Joe Gatewood, a slow-talking, humorous Mississippi boy whom everyone liked and whom we nicknamed, of course, "Gator," had a close encounter with a SAM and received moderate shrapnel damage to his airplane. The morning strike pilots returned with eyes wide and tales of MiGs and a sky full of "flying telephone poles," as the SAMs were called. In addition, every type of antiaircraft artillery North Vietnam possessed had been observed firing. I was flying on the afternoon strike.

Our target was an ammunition storage area just off the edge of the Cat Bi airfield. At this time in the war, even though the MiGs were becoming an ever-increasing threat, the Johnson administration would not let us hit the MiG bases for fear that the MiGs would begin to stage out of Red China, as the North Koreans had done in the Korean War. Until that policy changed, we would just have to deal with the MiG threat in the air. VA-212 would lead the strike with six bombers and four Iron Hand radar suppressors, our entire complement of available airplanes. VA-76 was likewise fully employed, with ten bombers. Ten fighters would provide flak suppression and fighter target combat air patrol (TARCAP). We would be carrying maximum bomb loads this day: ten five-hundred-pound Mark-82s, six on the TERs and four on a centerline MER. This meant we would have to refuel from a tanker on the way to the target in order to have normal reserves for the recovery. The XO, Commander Quaid, led the air wing briefing and the strike. We copied the SAM and MiG code words for the day and all the radio frequencies we might use on our mission strike cards. The *Ticonderoga* and *Kitty Hawk* air wings were hitting targets in the area just before we were to coast in but should be clear of the area before we popped up for our runs.

The run-in would be at three thousand feet, and we would coast in at the mouth of the Black River. Our initial point for the pop up to the bombing run was to be a bridge over one of the numerous tributary streams of the river. VA-76 would split off its element to hit a different target in the same area. After the air wing briefing we adjourned to VA-212's ready room for our own briefing and the signal to man airplanes. Commander Quaid would be in ship 220, and I was his number two in ship 221. Lt. Cdr. Arv Chauncey would lead the second section in ship 232, and his wingman was Lt. (jg) Davy Wolf in ship 233. Lt. Tom Taylor would lead the second element in ship 230; his wingman, our tail-end Charlie, was Lt. (jg) Al Crebo in ship 225.

After the briefing, the terrible waiting began. Frankly, I was very scared. The tales told about the morning strike proved beyond doubt that this would be our toughest mission yet. I tried to reassure myself with the fact that the target was very close to the water. Unless I was hit so hard that the airplane wasn't flyable, I should at least be able to make it out over the water before punching out. The ready room teletype began to clatter, struggling to send the command to man airplanes. As usual, the typing was a bit off. At the command PITONS, MAN YOUR PLAQUS, I grabbed my helmet bag and headed for the flight deck. Why was it that the damned escalator to the flight deck was always broken when I was most scared? Fear attached lead clamps to my legs. It was physically all I could do to make one foot go ahead of the other during the interminable climb to the flight deck.

Strapping in the cockpit after the preflight walk-around I was too busy to dwell on my fear. Just as soon as we started engines and the radios came to life, a transmission came over the guard channel. "Hallmark, Hallmark, Bravo Foxtrot Two, twenty-five sixteen fifteen, Petunia Four-Five, out." Petunia Four-Five was an EC-121, an old Super Constellation that the Navy had converted to a radar surveillance airplane with huge radar antennas both on top of the fuselage and underneath. We used to joke that the airplane had a swimming pool in the belly and the extension on top was a diving tower. Petunia's job was to detect SAM radar activity or MiG activity over North Vietnam while orbiting safely off the coast. "Hallmark" was the SAM code word for the day, and BF2 indicated the map sector in which our targets were located. The rest of the numbers were the date and Zulu time of the transmission. The guard channel frequency was always monitored by military radios and was on anytime the radio was. "Hallmark, Hallmark, Bravo Foxtrot Two, twenty-five sixteen seventeen, Petunia Four-Five, out," came over again as I taxied to the catapult for launch. Jesus, I thought, the Tico and *Kitty Hawk* must really be catching hell. Just after I launched and began the turn to the rendezvous the guard channel came to life again. "Hallmark, Hallmark, Bravo Foxtrot Two . . ." Alright, already, Petunia, I thought. Give it a rest! The transmissions continued sporadically until we finished taking on fuel and the strike group was headed toward the target. Petunia finally gave up and called, "Eagle Leader, this is Petunia Four-Five, be advised that your entire target area is Hallmark, over." Commander Quaid rogered and asked Petunia to forgo any further warnings. We were well aware of the threat.

As we approached the coast, one of our fighter escorts called bogeys at twelve o'clock. I glanced ahead and saw three black dots headed toward us on a collision course. "Bogey" meant that they had not yet been identified and were potential hostiles. MiGs! was my first thought. I had to resist the impulse to slide in closer to Eagle Leader for protection. Starkly aware of the vulnerability of my bomb-laden airplane in the face of a MiG attack, I could only hope that our F-8s could counter the threat. The three dots soon streaked over the formation. They were F-4 Phantoms from the *Kitty Hawk* coasting out after their attacks. Commander Quaid called, "Eagles, arm switches," as we crossed the coast. He began to lead the strike group in a slow side-to-side jink to foil any flak gunners tracking us as elements began to split off to their target assignments.

Our electronic countermeasures system included a small threat detector mounted on the glare shield that sounded a warning if the airplane was painted by antiaircraft radar or Fansong SAM radar. The former produced a high-pitched buzz in the headset and lit a red AAA light in the box. Fansong SAM tracking radar made a sound in the headset like a rattlesnake's rattle, and the box would generate a slow warble accompanied by a steady red light that read SAM. If the system detected L-band guidance radar, which the North Vietnamese used to guide the SAM into the radar beam that was locked onto the targeted airplane, then the slow warble would switch to fast and the red SAM light would flash. Just as we approached the bridge that was our initial point for the pop-up to the run-in, my threat detector lit up a steady SAM light and began its warning song: *deeduuldeeduul*. As we hit the initial point and started our pop-up, the light began to flash and the song became an urgent *DEEDUULDEEDUUL*. My heart jumped, and radio discipline, which was never very good in an alpha strike, went to hell. "*I got a SAM light!*" I broadcast blind, forgetting to identify myself. The light meant that the dreaded SAM was tracking *me*!

We had been told that a thirty-degree dive-bombing run was a sufficiently steep dive to foil a SAM's tracking radar. This day would teach us the fallacy of that bit of intelligence. All through the climb to roll-in altitude the deadly song continued in my ears. *DEEDULDEEDULDEEDUL*. It was with considerable relief that Eagle Lead and I reached roll-in altitude. Since I had ended up on the inside of the roll-in turn, the XO rolled toward me to start his run. I should have let him dive under me while I continued wheeling around the target to get more distance between us. I suppose the urgency of the SAM warning caused me to roll in early, and I ended up much closer than I would have liked to the XO's airplane during the dive. This error very nearly allowed the North Vietnamese to score a double with their SAM. Relief swept over me as I got my nose down in the run, thinking that the SAM couldn't get me now. I was only about two hundred feet behind the XO's airplane, scanning between his A-4 and the target, when I saw his bombs release. I pickled off my bombs just a second later, using his release point for my own.

We had just finished the pullout with our noses coming up to the horizon when a huge explosion ripped across my windscreen and the XO's airplane disappeared in a fireball and orange smoke. The SAM's rocket motor, which was still burning, spun right in front of me. I yanked back hard on the stick, putting who knows how many Gs on the air frame, and just missed colliding with it. My airplane flashed on through the debris from the exploded SAM and pieces of the XO's airplane and emerged to see Eagle Leader's A-4 enveloped in a cloud of streaming fuel and hydraulic fluid. "Eagle Lead, you're hit! Head for the beach," I transmitted. That was unnecessary because our run-out heading was toward the Gulf anyway. I received no response. I firewalled the throttle to join on the stricken leader and called him again on the radio; still no response. About this time my SAM detector came alive again and an 85-mm antiaircraft gun on a quay jutting out into Haiphong Harbor, close aboard on our left, took us under fire. We were so close to it that I was amazed that the shells had time to arm, but the black puffs of exploding flak bursting around us were proof that they did. The XO still wasn't responding to my calls, so I slid in for a closer look and saw him slumped forward with his head down. Shit, I thought, he's dead!

The SAM that had caused the second warning was flying level now, coming fast off our starboard quarter. As I watched it approach, Al Crebo, our tail-end Charlie on the roll-in, transmitted, "This is Eagle Six. I'm hit and I'm losing control." Fortunately, the SAM off our port quarter either ran out of steam or lost tracking because it nosed over and crashed into the water behind us and we flew out of range of the 85-mm gun. The XO's ram-air turbine (RAT), the backup electrical power source, flipped open on the side of his fuselage and began to spin, and I realized that the XO wasn't dead after all. The SAM hit had taken out his electrical power and he hadn't heard my frantic radio calls. In my concern for his condition I stupidly blurted out, "XO, do you know you're hit?" "Do I know I'm hit?!" he snapped back. "Yeah. How bad is it?" I slid in close and began to describe the damage I could see. The right wing and the fuselage aft of the trailing edge of the wing all the way to the tail were full of holes. He had lost all his wing fuel and hydraulic systems and was flying with the backup control system. A carrier landing in this condition would be dicey at best.

After I described the extent of his visible damage, we turned to join the rest of the Eagle bombers, who were clustered around what remained of Al Crebo's airplane. One of them looked me over because the XO's airplane was in no shape for him to fly formation on me. I was amazed to hear that I had no visible damage. How had I flown through all that exploding debris and flak and come out untouched? The fact that Al Crebo's airplane was still flying was even more astonishing.

About the time the first SAM hit the XO, Al Crebo was just about to start his roll-in. As he was the last to make his run, he had to hang up at the top of the roll-in waiting for enough separation from his leader. He was down to about 220 knots by this time, which made him a sitting duck for the SAM shooters. Needless to say, this flaw in our tactics and the pounding we took that day as a result caused some changes in Air Wing 21's future attack procedures. Al's slow speed rendered his deception jammer ECM equipment ineffective, and the SAM locked in on him. The missile must have exploded within feet of Al's airplane because the explosion flipped the little A-4 over on its back. When Al recovered from the effect of the explosion his nose was pointed at the target, so he elected to continue his bomb run. He began losing various airplane systems during his run-in, but he was able to punch his bombs off before he lost his internal electrical system. Just as his nose came up to the horizon, he lost his primary flight control system and the airplane rolled upside down three thousand feet above the ground. Now, the A-4 had a backup flight control system that was a direct cable linkage with the flight control surfaces. It was strictly a manual system with no hydraulic boost, and a lot of muscle was required to overcome the resistance of the air stream even at fairly slow flying speeds. The *Naval Air Training and Operations Procedures Standardization* manual (NATOPS) had a procedure for testing the manual flight control system. It called for the airplane to be in the landing configuration and on final approach headed straight for the runway (so no large turns would be required), with airspeed below 200 knots, before disconnecting the hydraulic boost. The control stick in the A-4C model could be rotated a half turn and then extended up an additional foot, giving the pilot better leverage to overcome the stiff resistance of the air stream. Al was doing more than 450 knots when his airplane rolled upside down out of control. He reached down in the cockpit, disconnected the primary system, and rolled the airplane upright. Later, he didn't remember that maneuver taking a lot of effort, but then again, his adrenalin was really pumping at the time.

The Flying Eagles gathered around Crebo's crippled airplane began to assess the extent of the damage. That it was still airborne defied imagination. The rudder was completely gone and only about half of the vertical stabilizer remained. The turbine section of the J52-P8A ended at the trailing edge of the wing, so the A-4 had a very long tailpipe. There were at least a dozen holes in Al's tailpipe, some of them large enough to see daylight through the other side. In fact, there were holes just about everywhere on the airplane except in the cockpit area, and the concussion from the SAM's detonation had popped open every access panel on the airplane. If the shrapnel that went through the tailpipe had hit in the cockpit area Al would surely have been killed. As it was, he was incredibly lucky; the shrapnel had come very close. Al's section leader, Lt. Tom Taylor, had a hand-held camera with him and took several photos of Al's airplane. Some of these were later sent to McDonnell-Douglas Corporation. One photo showing a side view of the airplane was blown up to sixteen by twenty inches and sent back to us. We hung it in the squadron ready room ashore as a tribute to the gutsy little A-4. If it didn't get shot in the engine and they couldn't blow it up, the A-4 would just keep on flying!

Al had no idea how much fuel he had left because the fuel gauge was inoperative. As we neared the ship, he decided to see what worked and if he should attempt a carrier landing. When he tried to lower the tail hook and landing gear, only the nose gear would extend. The wing plates were so badly buckled that the main mounts were jammed in the wheel wells. That pretty well decided the issue. Al would try to climb to ten thousand feet, the altitude NATOPS recommended for ejection, and punch out. He made it to six thousand before the engine finally flamed out from fuel starvation. Al grabbed the secondary ejection handle between his knees, pulled it up sharply, and became the first VA-212 pilot of the 1967 cruise to eject. He would not be the last.

The XO landed safely even with a manual flight control system, a feat of superior skill in airmanship. The rest of the strike force landed without incident. Later we learned that more than thirty SAMs had been fired at the air wing, but only two hit their targets. Nevertheless, the events of the day proved that the information we had used to develop our tactics was flawed. After further review, we decided to change our approach to the target to a higher altitude, using a twelve-thousand-foot roll-in and a forty-five-degree dive with a five-thousand-foot release. Our combat losses—two airplanes heavily damaged and one lost—had reduced our combat effectiveness somewhat. It would be a couple of days before I flew another combat mission because we simply didn't have enough airplanes to go around.

On 29 April the USS *Bon Homme Richard* enjoyed a singular event. Rear Adm. Vincent de Poix, ComCarDivSeven, transferred his flag to the Bonnie Dick and we became the flagship of the carrier division. The ship was given a day off from the war to celebrate, and we were treated to a barbecue on the flight deck. The fighter pilots still had to man a "launch five alert" in case the North Vietnamese air force decided to attack the Seventh Fleet, so they had to sit in the cockpits of two F-8s that were spotted on the catapults while the rest of us enjoyed the holiday all around them. They stood two-hour alert watches, though, so they also had a chance to enjoy some of the festivities. The mess cooks set up barbecue cookers in safe areas of the flight deck and began to roast large chunks of beef. Sailors engaged in games of volleyball and catch, and sunbathers lounged everywhere. It was a grand break from the frenetic pace of flight operations, and the barbecue was delicious.

The first day of May 1967 marked one of the most successful strikes of the war for Air Wing 21. The Johnson administration had finally agreed to let us go after the increasing MiG threat, but in typically timid fashion because they were still afraid that the MiGs would began seeking sanctuary in Communist China if we destroyed the MiG air bases in North Vietnam. We were allowed to use only "soft ordnance" that wouldn't crater the runways. The MiGs themselves, on the ground or in the air, were fair game. Air Wing 21 was given the MiG airfield at Kep, some forty miles northeast of Hanoi, as a target. Terry Rieder and I normally alternated on missions, and he was tagged for the Kep strike. Even though I knew this would be a very dangerous mission, I was a little envious of Terry. It was only fair, though; this would be Terry's first alpha strike, and I had already been on three.

The route the alpha strike took on the way to Kep was much farther north into North Vietnam than anyone in the air wing had ever been before. The force flew very close, and roughly parallel, to the Chinese border. It was a long drive in there, about ninety miles from the coast, but the mostly mountainous terrain was relatively sparsely populated, so there were few air defenses to worry about en route to the target. Terry was a flak suppressor on this strike, carrying CBUs. The airfield itself was heavily defended by antiaircraft batteries, so Terry and the other flak suppressors would have plenty of work to do. The strike group was nearing the target when the first flights of airborne opposition attacked the formation.

Lt. Cdr. T. R. Swartz, a VA-76 pilot, was also a flak suppressor this day, but he was armed with air-to-ground Zuni rockets. The Zuni was a ballistic weapon with no internal guidance or homing system. T. R. spotted a MiG-17 closing fast on one of his squadron mates in the bombing division. The MiG was almost in firing position, but T. R.'s frantic warning over the radio was lost in the babble of the excited voices of men in battle. He happened to be in a pretty good perch position on the MiG, so he rolled in just as he would have on a gunnery banner. T. R. had no idea how much to lead the MiG with a Zuni, but he tracked the MiG through the low reversal and fired off the first Zuni, intending only to scare the MiG away before it got off a shot at his squadron mates. T. R. was pulling three Gs or so, and the Zuni curved sharply away, far behind the MiG. T. R. yanked the nose of the A-4 hard ahead of the MiG, put the 100-mil ring of the gun sight on the canopy of the sleek little Russian-built fighter, slowed the airplane into a one-G flight, and fired the second Zuni. The rocket and the MiG arrived at the same point in space at the same time. The Zuni exploded just behind the MiG's cockpit, blowing the airplane into pieces, and T. R. Swartz became the first A-4 pilot in history to down a MiG, and the only A-4 MiG killer of the Vietnam War.

As the strike group approached the target, things got hot quickly. The TARCAP F-8 fighters were already engaged with MiGs swarming up from Kep to meet the attack. Terry Rieder had no trouble identifying his flak site because it was illuminated with muzzle flashes and took him under fire even as he started his roll-in. Streaks and flashes whizzed past the canopy and through the gun sight. Terry had never seen such a concentration of flak. A solid stream of fire seemed to be pouring from the guns fixed in his bomb sight pipper. He reached release altitude and punched off his CBUs, then pulled out hard and jinked right and left. Tracers continued to pour past him and over the top of his wing. Damn! he thought. The CBUs should have got them by now. He looked back down toward the flak site and saw a sight that chilled his blood. The flak site had indeed been silenced by his attack; the tracers were coming from the nose of a MiG-17 that was almost in parade position on his left side. Fire wreathed the nose of the MiG as a stream of 30-mm cannon shells hosed Terry's airplane. "This is Eagle Two. There's a MiG on my six!" Terry's panicked call cut through the babble of alpha strike chatter and came in clearly over the loudspeaker in Strike Ops back on the ship. "Thars unhhhh a MiiiiGGGG on maah siiixxx," came the next transmission, made at about eight Gs as Terry broke hard toward the ground. His only chance was to get as low as he could and try to keep some angle off the MiG to keep his pursuer from being able to pull lead on him. Terry flew down into a little valley, jinking hard, trying to shake the MiG off his tail. His cries for help had been heard, and two TARCAP F-8s were desperately trying to get a shot off at the MiG. But the enemy fighter was so close to Terry's A-4 that they couldn't be sure whose tailpipe heat their Sidewinders would home on. Their break came when Terry, running out of room in the valley, rolled hard up and inverted over the top of a ridgeline and down the other side. The MiG had to break off pursuit when he nearly pancaked into the side of the ridge trying to follow Terry's maneuver. The MiG pilot pulled up sharply to yo-yo on Terry and gave the F-8 lead the separation he needed. The Sidewinder growled its deadly song in the Crusader pilot's headset, and the pilot pressed the trigger. The slender missile whooshed off the launch rail, locked onto the MiG's exhaust heat, and blew the MiG apart.

The first Kep strike was a huge success. Not a single Air Wing 21 pilot was shot down on the raid, and everyone was safely recovered, still in the grip of the adrenalin high that accompanied the realization that they had survived the mission. Pilots ricocheted off the walls of the ready rooms as they competed to tell their stories. Eleven MiGS had been destroyed in the air and on the ground; it would be the most successful strike of the war. As we celebrated the triumph, we had no way of knowing the terrible price that would be exacted from the air wing during the rest of May.

After the success of the Kep MiG base strike on the first of May, the rest of the week was anticlimactic. We had laid on a major alpha strike to Haiphong on 4 May, but bad weather over the target aborted the mission. The remainder of the week's missions were individual squadron targets in the lower package areas or diversions to Hillsborough in the South.

Our second line period ended on 8 May and the ship set course for Subic Bay, our home away from home in WESTPAC. Although our second line period had lasted only twenty-five days, it had been a momentous period—a real baptism by fire that had inflicted some losses. We had emerged wiser, but the lessons painfully learned were but a prelude of what was to come.

We left Yankee Station during the afternoon after the final recovery of the line period was complete and flight quarters had been secured. The arrival of an aircraft carrier was a routine event in Subic Bay, and at midmorning on 9 May the Bonnie Dick slipped quietly into the channel without fanfare and was nudged alongside the carrier pier by the tugs.

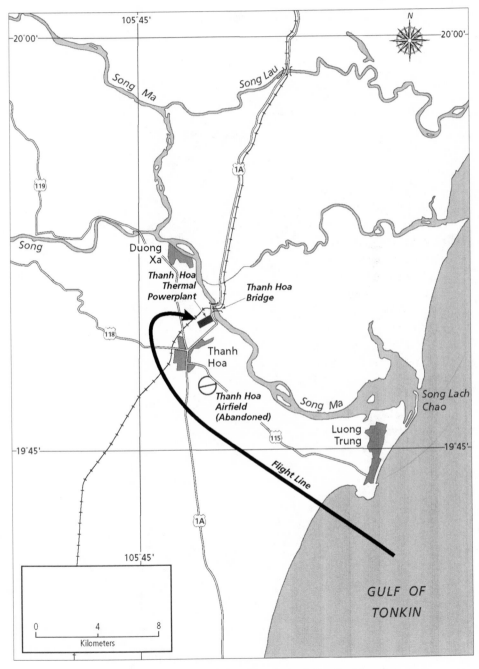

The Thanh Hoa thermal power plant and Thanh Hoa Bridge strikes.

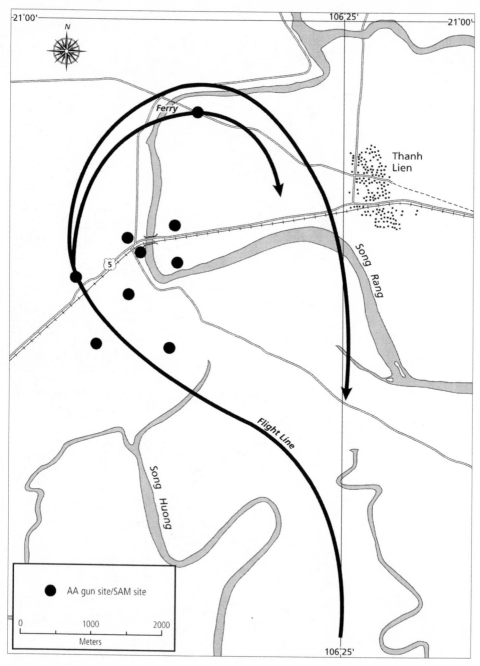

Attack on the suspected POL site near Haiphong where I marked the aim point for the bombers by bombing the river. Approach and attack headings with minute marks on the petroleum storage site.

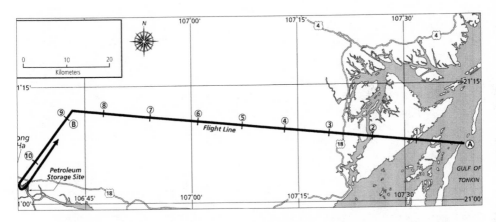

Thanh Lien railroad siding and bridge complex showing some of the antiaircraft gun sites and surface-to-air missile sites. This was the map used in the "Dr. Pepper strikes."

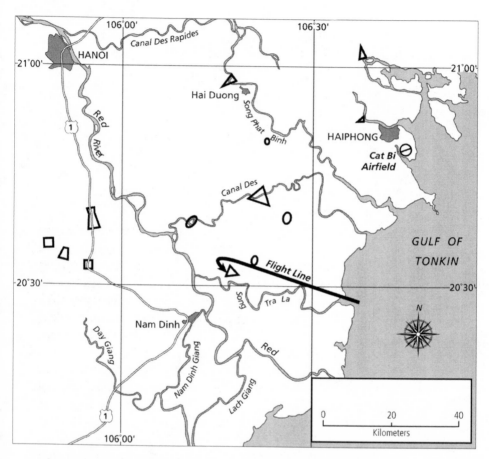

Map of Route Package 6A showing Hanoi, Haiphong, Hai Duong, and "the sleepy little textile village" Nam Dinh. On one of the Dr. Pepper strikes, the author noted the positions of ships anchored in Haiphong Harbor. The lower portion of the map shows the "hourglass" area.

14

Battle Losses

We quickly settled into an in-port routine. After completing the day's minimal military duties, officers not in the duty section would generally go to the officers' club for lunch before engaging in the recreational activity of the day. The air wing's pilots would all head for the Cubi Point Officers' Club while the "black shoes"—the nonflying ship's officers—would head for the naval station officers' club on the other side of the bay. The term "black shoe" refers to the days when aviators had a separate green working uniform with which they wore low-cut brown dress shoes. Nonflying officers had no such uniform and wore black low-cuts with their khaki and blue uniforms. Aviators thus became known as "brown shoes," and deck officers as "black shoes."

After lunch we could choose golf, tennis, swimming, or skeet shooting as diversions to while away the time until happy hour. The main activity from that point on was to drink alcohol in various guises and large quantities while trying to remain conscious until the club closed around 0200. The old Cubi O Club was a place wonderfully designed for aviators to relax and get knee-walking drunk while engaging in various activities aviators call "setting your hair on fire." Black shoes are generally a more morose group than aviators, so the atmosphere at the black shoe officers' club didn't encourage roaring around with your hair on fire. It was designed more for solitary, quiet drinking. Way up the canyon in which the officers' base housing was located was the Callian Officers' Club. The Callian Club was primarily for the families stationed at Subic Bay, and rowdy, drunken activity was expressly forbidden there. One went to the Callian Club for a quiet, refined dinner and cultural entertainment. But at the old Cubi Club, almost anything went.

The old Cubi O Club was a low-rent, thatched roof and bamboo pole affair. Perched close to the edge of a cliff that overlooked the runway at the air station, it had a veranda with a bamboo railing right on the lip of the cliff. An overhanging thatched awning provided shade, and it was pleasant to sit on the veranda and sip something cool in the late afternoon while enjoying an unobstructed view of the spectacular Pacific sunset. One afternoon several of us were enjoying the air on the veranda when one of our number exclaimed, "Gawd damn, looka there!" Outlined against the backdrop of the steep, rocky cliffs east of the field, painted gold by the setting sun, was the form of an F-8 Crusader in a sixty-degree dive toward the runway a thousand feet below us. Vapor clouds flashed on and off its wings as sonic shock waves caused the humid tropical air to condense and vaporize intermittently. Leveling off about fifty feet above the runway, which put it about nine hundred feet below us awestruck observers, the F-8 flashed beneath our feet. *Ka-Kaboom!* The shock wave was a palpable thing, a blow to the chest that nearly knocked us off our feet and raised dust off the thatched roof. The F-8 pulled up in a series of victory rolls and completed a wide downwind turn for landing. We were impressed. The pilot, a fellow named Bert Hardin who had gone through flight training with us, had requested a low-altitude, high-speed pass up the runway, which had been approved by the tower. Bert was finishing up a test hop of an airplane just out of maintenance and decided that the tower and ramp personnel at the air station might enjoy a little air show—which they always did whenever a fighter pilot got the opportunity to do a little hot flying. What the tower personnel didn't know was that Bert, whom we had nicknamed "Hard Rock," tended to stretch the envelope from time to time and "high-speed pass," to him, meant as fast as he could get the F-8 to go. We estimated his speed as he passed the control tower to be somewhere around Mach 1.5. The shock wave broke nearly every window in the tower. Bert's exuberance earned him two weeks' confinement in his room, but he carved out a niche for himself in naval aviation lore.

No description of a Subic Bay in-port period would be complete without mention of Olongapo, the town outside the gate. Olongapo was the most awful place I had ever been. The Olongapo River, which separated the base from the town, was an open sewer. The town side of the river was crowded with huts built on bamboo poles out over the river whose toilet facilities consisted of a hole in the floor. Preteen children would sit in outrigger canoes under the bridge linking the town with the base and exhort the sailors crossing the bridge into town on liberty to throw coins into the river for them to dive after. On reaching puberty, the little girls in the canoes would graduate to hustling drinks in the town's bars. The street on the town side of the Olongapo River Bridge was lined for the first couple of blocks with stalls that sold black-market goods illegally brought out of the Navy Exchange by Filipino employees of the base. These workers were given exchange shopping privileges as a condition of the contract the U.S. government negotiated with the Philippine government to keep U.S. military bases on Philippine soil. The civilian workers were supposedly bound by the same regulations concerning goods purchased in the Navy Exchange that military personnel had to follow, but the Navy didn't enforce them for fear of creating problems with the Philippine government. Appliances, sporting goods, clothes, shoes, and the like were out of bounds for Seventh Fleet sailors in the base exchanges because the five-thousand-man complement of an aircraft carrier—not to mention the crews of their escort vessels—would have overwhelmed the exchanges, which were designed and stocked to serve permanent base personnel, a much smaller number. So the black-market stalls did a brisk business with the Seventh Fleet sailors on liberty. There were some legitimate businesses in downtown Olongapo—craft shops that sold excellent wood products, rattan furniture, and artworks. The wood of the monkey pod tree, a softwood tree indigenous to the Philippines, was perfect for carving, and Filipino artisans made all manner of products that were eagerly purchased by foreign shoppers. For the most part, though, the remaining businesses in Olongapo were bars.

Sailors had a special name for the liberty regulations in Subic. They called it "Cinderella liberty" because nonrated enlisted men had to be back on board ship at midnight. All U.S. military personnel had a midnight curfew that decreed that they had to be either back on board the naval station or off the streets of Olongapo by then. Accordingly, the bars all closed at 2330. But between opening time just after the expiration of curfew until 2330, the Olongapo bars provided entertainment that many young sailors had never imagined even in their wildest dreams. It was all SEX. Every bar had dozens of fourteen- to eighteen-year-old "hostesses" whose profession was selling drinks for the bar. They were not selling their bodies. This had nothing to do with their virtue; the hostesses simply made much more money hustling drinks than they would by renting their bodies to a succession of horny sailors. It was a lot less risky, too. All the girls carried a ring that held little tags. For each drink they got a sailor to buy, they got another little tag, which represented a commission on the drink. At closing time, they would line up to cash in their tags. The girls drank watered down Coca-Cola for which the sailors paid scotch whisky prices—about three bucks per "scotch." The sailors typically ordered San Miguel beer for themselves. In return for a drink, the "hostess" would sit in the sailor's lap, grab his crotch, and allow herself to be fondled as long as the sailor continued to buy drinks. At 2330, the sailor had to head back to "sheep," desires unquenched, while the bar girl left to spend the night with her base personnel U.S. Navy boyfriend. The Navy base personnel were allowed to RON in town as long as they observed the curfew.

Unknown to the air wing as we went about our various pursuits of happiness, Cdr. Homer Smith had flown to Guam with Adm. U. S. Grant Sharp, the commander of the Pacific Fleet, for a conference with President Lyndon Johnson. The Johnson administration was trying hard to convince the North Vietnamese to begin peace talks by trying to make life increasingly difficult in North Vietnam. Electrical power plants had become priority targets because their loss would be a major inconvenience. The Hanoi thermal power plant had not been included in the list of new targets for conventional bombing because it was located in a heavily populated residential area of Hanoi. Commander Smith was in Guam to present a plan for a surgical strike of the Hanoi thermal power plant using the new Walleye. President Johnson bought the plan and Air Wing 21 was ordered to implement it.

The *Bon Homme Richard* was under way for the Gulf of Tonkin soon after Commander Smith returned from Guam. We left port three days early and steamed at flank speed toward the launch point for the Hanoi thermal power plant strike. We arrived on the line the afternoon of 15 May, but the weather was bad over Hanoi and the strike was canceled until the sixteenth.

The bad weather in Hanoi continued for three days, so on 18 May the air wing's attack squadrons concentrated on individual division interdiction targets in Route Package 2. I was assigned the strike tanker job on one of our morning launches, ordered to hold a position about three miles off the coast in case battle damage required refueling or one of our planes was shot down and a search-and-rescue mission was necessary. Lt. Cdr. John Kirkpatrick, VA-212's maintenance officer, was leading a division on an armed recon mission when he took a 37-mm antiaircraft round in his right wing. The round exploded inside the fuel cell in the right wing, blowing a three-foot hole all the way through the wing. All the fuel in both wing tanks vaporized and escaped out the cavernous hole in the wing (the right and left wing tanks were one continuous tank in the A-4). Shrapnel from the exploding round penetrated the fuselage tank, and most of the eleven hundred pounds of fuel it held was lost, too. John was left with about one hundred pounds of fuel, only five minutes' flying time. I was monitoring strike frequency and heard John call hit and his fuel state. Turning toward the coast, I headed in the flight's direction and transmitted my TACAN position off Red Crown, the north SAR destroyer. A thin white trail of streaming fuel marked John's stricken A-4 as he passed over the coastline. Had he been hit a few miles farther inland he never would have made it to the water. I began a turn across his flight path and streamed my refueling drogue to make his join-up faster. John plugged me right away, and the flip-flop window on the tanker package control panel flipped from barber pole stripes to "Xfer," indicating that the tanking airplane was ready to receive fuel. I flipped the switch to the "Xfer" position and saw the fuel transfer counter begin to click off pounds of fuel as John's thirsty engine began to drink directly from the tanker's store.

The immediate need taken care of for the moment, John and I discussed our next move. John said that although his airplane was difficult to fly with such a large section of lift gone from his wing, he thought he could save the airplane and wanted to try to land aboard the ship. John's wingman gave the damaged airplane a look-over while John was plugged into my tanker. After hearing his description of the damage, I was amazed that John was able to fly it at all, much less well enough to rendezvous with me and plug the tanker drogue. John told me what he had decided to attempt and the role I was to play. I was to make a long, straight-in approach to the ship, descending to six hundred feet above the water and lowering my landing gear and flaps at the ten-mile gate with John remaining plugged in all the way. I would fly into the glide path and then add power to pull the drogue away from John's airplane as he attempted to land. I would remain at six hundred feet on the heading of the angle deck. If John had to go around or bolter, he could simply climb to six hundred feet and replug the tanker to avoid flaming out from fuel exhaustion. He would have to hit the drogue on the first try, though, because at the higher power setting he would have to use to go around, he would have only a couple of minutes of fuel left—if his fuel gauge was accurate. It wasn't designed to give accurate readings below the hundred-pound level.

The flight seemed to take much longer than the fifteen minutes that separated us from the Bonnie Dick. Strike Operations had notified the air boss of John's predicament, and Rocket Tower informed us that we would have a ready deck on arrival. I was taut as a bowstring, trying to fly a smooth and level path to make John's job of flying formation on me and staying plugged in easy as possible. At ten miles behind the ship it was time to configure for landing. I called John on the radio. "OK, John, time to dirty up, landing gear . . . now," I said as I flipped my own landing gear handle down. I hesitated a few seconds to let John adjust to the new trim and power requirements. The fuel transfer counter continued to click away, indicating that John had made the landing gear transition. Next I called, "OK, John, flaps . . . now." Lowering the wing flaps requires an even larger pitch and trim change, but the fuel transfer counter never missed a beat. I had saved the speed brakes for last since we had already slowed to approach speed to conserve fuel in case John became unplugged. After calling the speed brake extension, I had to catch myself to keep from dropping my own tail hook, which would have interfered with the refueling hose. I reminded John to check hook down as we flew up the wake of the ship toward the glide slope. Rocket approach began to call off the distances so that I didn't have to cross-check the DME gauge and could keep my scan on the lineup and angle of attack. Just as the amber ball appeared in the top of the lens I called, "OK, John, you're on the ball. I'm pulling away." I went to full power and felt the hose pull free of John's airplane. The LSO began to talk to John, but he was right in the groove and trapped with an OK 3-wire, three-foot hole in the wing be damned. I marveled at the feat John Kirkpatrick had just performed. Keeping his severely damaged airplane plugged in to the tanker during all the speed and configuration changes, and then flying a near perfect carrier landing was a demonstration of superior skill.

I later learned that the rest of Air Wing 21 didn't fare as well as Commander Kirkpatrick. VA-76's XO, Cdr. Ken Cameron, was hit hard right over his target and had to eject in the target area. People were waiting for him on the ground, and he was surrounded as soon as he touched down. I met Ken when I went through the RAG; he carrier qualified with my class, so I got to know him personally. Ken wasn't the only casualty. A photo RF-8 from VFP-63 had been hit by antiaircraft fire but was able to limp into Da Nang, and our prospective XO, Cdr. Fred Whittemore, had his airplane hit by small-arms fire but was able to return to the ship.

———◦———

Finally, on the afternoon of the next day, the weather over Hanoi became marginally good enough to attempt the Walleye strike on the Hanoi thermal power plant. After we had learned that the essential factor in evading an SA-2 surface-to-air missile was being able to see it, Air Wing 21 had adopted a policy that required six-tenths or less cloud cover below the strike roll-in altitude. The SAMs accelerated to four times the speed of sound within ten miles of launch. At that tremendous velocity, the SAM's turn radius was huge and any fighter-type airplane could easily outmaneuver it. But if the SAM emerged from an undercast only a few thousand feet from its intended target, the pilot wouldn't have time even to react, much less to outfly the missile. This factor coupled with the essential requirement that the Walleye camera have a completely unobstructed view of the target meant that the sky in the target area had to be nearly clear of clouds. This day the weather surveillance reported only 30 percent cloud cover over Hanoi. While there was a 70 percent chance that clouds would not obscure the target, though, there was also a 30 percent chance that the target would be obscured and the mission would fail.

Only two Rampant Raiders from VA-212 went on the strike. Commander Smith chose the two most qualified Walleye pilots for this important mission: himself and Lt. Cdr. Mike Cator. The alpha strike would be quite small as well. There would be little flak right in the target area, and that made flak suppressors impractical on this mission. So the strike group consisted of fighter TARCAP, some Iron Hand cover, and the two Walleye airplanes.

The mission did not go well. Clouds partially covered the target, and the skipper and Mike were able to lock onto only the parts of the power plant complex they glimpsed through the clouds. As was always the case when we attacked Hanoi itself, the North Vietnamese threw everything they had at the strike group. The TARCAP acquitted itself well, shooting down four MiGs, but a SAM and the flak took down two F-8 Crusaders, one piloted by Commander Russell of VF-211, and the other by Lt. (jg) William J. Metzer of VF-24. Since the pilots had to eject in the outskirts of Hanoi, there was no chance for a rescue mission and both were captured. The rest of the strike returned to the ship safely, but we would not learn the results of the strike until the next day because the photo recon airplane from the USS *Kitty Hawk* was shot down while trying to photograph the strike damage.

Commander Smith was due to be relieved as commanding officer of the Rampant Raiders. He had some latitude in selecting the date of his change of command, though, and he had elected to finish the operational evaluation of the Walleye and conduct the Hanoi thermal power plant strike because he had personally presented the strike plan to the president. He had another, more personal reason to delay his relief: he wanted to complete two hundred combat missions, and this line period would be his last chance to do so. When he left Air Wing 21, he would take command of an air wing on the East Coast that was not slated for combat duty in Vietnam.

On 20 May 1967, Commander Smith launched on his 197th combat mission. He was leading Lt. Tom Taylor on a two-plane Walleye strike on the Uong Bi thermal power plant about twenty miles east of the North Vietnam city of Bac Giang. Lieutenant Taylor was the Walleye project officer and a temporary Rampant Raider. He was really assigned to the research and development squadron, VX-5, at NAS China Lake, California, and was just TDY to VA-212 while the Walleye was being evaluated, although he flew many combat missions that did not involve Walleyes. He stayed with us for the entire combat operation evaluation although officially he was on shore duty this entire time.

Commander Smith's airplane was hit hard by antiaircraft fire during the pullout after releasing his Walleye. He continued flying for a short time, but his airplane began to roll right and his nose dropped dangerously low. Lieutenant Taylor called him to pull up, but the skipper was forced to eject from his now uncontrollable airplane. People were waiting for him when he landed in his parachute and took him captive when he stood up to unbuckle his torso harness. He was up and walking when they led him into the brush. Sometime during 1969–70, the Navy notified Jean Smith, Homer's wife, that Commander Smith had died while a captive of the North Vietnamese. The release of this information, presumably obtained by the International Red Cross, was surprising because it occurred before some of the POWs had even been allowed to write letters home confirming their status as POWs. The capture of our skipper was a blow to VA-212. He was the first of the Rampant Raiders to join the casualty list. The stress of the increased intensity of combat was beginning to take its toll, and I began to doubt my own chances of returning home from the cruise.

The Johnson administration, exhibiting complete ignorance of North Vietnam and its people, decided to try a carrot-and-stick approach to entice the North Vietnamese to the conference table. On 23 May, Buddha's birthday, President Johnson ordered a unilateral, one-day ceasefire for U.S. forces. The Seventh Fleet launched a limited flight schedule that day, with the *Bon Homme Richard* launching the barrier combat air patrol (BARCAP) to protect the fleet from surprise air attack, and tanker and surveillance missions. Whenever a surveillance airplane happened to come within range, the Vietnamese Communists demonstrated their appreciation of the ceasefire by opening up with all they had.

The admiral took this opportunity to have VA-212 fall in on the forecastle to hear the reading of the orders officially transferring the command of the Rampant Raiders to Cdr. Marv Quaid, USN. Cdr. Fred Whittemore would become the new executive officer. Commander Quaid delivered a speech praising our effort so far and urging continued dedication to duty. The new CO's excellent leadership would go far in helping me cope with the terrible demands of combat that I would face in the coming months.

We resumed strike operations the next day. Nearly all the strikes planned for the daily schedule were targeted on the new areas opened up to us around

Haiphong and Hanoi, but with the hit-or-miss weather in the North, about three-fourths of the strikes were canceled and we hit interdiction targets in the lower route package areas instead. It immediately became obvious that the North Vietnamese had used the respite of Buddha's birthday to reload their guns. I was flying Lt. Cdr. Pete Yonke's wing on an armed reconnaissance mission in Route Package 2. We attacked some barges on the Song Ca River and got some lively 37-mm and automatic weapons fire in return from a normally quiet area.

The following day tragedy visited Air Wing 21 yet again. Ens. Dick Graves, a Spad pilot from VA-215, was killed when his Skyraider flew into the water just off the coast of North Vietnam. Whether he was hit by ground fire or experienced some malfunction was never known. I had come to know Dick quite well because we were both ensigns. He was a very nice young man, with unfailing good humor. His loss affected me deeply. His death made eight Air Wing 21 pilots either killed or captured. The war was taking a terrible toll during this line period.

On 30 May, a major railroad and highway bridge complex at Phu Ly, thirty miles south of Hanoi, was under clear skies, and Air Wing 21 laid on an alpha strike to get the bridge. CAG, flying with VA-76, call sign "Sunglass," would lead the strike with the first division of bombers; VA-212 would make up the second division. To ensure the bridge's destruction, we would be carrying maximum bomb loads. VA-76's A-4Cs would have three Mark-83 thousand-pounders on their centerline MERs, and the Flying Eagles would carry three of the big bombs as well—two on the wings and one on the centerline. As we would be carrying no centerline fuel tank, VA-212 would have to refuel. VF-211 and VF-24 would be supplying flak suppression and TARCAP, and VA-212 would provide Iron Hand antiradar cover. VAH-4 would have a KA-3B orbiting a TACAN fix off the north SAR destroyer to provide refueling, and an A-4 tanker would be circling above the ship.

The various elements of the alpha strike launched separately. Our soon to be XO, Cdr. Fred Whittemore, was leading the Flying Eagle division with me as his number two and Lt. (jg) Al Crebo leading the second section. Commander Whittemore launched first and led the rendezvous. The launch lineup on this day was unusual, and Commander Whittemore had launched well ahead of the rest of the Flying Eagles. This would become significant later in the mission. After we all joined, Commander Whittemore signaled that he had no radio and passed the lead to Al Crebo. Rather than taking himself out of the mission, which would have been the wiser course, he passed the section lead to me and crossed under me to take up the number four position. Al led our division to join up with the rest of the alpha strike and we headed for the coast. The strike leader called for us to check switches as we crossed the coast. The route to the target would take us past the large village of Nam Dinh. The formation was jinking gently, with each division moving side to side and varying altitude as much as possible while retaining formation integrity. Journalist Pierre Salinger, President John F. Kennedy's former press secretary, who had become a prominent opponent of the Vietnam War, had recently toured North Vietnam. On his return he described Nam Dinh as a "sleepy little textile village" and reported that the largest piece of ordnance he saw there was "a pistol on a policewoman's hip." His words, reprinted in *Time* magazine, came back to me as the first cluster of radar-directed 85-mm and 100-mm antiaircraft bursts began exploding off to our right. Sleepy little textile village indeed! The flak suppressor F-8s had split off earlier to beat us to the target, but they swung a little too far wide, and that messed up the timing of the attack.

The highway and railroad bridges at Phu Ly were a major link on Highway One from Hanoi to Nam Dinh, and the North Vietnamese protected them with heavy flak. Dark gray 57-mm shells were exploding around us and white 37-mm bursts were creating an overcast as we reached the roll-in point. I delayed my section's roll-in as long as I could to get the maximum offset in the bomb run from the previous section's track over the ground. Consequently, I could see the first group's bombs hitting long and exploding in the river. The Flying Eagles corrected the aiming point, and as I reached release point and felt my own bombs come off the racks, the first of the Flying Eagles' bombs were exploding smack in the center of the bridge.

A large 57-mm gun emplacement just north of the bridge with at least a dozen revetments had been hammering away at us since before the roll-in, and the F-8 flak suppressors were just beginning their belated runs. Just as my nose came above the horizon and the G forces from my pullout eased enough for my vision to return to normal, my windscreen was filled with a side view of an F-8. Our flight paths were perpendicular, and my brain recorded the fact that we were going to collide. There wasn't time to even move the stick. It was simply an instant frozen in my memory for all time, like a mental snapshot. The F-8 flashed past me and I noted that he was firing his Zunis as my airplane passed within inches of his vertical stabilizer. Intent on his attack run, he never even saw me and I simply had no time to be frightened; that would come later. As I jinked left, I looked back to see that the entire bridge, from bank to bank, was a pile of smoking, twisted girders down in the river. The strike group split into individual units as we streaked toward the safety of the Tonkin Gulf. I timed my jinking turns to close on the two specks ahead that were Al Crebo and his wingman.

When we joined up off the coast, we began the ritual look-overs to check for battle damage. Commander Whittemore completed his examination of my underside and gave me a thumbs-up indicating that I was unscathed. I passed the lead to him and slid back and under him looking for any holes in his airplane. The lead section had already completed their look-overs, and I heard Al switch us to tanker frequency as he headed the division toward the strike tanker. Now, Fred Whittemore had been a division leader for years, and he simply wasn't used to being a wingman and flying formation on someone else. And because his radio wasn't working he didn't hear the turn toward the tanker or the switch to tanker frequency. He just flew straight ahead and didn't even look toward the first section as they peeled off toward the tanker. After I finished looking over his plane, I pulled up on Fred's left wing and gave him the signal to take the lead. He responded with a drinking motion and held up five fingers signifying that he had only five hundred pounds of fuel remaining—only about fifteen minutes of flying time. Damn! I thought. Why is he so low on fuel? I still had about twelve hundred pounds. Then I remembered that he had launched well ahead of the rest of the flight and had burned a lot of fuel waiting on the rendezvous.

I looked around, but Crebo and his wingman were nowhere in sight. I switched to tanker radio frequency and called Al for his position. "We're on the Red Crown three-four-zero for twenty, Eagle Three. Where are you?" I looked down at the RMI to get the radial and DME off Red Crown. My TACAN needle was spinning uselessly around the dial, signaling that my TACAN had gone inoperative. Fred's fuel situation had just become critical. "Eagle Lead, Three, I've lost my TACAN. Four is low state. I'm going to take him to the ship for the overhead tanker." I reasoned that we had been heading in the general direction of the ship since going feet wet and were probably as close to the A-4 circling the ship as to the strike tanker. In any case, Fred didn't have enough fuel to spend a lot of time looking for the tanker and the rest of the flight. I could use my ADF on the ship's nondirectional radio beacon to find the ship even without TACAN. I switched to the Rocket Strike Operations frequency without getting a reply from Al Crebo. A motion caught my eye, and I looked to see Commander Whittemore waving and emphatically signaling that he was down to four hundred pounds. Having reassumed the number four position, he was now aware that the lead section was not with us and he was wondering where they were and why we were not joining on the tanker.

"Rocket, Flying Eagle Three, inbound with flight of two, one low state, need the overhead tanker, over," I called.

"Ah . . . Flying Eagle, Rocket. The overhead tanker went down before launch and we didn't launch a replacement, over."

Shit! I thought. "Rocket, you better launch one most skosh or two Flying Eagles are going swimming, over."

"Roger, Flying Eagle. We'll get you a tanker ASAP."

Commander Whittemore frantically signaled three hundred pounds. Aw, Jesus, I've really screwed this up, I thought. If that tanker is buried in the pack for the next launch, they'll never get it up here before the commander runs out of fuel. I should have used my ADF to try to find Al and the other tanker. Fred was pounding at me with his fist on the canopy and signaling two hundred pounds left. Finally, I saw the relief tanker squirt off the port catapult and climb toward us. He streamed the hose and drogue on the way up, and I turned the section to join up behind him. I gave Commander Whittemore the kiss-off signal and pointed toward the tanker. He plugged right away on the first pass at the basket and I gave a sigh of relief as I saw the amber light on the tanker package turn green indicating fuel transfer. About this time, Al and his wingman arrived overhead along with the strike tanker. "Eagle Three, dammit, where the hell have you been?" came the irate call from Crebo. Only now did I realize that he had never heard my transmission about losing my TACAN and taking Commander Whittemore for the overhead tanker.

After I refueled, we all landed without incident and a furious Commander Whittemore convened a private debriefing for us in the tiny operations office off the ready room. I was standing by to be court-martialed at the very least for nearly putting him in the drink. But when Fred learned that he had confused the airplane numbers and had given number three the lead and number two the section, that ended the matter. I never did get the chance to explain why I had led him to the ship. It was as if he figured, "Aw heck, what can you expect from an ensign anyway?"

During the Bonnie Dick's previous off-line period, the Johnson administration had finally been convinced that the North Vietnamese MiGS were unlikely to begin operating out of China if we bombed their runways, and the Air Force had been allowed to bomb Kep airfield with "hard bombs." Their bombs cratered the runway, and the airfield had been closed since that attack. Recent reconnaissance photographs showed just one inoperative MiG with its tail section removed and some construction equipment on the runway. Perhaps because the air wing had enjoyed such great success on the first Kep strike, the admiral laid on another, billed as a "harassment strike," even though the recon photos showed little of value to hit. VA-212 received the strike order on 30 May, and the alpha strike was scheduled for the next day. VA-76 would lead the strike with six bombers to further tear up the runway. VA-212 Flying Eagles would provide four flak suppressors and two Iron Hand antiradar airplanes. The skipper, Commander Quaid, would lead the Iron Handers with Lt. (jg) Mark Daniels flying his wing, and Lt. Cdr. Arvin Chauncey would lead the division of flak suppressors with me flying as his number two.

Arv Chauncey convened a briefing for the flak suppressors the night before the strike to detail the latest photo intelligence showing occupied flak revetments. With so much flak around the airfield, each of us would be assigned an individual flak position to attack, and Arv wanted to work out the details before the full air wing briefing the next morning. Because this was such a dangerous target—very heavily defended and far inland—I was really scared, and my fear made me angry. Although I knew it would do no good, I complained bitterly to Arv that this was a "goddamn useless mission for nothing." Arv finally had to rebuke me. It didn't matter what I thought of the mission, he said. Orders were orders, we had been assigned the mission, and that was that.

Kep was a difficult target for many reasons. Its inland location made fuel a problem. Further, the number of routes to the target was limited. The shortest one would subject the strike group to a continuous gauntlet of the heaviest air defenses North Vietnam could muster, and coming in from the west over northern Laos would require too much fuel to be practical. That left the route we had taken on the first Kep strike: flying up the Tonkin Gulf to a point just south of the Chinese border, then paralleling the border to an initial point about fifteen miles northeast of Kep, where the strike group would climb to attack altitude and wheel southwest toward the airfield. This was the least heavily defended route. The strike planners decided that we would fly in fairly low, at about four thousand feet, to keep us below the radar horizon of the SAM sites west of Haiphong and around Hanoi. Two KA-3B tankers would orbit about five miles off the coast to give tanker support.

The *Bon Homme Richard* had a constant companion—a Russian navy "fishing trawler." Its "fishing" was done not with nets, though, but with antennas that sampled the Bonnie Dick's electromagnetic emissions—radio transmissions, radar, sonar, and so on. Because the Bonnie Dick was operating in international waters, we could not do anything about the Russian ship's intelligence gathering. The launch of the Kep strike was no doubt known in Hanoi from the moment the first airplanes were catapulted off our bow.

Although Hanoi didn't know the exact target, they could track the progress of the strike group and put all their air defenses on full alert. They were ready and waiting for us.

The rendezvous of the strike group went smoothly, and we headed north up the Gulf of Tonkin. I glanced around and as always thrilled at the sight of the alpha strike formation. I felt as if I were a part of a mighty armada and took strength from the powerful force we represented. The area just off the coast of North Vietnam that was our coast-in point was a fantastic and foreboding-looking place. Sharp, jagged karst islands thrust vertically up from the water, some up to a thousand feet tall. I mentally called these islands the "Dragon's Teeth." We were only about twenty-five miles south of the Chinese border when we wheeled west and headed inland. Our old friend "Petunia," the EC-121 patrol aircraft, was on station and began to broadcast border warnings. Policy called for the border-warning code word of the day to be broadcast on guard frequency any time a U.S. airplane got within thirty miles of the Chinese border. Petunia was in full compliance, broadcasting the border warning every minute or so. It seemed to me that he should have been able to figure out that we were an alpha strike flying deliberately in the buffer zone and to shut the hell up. The strike leader called for us to arm switches as we crossed the coast and went feet dry. The adrenaline began to rise as we penetrated into North Vietnam. I caught glimpses of the rugged terrain below as the force jinked slowly, each formation within the strike weaving side to side and climbing and descending to make tracking more difficult.

Our airplanes had new chaff dispensers that had been installed in the tailpipe section behind the wings' trailing edge. Designed to confuse the enemy's radar, the chaff comprised bundles of aluminum strips cut to length to match the wavelength of the enemy's radar transmissions. The chaff presented a much stronger return on the enemy's radar scopes than the skin paint of the airplane's surface, and—we hoped—obscured the airplane and caused the radar to lock onto the chaff instead. Before the chaff dispensers were installed, we used to stuff chaff into the speed brake wells. The pilot released all of the chaff at once by cracking the speed brakes open momentarily. Occasionally someone would accidentally bump the speed brake switch while taxiing up the deck for launch and the flight deck behind him would sparkle in a blizzard of aluminum foil. The chaff dispensers eliminated this problem. We now had twenty-five one-inch tubes of tightly packed chaff strips that we could punch out one at a time by pressing a switch on the throttle. Nervous fingers hovered over chaff buttons as we jinked just above the radar horizon of the waiting missiles and guns, and it took an act of will to hold off when our threat receivers picked up a burst of radar signal.

We reached the initial point, a large reservoir, and the strike leader began to climb the force to attack altitude. Without warning, because the enemy had been optically tracking us without using radar, heavy antiaircraft shells began to burst right in the formation. Without being aware of it, because we had little intelligence on this area of North Vietnam, the strike leader had led us close to a very large concentration of heavy antiaircraft guns protecting the northeast railroad that ran from China to Hanoi. The first flak burst I saw hit Arv Chauncey's airplane just behind the right wing. I was flying on Arv's port side, stepped down slightly, and the explosion momentarily shrouded Arv's tail section in black smoke. Almost immediately, what looked like a bushel basket of sparks poured from Arv's tailpipe, accompanied by pale red flames. The cohesion of the strike group disintegrated as individual elements took evasive action. Their problems had just begun, but Arv and I were already in serious trouble.

Arv called, "I'm hit and heading back," as he rolled into a left turn. I crossed above and behind him, trying to get a look at the damage to his right side as we fell out of the strike formation. He called to jettison our CBUs, and I saw him begin to drop his bombs. I punched my bomb pickle four or five times just to be sure all of mine released. "Steve," Arv radioed, "I'm losing my engine and can't make it to the coast. I'll try for those mountains." My heart sank. It was obvious that Arv wasn't going to make it back over water because we were steadily losing altitude and slowing down. The flak guns were hammering us badly, and Arv couldn't do anything but fly straight and try to stretch his glide. The high-pitched buzz of antiaircraft tracking radar filled my headset as the gunners on the ground locked us up solid. I began punching out bundles of chaff, trying to break their lock as the heavy shells continued to burst all around and in between us. I had no idea where the flak was coming from because I hadn't seen the guns. As we descended below twenty-five hundred feet, the flak stopped as suddenly as it had begun. I was flying a hundred feet above and to the right of Arv's airplane. The mountain he had referred to—a two-thousand-foot-tall ridge covered by heavy forest—was still a couple of miles ahead, and it didn't look as if he could glide that far. Huge tongues of yellow flame began to pulsate out of Arv's tailpipe as his engine continued to disintegrate. Afraid that his airplane was about to explode, I transmitted, "You're burning pretty bad now, Arv. You better get out." His canopy flew off almost immediately, and the rocket-powered seat lofted Arv clear of the burning A-4.

I looked down at the radio dial and switched to 243.0 MHz, the guard channel. "Mayday, mayday, mayday," I transmitted. "Flying Eagle two-two-six has ejected five miles east of the reservoir. Good chute. Get the rescue chopper on the way. This is Eagle two-two-three, over." I waited for a response as I watched Arv drift slowly down in his parachute. Arv's burning airplane struck the side of the ridge and exploded. I called again on guard and still received no answer. Then it dawned on me that I was too low and had to get higher than the surrounding mountaintops before Red Crown could receive me. I popped up above the ridge, circling north of Arv's parachute, now far below, and called Red Crown again. This time they answered that the helo was on its way. The hiss of antiaircraft radar filled my headphones again, and I caught a glitter of light off to my right. Looking that way, I saw the muzzle flashes of the heavy guns as the second volley of shells sped my way. There! There's the flak, I thought as the first volley of shells exploded around me. I punched out some more chaff and radioed to Red Crown that the rescue helo could come low up the valleys from the southeast and stay below the flak.

Arv had come down on a small, scrub-covered hill separated from the ridge by a deep chasm that had a small stream at its bottom. As I ducked below the ridge top to get below the sight of the guns, Arv came up on guard channel: "Steve, I'm OK and I'm going to lay low in some bushes here." "Roger, Arv." I answered. "Hang on. The rescue helo's on its way." I climbed again to radio altitude and relayed to Red Crown that Arv was in good shape on the ground and would hide in some bushes. I spotted a small village only about two miles west of Arv's hill and asked Red Crown to hurry the helo. The radar-controlled guns had locked me up again when I popped above their horizon, and I punched out some more chaff to throw them off. Shells began to explode seconds later, and I ducked below the horizon once more. Arv's parachute was lying in plain sight on the hilltop. I swung far west of the hill to avoid flying over Arv's position and giving away his location to any observers on the ground. All that remained was to wait on the helo. I figured it would take him thirty to forty minutes to get in there, and I would be getting very low on fuel by then. I tried not to think of the paltry few rounds of 20 mm that was all the protection I had if the MiGs decided to show up. I was all alone over North Vietnam.

The strike group encountered more heavy antiaircraft fire a few miles farther west of the point where Arv had been hit. A SAM launch from the vicinity of Kep had forced the formation to dive to take evasive action, and they exposed themselves to the flak at a perilously low altitude. Five of the six lead bombers were hit within seconds, and the strike group was hopelessly scattered. Not one airplane made it to the target. Commander Quaid took a hit in one of his Shrike missiles that started the propellant burning out of the shrapnel hole. He was forced to jettison his entire external stores load—racks, fuel tank, and all—before the rocket exploded under his wing. Luckily, none of the damaged airplanes went down, and Arv remained the only search-and-rescue mission. The battle damage did result in much lost fuel, however, and our tanker resources were overwhelmed with low-fuel-state airplanes. Having switched to guard frequency, I was unaware of the fate of the strike group, but the lack of on-station fuel was going to have enormous consequences.

"Flying Eagle Two, Wild Eagle, over." I recognized Mark Daniels's voice over guard channel.

"Roger, Mark. Eagle Two here. Go ahead, over," I answered, relieved that I was at least talking to another airplane from VA-212.

"Steve, the skipper was hit and had to jettison his Shrikes. We're heading back to you. Go air-to-air TACAN, over." Air-to-air TACAN allowed each airplane's TACAN receiver to send and receive distance-measuring data, but it would not indicate direction. Mark was using the airplane's ADF needle to home on me, and the DME readout told him how far apart we were.

"Roger, Mark. Stay below three thousand. The flak is coming from north of the ridgeline to your left." A few minutes later I spotted the two A-4s slipping in to join on my left side as I circled south of Arv's position. The skipper, despite the fact that his airplane had received battle damage, joined on me while Mark Daniels climbed up to act as radio relay for the rescue mission. I was trying to describe Arv's position to the skipper so that he could assume command of the SAR. Arv's parachute was still lying in plain sight on the hill, but the skipper was having difficulty spotting it while flying formation on me. I knew exactly where to look whereas he didn't, and I had us circling well south to keep from exposing Arv's position. The skipper didn't want to take the lead without knowing exactly where Arv was, so I decided to make one pass closer to Arv's hill to get Commander Quaid a visual on the parachute. We heard Mark Daniels transmitting to Red Crown more detailed map coordinates and assuring them that there was no ground fire in the area and that the helo could safely approach from the valleys to the southeast. That was the last we heard from Mark.

I swung the formation east of Arv's hill within about a mile of the parachute and saw four black pajama–clad figures climbing up Arv's hill whom I took to be local militia from the nearby village. I called on guard frequency, "Arv, there are four bad guys coming up your hill. Your parachute is in plain sight. Can you get to it to roll it up?" The skipper radioed me, "Steve, can you put some twenty mike-mike over their heads to scare them off?" "Roger, Skipper. Rolling in now," I answered. Rolling left, I began a shallow dive north to south while rolling the gun sight depression knob to zero mils. I wanted to fire close enough to frighten them without hitting anyone. The last thing I wanted to do was kill any of the bad guys on the ground, because if the rescue attempt failed, they would undoubtedly exact retribution on Arv. Stabilizing in the strafe run, I saw the militiamen dive for cover as I fired a short burst over their heads into the face of the opposite hill. Arv called, "Good shooting. . . ." The rest was garbled, but he said something about his position.

Arv's position was doubtless known to people on the ground now, so there was no longer any reason not to over fly him. I pulled out of the run and rolled left for another pass if necessary. The skipper rejoined outside my turn, and I noticed that Arv's parachute was no longer visible. Whether the bad guys had retrieved it or Arv had rolled it up, I never knew. As we completed one more circle of Arv's hill he called on his survival radio one last time. "Steve, this is Arv." And that was all. He never completed the call, and there was something in the tone of his voice that sounded like resignation. Those were the last words I heard from Arvin Roy Chauncey until after his release from a North Vietnamese POW camp in 1973.

Passing north of Arv's hill, motion high and to my right caught my eye. Flak was bursting high above, and I wondered what they were shooting at when the silhouettes of four Skyraiders surrounded by black puffs of smoke came into sight. The Barn Owls' RESCAP had arrived on the scene. "Barn Owls, dive right below the ridge and they can't shoot at you," I called. The four Spads complied quickly and I gave Barn Owl Leader, VA-215's skipper, the description of Arv's position and where the flak was located. He rogered and took station overhead. Commander Quaid called and asked for my fuel state. I had been flying at low altitude at a fairly high fuel-flow rate for quite a while now because it wasn't wise to fly slowly over enemy territory. Commander Quaid acknowledged and told me we had to leave right now.

Quaid took the lead as he headed us east toward the Tonkin Gulf. He was much better off on fuel because he had cleaned off all his external stores when he had jettisoned his missiles and external tank. His "clean" airplane had much less drag than mine and consequently could fly at the same speed with lower fuel consumption. It hadn't occurred to me to jettison my empty bomb racks and fuel tank because I had been so busy with the SAR. It was a mistake that nearly cost me my airplane. We still had nearly sixty miles of North Vietnam to cross before reaching the safety of the Gulf, and I would be really skosh on fuel by the time we got there. We flew at about 360 knots—about three-quarters of the available thrust from the engine—until only a few miles of flat alluvial plane lay between us and the coast. The skipper called, "We had better push it up across here, Steve." I really hated to push the throttle to full power and watch the fuel gauge unwind at that high fuel-flow rate, but we accelerated to above 400 knots as we crossed the coast. I had only three hundred pounds of fuel remaining, and the tankers were nowhere in sight.

While I had been involved in Arv's attempted rescue, the remainder of the alpha strike had been scrambling to survive. The battle damage they suffered had overwhelmed the tanker resources we had on station. There simply wasn't enough fuel to go around, and Air Wing 21 was almost certainly going to lose some airplanes because of it. Frantic calls went out for any airborne fuel assets to divert to the north Gulf. A U.S. Air Force KC-135 tanker with a drogue attached to his refueling boom heard the frantic situation unfolding far to the north. Without waiting for permission, the Air Force tanker skipper headed up toward Haiphong and saved the rest of the strike group. The fuel situation was so critical when the KC-135 arrived that a Navy KA-3B tanker plugged the Air Force tanker and an emergency low-state F-8 Crusader plugged the KA-3 and took on fuel straight through from the KC-135. All this refueling activity had pulled the tankers about twenty miles farther south than they were supposed to be.

By the time Commander Quaid and I got a visual on the tankers I was down to less than two hundred pounds of fuel and was starting to panic. Three KA-3Bs were flying in formation, but only one of them had fuel to transfer. After pointing the tankers out to me, the skipper detached me to refuel first because my need was much greater. "Which tanker do I plug?" I called, knowing that I had to make a successful coupling on the first pass; there would be no second chance. "Plug the one with his hose out," came the reply. All three tankers had their hoses deployed. "They all have their hoses out!" I called, panic edging my voice. Two of the hoses promptly retracted, and I took a bead on the remaining drogue. My fuel gauge showed the needle somewhere around the first increment above zero, which was one hundred pounds, and I fully expected the engine to flame out before I could plug in. Finally, the probe slipped inside the basket, and I let my forward momentum push the hose in a few feet. The green light on the tanker belly came on indicating fuel transfer, and a wave of relief washed over me. I was going to make it.

While I was taking on fuel, the Barn Owls' skipper called to tell us that the SAR had been called off. They had seen Arv being led down the hill by his captors. The rescue helicopter was only about halfway in to Arv's hill when the SAR was terminated. It seemed the admiral had refused to let the helo start inland when I had originally called for it because of a false report of MiG activity in the area. By the time he gave permission for the helo to go inland, it was low on fuel and had to land back aboard the north SAR destroyer to refuel.

Marv Quaid had been trying to raise Mark Daniels since we had left the SAR area. While Commander Quaid was refueling, Red Crown called to notify us that Mark had been picked up from the water and was aboard the destroyer. Mark had been hit while he was relaying radio calls for us and had lost his radio. Unable to find the tankers, he had ejected close to the north SAR destroyer when his airplane ran out of fuel. Mark's left knee was damaged severely when he ejected, and he spent the rest of the cruise in the hospital in Subic Bay.

During the long flight back to the ship, Commander Quaid rested his helmet on the glare shield. Waves of emotion broke over me when I saw this expression of grief. The aftermath of fear and the anguish over Arv's capture hit me, and I sobbed into my oxygen mask. We were the last two airplanes of the ill-fated strike group to land on the Bonnie Dick. We had been airborne for nearly three hours. Air Wing 21 had suffered a total defeat, and I considered 31 May 1967 to be the worst day of my life.

Arv Chauncey's capture just two weeks after Homer Smith was taken prisoner had left us numb. We missed the cheerful presence of Mark Daniels after he was transferred to the hospital at Cubi Point. Attack Squadron 212 had little time to dwell on its losses, though; operations continued at a heavy pace. The weather continued to dictate what targets we could attack, and we got a much-needed respite the day after the disastrous Kep strike. VA-212 was now hurting for airplanes. Arv's and Mark's had been lost, and the skipper's was heavily damaged. But even with the shortage of airplanes I flew one combat hop on Lt. Cdr. Pete Yonke's wing when we bombed some barges in the Son Ca River south of Vinh. For the first time in weeks we didn't see any return ground fire and the hop was uneventful. Early on the morning of 2 June, I launched on my first night combat hop of the cruise, but my radio was rendered inoperative when something jarred loose during the catapult shot. I joined on my flight leader and signaled no radio, so we just orbited the ship until the next recovery. On the next launch, tragedy struck yet again when Lt. Cdr. Rex Wood from VF-24 simply disappeared after launching. He failed to make the rendezvous with his wingman and was never seen again. We began searching for him at first light, but there was no trace of his airplane. Our terrible losses continued to mount.

There was a bit of good news, too. Terry Rieder was promoted to lieutenant (junior grade) on 1 June, and Lt. Dick Thomas became Lieutenant Commander Thomas the same day. This left me as the only ensign in VA-212—and indeed, in the entire air wing—so I had the dubious distinction of being the wing's junior pilot. Terry's promotion to j.g. was punctuated by a 57-mm shrapnel hole in his right wing the next day, but he was able to get back to the ship and land safely.

15

Deadly Combat

I flew my fiftieth combat mission on 4 June 1967. Lt. Cdr. Pete Yonke and I had been assigned to fly flak suppression for some VA-76 bombers on a mini–alpha strike, but it was canceled at the last minute so Pete and I flew an armed reconnaissance mission instead. Armed recce hops were simply hunting missions looking for targets of opportunity. We were armed with 5-inch Zuni rockets, loaded four to a pod with two pods on each wing. The Zunis in each pod had two VT-fused warheads and two high-explosive incendiary warheads. The VT fuses were small radar sets in the nose of the rocket that would detonate the warhead on receiving a strong enough signal from the object the missile was about to hit. The VT heads would cause the rocket to explode anywhere from ten to thirty feet prior to impact to maximize the spread of shrapnel. They were designed to be antipersonnel weapons and were effective as flak suppression weapons because the purpose of flak suppressors was to silence the gun by killing the gun crew. Pete located some barges in the Song Ca River just a few miles South of Vinh. It was Sunday, but the gunners in Vinh obviously were not in church because they lobbed about a hundred rounds of heavy 85-mm antiaircraft fire at us. Our attack on the barges was inconsequential in that we didn't observe any secondary fires or explosions from our attacks. The flak missed us, too, so I guess we quit even on that engagement.

Flight operations were halted early on 5 June because of inclement weather—but not before we suffered yet another casualty. Lt. Cdr. Colley Haines, the officer in charge of the VFP-63 photo recon detachment, was hit by 37-mm and automatic weapons fire. His escort fighter saw no ejection or parachute from the stricken RF-8 before it crashed and exploded, and he thought Colley might have been hit in the cockpit. Colley's loss brought the total number of Air Wing 21 pilots killed or captured on this cruise to fifteen.

Two weeks remained in this, our third line period. We were due to rotate off the line on 19 June for a short R&R period in Subic Bay, and God knew we needed it. Fatigue and the relentless pace of combat had us walking around like zombies, and I now understood the true meaning of the phrase "thousand-yard stare." The USS *Enterprise* was on Yankee Station with us while the USS *Hancock* was on a short off-line period. The *Hancock* would return to the line for a short seventeen-day line period at the end of June and would be relieved by the USS *Oriskany*. The *Enterprise* was to end its 1967 combat cruise in the middle of July on being relieved by the USS *Forrestal*, and we were scheduled to leave for home at the end of July on being relieved by the USS *Coral Sea*. But mid-July was six hard weeks away, and I hardly dared to think of going home. The combat pilots on the Bonnie Dick had suffered an almost 15 percent casualty rate, and the dry season was just starting in North Vietnam. From here on the intensity of combat would steadily increase.

Weather and a shortage of flyable airplanes had restricted our operations mainly to cyclic launches—the normal hour-and-forty-five-minute cycles of launches and recoveries when the ship was launching individual squadrons rather than alpha strikes. But on 10 June the weather cleared over North Vietnam, and Cdr. Marv Quaid led a flight of four Walleye-carrying airplanes against the Hanoi thermal power plant. Homer Smith and Mike Cator had failed to knock the power plant out of commission on the original power plant strike back in May due to bad weather over the target. VA-212 got the job done on this strike, but two of the four airplanes were hit. One was too badly damaged to salvage, but again the gutsy little A-4 got its pilot back home. VF-24 wasn't as fortunate. Lt. Cdr. Tom Hall was flying MiG CAP cover for the strike. He was hit by a SAM or flak, had to eject practically over downtown Hanoi, and was taken prisoner.

VA-212 was very low on airplanes now. In addition to the two we had lost on the Kep strike, four had heavy battle damage. This left the division with only six airplanes, and one of those was being used as a tanker. We were supposed to get three new airplanes as replacements this in-port period, and the airplane I had left in Udorn was ready to be returned. We could refresh and replenish our airplanes, but refreshing our spirits was more difficult.

Continuing President Johnson's policy of making life difficult for the North Vietnamese, on 11 June Commander Quaid led VA-212's four remaining airworthy combat airplanes against the Uong Bi thermal power plant north of Haipong—the target that had claimed Homer Smith in May. The strike was successful and did heavy damage to the power plant. One of the F-8 MiG CAPs was shot down, but the pilot was able to eject over a high ridge covered in heavy jungle. Quaid led the rescue effort, and they got the pilot out uninjured.

———•——

Clang, clang, clang. . . . The general quarters klaxon rousted us out of exhausted sleep at 0200 on the morning of 12 June. "Fire! Fire! Fire! . . . Fire in the starboard catapult machinery room," the ship's PA announced. Fire on an aircraft carrier is always serious, and this was no drill. Thoughts of the disastrous *Oriskany* fire invaded my mind as I struggled to pull on flight suit and boots and raced to my battle station in the squadron ready room. Most of the USS *Oriskany*'s air wing pilots had asphyxiated from smoke inhalation in their staterooms during that fire. As a result, every compartment on the Bonnie Dick had emergency oxygen breathing devices (OBAs) for each man in the compartment. But the OBAs were dubious protection from thick black smoke from a chemical fire, and I didn't want to be trapped in the rabbit warren of the forecastle in a fire. It was all over in about twenty minutes. Damage control parties extinguished the fire with minimal damage to the machinery room and we returned to fitful sleep.

The thirteenth of June had Air Wing 21 flying yet another alpha strike deep into North Vietnam. This time the target was the Cam Li ammo storage area about thirty-five miles northeast of Hanoi, not far from Kep. Fortune smiled this time, and the strike group got in and out without a shot being fired at them! All the VA-212 airplanes on this mission were flying Iron Hand cover. I was not yet qualified on that mission, so I flew the strike tanker orbiting over the Dragon's Teeth. On returning from the mission I got the great news that I could move into a stateroom. No more JO Jungle! I moved into a very nice two-man room just under the forward part of the island. A very nice fellow, Lt. Bill DeRousie of VA-215, was my roommate.

The ship got a delightful break from the hard routine of flight operations on the fourteenth. Actor Hugh O'Brien and most of the original Broadway cast of *Guys and Dolls* put on a performance while we took a day off from the war. The cast had arrived the day before on the mail delivery C-2A Greyhound from Cubi Point. Two of the female members of the troupe were invited to observe the alpha strike recovery from the LSO platform and were given a radio headset and microphone. When the pilots made their "on the ball" report to the LSO as they rolled into the groove for final approach, one of the girls would answer, "Roger, ball," in a sultry, sexy voice. The physical jolt caused by hearing a female voice after a month at sea was amazing! Each airplane would sort of bobble and wiggle in the groove when its pilot heard the sound.

Hangar Bay One was converted into a theater by lowering the number one aircraft elevator and halting it about four feet above the hangar deck. Folding chairs were set up in the hangar bay for the performances, but there were far more sailors to see the shows than there were chairs available, so sailors were hanging from every possible vantage point. The troupe put on two shows, with half the ship's company present for each. For a few magical hours elevator one was a Broadway stage. The performers coped with the vagaries of using the hangar bay as a theater like the true professionals they were and produced a wonderful show. Actress Joey Heatherton did a preshow song-and-dance number that really wowed the troops. She came out wearing a skintight leotard that outlined all her female charms perfectly. The ship's photographer, armed with a five-by-seven professional press camera, took several highly revealing shots from a point just under the four-foot stage and later produced a number of glossy eight-by-ten blowups that clearly showed the outline of Joey's most intimate places. These pictures got immediate and widespread distribution about the ship. The Bonnie Dick's public information officer was horrified at the lewdness of the photographs and tried to confiscate them, but VA-212 refused to relinquish its copy, which had been given an honored place under glass on the squadron duty officer's desk in the ready room. Each of us would give Joey's pussy an affectionate pat for luck on our way to man airplanes for a strike.

I had begun this line period with a vow to improve my carrier landing performance. The LSOs graded each pilot's landings on a four-point grading scale, and cumulative averages of each pilot's landing grades were displayed on a board in the ready room. At the end of the first two line periods I had been dead last. As the junior pilot in the air wing, I suspected that I was graded more harshly than more senior pilots, but since good grades in carrier landings were synonymous with staying alive, I was determined to improve my standing in the competition. Someone had suggested that I might improve my landing skills by observing as many landings as I could from the LSO platform, so during recoveries on which I wasn't flying, I would stand behind the duty LSO and watch each pass. It was instructive and helpful to see the areas in the approach where errors in flight path control were likely to occur and to understand what corrections were necessary to return to a perfect pass.

Knowing this allowed me to better anticipate corrections, and I could fly farther ahead of my airplane, so to speak. I also concentrated on remembering each detail of my own landings and graded myself even more harshly than the LSO did. My efforts paid off, and at the end of our third line period I was fifth in the squadron in landing grade average.

During one memorable recovery, the LSO team and I witnessed an epic battle between man, machine, and the sea. Recovering battle-damaged airplanes had become rather commonplace by this point in the cruise, so when Lt. (jg) Mike Wallace reported that his F-8 Crusader had battle damage, no one on the LSO platform was particularly concerned. Designed for carrier operations, the F-8 had a long, slender fuselage with top-mounted wings and a unique aerodynamic design. The fuselage would remain level while the wings were raised hydraulically to increase the angle of attack in the landing configuration. Any former F-8 driver will tell you that the Crusader was a superb fighter plane but a bitch to land. The variable-incidence wing incorporated a leading-edge high-lift device called "droop" when the wing was raised for landing. The "droop" was a hinged portion of the leading edge next to the fuselage that formed a curved surface to increase the aerodynamic camber of the wing.

Mike was aware that his left wing's leading edge had been hit by flak, but he had no idea that his entire left wing droop would separate from the wing when it was raised for landing. Believing that his damage was minor, Mike flew a normal traffic pattern at the ship, turning into his damaged left wing. Just past the point where he began his crosswind turn to final approach, the left wing, lacking its droop, stalled and the F-8 began an uncontrolled roll to the left. The nose pitched sharply down, and Mike found himself in a steep, rolling dive toward the water only six hundred feet below. Mike reacted to his training and did the proper thing: he pulled the face curtain sharply down to eject. Nothing happened. He grabbed the alternate ejection handle between his thighs and pulled up hard. Nothing happened. We watched in horror as the F-8 spiraled ever more steeply toward the water. "*Eject! Eject! Eject!*" screamed the LSO over the radio. But Mike couldn't eject, and the F-8 disappeared in a huge cloud of spray. A heartbeat later, it reemerged from the cloud of spray in full afterburner and for a few seconds did the deadly "Sabre dance" across the water, kept airborne mainly by the thrust of the afterburner. Somehow, perhaps because it was dead calm without a ripple to disturb the surface of the Gulf that day, Mike's F-8 generated enough lift from ground effect during its wild gyrations to allow the left wing to accelerate out of the stall, and he was able to regain control and climb out of a watery grave. The aerodynamic forces separating him from crashing must have been measured in micrometers.

Mike took the F-8 far behind the ship and made a long, gingerly, straight-in approach. Keeping his speed up to compensate for the lack of left wing droop, he made a near perfect pass and was yanked to a brutal stop by the 3-wire. But he was alive and safely aboard. Mike's airplane had flown three combat missions since returning from the overhaul facility in Cubi Point, not counting the flight from Cubi to the ship, but maintenance inspections had failed to reveal that the ejection seat initiators had not been reinstalled after the seat was removed during the airplane's overhaul. So Lt. (jg) Mike Wallace became one of the very few aviators ever who lived to write "Ejection seat inop." in the airplane maintenance discrepancy log.

Mercifully, our third line period ended on 18 June. That morning, three of us flew the final strike of the line period against a small bridge across an irrigation canal that fed some of the innumerable rice paddies in the coastal plain just north of Thanh Hoa. Commander Quaid led the strike; I was his number two, and Lt. (jg) Davy Wolf was number three. We carried a mixed ordnance load of Mark-82 bombs and big Bullpup missiles. After dropping the bridge, we were to expend our remaining weapons on the remains of a train that an armed reconnaissance mission had surprised the day before. Terrain considerations dictated a south-to-north run at the bridge. There wasn't much flak right in the target area, but we knew that we could count on some heavy stuff from Thanh Hoa.

Just a mile or so north of the bridge on the east side of the canal was a large cathedral, a remnant of the French Catholic colonial influence in Vietnam. Just what stature the church retained in Communist North Vietnam wasn't clear to us, but we certainly didn't want to blow up a church. Commander Quaid carefully indicated its location to us in the briefing, relating an experience he had in the Korean War when his group had attacked a target very close to a Buddhist temple. Commander Quaid repeated the admonishment he had received as a junior pilot in Korea: "Don't hit the pagoda."

The big Bullpup was a larger version of the AGM-45B, which we called the Smallpup. The Smallpup was launched from a rail, while the Bigpup, which had a much larger thousand-pound warhead, was dropped from the bomb rack just like a bomb. After falling clear of the airplane, the Bigpup's rocket motor would ignite and the pilot would guide it to the target. The guidance principle was simplicity itself. The missile had a bright flare burning in its tail that the pilot simply flew into his line of sight to the target and then guided to the target pipper with a joystick mounted on the left console in the cockpit. The pilot flew the A-4 with his right hand and the missile with his left. Success required two absolutely steady hands.

The skipper gave me first crack at the bridge. We had observed some heavy 85-mm flak out of Thanh Hoa on the way in to the target, but they were shooting at extreme range and we had no trouble avoiding the bursts. Without antiaircraft defenses to disrupt my run, I had a clear shot at the bridge. Stabilizing in the run, I pressed the bomb pickle and felt the airplane lurch as the Bigpup left the wing. The rocket motor ignited perfectly and I saw the missile accelerate out ahead of me in a shower of orange sparks. I focused all my concentration on flying the bright flare into the line of sight formed by my gun sight pipper on the bridge. Everything went well and I held the missile right on target until about five seconds before impact, when it stopped responding to my control inputs, veered sharply left, and exploded in a haystack about a hundred yards left of the bridge.

I swallowed my disappointment and broke right to circle clear while Davy Wolf tried his hand at the bridge. Davy had the bridge nailed! But just before impact his missile pulled up sharply and streaked level just a few feet over the bridge. Again, either local radio interference or a transmitter/receiver failure had broken Davy's control of the missile. The Bigpup continued up the canal just a few feet above the level of the banks, began a slight turn to the right, and flew right through the front door of the church, exploding inside and blowing the roof off the building. "Aw, Davy," the skipper exclaimed. "You hit the pagoda!"

Commander Quaid began his run on the bridge while Davy and I circled to the east. He nailed the target dead center, and his Bullpup took out the whole bridge. When the smoke cleared, the bridge was gone, from bank to bank. We bombed what was left of the train that the armed recce pilots had mostly destroyed the previous day and recovered without incident. I claimed a "fuel storage area for water buffalo" on my after-action report. I don't know how Davy characterized his hit, but I do know that church needed a new roof.

The ship left the line at 1300 after launching the airplanes being flown to the corrosion control facility. I envied the fly-in pilots, but we had an afternoon full of nuclear weapons loading drills, and I had several loads scheduled. After that, I had the midnight-to-0400 flight deck integrity watch. The ship would pull into Subic Bay at 0800 the next morning, and I would be duty free for the entire in-port period. I intended to catch up on all the sleep I had lost during the line period and to drink a lot to try to keep from thinking about the next line period just eight days away.

The ship had already docked alongside the long quay on the Subic side of the bay by the time I rolled out of bed. We were on the Subic side because the USS *Enterprise* was docked at the carrier pier at Cubi Point preparing to head for home. The other Seventh Fleet carriers always began their Pacific transit from Japan, but since nuclear power was politically sensitive at the time, the *Enterprise* did not make port calls in the Japanese home islands. She would head straight for home from Subic Bay.

Lt. (jg) Tom Green, one of my old roommates from Preflight, was an F-4 pilot on the USS *Enterprise*, and I headed over to look him up. I found Tom in high spirits, as were all the *Enterprise* pilots on the eve of their departure for America and home. Most of them would get to fly home rather than having to ride the ship because no flight operations were planned for the transit. Since this was my first visit to the world's first nuclear-powered aircraft carrier Tom took me on a tour. The ship was immense and, compared with the World War II–vintage Bonnie Dick, very modern. The staterooms were spacious and well appointed, and I stood and gawked at the gargantuan flight deck. With both waist and bow catapults and a large parking area behind the island, the huge flight deck could accommodate simultaneous launches and recoveries. I teased Tom by telling him that any pilot who got a 1-wire or boltered on this huge flight deck ought to have his wings yanked! Trying to keep the envy out of my voice, I bid the *Enterprise* pilots bon voyage and headed over to the O club for lunch.

After lunch, I joined a few other Rampant Raiders for a round of golf on one of the world's most unusual golf courses. The sprawling military complex at Subic Bay—including the Subic Golf Course—had been carved out of tropical jungle. The fairways were beautiful and well groomed, but there was no rough in the usual sense of the word. The "rough" was virgin jungle, and one entered there in search of a hooked or sliced ball at one's peril. Many poisonous snakes were indigenous to the region, and I had no doubt that many made their home right there in the jungle surrounding the golf course. The prudent thing to do in the event of a ball off the fairway was to drop a new ball and take the one-stroke penalty. The course even had a rule allowing a player to drop a new ball without penalty if one of the numerous wild monkeys that lived around the course should scamper across the fairway and steal the old one.

One of the holes had a large sign adjacent to the tee cautioning anyone with a bad heart to bypass it and go on to the next hole. The tee faced a nearly vertical hill about fifty yards away and across a small stream. Once safely at the base of the hill the golfer looked up about two hundred feet to a target at the top of the hill (the pin on the green was located out of sight over the lip of the precipice). Between the level fairway and the tiny green at the summit were two terraces cut into the side of the hill. The gutsy shot was to try to chip all the way to the green from the bottom in one shot, but if one hit short, the ball would plummet back down and roll into the stream. Far safer to chip up to each terrace and try for the green from the second. Alongside the breath-takingly steep path to the top of the hill was an electrically powered ski lift rope tow that assisted golfers up the slope. After completing a more or less conventional hole on the summit of the hill, one turned to a tee on the edge of a two-hundred-foot-tall rock cliff. The L-shaped fairway below had the green at the toe of the L. Again, the safe shot was to drive off the cliff to the juncture with the bottom leg of the L; the gutsy shot was to drive straight for the green over the hundred-foot-tall jungle canopy below. I don't recall the scores we shot, but the mental exercise of pursuing the little white balls took our minds off the upcoming line period for at least a few hours.

As on our last in-port period, regardless of the exercise of the day, we inevitably ended up in the O club for dinner and then drank until the club closed. The in-port period passed quickly, and the six short days became a blur. By the time the ship pulled out of Subic Bay on 26 June we were as rested and ready to tackle our final line period as we could be. But fear of what lay ahead was a constant presence in the back of my mind.

The fourth and final line period of the 1967 cruise began on 28 June. VA-212 was back to its normal airplane complement with battle damage repaired and the receipt of four refurbished A-4Es. We began by flying cyclic operations the first day to refamiliarize ourselves with our airplanes and carrier operations before resuming alpha strikes. I flew two missions, bombing small highway bridges just north and south of Vinh. I hadn't flown in nine days, and the airplane didn't feel quite comfortable for the first hour or so until my proficiency level returned. The first carrier landing in more than a week felt more difficult than usual, and I had to push myself to speed up my scan and sharpen my responses to corrections needed to stay in the groove. But after the second hop and recovery I was back up to speed. The two strikes were uneventful. We successfully dropped both bridges and observed only some light automatic weapons fire in opposition. It was a good way to reacclimate to combat. We would resume the terrible alpha strike regimen soon enough.

The oppressively hot weather made life on Yankee Station miserable. Summer was in full swing in the Gulf and many days were dead calm with little or no prevailing wind, forcing the ship to accelerate to nearly thirty knots to get the wind across the deck necessary for launch and recovery. The maximum-speed steaming ate up the ship's available sea room in a hurry, so between launches the ship would steam dead slow with just enough way on to maintain rudder control. These between-launch periods were the worst of all—no breeze across the deck, temperatures in the high nineties, and relative humidity close to 100 percent. Adding to the sweaty misery of the flight deck crews were the emissions from the ship's smokestack and galley exhausts, which blanketed the flight deck with no breeze to dissipate them. Choking stack gas would make eyes water and saliva taste like copper. The flight deck crews had to perform hard physical labor at a frenetic pace in these conditions to ready the flight deck for launches and recoveries. Ordnance men loaded iron bombs, missiles, ammo cans, and the myriad other airborne tools of war using human muscle alone. Airplanes had to be shoved around the deck by hand, tie-down chains and chocks had to be carried from place to place, heavy refueling hoses had to be dragged to and from airplanes, and a hundred other things had to be done against the ticking clock before the next recovery— heat, humidity, and stack gas be damned. And damned they were, often and fluently by the sailors toiling in these unglamorous and unsung jobs.

The ship would still be wallowing in the greasy troughs of the gentle swells when the pilots manned their airplanes. The relief of the breeze created when the ship began to accelerate to launch speed was indescribable as sweat-soaked flight suits gave up some of their moisture to evaporation. The relief was short-lived, however, when engines were started and the flight deck was bathed in jet fumes and heat from exhausts. The F-8 fighters were usually launched first, and when they were carrying external stores they had to use afterburners for launch. This made life on the flight deck even more miserable. Planes waiting for launch would have to lock their canopies down tight—not even a small crack between the canopy rail and canopy for ventilation—when the F-8s were using burners for takeoff. The greenhouse effect of the sun beating down on the Plexiglas would raise the temperature inside the cockpit to 130 degrees within minutes. The air conditioner on the A-4 was a compression-expansion type system that depended on engine RPM for volume of output. At idle RPM only a whisper of cool air would emanate from the cockpit's eyeball vents. To get what little cool air flow we could, we would turn the temperature knob down to full cold while at idle power taxiing for launch or waiting in line.

All of us experienced A-4 pilots had learned at one time or another to turn the temperature control to about half hot when we ran the engine up to full power for takeoff. If this wasn't done and the temperature control was still on full cold, the air-conditioner would produce billowing clouds of thick, white condensation fog that looked like white smoke and would scare the shit out of the pilot, who would think he had a serious electrical fire. VA-76 had received a new pilot replacement during the off-line period, and the young lieutenant (jg) was making his debut launch with VA-76. Fresh out of the A-4 RAG, the new man was understandably nervous about his first launch with his new squadron, and was no doubt frightened because this was also his first combat mission. For these reasons or simply because he didn't know any better, he forgot to turn his temperature control up when he was positioned on the catapult. About halfway down the deck on the cat stroke, thick white clouds billowed up around his legs. As his A-4 clawed for altitude off the catapult, the pilot screamed over the radio, "Rocket Tower, Sunglass six-eight-six. I've got cock in the smoke pit." He never lived it down.

The Bonnie Dick really showed her age when trying to get up to the thirty knots required to launch. Small warps in the shafts driving the four giant bronze screws that thrust the big ship through the water would create a heavy vibration in the aft part of the ship. When the ship was straining to get thirty knots, a person could tap dance by standing still on the fantail. It wasn't uncommon for pilots taxiing up to the blast deflector to hear the air boss ask, "Eagle X, will you accept three knots of excess?" meaning that the catapult shot would accelerate the airplane to only three knots above stall speed as it was flung into the air. That was simply a pro forma call to make it official that the pilot accepted the responsibility of flying his airplane with only a three-knot margin of error, thereby relieving the ship from any blame if the pilot and airplane should wind up in Davy Jones's Locker. None of us ever said no; that wasn't an option. So we would be launched off the bow into immediate stall buffet as the little A-4s struggled to overcome gravity and fly. Our left hand would shoot off the throttle as soon as the G forces of the cat shot relaxed and hover over the red-and-white barber-pole jettison handle, which if pulled would clean off all external stores and suddenly make the airplane about seven thousand pounds lighter. If the engine merely coughed and lost any thrust at all, the airplane was surely in the drink. The onset of stall buffet was accompanied by a sinking feeling as the airplane mushed and settled off the bow to within thirty feet of the water. Sometimes the air boss would scream "*Pull up!*" over the radio, and the pilot, trying to milk flying speed out of his struggling airplane, would think what the hell do you think I'm trying to do? We had no idea just how far we were settling off the bow until someone in the plane guard helicopter shot some profile movies of an A-4 launch. We were horrified to see that we were so close to the water as we accelerated to flying speed that the jet exhaust of the engine at full thrust was blowing spray back over the bow of the ship! We never lost an airplane this way, but we were definitely flying at the margins of the envelope.

By 30 June, Air Wing 21 had resumed a full alpha-strike schedule. Only bad weather would be allowed to alter the planned schedule of three alpha strikes per day for the remainder of our line period. The Johnson administration was determined to inflict so much damage on North Vietnam's infrastructure that the North Vietnamese would be forced to the conference table to begin peace talks. It was yet another example of the complete misunderstanding of the proper use of military force and the misapplication of air power that so characterized America's involvement in the Vietnam War.

The United States never enjoyed air superiority over North Vietnam because our military forces were never allowed to attack the source of the air defenses arrayed against us. The main resupply point for North Vietnam was the harbor and dock complex in Haiphong, but the ships bringing in war matériel and the dock facilities remained off limits to U.S. air power because it was "not politically feasible" to attack them. In this sense, our bombing raids in the summer of 1967 were strategic rather than tactical in nature because they were designed to pursue a diplomatic solution to the efforts of the North Vietnamese Communists to reunify Vietnam and force communism on South Vietnam. The Johnson administration never understood that by attacking the shipping in Haiphong Harbor and mining the harbor against future resupply they would have denied the North Vietnamese the ability to wage war in the South. But Lyndon Johnson and his advisers had decided that military victory in the conflict was impossible and refused to hit the one target that could have won the war.

The change in target assignments also meant that except for sporadic cyclic operations when the weather prevented alpha strikes, U.S. air power was not patrolling the supply routes in the lower route packages of North Vietnam. Meanwhile, the enemy was rapidly repairing and rebuilding the bridges and roads we had previously knocked out. Ignoring these interdiction targets allowed the North Vietnamese to move the massive amounts of military equipment into South Vietnam that were required for the Tet Offensive of January 1968.

I was the squadron duty officer on 1 July 1967, and Commander Quaid chose that occasion to approve and present my promotion to lieutenant (junior grade). The senior officers of VA-212 had been yanking my chain by telling me that they wouldn't allow my promotion to j.g. until another ensign was transferred in to replace me, and I had been starting to believe them. The promotion changed nothing. I was still the junior officer in the squadron, but at least I wasn't a nugget anymore. My dad sent me his old lieutenant (jg) bars and shoulder boards from his World War II uniform, and my reflection in my stateroom mirror showed a flush of pride as I pinned them on. My logbook showed that I had accumulated sixty-three combat missions as an ensign.

The second, third, and fourth days of July began a series of alpha strikes that would become known among the pilots of Air Wing 21 as the "Dr. Pepper strikes." U.S. air losses in the heavily defended Route Package 6A area had reached unprecedented levels, and U.S. airmen were being lost or taken prisoner almost daily. In a desperate attempt to improve our countermeasures the admiral decreed that Navy strikes had to have active electronic countermeasures (ECM) jamming covering any target located in a heavy antiaircraft radar environment—which included nearly all the targets in the Hanoi or Haiphong area. The Navy had no such active jamming capability in the area, so we relied on a U.S. Air Force EB-66 out of Takhli air base in Thailand. The EB-66 had to fly into the Tonkin Gulf south of the DMZ, then up to a station just off the coast near Haiphong. Our strikes were timed for his on-station times and occurred at approximately 1000, 1400, and 1600—or ten, two, and four—hence the name "Dr. Pepper strikes" from the old advertisement slogan, "Drink a bite to eat at ten, two, and four." In addition to being tied to certain times of the day, we also had a relatively narrow corridor to the targets that could be jammed and thus had to approach the target from the same direction each time. We used to joke that the North Vietnamese gunners would glance at their watches, declare that it was about time for the ten o'clock strike, drop their poker hands, aim their guns at our entry point, and be waiting for us when we arrived.

The target that prompted the Dr. Pepper strikes was in Hai Duong, a city roughly halfway between Hanoi and Haiphong that was a major railroad and highway transshipment point. The Red River Delta lies in the alluvial plain between Hanoi and the coast of North Vietnam. Many secondary channels and tributaries split off the main Red River Channel in the delta. A number of railroad and highway bridges crossed these channels at Hai Duong, and they had been a high-priority target since April. The extensive air defenses in and around Hai Duong were a sure sign of the importance of these bridges to the North Vietnamese transportation system. An actual photographic count showed more than one thousand antiaircraft gun barrels around the area. Many prepared SAM sites lay within SAM range of the area, and our intelligence estimated that at least fifteen SAM batteries containing five to ten SAMs each were somewhere in the area at any time. The targets were also a short flight time from the MiG bases at Phuc Yen, Kep, Bac Giang, and Cat Bi. In other words, Hai Duong was one of the most heavily defended pieces of real estate in the history of aerial warfare.

Our main target in Hai Duong was nothing so glamorous as a bridge. The bridges had long since been blasted away by previous strikes. When the main railroad and highway bridge was destroyed, though, its center support structure remained standing in the middle of the Black River Channel. This concrete cylinder was about thirty feet in diameter and extended perhaps ten feet above the surface of the river. Seventh Fleet target planners had decided that the North Vietnamese were stringing cables across the river at night and pulling bridge sections into place, using the old bridge piling for the necessary support in the center, so they decreed that the bridge support had to be destroyed or rendered unusable. I cannot imagine a more difficult task for bombers. The best we could do with Mark-82 and Mark-83 bombs was blast chunks off the piling until we chiseled it down below the surface. A miss of inches into the river was a wasted bomb; only a direct hit would damage the chunk of concrete. Out of a forty-plane alpha strike, only four or six would be bombers. All the others would be support airplanes for the bombers: flak suppressors, Iron Hand cover, TARCAP, tankers, and, of course, the Air Force jamming airplane.

To reach the target and remain within the jamming cover of the EB-66 we had to fly within easy visual range of the anchorage and docks of the port facility in Haiphong. We saw as many as twenty large transport ships busily unloading war matériel for North Vietnam in the harbor each time we flew to Hai Duong. For every missile and artillery shell fired at us, replacements were already being unloaded in Haiphong. As badly as we wanted to hit the harbor, and as useless as we felt the assigned target to be, none of us deviated from our assigned targets. Orders were orders, and we were sworn to obey. We wished mightily that the top people in the Johnson administration would come to their senses and let us hit the harbor, but they never did.

It was a long way in to Hai Duong—about thirty miles from our coast-in point, with enemy air defenses all the way. On the Fourth of July, I was flying my third trip to Hai Duong as Lt. Cdr. Pete Yonke's number two. Pete was leading the entire alpha strike with a division of flak suppressors. The attack was straightforward; the flak suppressors leading the bombers would roll in ahead with the bombers in our wake. I had been assigned a large 57-mm gun site that recent photo reconnaissance showed to be occupied. My target would be easy to spot; it was located in the only bend in a long, straight stretch of highway that was closely paralleled by railroad tracks. The second section of flak suppressors was led by the XO, Cdr. Fred Whittemore. Two

F-8s from VF-211 and two from VF-24 would also provide flak suppression with their Zuni rockets. The three A-4s in the lead division had hard targets assigned, but there were many more guns in the target area than there were flak suppressors. We had targeted the gun sites that posed the most hazard to the bombers. Commander Yonke told us that he would pick his target from the remainder on the way in. Whichever untargeted site was firing the most would be his.

The launch and rendezvous went as planned, and Pete headed the strike group due north up the Tonkin Gulf toward the coast-in point. We had climbed to twelve thousand feet for the run in, and Pete accelerated the formation to 450 knots as we neared the coast. It was a hazy, gray day with a high, thin cirrus overcast about ten thousand feet above us that would silhouette our airplanes against the sky, making optical tracking easier for the North Vietnamese gunners. Pete called for us to arm switches as the force went feet dry and started us gently jinking. About halfway in to the target, black puffs began to burst ahead and to the left of the formation. Each sooty black puff marked the origin of a small, deadly cloud of whirling chunks of steel. Radio discipline went to hell as many voices tried to report the flak simultaneously. The 85-mm gun site that had taken us under fire was easy to spot. It was a large concentration of guns, and their muzzle flashes stood out clearly in the subdued light of the cloudy day. Pete startled me with the transmission, "You have the lead, Eagle Two. I'm going after that guy." I had no time to react as I watched the belly of Pete's airplane turn up as he rolled in on the flak site.

There wasn't much leading required at that point. We were headed directly toward the target about fifteen miles ahead. All I had to do was kiss off the second section in time for them to acquire their own targets. But I had never expected to be leading the entire alpha strike. For about two minutes I was the point of the spear. In my usual position as a wingman, I divided my attention between keeping formation on the lead and glimpsing the ground en route to the target. The only time I had my attention solely on the ground was during my bombing run, and that was only on the small area of my immediate target. Throughout the recovery and retirement, my attention focused on rejoining the leader. So this was the first time the entire panorama of the battle arena was visible to me undistracted by the requirements of station keeping. I had the general target area in sight from the time Pete passed me the lead. The Black River Channel was the largest of the meandering watercourses in the Red River Delta, and the village of Hai Duong was the largest in the collection of many small villages in the area. The ground ahead of me began to twinkle and flash as the Hai Duong gunners opened up on us. The other elements of the alpha strike began to split off to set up for their attacks. I turned right in the cockpit and threw a kiss to Commander Whittemore signaling him to break off for the second section's attacks. I could see my target dead ahead, the intensity of the muzzle flashes actually reflected by the water in the surrounding rice paddies.

Since my target was exactly at my twelve o'clock, a roll-ahead maneuver was required to set up my bomb run. I bored ahead level until the target almost disappeared under the nose. Then I pulled the nose up about twenty degrees and snap-rolled the A-4 inverted. Acquiring the target through the top of the canopy, I pulled the nose down until the target crossed the canopy bow and then snapped the little airplane upright and picked up the target in my gun sight, cross-checking for forty-five degrees in the dive. The gun site had been delivering barrage-type antiaircraft fire, concentrating on blanketing an area of sky with bursts. The disciplined pattern of muzzle flashes resulting from the barrage fire began to falter as individual gunners saw me and shifted their fire to blast me out of the sky before I could get them. The larger antiaircraft guns did not use tracer streams to direct their fire, so I could not see how close the shells were coming, but even through the canopy and helmet I could hear the staccato *pop . . . pop . . . pop* from the shock waves of the supersonic shells as they passed very close to me. Something in me snapped. All the months of fear and stress finally became more than I could endure. I was overwhelmed by black rage and an intense desire to kill. Gone were any objective thoughts of silencing the site; this was very personal now, between the gunners and me. I wanted them to die. "*YAAAA!*" I heard myself scream into the oxygen mask. "I'm going to get you bastards!" Reflex caused by training and habit made me punch the bomb pickle and begin pulling out of the dive, for at that moment I would have dived right into the middle of the gun site, ensuring the gunners' destruction as well as my own. *Whoomp . . . whoomp!* My airplane was jolted violently as I passed through someone's jet wash, jarring me back to reality. "Good bombing, Buddy," came the exultant voice of the XO over my headset, referring to my hits on the gun site. In my battle frenzy I had not even looked for my hits.

The strike group retired from the target without losses, and Pete rejoined us feet wet after having really pasted the 85-mm site. There was some exuberant chatter over the radio on the way back to the ship, but I couldn't join in. I was still shaking from the intensity of the emotion I had felt. Later, in the quiet solitude of my stateroom, I wrote a letter to my dad expressing my fear that I had become devoid of normal compassion and humanity and asking if he had a similar experience fighting the kamikaze in World War II. He wrote back assuring me that I would recover from these feelings once I left behind the stress of combat. But I knew with deep regret that my psyche had been scarred forever and I would never again be the same person.

At about this time, in July 1967, a group of U.S. citizens opposed to the war made a pilgrimage to North Vietnam. This group was by no means the first. Several such groups had visited Hanoi to atone for their government's policy of waging war on the peace-loving people of North Vietnam. The North Vietnamese government was delighted to have these groups as guests because their visits provided valuable propaganda for the Communists, who could show the world that the people of the United States wanted no part of the war that the "imperialistic, warmongering government of the United States was forcing on its people." A popular young film star named Jane Fonda had decided to become an antiwar activist and had accompanied this latest group of supplicants, providing media interest because of her public persona. She traveled about Hanoi giving whatever aid and comfort she could to the enemies of her country—the country that had nurtured her, pampered her, and made her wealthy, and whose principles of freedom made it the only country on Earth that would not make her stand trial on charges of treason for her activities. One day while providing propaganda photo opportunities for the international press, Jane climbed up onto the trainer's seat of a North Vietnamese antiaircraft gun. Squinting through the optical gun sight while the press corps was busily filming and snapping pictures, she quipped, "I wish I had one of those Yankee air pirates in my sights." Well, Jane, the feeling was and is mutual. I wish I had known what gun you were sitting on.

By 5 July the *Bon Homme Richard* and Air Wing 21 had established a record for the number of alpha strikes flown—forty-four, the most of any unit in the Navy. We were flying three alpha strikes a day, and so far in this line period had not lost anyone in combat. It seemed that changing our tactics to a twelve-thousand-foot run-in with a forty-five-degree dive and five-hundred-knot, five-thousand-foot release was paying off in decreasing our casualty rate. But I still had to wonder how long our luck would hold.

The first strike that day was on a suspected oil storage site. At the briefing we griped about wasting our time on a nothing target. Because suspected POL sites in the lower route package areas rarely yielded secondary explosions or signs of petroleum, we were convinced that this was just another bomb dump exercise to add to our sortie count. The recon photos did nothing to alter that view. The target was located on the north bank of one of the numerous meandering channels of the Black River not far from the village of Luu Trong, which was about ten miles northwest of the port facilities in Haiphong. The reconnaissance pictures showed what appeared to be a plowed rectangular field covering about fifty acres.

CAG Monger would be leading the strike with two divisions of VA-212 bombers followed by two more divisions of VA-76 bombers. This would put ninety-six Mark-82 500-pound bombs and sixteen Mark-81 250-pound bombs in the fifty-acre field, enough to cover all of it adequately. Two more VA-212 Flying Eagles would provide Iron Hand coverage, and a division each of fighters from VF-24 and VF-211 would escort the strike as TARCAP. No flak suppressors would be needed for this mission because no flak had been observed near the target—another factor supporting our conviction that this target was something the Seventh Fleet target planners had ginned up because they were running out of worthwhile targets in Route Package 6B.

After the air wing briefing we retired to the Rampant Raiders' ready room for the division briefing. I would be flying as CAG's wingman in the number two slot. The meteorological brief of weather conditions in the target area forecast surface winds from the south at about fifteen knots, a fairly stiff breeze. We needed correct surface wind information for bombing accuracy since our bombing was entirely ballistic, but we rarely had wind data from the target, so the surface wind was always a guess. CAG told me in the division briefing that he would use the center of the river channel as his aim point and I should aim at the north bank of the river. If the wind forecast was accurate, our bombs should be right on target. If we hit the river, the trailing bombers would know there was no wind and to bomb pipper to bull. CAG was very thorough in his briefing, and by the time he finished it was time to man airplanes.

CAG led the alpha strike feet dry about ten miles north of the port facility at Hon Gay, about twenty miles northeast of Haiphong, over mountainous terrain that was sparsely populated and had few air defenses. We would head due west until reaching a point northwest of our target, then wheel south and make our bomb runs from west and southwest on an easterly heading. Recovery would be to the northeast over the same mountainous terrain, and we would go feet wet at our original coast-in point.

Everything was going well as CAG started our wheeling turn to the target. No flak had been seen, and the Iron Handers were keeping the SAM radars from coming up for long enough to get a lock on our track. In addition, it was difficult for the North Vietnamese to decide which area we were going to hit because there were many sites we had bombed before that we could attack from our position. CAG rolled in from ninety degrees off the target heading to give the trailing bombers ample time to separate and make individual runs. It was here that he had a problem. The CAG had to be able to fly all the tactical airplanes in his air wing, and it was quite a feat to be current and proficient in all the different types simultaneously. But the A-4C had just the opposite configuration from the A-4E, and had external fuel tanks on the wings and the bombs on the centerline. CAG got the switches set for an A-4C and punched the button to release the external fuel tank instead of the bombs. He called, "Eagle Lead off target. No drop," as he recovered from his bombing run.

I had just begun my bombing run and it was easy to shift my aim point to the center of the river to provide marking hits for the rest of the bombers. Five thousand feet, five hundred knots, and forty-five degrees of dive all came together, and the A-4 jumped and bucked as the bombs rippled off the wings. Jinking right to keep CAG in sight, then left to look back and see my hits, I saw huge fountains of water erupt from the center of the river. "There's no wind! Bomb pipper to bull, pipper to bull," came the call from Eagle Three to the rest of the bombers. I saw the bombs dropped by Eagles Three and Four hit and walk from the southwestern edge of the target toward the center. Huge yellow fireballs from secondary explosions rolled up through the bomb smoke and dirt, with more yellow fireballs embedded in the thick black petroleum smoke billowing up from the target. Massive secondary explosions accompanied every bomb hit. This time the strike group had struck oil.

Not a shot had been fired at us as we rejoined and headed for the ship, leaving behind a column of smoke that rose vertically from the target to at least twenty thousand feet and then stretched across the Tonkin Gulf all the way to Hinan Island. We could still see flames in the base of the column from ten thousand feet above the ship sixty-five miles south of the target. With no casualties, this had been one of the most successful strikes of the cruise. Later, during the high-spirited exaltation over the success of the mission, other pilots began to rib the hell out of me for hitting the river. It did no good to protest that CAG had briefed me to do that to check the wind forecast and that if they hadn't known to bomb pipper to bull we might have missed some of the oil. No, for a few days I was the butt of jokes about killing fish and attacking the food supply. Ah, the vagaries of war.

16

End of the Line

Our fantastic luck, coupled with the change in our bomb delivery profile, continued to hold, and by the end of the first week of July we still had not lost anyone or even had serious battle damage. July seventh was another three-alpha-strike day for Air Wing 21, and it was back to the bridges at Phu Ly. We had dropped the main railroad and highway bridge on 30 May, but the ever-resourceful North Vietnamese had built a bypass bridge and were busily reconstructing the main bridge. VA-212 was assigned to bomb this new construction with two divisions of bombers—one on the bypass and the other to destroy the repairs that had been made to the main bridge. VA-76 and VF-211 would fly flak suppression. I was going to fly tail-end Charlie for a change, and my position as the second section wingman, or number four, meant that I would have the bomb damage assessment camera mounted in my centerline bomb rack. I would be able to film the hits of the first two airplanes in the division, and with enough separation, possibly some of number three's hits. The VA-212 bombers were each carrying four of the 750-pound bombs we called "Bridge Busters." The Sunglass flak suppressors from VA-76 would have six Mark-81 250-pounders on their centerline MERs. The Mark-81s were fitted with VT fuses designed to detonate the bomb fifty feet above the flak guns, spewing high-velocity steel shrapnel through the site to kill the gunners. In addition, the F-8 flak suppressors would hose down the gun sites with 5-inch Zuni rockets with warheads designed to produce thousands of rifle bullet–sized pieces of shrapnel that would rip through the target area at nearly supersonic speed.

Phu Ly was heavily defended by 37-mm and 57-mm antiaircraft artillery, but we had never located any SAM sites in the area. The North Vietnamese seemed to want to keep their SAM assets closer to Hanoi and Haiphong. Phu Ly was just close enough to Hanoi that if the strike group swung a little too far north, it would inevitably draw at least one SAM from the area south of Hanoi, which was within easy SAM range of Phu Ly. I wished that we could call the North Vietnamese on guard channel and tell them we weren't coming to Hanoi today so they could save their SAMs on this strike!

It was a long flight in to Phu Ly and we met scattered enemy air defenses along the way, so the strike group had to keep jinking en route to the target from the time we went feet dry. The strategy for this day was to split the strike group about ten miles east of Phu Ly, with the flak suppressors turning southwest and the bomb group swinging north of the target. The intent was to time the split so that the flak suppressors would make their attacks, rolling in from the southwest and running out to the northeast, and their ordnance would be exploding in the flak sites just as the bombers were rolling in from west to east. Also, splitting the strike group forced the Phu Ly gunners to divide their fire to cover both groups as we passed north and south of their positions. The guns were in full throat as we approached our roll-in points, and a thin, gray cloud was forming over the target from the flak bursts.

The main river channel, fed by numerous smaller tributaries from the Annamese Mountains to the west, split at the village of Phu Ly, with one channel running roughly east to the Red River and the other running south toward the "hourglass" area of the Red River Delta. The main railroad and highway bridges that we had dropped in May spanned the east-running channel, and the bypass highway bridge ran across the main channel before the split. A very large 37-mm gun site was located on the west bank just across the road from the bypass bridge, and there were two 57-mm sites on the north bank of the easterly channel. The F-8 with which I had nearly collided on the May strike had been attacking one of these sites.

Our timing was off, and the bombers rolled in too far behind the flak suppressors. Heavy dust and smoke covered the flak sites as we rolled in, but some of the guns were recovering and opening up again. I had seen VA-76's bombs exploding on the 37-mm site as we swung around for our roll-in. Two guns never missed a beat; their muzzle flashes continued to pound away even as the bombs were exploding fifty feet over their heads. I had to admire the courage of the gun crews who remained at their posts in spite of the hailstorm of death killing their comrades on the other guns.

I flipped on the camera switch as I began my roll-in. As the last airplane over the target, I had a panoramic view of the battle scene as I rolled over for the dive. Long streams of smoke and dust trailed nearly horizontally away to the north of the 37-mm site, indicating a stiff ground-level wind blowing from the south. Two of the guns in the site continued to twinkle and flash as they shifted their tracking to the bombers. The first division's bombs were causing huge gouts of earth to fountain skyward from the new construction on the main railroad and highway bridges to the east. Eagle Lead hit just a little long, missing the bridge but cratering the road east of the river. Eagle Two, Lt. (jg) Bernie Smith, was right on target with one bomb exploding dead center of the bridge and blowing it apart. I shifted my aim point to the approaches on the west bank and felt the familiar buck and jump as the four Bridge Busters rippled off my wings in pairs. Grunting against the Gs and trying to keep the small spot of vision remaining to me on my leader, I relaxed the pull and jinked left to see my hits as soon as my nose came up above the horizon. Eagle Three's bombs were exploding in the river where the bridge had been, and my bombs hit the bridge abutments and cratered the road. In spite of all the flak and the error in timing the attack, our good luck held and no one was hit. Everyone landed safely, and it was another very successful strike. This strike marked my seventieth combat mission and my ninety-seventh landing on the Bonnie Dick.

The next day, 8 July, was a stand-down day for the *Bon Homme Richard* and Air Wing 21. The break allowed us to perform some much-needed maintenance and catch up on a backlog of administrative details. Enjoyed by all the combat pilots in the air wing, this break in combat operations was one less day of exposure to hazard and one more day closer to the end of combat operations for this cruise. But the next day we were back in the thick of the war.

A petroleum storage area just five miles from downtown Haiphong was our first target. I was tail-end Charlie again, and number ten in the bomber group—the last plane to roll in. VA-212 had launched all its airplanes on this strike except for two A-4s configured as tankers. Lt. (jg) Terry Rieder was also on this mission, one of the few times both of us flew on the same strike. VA-76 was providing flak suppression along with elements from VF-24 and VF-211. About two minutes from the target, a SAM site opened up on us by firing two SAMs at the strike group. Formation integrity disintegrated as we split up to take evasive action. Evasion was not difficult this time because we had seen the launch and had visual on the SAMs from liftoff. The flak suppressors all went after the SAM site, because SAMs had been declared a priority target, and destroyed it along with several missiles still on their launchers. By the time the bomber group rejoined, though, a thunderstorm of flak was building around the target. The ground toward the target looked like a solid carpet of gun flashes as flak puffs began bursting all around the bomber group. White 37-mm puffs, gray 57-mm puffs, and heavy black 85-mm and 100-mm bursts dotted the sky all around us.

I was flying wing on the XO, Commander Whittemore, who was leading the trailing section behind the two divisions of bombers. The bomb group split up to make runs from diverging directions, and the XO swung us wide to set up for our roll-in. The flak gunners were leading us, though, and a huge concentration of 85-mm flak began to burst off our right wing just as he began his roll-in to the right. Whittemore reversed his turn with a hard rolling pull to the left to avoid the flak, and I gritted my teeth and screamed against the diaphragm bladder of my G-suit, trying to keep from blacking out from the Gs of the turn while I fought to maintain formation on him. By the time we reversed back toward the target, we were far out of position and way behind the rest of the bomb group, which was already recovering from the bomb run. When we reached the roll-in point, we were the last two planes in the target area. Every gun that was still operational took us under fire. The target was difficult to see because the flak bursts had formed a thin cloud layer between us and the target. Flak was everywhere and close—even more than I had seen when Arv Chauncey had been shot down. Flashes from exploding shells were reflecting off the Plexiglas canopy and the glass faces of the gauges in the cockpit. It seemed impossible to survive this maelstrom of shrapnel, and I thought we were dead. I had been focusing all my attention on following the XO's evasive maneuvers and maintaining formation integrity, and by the time we were in the bomb run I was too close on the XO to make my own run. I simply pickled my bombs off when he dropped his and hoped he had a good target picture when he dropped. At that point I really didn't care if we hit the target or not, I simply wanted to get as much air space between me and those guns as I could, as fast as I could get it.

We sped out of range and went feet wet soon after bomb release. I was shaking so violently that I had trouble keeping the airplane steady as I crossed under the XO looking him over for battle damage. Miraculously, neither of us had been hit; somehow we had managed to be where the deadly little clouds of steel fragments were not. Terry Rieder had not been so lucky and returned to the ship with a few holes in his airplane. While not serious enough to keep him from a good pass and landing, this marked the fifth time Terry had been hit in combat, and we changed his nickname from "Buff" to "Magnet Ass." Our streak of good luck rolled on, but all of us wondered how long it could hold.

The EB-66 electronic jamming idea had been scrubbed. There was no clear evidence that the jammer's countermeasures were an effective deterrent to enemy radar, and having to tie our strikes to his on-station time put too many constraints on our targeting. Instead, SAM sites had been declared a priority target and air strikes focused on locating and destroying as much of North Vietnam's SAM capability as possible. On 11 July, Terry Rieder returned to the ship brimming with excitement over having pasted the hell out of a large SAM site. We gathered around him as he described his group's hits on the site. The rocket booster of one SAM ignited from a near hit, and the SAM went snaking off across the ground, raising hell in the site and contributing to the destruction of another missile. Terry also told us in an amazed voice that the missiles had been painted bright turquoise. "Aw, bullshit, Terry, you were so scared you just thought they were blue," was the disbelieving response from one of his listeners. We learned the next day, though, that Terry was right.

The 12 July target was a military barracks area on the outskirts of Hanoi, southeast of downtown. I was flying number two on Commander Quaid, who was leading the entire strike. We were bombers this day with VA-212, making up two divisions and carrying our usual load of six Mark-82s and two Mark-81s. This was a very dangerous mission because the target was so far inland and the only practical route would take us over the heavily populated and defended Red River Delta. We would have to run a gauntlet of antiaircraft fire all the way in to the target and all the way back to the safety of the Gulf. We were only about twenty miles inland when a SAM site fired three missiles at us ballistically rather than using targeting radar. SAM operators often used this tactic to prevent us from locking on to their acquisition radar with our Shrike missiles. They would fire the SAMs much as a duck hunter would lead a duck, then switch on the L-band guidance radar for the last few miles to the target, giving them very little exposure time to counterbattery fire from antiradar missiles. So, without any electronic warning, three missiles whooshed off their launchers about eight miles dead ahead of the strike group.

The sky was clear with bright sunlight and nearly unlimited visibility, and the SAM booster rockets left huge, orange smoke trails as the missiles streaked toward us. Many voices from the strike group called out a warning. A few seconds later the threat detector lit up like a pinball machine, with the high warble warning tone and flashing red SAM light indicating that the L-band guidance signal had been switched on. The first missile, still under booster thrust, was headed toward the skipper and me, and the other two were spread out to its right. I decided to break right and down, since the second section was off to the left, and rejoin the skipper after evading the missiles. Timing the break was critical because moving too early would allow the missile controllers to correct and follow. About the time I began to move the stick, the missile streaked past, slightly high, over my left wing. The damned things were capable of Mach 4 by the time the booster was jettisoned, and the closure rate was unbelievable. I wasn't hit only because I was too close for the controllers to capture the missile with their guidance system and the missile was still ballistic when it passed me. As the missile streaked by, my startled mind registered the fact that it was bright turquoise blue with a bright white flame plume out the booster. The missiles detonated high above and behind the strike group, but the orange smoke clouds still hung in the still air over their launchers, clearly marking the location of the site.

The skipper called a strike on the SAM site and seconds later began his bombing run. I held my heading for a few seconds and then rolled in behind him. The North Vietnamese had concealed the SAM site in a village, trying to take advantage of our much-publicized policy of avoiding civilian populations in our attacks. The launch smoke was still visible when we started our runs, and I had no trouble finding a target. I picked out a missile still on its launcher and flew the pipper to the target. About ten flak sites with six to ten guns in each ringed the SAM site, and they began a furious barrage of antiaircraft fire. Tracers crisscrossed in front of me as I punched off the bombs and jinked hard right and left during the pullout. I don't know if any civilians still occupied the village after the SAM battery was set up in their midst, but the entire area was destroyed. Forty-eight 500-pound bombs, forty 250-pound bombs, and sixteen 5-inch Zuni rockets blanketed the area. Many fires were burning in the village, and secondary explosions were still evident even after we had gone feet wet. No one had been hit and we hadn't had to go all the way in to Hanoi—it was altogether a very successful strike. And that particular SAM site wouldn't be firing any more missiles at us.

Later that day, 37-mm fire struck Lt. Cdr. John Kirkpatrick's engine while he was returning from a target far inland toward Hanoi. Once again the route out was over the heavily populated Red River Delta. The area was all rice paddies and villages, and there was no cover for a downed airman. Ejecting here meant certain capture. I had the strike tanker and was holding about five miles off the coast due south of Haiphong and east of Nam Dinh. John's engine was developing only about 80 percent thrust, and he was losing altitude and airspeed. The engine was running very rough as it shed turbine and compressor blades out the back. Down to about two hundred knots and three thousand feet with more than twenty miles to go before reaching the safety of the Gulf, John clearly didn't think he would make it out. His voice sounded resigned as he described his engine readings to his wingmen and prepared to eject. But the rugged little J52-P8 just kept chugging along while it ate itself. At two hundred knots John was a sitting duck for flak and SAMs, but as the miles slowly dragged along beneath his airplane and the coastline came into view, hope began to creep into his radio transmissions. There were a few sandbar islands a few hundred yards off the coast, and John began to think that he might be able to make it to one of the sandbars. The rescue helicopter, on station a few miles out over the water, was monitoring John's transmissions, and the pilot called to say he didn't know if he could go in to the sandbars without permission from the admiral. John answered him passionately. "Goddammit, Helo, if you don't come in to pick me up, I'll crawl, swim, or fly out there and shoot your ass down!" One of his wingmen echoed the threat. John's sturdy A-4 got him three miles out over the water before the tortured engine gave up the ghost, but three miles was plenty. The rescue helo was on the scene when John ejected and picked him up uninjured within five minutes. I was elated that John made it out safely but somewhat saddened by the loss of the airplane. John was flying ship 228, the airplane I had left in Udorn after the premature explosion of my bomb back in February. But the little airplane got two of its pilots to safety from extremis in its short life, and I'm sure it has a place of honor in Davy Jones's Locker.

Air Wing 21's amazing run of good luck came to an abrupt end on 14 July. VA-76 was the hapless squadron this time. We were attacking the Cao Tri Bridge about twenty miles south of Hanoi when a barrage of SAMs from Hanoi streaked toward us. VA-76's skipper, Cdr. B. I. Fuller, was hit right over the target area and immediately ejected. As his parachute floated down almost directly over the target, we saw to our horror a 37-mm gun firing at him. The parachute canopy was riddled with holes, and some of it was smoldering when he hit the ground hard just yards from the revetment of the flak site that had been shooting at him. Commander Fuller lay motionless after hitting the ground, and enemy gunners swarmed out of their revetment to take him captive. SAMs hit two other VA-76 airplanes at the same time. One was heavily damaged, but the pilot was able to make it out over the Gulf before ejecting and was rescued unharmed; the other had only minor damage and the pilot was able to return to the ship.

All the pilots who saw Commander Fuller go down were convinced that he was dead. But confirming the wisdom of the Defense Department's policy of listing downed airmen as "missing in action" until their death has been positively confirmed, Fuller's name was released on a POW list three years later. He was the first former POW off the plane that delivered the repatriated POWs to Clark Air Force Base in the Philippines after the Paris Peace Accords were signed in January 1973. An A-4C bearing Commander Fuller's name is on display at the Smithsonian Institution's National Air and Space Museum in Washington, D.C.

The USS *Oriskany* had relieved the *Hancock* on Yankee Station around 11 July. After a couple of days of cyclic combat operations in the lower route packages, the *Oriskany's* air wing joined those from the *Kitty Hawk* and the *Bon Homme Richard* in the alpha strikes against heavily defended targets in Route Packages 4 and 6B. The new pilots were in no sense ready for what lay ahead. The *Oriskany* had experienced a terrible fire in October 1966 while in the Vietnam theater of operations. An ordnanceman sailor had accidentally activated a parachute flare during an ammunition unrep and in his panic had kicked it into a locker full of flares. The resulting fire on the hangar deck did major damage to the ship, but even more tragic, most of the air wing's pilots were asphyxiated by smoke inhalation in the ship's forecastle. The *Oriskany* had been out of action for a year and a half in consequence and had a new and very green air wing aboard. Few if any of them had previous combat experience, and they began combat operations during the most intense period of air warfare in the Vietnam War. The consequences of this inexperience would bring further tragedy to the *Oriskany*. During the period July–October 1967, many of the ship's pilots would be killed or captured.

On 15 July it was back to Phu Ly again. The North Vietnamese simply rebuilt the highway bridges we destroyed, sometimes in as little as one day. So we went after the rebuilt bridge that Bernie Smith had destroyed so spectacularly a few days before. We fired big Bullpups at the bridge, but all of us missed. Some light 37-mm fire came up from the irrepressible gun site west of the river, but no one was hit, so we broke even on that strike. Air Wing 21 had flown most of the previous night on a spurious PT-boat alert during which another of VA-76's A-4Cs had been shot down. That made five planes VA-76 had lost in just three days. Not all of these airplanes had been lost on strikes, but those that made it back to the ship were so badly damaged that they would never fly again. The sixteenth was another stand-down day while we shifted our hours for flight quarters to include some planned night strikes. A strike in Nam Dinh, Pierre Salinger's "sleepy little textile village," had been planned for the seventeenth, but bad weather at the target diverted us to a railroad siding south of the city.

The night of 17 July was clear with a nearly full moon. I was flying a two-ship hop with the skipper—my first night combat operation. At night we flew sections because it was too difficult to keep everyone separated if we tried to fly division formations. Once over the beach it was external lights out, and the wingman separated from the leader and kept track of his position using air-to-air TACAN, which gave only the distance between airplanes, not the direction. We kept track of one another's position with verbal position reports relating to some point on the ground. We were truck hunting, a futile exercise with a full moon because the North Vietnamese truckers drove with their lights off, using moonlight to stay on the road. We finally dropped flares to illuminate a likely truck parking place where a ferry was reported to be operating across a river, but no ferry or trucks were visible in the crazily swinging light of the flares. So we bombed the road, creating job opportunities for the road repair crews. The night landing aboard the ship, my first in months, was fairly easy under the bright moon, and I was relieved to have my first night combat hop behind me.

Two of the *Oriskany*'s A-4s were hit at Phu Ly during the day of 18 July. Both airplanes made it to the mountains west of the target; the pilots ejected and a massive rescue effort was launched. The first pilot was rescued, but the second rescue helicopter was shot up badly; one crewman was killed and the other severely wounded. The downed pilot had to wait until the next day for another rescue attempt. An *Oriskany* F-8 had been downed in the same area the day before, but the pilot had been rescued unharmed. This made seven *Oriskany* planes shot down in six days on the line. There was worse to come.

The next day it was business as usual on Yankee Station, but it was a day of tragedy and resignation for the hapless *Oriskany* pilot evading the North Vietnamese in the hills west of Phu Ly. Another rescue effort was mounted at first light, but the North Vietnamese had used the hours of darkness to set up a deadly trap for the SAR forces they knew were sure to come. Cunningly, they held their fire until the rescue chopper was about to pick up the downed pilot and then opened up with all they had. The rescue helo was hit immediately and exploded in midair, killing all five crewmen. A RESCAP A-4 from the *Oriskany* was also hit, and the pilot barely made it out over the Gulf before ejecting. This made six men killed, one severely wounded, and several airplanes lost or damaged in an attempt to rescue one pilot. The rescue effort was called off and the hapless *Oriskany* pilot was abandoned to his fate.

Air Wing 21's first target that day was a group of low buildings just south of Co Tri. Skipper Quaid was leading the alpha strike with two divisions of VA-212 bombers and I was his number two. He had planned to swing west of the Red River Delta and keep a ridge of mountains between the strike force and the target, then to fly the strike group up a valley that ran north and south and wheel sharply east to attack the target, picking a narrow pass in the mountain ridge as his initial point. If our luck held, the North Vietnamese air defense people wouldn't know the target's identity until the last minute and would be able to mount only a limited response. It was a brilliant plan in concept but not in performance. The ridge contained many narrow gaps into the delta to the east, and Commander Quaid went one pass too far before turning the strike east to the target. He realized that we were too far north of the target very soon after we crossed the mountains and arrived over the delta. About the time he realized his mistake—which had put us very close to the south side of Hanoi—a SAM battery fired three SAMs at the strike group. The skipper called a hard turn to the left, and we dived to avoid the SAMs. Two of the missiles had locked in on the first division and followed us down. Quaid took us down very low over the rice paddies, to within two hundred feet or so of the ground. As soon as he saw the two missiles diving down to our altitude and closing fast, he began a sharp pull-up. At their great speed, the missiles had too large a turn radius and crashed into the rice paddy trying to follow our turn. The third missile exploded high above us. We had time to rejoin the bomber group during the few miles we had to fly south to get to a roll-in point southwest of the target. We rolled in from south to north, completely destroyed the target, and recovered to the west over the mountains.

To ensure adequate coverage of the target area we were carrying maximum bomb loads with no external fuel, making this a must-refuel mission. On the way to rejoin the skipper after the bomb run, I checked my fuel and was shocked to see just four hundred pounds remaining. I knew the extra turn and extra miles to the target had cost some fuel, but even so I should still have had around a thousand pounds. The skipper had planned to run us out over the mountains for a while so that we could minimize the time spent over the heavily defended delta. After rejoining him, I called that he better get the tanker headed in to join us as soon as we went feet wet because I was going to be critically low on fuel by then. Quaid sounded a little disgusted with me as he called the tanker with a new rejoin radial and DME and sent me to plug in ahead of the rest of the flight. I had just two hundred pounds on the gauge when I plugged and was reliving the fright I had experienced after Arv was shot down. Everyone refueled after that, and the flight back to the ship and recovery were uneventful.

To make room on the flight deck for the next strike, the skipper's airplane and mine were struck below to the hangar deck. I was still in the cockpit unstrapping, trying to recover my composure, when the skipper walked up to the side of my airplane and inquired if he should climb up or would I join him on the hangar deck so he could kick my ass. Now, I respected the skipper above all other men except my own father, and I viewed him as a father figure, but his words stung like a lash and I swarmed out of the cockpit with rage in my heart and blood in my eye. Jumping the last three steps off the cockpit ladder, I flung my helmet bag to the deck, stomped over to the skipper, balled my fists, and said, "Yeah!?! Well here I am!" The skipper was just as furious and began an earnest ass chewing for my girlish squeal over the radio asking for the tanker. I very nearly ended my military career right there. I was struggling to keep from punching his lights out when my plane captain, no doubt uncomfortable to witness this exchange between officers, decided to intervene. "Mr. Gray, Mr. Gray, do you know you were hit?" he asked. "You have a hole in your wing." The skipper and I looked at each other for a moment and then walked over to the right wing. Sure enough, there was a 12.75-mm bullet hole roughly in the center of my right wing—mute explanation of why I had been eight hundred pounds lower on fuel than the rest of the division. Apparently, no one had seen the thin stream of fuel vapor marking my battle damage, and the skipper had missed seeing the hole during his poststrike look-over of my airplane. That was understandable; the entry hole on the bottom side of the wing was only about the size of my thumb, and the exit hole on the top of the wing was about the size of a silver dollar with the aluminum skin pushed up around it. "Well, Steve," the skipper said, "I guess that explains your low state. I understand your call now and I'm sorry I jumped you. I guess I'm just pissed that I screwed up the nav to the target." My anger evaporated just as quickly as it had flashed to the surface.

Later that day the skipper apologized publicly to all the pilots on the strike for making like Magellan and exploring North Vietnam trying to find the target. His mistake was certainly understandable. Trying to eyeball a narrow gap in the mountains in an area you have never seen before is difficult; doing it while leading an alpha strike over enemy territory is extremely difficult. His ability to orient himself and locate the target after realizing his mistake showed great skill and indicated careful and detailed preparation. Accepting the blame for the mistake without offering excuses showed true leadership. Commander Quaid taught me a huge lesson in leadership that day.

That afternoon I flew on another strike to the Do Son POL storage area. This time we bombed the craters the rest of the strike group had left on the target while I had bombed the river. We got no secondary explosions, indicating that the North Vietnamese had not tried to use the area again to store fuel. As they also did not fire a shot at us, the mission was another draw. The afternoon did not go as well for the *Oriskany*, where misfortune continued unabated.

We had just finished recovering all but the tanker from the Do Son strike when one of the *Oriskany*'s F-8s appeared two miles behind the ship declaring an emergency and his intent to land aboard the Bonnie Dick. The LSO had little time to prepare the deck for him. The F-8 pilot reported severe battle damage. He had only two hundred pounds of fuel, a damaged hydraulic system, and diminished control movement, and he had a hung 750-pound bomb under one wing and couldn't lower his flaps. I was watching the F-8's approach on the closed-circuit TV in the ready room. The F-8 looked good until it crossed the ramp. Then suddenly the nose swung wildly right and the airplane slammed down hard on the deck. The force of the impact broke off the landing gear, and flames streaked out from under the fuselage as the airplane slid forward off the angle deck and disappeared in a huge splash off the side of the ship. The waves closed over the white patch of foam that marked the point where the F-8 went into the water. When the foam dissipated, nothing remained to mark the grave of this pilot, the XO of one of the fighter squadrons in the *Oriskany*'s air wing. No one knew why he had tried to save such a crippled airplane, but his decision to try to land the airplane instead of ejecting cost him his life. This brought the *Oriskany*'s toll up to nine airplanes lost, two pilots killed, and one captured in just seven days on the line. And still it wasn't over.

July twentieth was a bad day for the XO, Commander Whittemore. First, he was hit by antiaircraft artillery fire while on a strike to the Hi Dong area. The airplane was hit in the control package where the hydraulic boost was added to the cable-actuated flight control system. After the hit, Fred was dismayed to discover that the control stick was no longer connected to anything! It just flopped around loose in his hand. He was far out over the flat delta where ejection meant certain capture. The good news was that he still had rudder control and electrically operated pitch trim. Now, the A-4 was inherently aerodynamically unstable; it had to be to operate in the wide range of flight regimes its mission required. Continual small control inputs had to be made to keep the airplane in any attitude of flight. Without the control stick, the airplane soon began to roll and dive for the ground. The XO was determined not to eject over enemy territory, so he used rudder control to roll the airplane upright and used pitch trim to get the nose up. But doing this caused the airplane to pitch nose up and climb, losing airspeed. So he had to rudder roll inverted to get the nose down and then roll upright again. In this fashion, with a series of roller coaster vertical moves, the XO worked himself far enough out over the water to eject. He was rescued without injuries—further proof that if the engine was running, fire wasn't burning the pilot out of the cockpit, and any control remained to the pilot, the gutsy little A-4 could get its pilot out of harm's way.

The twenty-first was a much better day for Air Wing 21. I flew a strike against a warehouse complex just a half-mile from the famed Thanh Hoa Bridge. We took a lot of 37-mm fire from Thanh Hoa, but no one was hit and we inflicted heavy damage on the target. But the first hop of the day, which I missed, had all the excitement. A flight of ten MiG-17s jumped the morning strike and were engaged by the F-8 TARCAP. The fighters shot down three of the MiGS, got a probable kill on a fourth, and damaged two more. The MiGS were completely routed and did no damage to the strike group. Three more names were added to the list of *Bon Homme Richard*'s MiG Killers.

The Russian intelligence-gathering "trawler" that was our constant shadow was getting more aggressive in its attempts to harass our launches and recoveries. Since the U.S. government had proclaimed the waters of the Gulf of Tonkin three miles off the coast of North Vietnam and Hinan Island, People's Republic of China, to be international waters, American ships in the Gulf were bound to obey the international rules of the road for ocean navigation. This meant that if the Russian ship maneuvered herself into the path of an aircraft carrier where she had the right of way, the carrier had to give way even if she was engaged in launching or recovering aircraft. The navigation officer was constantly trying to maneuver the ship so that the trawler wouldn't be able to get in position to abuse the rules of the road and gain the right of way. Sometimes he was successful in sucking the trawler out of position, but the room available for the ship to maneuver was limited by our on-station requirements, and sometimes the trawler was successful in interrupting our flight operations. The pilots of the air wing were strictly forbidden to take any action against the Russian ship, but on this day Cdr. John Wunche, the commanding officer of the heavy tanker detachment, had finally had enough of the Russians' antics.

John Wunche was a big man with bright red hair and a flaming red handlebar mustache. He was a frustrated fighter pilot whom fate and the Bureau of Naval Personnel had put into the cockpit of a former heavy bomber now employed as a carrier-based tanker. Commander Wunche flew the tanker like a fighter and frequently delighted the tactical pilots by rolling the "Whale," as we all called the KA-3B tanker, on completion of a tanker mission. Consequently, John's nickname was "the Red Baron." On 21 July 1967 he proved just how appropriate that name was.

The Bonnie Dick had nearly completed a recovery. The Russian trawler had been steaming at full speed to try to cut across our bow, and the bridge watch had been keeping a wary eye on the intruder. For a while it looked as if the Russian would be too late and we would finish the recovery before having to give way to the trawler. But a couple of untimely bolters extended the recovery and the *Bon Homme Richard* had to back down and change course to comply with the rules. The LSO hit the wave-off lights when the Whale was just a few yards from the ramp. John crammed on full power and sucked up the speed brakes for the go-around. The Bonnie Dick began a sharp right turn to pass behind the Russian, causing the ship to list steeply, and there, dead ahead of John, was the Russian trawler. He couldn't resist. He leveled the Whale about a hundred feet off the water and roared across the mast of the trawler with all fuel dumps open like a crop duster spraying a field of boll weevils. The Russian disappeared in a heavy white cloud of jet fuel spray, then reemerged with JP-4 jet fuel glistening from her superstructure and running lip-full in the scuppers. The Russian trawler immediately lost power as the ship's crew frantically tried to shut down anything that might generate a spark and ignite the fuel. She was rolling dead in the water in the *Bon Homme Richard*'s wake, the crew breaking out fire hoses to wash down the fuel, as we steamed out of sight completing the recovery of the Whale. The Red Baron was an instant hero to the entire ship's company.

After a long dry spell the weather over the northern route package areas closed in again with rain and thunderstorms generated by the summer heat and humidity. On 24 and 25 July, Air Wing 21 flew cyclic operations to the lower package areas after the weather canceled our planned alpha strikes. The combat pilots greeted these cancellations with relieved glee. By this point in the cruise we were having a hard time maintaining a patriotic attitude toward our missions. Only a few days of combat remained for us, and we were reluctant to expose ourselves to any more hazard so close to the end. A letter I wrote to Alma on 27 July expressed my personal views.

We really must seem reluctant to you for wishing for all this bad weather. But we have done our part, and since this isn't a real war (except that people do get killed), and since it won't affect the outcome of the whole Vietnam mess if we fly those alpha strikes tomorrow, and since it is so near the end, we just can't get too fired up to get shot at again. If any of us thought our strikes were doing any good, and if we thought it would shorten the war one damn bit, then we would all be raring to go and hit any target in North Vietnam. But it is painfully obvious that the outcome of this war will be decided in conference rooms by diplomats speaking oh so politely to one another over a glass of fine brandy. It won't be decided by guns or bombs or numbers of men dying. Until our scared, cowardly State Department and policy makers decide to develop a fighting attitude, then those of us who must fight will fly our missions when we must and continue to pray for bad weather. Anyway this war has taught all of us who fight the same hard lessons that all other fighting men in all other wars have learned.

There is no glory in war, circumstances determine heroes, all of us are just as scared as the next guy, and medals don't mean a damn thing to those who earn them.

On the night of 25 July, the *Oriskany* lost another pilot, who inexplicably flew into the ground during his attack. The ship's total now was eleven planes and three pilots lost in less than two weeks. Air Wing 21 had lost twenty-two planes and fifteen pilots killed or captured on the entire cruise, and our wing had flown more alpha strikes against more heavily defended targets than any other carrier in history. Even so, our losses had been no worse than those of any other air wing in the Vietnam theater. The lack of combat experience in the *Oriskany*'s air wing took a terrible toll.

The night of 28 July, Air Wing 21 was briefed for what we thought would be the last combat day of the 1967 cruise. Only two strikes were scheduled for the next day, the first to a truck parking area in Phu Ly, the other against the Thanh Hoa Bridge. To my disappointment, I was on the first strike to Phu Ly; I really wanted to be on the Thanh Whore Bridge strike. The air wing had a backlog of Mark-84 two-thousand-pounders and was going to expend them all in an all-out attempt to drop the Thanh Hoa Bridge. The skipper picked the best bombers to go on that strike and selected Terry over me. The legacy of the river bombing still haunted me. But I couldn't disagree with his choice. Terry was a very good pilot and probably a better bomber than I was.

The Phu Ly truck park strike went off without a hitch. We got in and out with no one hit. The usual flak from the Phu Ly gunners dotted the sky over the target, but the flak seemed as halfhearted as our bombing of what turned out to be an empty area with no trucks in sight. The pilots were an elated bunch after the recovery, and I got down to the ready room in time to give good wishes to the men going after the Thanh Hoa Bridge. My elation and relief overcame my disappointment at not getting a crack at the bridge; after all, we were through with combat this cruise. Or so we thought.

The screen in the ready room typed out PILOTS MAN YOUR PLANES. We gave last encouragement to the Thanh Hoa Bridge busters and settled down to watch the launch. The telephone at the SDO desk rang while the pilots were manning their planes. The SDO had a stricken look on his face he announced to us, "The strike is canceled. The USS *Forrestal* is on fire and we are steaming to give assistance." Those of us in the ready room left at a run for the flight deck. The ship was turning out of the wind and toward the *Forrestal* and accelerating to flank speed as we arrived on the flight deck and joined pilots in their flight gear staring toward the horizon. The

Forrestal was still hull-down on the horizon, but a thick black column of smoke marked her position. Reddish yellow flames were billowing up at the base of the smoke column. Long before arriving alongside the stricken carrier we began to encounter floating debris that had been blasted far out from the ship. It was clear that a disaster of major proportions had befallen our sister carrier.

The closer we came to the *Forrestal* the more evidence of tragedy we encountered. Dented drop tanks that had been blasted from their planes floated half submerged, buoyed up by air trapped during their flight. Grisly evidence of the human toll began to appear as we pulled within a few hundred yards of the burning carrier. By the time we arrived alongside, the fires on the flight deck had for the most part been extinguished. The flight deck aft of the island was a tangled wreck of blackened, smoking debris. Parts of what had been airplanes were visible amid the wreckage—part of a vertical stabilizer here, a wing tip there, part of the nose of an A-6. Huge holes had been blasted into the steel flight deck, exposing the hangar deck below. Other bombs blasted free from their racks had rolled through the holes, dropping twenty feet into the hangar deck and exploding, spreading destruction to the hangar deck and aircraft parked there. Holes had been blasted completely through the armored hangar deck as well, and bombs had fallen as many as three decks below into crew berthing spaces. Many of the fires the explosions caused below decks were still burning out of control when the *Bon Homme Richard* arrived to render aid.

The Bonnie Dick's helicopters made continuous round trips to the stricken *Forrestal*, ferrying seriously wounded sailors to our sick bay for emergency first aid. The USS *Repose*, a hospital ship serving as a floating surgery off Da Nang, left her station and steamed to join the growing flotilla of ships attending the *Forrestal*. There were just so many casualties, mostly badly burned. Our sick bay and those of the other ships were filled with them, and still the stream of victims continued. Finally, late that evening, all of the wounded were being treated and the *Forrestal*, with damage control parties keeping a wary eye on still smoldering compartments, left for Cubi Point under her own power, escorted by a fleet tug.

We learned the cause of the catastrophe much later. The *Forrestal*, which had been on the line only five days, was preparing to launch an alpha strike. A-6s, F-4s, and A-4s fully fueled and loaded with bombs and missiles packed the flight deck aft of the island. As a safety precaution, forward-firing ordnance such as rockets, guns, and missiles were not enabled until the airplane was on the catapult with nothing but open sea ahead so that an accidentally discharged weapon would fall harmlessly into the ocean. The electrical firing leads to missiles were not connected until the airplane was on the catapult.

An ordnanceman with an ammeter checked each firing lead to make sure that no current was present before hooking it into its receptacle in the rocket pod or missile. Somehow, during the current check a missile from an airplane behind the one ahead of it on the catapult was fired. The missile struck the airplane on the catapult, which immediately exploded. Shrapnel from that explosion ripped into the plane's fuel tanks, igniting thousands of gallons of jet fuel. The ship had accelerated to get thirty knots of wind across the deck for the launch, and the wind spread the fire rapidly among the parked airplanes. The entire area aft of the island was engulfed in flames within a minute of the initial explosion. Shortly afterward the first bombs began to cook off. The explosive used in the Mark-80 series bombs was extremely stable. During the *Oriskany* fire, bombs glowing cherry red from the heat of the fire had been shoved overboard without exploding. But those bombs did not have fuses installed. All the bombs loaded on alpha strike airplanes had fuses. Fuses are made of very sensitive explosives, and the heat of the fire was sufficient to cause them to detonate, initiating the main explosive in the bomb.

Fire on an aircraft carrier—which is essentially a tank farm full of fuel and thousands of tons of high explosive—is the crew's worst nightmare. Had the catastrophe that befell the *Forrestal* happened on the Bonnie Dick, we would likely have sunk. The *Forrestal*, fortunately, was a much larger and more modern ship with armored flight and hangar decks. The explosions that ripped through her decks would probably have blasted through the bottom of the *Bon Homme Richard*'s hull. As it was, the *Forrestal* was still not out of the woods. During the night of her journey across the South China Sea to the Philippines, fires smoldering below decks broke out again, and for a while the future of the ship was in doubt. But the *Forrestal* survived this threat too.

The heroic efforts of the *Forrestal*'s damage control teams saved her. Some lost their lives in the fight to save the ship. A closed-circuit TV camera on the ship's flight deck recorded the last moments of life for seven *Forrestal* sailors. A chief petty officer was leading a hose team of six sailors advancing on an A-6 Intruder that was engulfed in flames. They were trying to cool the bombs under the A-6's wings with a fog nozzle on a four-inch fire hose when the bombs exploded and a huge fireball obscured the scene. When the smoke cleared, the camera showed an area littered with burning piles of debris and the unmanned fire hose lashing wildly about like a headless serpent. Of the seven men nothing remained. They simply vanished in the fury of the explosion, blown into pieces too small to be found.

In the aftermath of the frantic effort to give aid to the *Forrestal* and treat her wounded sailors, a mood of bleak despair settled on the ship's company of the *Bon Homme Richard*. It was a foregone conclusion that the Pacific Fleet's commander would extend the Bonnie Dick's duty until a replacement carrier could get to the line, and that would probably take at least six weeks. Commander Task Force 77 had in fact recommended this. I was positive that I would not survive six more weeks of combat. I felt sorry for the *Forrestal*'s sailors and the tragedy that had befallen them, but I was also feeling sorry for myself. It was a black night.

I was shaving early the next morning when Captain Ruiz addressed the crew on the ship's PA. Our orders were to assume the *Forrestal*'s strike schedule for that day; then we would leave the line as scheduled and begin the journey home. Cheers broke out all over the ship as we realized that the six-week sentence we had been dreading had been commuted to one day. I hurried to finish shaving and dress in flight gear to get to the ready room to find out what my schedule would be.

Three strikes on the schedule were ruled out due to aircraft unavailability. We were worn out, and so was our equipment. Finally it was decided to launch one alpha strike against the Hon Gay port facilities. Hon Gay was on the coast of the Tonkin Gulf in the area of the ten thousand islands I called the Dragon's Teeth. I would be flying the strike tanker on this mission, so I would be safely out over the Gulf, out of harm's way. The mission went very well; the port facilities were severely damaged and Air Wing 21 took no casualties. This time, however, we weren't so ready to celebrate. We all knew that there was still a chance we could be extended, and we wouldn't feel safe until we were actually headed home.

Epilogue

A nd so ended the combat portion of the 1967 cruise for the USS *Bon Homme Richard* and Air Wing 21—not with a bang, but with a whimper of relief from me. After the Hon Gay strike we left for two days in Cubi to offload ammunition, then steamed to Japan to conduct relief briefings and transfer Yankee Team assets to our replacement, the USS *Coral Sea*. The *Bon Homme Richard* and Air Wing 21 compiled a distinguished combat record during the cruise. We flew more than a hundred alpha strikes, more than any other ship and air wing in the Navy. VA-212 had flown 2,175 combat sorties and delivered more than six million pounds of ordnance—most of it loaded by hand—against the enemy. Air Wing 21 lost fifteen pilots killed or captured and twenty-two airplanes. VA-212 left two pilots prisoners of the North Vietnamese and lost seven airplanes. The Bonnie Dick would not be conducting flight operations during the trip home, so most of the combat pilots would get to fly back to the States, including all who would be returning to Southeast Asia the following year. Only a few of the squadron officers remained aboard to administer the squadron.

On docking at the U.S. Navy base in Yokosuka, Japan, the air wing pilots who would be flying home detached from the ship and proceeded to NAS Atsugi to await transport. We had until the ship crossed the International Date Line before flying home, because if the powers-that-be decided to send the ship back to Vietnam, it wouldn't do to have the pilots already home and scattered on leave. For some arcane reason, crossing the Date Line prevented the possibility of extending the cruise.

During the interminable wait at NAS Atsugi, we learned that good old COMFAIR Alameda had dropped the ball and no military charter airplane was available to fly Air Wing 21's combat pilots home. But the transportation officer at Travis Air Force Base came through like a champ and secured space for us on a regularly scheduled Northwest Orient flight leaving from Haneda Airport outside Tokyo. The flight to the States took all night, and we landed in Seattle as the sun was rising over the Cascade Mountains. Our first look at the United States since leaving San Diego seven months and a lifetime ago could not have been more beautiful. After a short stopover in Seattle we continued to San Francisco International. Walking down the air stairs I spotted Alma standing in the crowd behind the chain-link fence separating the terminal area from the tarmac. A few steps later I was in her arms and reunited with my bride.

The joy of reunion with my wife and the relief of being out of combat were tempered by the certain knowledge that I would be returning to Vietnam next year. VA-212 was rotating about half of its pilot force and would begin training their replacements after the air wing returned. Cdr. Marv Quaid, Cdr. Fred Whittemore, Lt. Cdr. Pete Yonke, Lt. Cdr. Dick Thomas, Lt. Wiley Decarli, Lt. Al Crebo, Lt. (jg) Bernie Smith, Lt. (jg) Terry Rieder, and I would be returning for the next cruise.

I tried to force the dread of the next combat cruise to the back of my mind, but the fear was never far away. To cope with it I drew on the same source of strength that had helped me muster the courage to fly my combat missions on the 1967 cruise. I would do what I must and fly my missions because of my pride in myself as a man and my pride in being a naval aviator, and because if I didn't fly my missions, one of my squadron mates would have to fly them for me. Also, I believed that we were doing the right thing in Vietnam; I just disagreed with the way the war was being managed. I believed that the spread of international communism by force had to be stopped. I believed that the principles of freedom and democracy had to be defended. And I believed that military service and sacrifice were necessary to secure the blessings of liberty for my family and my country. The concept of liberty embodied in the Constitution of the United States of America is worth the risk of capture and death. I believed it then, and I believe it now.

Index

About the Author

Steve Gray grew up in Duncan, Oklahoma. After graduating from Duncan High School, he attended the University of Oklahoma for two years before dropping out to join the U.S. Navy. He graduated from Navy pilot training and received his wings as a naval aviator and was commissioned an ensign on 25 June 1966.

After just six months of training to fly the A-4 Skyhawk, Steve joined Attack Squadron 212, making two cruises to Vietnam and flying more than 250 combat missions and 300-plus carrier landings. After seven years, Steve left active duty to pursue a civilian career, flying first as a corporate pilot and then with Delta Airlines, after earning an associate's degree in business. During his thirty years with Delta, Steve flew some thirty different types of aircraft and accumulated more than 24,000 flying hours. He and his wife, the former Alma Thumann, live in Texas. *Rampant Raider* is his first book.